TRAGEDY OF PARAGUAY

ALSO BY GILBERT PHELPS

FICTION

The Dry Stone
(*Arthur Barker*)
The Heart in the Desert
(*John Day, New York*)
A Man in his Prime
(*Arthur Barker & John Day*)
The Centenarians
(*Heinemann*)
The Love Before the First
(*Heinemann*)
The Winter People
(*The Bodley Head; Simon & Schuster, New York; available also in Penguin, and in an abridged school version in 'The Queen's Classics Series', Chatto & Windus*)
Tenants of the House
(*Barrie & Jenkins*)
The Old Believer
(*Barrie & Jenkins; Wildwood House; Random House; New York*)

TRAVEL

The Last Horizon: a Brazilian journey
(*The Bodley Head; published by Simon & Schuster as 'The Green Horizons'*)

GENERAL

Living Writers
(*Editor, Sylvan Press*)
Latin America
(*B.B.C. Publications*)
Latin America: an introduction
(*Bank of London & South America*)

CRITICISM

The Russian Novel in English Fiction
(*Hutchinson's University Library*)
A Short History of English Literature
(*Folio Society*)
A Survey of English Literature
(*Pan Books*)
Questions and Response: an anthology of English and American poetry
(*Cambridge University Press*)
The Byronic Byron: a selection, with introduction and notes
(*Longmans' English Series*)

Tragedy of Paraguay

GILBERT PHELPS

CHARLES KNIGHT
& COMPANY LIMITED

LONDON & TONBRIDGE

Charles Knight & Company Limited
25 New Street Square, London, EC4A 3JA
& Sovereign Way, Tonbridge, Kent, TN9 1RW

A Member of the Benn Group

Copyright © 1975 Gilbert Phelps

ISBN 0 85314 148 7

Printed in Great Britain by
Cox & Wyman Ltd,
London, Fakenham and Reading

Contents

	Introduction	ix
	The Main Persons of the Drama	xv
ACT ONE	Expulsion from Eden?	1
ACT TWO	Father and Son: Further Lessons in Autocracy	33
ACT THREE	The Napoleon of South America?	69
ACT FOUR	Offensive and Defensive	115
INTERLUDE		172
ACT FIVE	The Long Retreat	191
EPILOGUE		261
	Select Bibliography	278
	Index	283

Paraguay and its neighbours: the main scenes of battle in the War of the Triple Alliance.

List of Illustrations

List of plates

Between pp. 160–161

1 Francisco Solano López

2 Elisa Lynch

3 Landing of Brazilian and Argentinian troops in Corrientes

4 Argentinian troops in Paraguay

5 The battle of Tuyutí, 1866

6 Paraguayan prisoners

7 General Mitre

8 The conference at Yataíty Corá

9 The Allied attack of Curupaíty

10 The battlefield at Curupaíty

Introduction

When my imagination was first fired by the story of Paraguay and the War of the Triple Alliance, I saw it in straightforward, lurid colours as the tragedy of a nation led to its doom by an irresponsible dictator and his equally ambitious consort.

As I entered more deeply into the subject, of course, I had to modify this primitive picture. The main ingredients, it is true, remained as fantastic as anything in Jacobean melodrama, encompassing as they do intrigues and treacheries; acts of violence, cruelty and tyranny; ferocious battles, ingenious strategems, daring assaults, one of the most remarkable retreats in military history, and incredible acts of heroism and endurance. All set against exotic semi-tropical backgrounds – and to complete the scenario, an extraordinary stranger-than-fiction love interest. Perhaps Hilaire Belloc was right when he said that 'readable history is melodrama'.

But although the astonishing War of the Triple Alliance, in which from 1864 to 1870 the land-locked Republic of Paraguay fought alone against her two most powerful neighbours, Brazil and Argentina, aided by Uruguay (the Banda Oriental as it was then called), undoubtedly marks the climax of Paraguay's history (in the period covered by this book), it is no longer possible to regard it in isolation, or as the work of one man. Paraguay's destiny was a long time gathering, but it was inherent practically from the moment when, in August 1537, the Spaniards baptized the tiny wooden fort they had erected on the eastern bank of the River Paraguay some thousand miles from the Atlantic, Nuestra Señora de la Asunción, and made it the headquarters of all the vast area claimed by Spain in the southern part of South America. The steps that led up to the climax were slow and gradual, but they were endowed with an Aristotelian inevitability; and Francisco Solano López, the Marshal-President who led his nation into the war, must in many respects be seen as the product of previous history, and even to some extent as the mere victim of circumstance.

Most English accounts of the subject have cast the Paraguayan leader as the unmitigated villain of the piece, but these derive largely from Brazilian and Argentinian sources which are themselves mostly partisan, particularly, of course, in the period during and immediately after the war; as that indefatigable Victorian traveller Captain (later Sir) Richard Burton (who paid two visits to the seat of war in 1868 and 1869) said: 'those who write have in almost all instances allowed their imaginations and their prejudices to guide their judgment, and mostly they have frankly thrown overboard all impartiality'.[1]

In order to arrive at a true estimate of the character and actions of Francisco Solano López, it is little use, on the other hand, turning to Paraguayan sources. While he was alive, he allowed only the most favourable accounts to be published in a press which he controlled absolutely (though in that he was no different from most other rulers). After his death, it is true, a number of Paraguayans joined in the vilification, and hostile opinions continued to be expressed by Paraguayan liberals until comparatively recent times. In 1926, for example, Dr. Cecilio Baez wrote of him as 'a senseless governor, an inept general, and a monstrous tyrant'.[2] But quite early on the process of rehabilitation was also taking place, side by side with the denunciations, reaching a rhetorical climax in Juan O'Leary's panegyric[3] – in spite of the fact that the author's mother and other members of his family had, according to several sources, met their deaths at the Paraguayan dictator's hands.

In a decree of March 1st, 1936, the rehabilitation was completed, when the Paraguayan government declared Francisco Solano López to be the national hero 'sin ejemplar', and his remains now lie in the Pantheon of the Heroes in Asunción. The purpose behind the panegyrics, no doubt, was in the first place to revive the spirit of a defeated race, and in more recent times to strengthen and focus the fierce sense of national solidarity which has always been, for good or ill, Paraguay's distinguishing characteristic. In other words, López, like so much about the history of his country, has been translated into the realms of mythology, so that the truth is even more difficult to get at and will now probably never be known in full.

In the pages I have devoted to him here, I have done my best to present a balanced picture, though I have to confess that by the time I came to the end of my reading I found myself becoming increasingly ambivalent in my attitude towards him – or perhaps confused would be the better adjective. It was easy enough to reject the attempts at whitewashing, easy to see his mistakes and his crimes. What was curious was that every time I enumerated them to myself, another voice seemed to chime in with an 'explanation' or a 'justification'. Obviously he was a despot and a tyrant . . . but so were his predecessors and many of his contemporaries throughout Latin America – and was he any worse than they? Obviously he was guilty of cruelties and injustices . . . but couldn't some of them be explained, if not condoned, on grounds of harsh political or military necessity, or as the panic reactions of a typical *homme moyen sensuel* placed in a situation beyond his moral stature? Obviously it is difficult to forgive his disregard of human lives, especially those of his long-suffering soldiers . . . but he belonged to a fatalistic race, and other parts of the sub-continent could show examples of callousness every bit as bad if not worse. Obviously López's ambition to become a South American Napoleon strikes us as bizarre . . . but he was by no means the only one; General Santa Anna, for example, who had ruled Mexico twenty years or so before the advent of López, was styled the 'Napoleon of the New World'. Obviously López was irresponsible to have precipitated a struggle against such impossible odds . . . but it is likely that such a war was inevitable in any case. Obviously López was at fault in refusing (when he had the chance) to end a war which was destroying his country . . . but there is much to be said for the view that he had genuinely become the symbol of survival against enemies who sought to obliterate not only him but the nation he represented.

And so on and so on. At one moment one feels one *ought* to condemn him whole-heartedly; at another one cannot resist a sneaking admiration, and a kind of logic seems to emerge from even his wildest actions. What at any rate does seem certain is that the simple black-and-white portrait does not meet the case.

What is even more certain is that whether or not the main protagonists live up to the requirements of high tragedy, the Paraguayan people most unequivocally do, and it is they who are the real heroes. By the end of the war, battle, disease and starvation had accounted for more than half the population. War casualties were at least 220,000.[4] Of the survivors, only 28,000 were adult males (several thousand less according to some accounts); the women and children outnumbered them by fourteen to one, and women over fifteen by four to one.[5]

The ferocity of the struggle can be measured, too, by the fact that casualties among Paraguay's enemies were nearly as high, and the dead on both sides totalled at least 350,000 at a time when the populations of the South American countries were still comparatively small; this figure, in fact, is more than twice the population of Buenos Aires in 1864, and probably about equal to the combined populations of Rio de Janeiro and the whole of Uruguay in the same year.

No wonder that so many Latin American historians have regarded this 'War of the Triple Alliance' as the most calamitous in their history. Yet strangely enough it attracted little attention outside South America. In part this was due to the remoteness of the arena. In 1864, Paraguay was to most Europeans and North Americans a tiny and almost completely unknown republic – somewhere in the middle of the vast South American sub-continent. Burton tells us that when he returned home he encountered 'blankness of face whenever the word Paraguay . . . was named, and a general confession of utter ignorance and hopeless lack of interest'. But the main reason why the war received so little attention in the European papers was that these were fully occupied with events nearer home. Europe at the time of the Paraguayan War was under the shadow of growing Prussian power, and it took place in the uneasy interlude between the Crimean War and the Franco-Prussian War. In 1864, for example, the *London Illustrated News*, which prided itself (on the whole rightly) on the scope of its coverage, could only spare an occasional page for events in such a remote part of the world, while it treated practically every aspect of the Austro-Prussian War. What interest Europe did have in South America was more strongly engaged by the ill-fated attempt (between 1864 and 1867) of the French Emperor, Napoleon III, to instal the Archduke Maximilian of Austria as Emperor of Mexico – or even by Spain's abortive efforts to regain some of her old prestige in South America, notably through her seizure, in 1864, of the Chincha Islands from Peru, which was followed by war with both Peru and Chile.

As for the United States of America, although at ambassadorial level she was more directly involved than any of the European countries, there were tragic happenings closer at hand – the final stages of Civil War; the surrender of General Robert E. Lee on April 9th, 1865; the assassination of President Abraham Lincoln six days later; and the period of recuperation and reconstruction that followed. It was only in its last year that the Paraguayan War aroused any considerable American interest.

But Burton expressed the feelings of all those who came into contact with the Paraguayan War, when he wrote of it as 'a spectacle that could not fail to appeal to man's sympathy and imagination' and declared, 'Seldom has aught more impressive been presented to the gaze of the world than this tragedy; this unflinching struggle maintained for so long a period against over-whelming odds . . .'. Later students of the War have been filled with the same feelings of pity and awe. W. H. Koebel, for example, described it as 'one of the most remarkable wars the world has ever witnessed'[6] – and he was by no means the only one to compare it with the 1914–18 conflict, William E. Barrett, for instance, seeing it as 'a prophetic picture' and pointing out that there were even technical similarities, among them 'trench warfare' and 'a Hinden-berg Line'.[7]

Sometimes, indeed, one has the feeling that this obscure struggle in an obscure corner of the world, over a hundred years ago, was the real 'war to end wars'. The remoteness and obscurity in them-selves accentuate its symbolic, apocalyptic nature, isolating it, as it were, under laboratory conditions. Here, in miniature but highly concentrated form, are all the contradictions and ambiguities; all the vanities, ambitions and obsessions; all the cravings for power and paranoid preoccupations with security, prestige and face-saving; all the specious arguments and counter-arguments; all the courage, endurance and sacrifice ('Daring as never before, wastage as never before') that go to make up all wars – including, no doubt, some that are being waged at this moment.

In relating this story of the tragedy of Paraguay I have drawn wherever possible on first-hand contemporary accounts, which are obviously closer to the feel and spirit of the times than any later history can be, though I have also done my best to make allowances for the fact that some of these accounts are *too* close to the events to be free of personal passions and bias. The most important of these in English are *The War in Paraguay* by George Thompson, who was one of López's commanders; *Seven Eventful Years* by George F. Masterman, who was an employee, and later a prisoner, of the Marshal-President; *The Paraná, with Incidents of the Paraguayan War* by Thomas J. Hutchinson, who was British Consul at Rosario in Argentina at the time, and witnessed some of the events; *Letters from the Battlefields of Paraguay* by Richard F.

Burton, who visited many of the major scenes of conflict; and, to a lesser degree, *La Plata, Brazil and Paraguay during the Present War*, by A. J. Kennedy who was in command of a British ship on the river system during part of the war.

Inevitably these authors are quoted frequently (particularly Thompson) and it would slow down the narrative to give references in every case. The details of the book concerned, therefore, are given in the notes on the first occasion only of quoting.

The same applies to other major sources, and notably to Pelham Horton Box's classic *Origins of the Paraguayan War*. The story this book has to tell is an enthralling one which needs to be read without interruption, and the general reader would be irritated by too many bracketed numerals in the text, while it is assumed that any who wish to pursue the subject further would want to read such major sources in their entirety. Details of all books quoted, together with a selection of other important titles on the subject, are of course given in the Bibliography.

I should like to express my thanks to Mr Stephen Clissold for so kindly checking my typescript and raising a number of valuable points.

Gilbert Phelps

NOTES

[1] *Letters from the Battlefields of Paraguay*, Richard F. Burton. London 1870. Preface. Quotations from Burton are taken from this book.

[2] *El Mariscal Solano López*, Cecilio Baez. Asunción 1926.

[3] *El Mariscal Solano López*, Juan O'Leary. Asunción 1905; 2nd ed. Madrid 1925.

[4] See for example História da Guerra do Paraguaï, Max von Versen, in *Revista do Institute Histórico e Geografíco Brasileiro*, LXXVI, Part II, p. 57. Rio de Janeiro 1913.

[5] It should be borne in mind, however, that a disproportion between male and female births had always existed in Paraguay, especially among the Guaraníes.

[6] *Paraguay*, W. H. Koebel. London 1917. Quotations from Koebel are taken from this book.

[7] *Woman on Horseback: the biography of Francisco López and Eliza Lynch*, William E. Barrett. London 1938. Foreword. Quotations from Barrett are taken from this book.

The Main Persons of the Drama

Dr José Gaspar Rodríguez Francia, Dictator of Paraguay, 1814–40, and architect of Paraguay's independence.

Carlos Antonio López, Consul, then President of Paraguay, 1841–62.

Francisco Solano López, eldest son of Carlos Antonio López and his successor in the Presidency; as Marshal-President commanded the Paraguayan forces in the War of the Triple Alliance.

Elisa Alicia Lynch, Francisco Solano López's mistress and consort.

Dom Pedro De Alcantara, second Emperor of Brazil.

Bartolomé Mitre, leader of Buenos Aires in its struggles to avoid domination of the country's government by the provinces; President of the Republic of Argentina, 1862–68, and architect of modern Argentina. Commander-in-chief of the Allied forces during the greater part of the War of the Triple Alliance.

Justo José Urquiza, Governor of the Argentine province of Entre Ríos and leader of provincial interests against those of Buenos Aires. After his defeat of the dictator Juan Manuel Rosas became President of an Argentine Confederation, but was later defeated by Mitre when Buenos Aires rebelled. Later co-operated with Mitre for the good of the country.

Venancio Flores, one of the leaders of the Colorado Party in Uruguay, a friend of Mitre's and commander of the Uruguayan contingent in the Allied army.

Luís Alves de Lima e Silva, Marquês de Caxias, Commander of the Brazilian forces for most of the war.

Luiz Felipe Maria Fernando Gastão d'Orléans, Conde d'Eu, Son-in-law of the Emperor Pedro II of Brazil, and Commander-in-chief of the Allied forces in the last stage of the war.

Francisco Isidoro Resquín, one of Francisco Solano López's most trusted generals, who was with him to the last.

Father Fidel Maiz, a priest who had once been tutor to Francisco Solano López and who became his 'Grand Inquisitor' during the conspiracy investigations of 1868.

George Thompson, an English officer who served in the Paraguayan army as a Colonel, specialising in engineering and fortifications, and who became one of Francisco Solano López's most trusted commanders.

Charles Ames Washburn, U.S. Minister to Paraguay who was implicated in the conspiracy of 1868.

Martin T. MacMahon, the American General who succeeded Washburn as U.S. Minister in Paraguay.

ACT ONE
Expulsion from Eden?

From the sixteenth century onwards visitors to Paraguay have been struck by a sense of sylvan enchantment, combined with a curious 'time out of time' quality. References to the Garden of Eden, Arcadia, 'lotus land', Shangri-la have been commonplace.

In part, of course, the explanation lies in the very real beauty and charm of the country and in the simple, pastoral way of life (even today) of the majority of the inhabitants – though it must be borne in mind that Paraguay is divided into two distinct zones, with the Chaco, lying to the west of the River Paraguay and considerably the larger, an inhospitable, sparsely populated region consisting mostly of forest-scrub and nearly waterless prairie.

In part it is the actual remoteness of the country that is responsible. It is impossible to understand Paraguay's peculiar nature and destiny without taking into account her geographical isolation, her reliance for an outlet to the sea on a river which for most of its length runs through foreign territory, and the fact that she is jammed between the hinterlands of the two most powerful states of South America, Argentina and Brazil.

Most important of all is the nature of the people themselves. Although the ruling caste, together with the administrative and cultural framework, are predominantly Spanish, the Guaraníes (the most numerous of the indigenous Indian peoples at the time of the Conquest) have exercised a most potent influence on the development of Paraguay. In spite of its early administrative importance Asunción was so inaccessible and remote that the number of Spanish settlers was always comparatively small, and as they had brought few Spanish women with them miscegenation took place quickly and on a large scale, producing a remarkably comely mestizo race. In the process, moreover, the Guaraní culture survived more vigorously than most of the other Indian cultures of South America. Even today many family customs and popular beliefs derive from Guaraní traditions. Above all, the Guaraní language is still used by the mass of the people;

newspapers and books are published in it, and there is a Guaraní theatre. Paraguay, in fact, has been described as the only genuinely bilingual country in South America. Nowadays most Paraguayans speak Spanish as well, and there is evidence to suggest that the balance between the two languages is gradually changing. In time perhaps the status of the Guaraní language will come to be analogous to that of Welsh – a valuable rallying point for national-istic sentiment, but for most practical purposes a dead language. But this was certainly not the case during the period covered by this book. It was in Guaraní, for example, that Francisco Solano López joked with his soldiers and exhorted them to battle, for the simple reason that it was the only language most of them knew.

Among the earlier writers on Paraguay the references to Arcadia usually applied to the Jesuit 'state within a state', which constitutes one of the most remarkable chapters of all in Paraguay's history.

It was in 1604 that the Father General of the Order, Claudius Aquaviva[1] decided on the formation of a new Jesuit province in the region, and his plans received the royal seal of approval four years later. Although it was called 'Paraguaria' this new province com-prised an area far greater than that of the modern republic of Paraguay, covering the whole of the La Plata region, as well as modern Chile. The main centres of operation were on the eastern and southern banks of the Río Paraná, in areas which are now in-corporated in Brazil and Argentina. Of the thirty *reducciones* that were eventually established, in fact, only eight fell within the boundaries of modern Paraguay, mostly in the south-eastern part of the country.

The first of these communities was founded in 1610 at San Ignacio Guazú on the banks of the Paraná. Others quickly followed, most of them in the province of Guairá (now in Brazil). But a very considerable crisis was brewing.

Nearly eight hundred miles away, at São Paulo in Brazil (today the greatest industrial city in South America) a remarkably vigorous race, known as Mamelucos, had grown up out of the union of the original Portuguese and Dutch settlers with their Indian and Negro slaves.

The supply of slaves had, however, gradually begun to dry up, for two main reasons. In the first place, many of the Indians had died as a result of the ill-treatment or of the diseases bestowed on them by the white man. In the second place, during the 1620s the

Dutch gained control of the seas off the east coast of South America (in 1630 conquering and occupying the Brazilian province of Pernambuco), and commanded the trade routes from Africa along which Negro slaves had been shipped from the Portuguese colonies in Africa, in particular Angola.

The Mamelucos, who had already proved themselves ruthless slave-hunters, were in consequence spurred on to even greater efforts. When they had enslaved all the Indians they could lay their hands on in the neighbourhood of São Paulo, they organized themselves into armed bands, or *bandeiras* (hence another of the names applied to them – *bandeirantes*). Marching barefoot, accompanied often by their women and children, they advanced further and further into the interior, looting, killing and collecting slaves as they went.

The *bandeirantes* of course played a memorable part in pushing forward the frontiers of the Portuguese empire of Brazil (though it must be borne in mind that between 1581 and 1641, the crowns of Spain and Portugal were united). Inevitably, however, they became an increasingly serious threat both to the *encomiendas* – or feudal fiefs, granted by the Spanish Crown to some of the more favoured colonists – and to the Jesuit missions. The latter were a particularly tempting bait, both because the Indians in them were better cared for than those in the *encomiendas*, and because the Jesuits were at this stage forbidden to issue their charges with firearms.

In 1629, the Mamelucos attacked and destroyed several of the reductions. The Jesuits' Indians, armed only with bows and arrows or clubs, were no match for the well-trained Mamelucos of São Paulo, with their horses, guns and bloodhounds, and their savage Indian auxiliaries, armed with blow-pipes and poisoned arrows. By order of the Jesuit Superior, Ruiz de Montoya – one of the most remarkable among a remarkable group of men – two of the Jesuits, unattended and on foot, accompanied the captives, 'confessing those who fell upon the road before they died', Cunninghame-Graham tells us, 'and instant in supplication to the Paulistas for the prisoners' release'.[2] The main task with which the two Jesuits had been entrusted, however, was to plead with the authorities in Brazil. They did, in fact, obtain from the governor-general in Bahía, a decree against the encroachment of the *bandeirantes* on to Spanish territory, but to get it enforced in São Paulo was a different matter; the official who was supposed to promulgate it was too frightened even to make the attempt, and the two fathers had to return empty-handed to Guairá – and soon the Mamelucos were once again on the rampage.

What followed must surely be one of the most astonishing episodes in history – the evacuation of the remaining Jesuit flocks from Guairá to the area round the lower reaches of the Alto Paraná. This involved organizing at least ten thousand Indians into families, each individual carrying a bundle on his back; hacking paths through dense jungle, hitherto completely unknown except to the wild and hostile Indians who inhabited them; crossing rivers and streams and rapids by canoe and raft; and skirting the vast Guairá cataracts, a feat which in itself took eight days.

This extraordinary exodus (led by Ruiz de Montoya) was completed towards the end of 1631, though of the ten thousand who had set out half had died on the way, of hardship or starvation.

For some time the Jesuits and their Indians enjoyed a respite, though other reductions in Guairá had to be evacuated, while the Mamelucos also destroyed the Spanish townships in the province, thereby ensuring that it became part of Brazil.

Then in 1636, Mamelucos broke into the province of Tapé and overran several reductions there, so that a further exodus had to be carried out, the 'promised land' in this case being the territory between the rivers Uruguay and Paraná – which is now the Argentine province of Misiones – though even it was not out of reach of the Paulistas.

In the meantime, Ruiz de Montoya, accompanied by Diaz Taño (another Jesuit of remarkable qualities) had set out for Europe in order (among other objectives) to try to enlist the help of the Spanish king and the *Consejo de Indias* (the Council of the Indies), which administered the affairs of the Spanish–American colonies, and of the Pope himself, against the attacks of the Paulistas, to plead for more effective military assistance from the colonial authorities – and, above all, to press for official consent to the arming of their mission Indians with firearms.

While Ruiz de Montoya and Diaz Taño were in Europe, the third major Mameluco invasion took place. The Spanish authorities and colonists did little about it, but in 1639 Father Diego Alfaro, who had been left in charge of the missions between the rivers Uruguay and Paraná, engaged the enemy with his Indian Militia, which had been issued with firearms, at Caazapá Guazú, and defeated them, though he himself was struck by a Mameluco bullet and fell dead from his horse, musket in hand. A Spanish force, despatched belatedly by the Governor of Paraguay, took a number of prisoners, but to the indignation of the Jesuits let most of them go. The Jesuits in consequence became increasingly reluctant to ask for help from the Spanish garrisons, and there seems little doubt that about this time they not only purchased firearms for their Indians, but also managed to manufacture a number in the reductions themselves.

In April, 1640, Father Diaz Taño arrived at Rio de Janeiro armed with a bull reiterating the papal prohibition of slavery, with special reference to Brazil and Paraguay, and threatening all slave dealers with excommunication. Again it proved impossible to enforce, and at the beginning of 1641, a band of Paulistas, more determined than ever to destroy the Jesuit townships and to acquire their Indians as slaves, set out with a large fleet down the Rio Uruguay. On the Rio Mbororé, a tributary of the Uruguay, a force of reduction Guaraníes, two hundred of them armed with muskets, under the command of Domingo de Torres, a lay brother who was also a veteran soldier, and two Indian *caciques*, or chiefs, waited for them. After a bloody battle on land and water, the Paulistas were defeated, and forced to retreat with heavy losses.

These events more or less coincided with the arrival of the news of the 1640 revolution in Portugal, which ended the union of the Spanish and Portuguese crowns and put the Duke of Braganza on an independent Portuguese throne as King John IV. The 'Sixty Years Captivity' (as Portuguese historians have called it) had been a stormy one in any case – and it had never fundamentally altered the underlying imperial rivalry between Spaniards and Portuguese.

The threat of Mameluco invasions was now no longer a constant anxiety, though there were still periodic raids, and the Jesuits were able to settle down to a long period of more or less peaceful development.

What was unique about the Jesuit missions was not the idea itself, which had already been adopted by other religious orders, but the thoroughness and efficiency with which it was carried out. The Jesuit System was nothing if not orderly. The towns and villages, which ranged in population from about twelve hundred to about eight thousand, were all built on the same plan. There was a large central square of grass, on which sheep were pastured in order to keep it short. On three sides of this square were the dwellings of the Indians – long, low pent-houses, made of wattled canes or sun-dried bricks, accommodating a hundred families or more, divided into separate apartments by lath-and-plaster walls, but all under the same roof and with a communal verandah or with a wide portico forming a covered walk.

The fourth side of the square was taken up by a towered church; to the right of it the house of the Jesuits (they usually worked in pairs, and even in the largest of the mission towns there were seldom more than three) and the public work-shops, each enclosed in a quadrangle; to the left, a walled cemetery and a house for widows, also enclosed in a quadrangle; and behind all these, a large garden.

The life lived in the reductions was every bit as orderly as their design. As Robert Southey says in his *History of Brazil*, 'An Indian of the Reductions never knew, during his whole progress from the cradle to the grave, what it was to take thought for the morrow: all his duties were comprised in obedience. The strictest discipline soon becomes tolerable when it is certain and immutable . . . that of the Jesuits extended to every thing, but it was neither capricious nor oppressive'.[3] And Cunninghame-Graham has given us this vivid picture of a typical day in the life of the reductions:

> '. . . the Jesuits marshalled their neophytes to the sound of music, and in procession to the fields, with a saint borne high aloft, the community each day at sunrise took its way. Along the path, at stated intervals, were shrines of saints, and before each of them they prayed, and between each shrine sang hymns. As the procession advanced, it became gradually smaller as groups of Indians dropped off to work the various fields, and finally the priest and acolyte with the musicians returned alone. At midday, before eating, they all united and sang hymns, and then, after their meal and siesta, returned to work till sundown, when the procession again reformed, and the labourers, singing, returned to their abodes. . . . But even then the hymnal day was not concluded, for after a brief rest they all repaired to church to sing the "rosary", and then to sup and bed'.

In this 'perpetual Sunday school', as Cunninghame-Graham calls it elsewhere, music, it will be seen, played an important part. It was soon discovered that the Guaraníes possessed both excellent singing voices and a considerable aptitude for European musical instruments. Mass, in consequence, was celebrated with a full orchestra; in the inventories (taken after the expulsion of the Jesuits) oboes, violas, and other musical instruments are listed.

There were frequent religious festivals. In particular, the patron saint's day (each mission had its own) was a public holiday and an occasion for great excitement. It began at dawn with a discharge of rockets and firearms (when they were available) and a peal of bells. Then the whole population flocked to church for an early mass; inside the church the sexes sat or knelt separately, the various Indian church officers dressed in special uniforms; outside, those who could not gain admittance stood in long lines outside the doors, which remained open during the service.

Cunninghame-Graham describes how after mass there was an elaborate procession, with '*los caballos del Santo*' – 'the horses of the saint' – richly caparisoned and ridden by Indians in splendid costumes, specially kept for the purpose, with the various Indian officers even more gorgeously attired – the Jesuits were at pains to create numerous offices for their Indians, each with a high-sounding name and its own livery. At the very front of the procession rode the *Alférez Real* (the royal herald), mounted on a white horse, dressed in a doublet of blue velvet, decorated with much gold lace, a brocaded waistcoat, and velvet breeches gartered with silver lace; on his feet were shoes with silver buckles, and on his head a splendid gold-laced hat. He carried the royal standard in his right hand, and a ceremonial sword at his side. Just behind him rode the *Corregidor* (the highest of the Indian officials in a Guaraní reduction), magnificent in yellow satin, silk waistcoat with gold buttons, breeches of yellow velvet, and again, a splendid hat. Then came the two *alcaldes* (roughly the equivalent of town councillors) in strawberry coloured satin waistcoats, and with hats piped with gold. Lesser officials were no less gaily dressed – and at stated intervals in the procession, troops of dancers (the Jesuits made use of the Guaraníes' love of dancing as much as of their talent for music), who 'performed a sort of Pyrrhic dance between the squadrons of the cavalry'.

Occasions such as this, of course, were highlights, but there were quite a number of them. If the life of the mission Indians was a 'perpetual Sunday', it is evident that it was not a drab English one.

In the everyday life of the communities, there were also a number of Indian officers – carefully selected and supervised by the Jesuits. The Indian *caciques*, for example, held commands in the armed militia – though with soldier-priests at their sides. These chiefs, incidentally, received preferential treatment in other ways; they had their own Indian guards and servants, and they received better food than the rest. The police officers were also Indians chosen by the Jesuits, and the missions had their own gaols.

The economy of the reductions was a kind of primitive communism. As Southey puts it, in his romantic Utopian vein:

> 'the first object (of the Jesuits) was to remove from their people all temptations which are not inherent in human nature; and by establishing as nearly as possible a community of goods, they excluded a large portion of the crimes and miseries which embitter the life of civilized man'.

A certain amount of private property was, in fact, allowed, the head of every family having a plot of land assigned to him for his own use; but if he failed to cultivate it properly, when he grew too old to do so, and on his death, it was allocated to someone else, not necessarily a member of the family. All the rest of the lands, and all the equipment, oxen for ploughing, seed and so on, were the property of the community. The produce from these communal lands was placed in a common storehouse, for the upkeep of widows, orphans, the children generally, and for the sick and aged. The common stores were also drawn upon for the needs of the churches (including the feasts and processions) and for other public purposes. The tribute, which from 1649 was paid direct to the king, in return for various exemptions (particularly from the labour demands of the colonists) came from the same source – though it must also be remembered that the Jesuits were considerable traders, both among the various reductions (by an intricate barter system) and with the outside world. Their main exports as far as external trade was concerned were cotton, linen cloth, tobacco, hides, hardwoods – and most important of all, *yerba-mate*, which was already (as it still is in many parts of South America) a necessity rather than a luxury, probably because it is rich in various vitamins that are usually lacking in the rest of the diet.

The mission Indians, in return for their labour, received rations of food and clothing (more or less on the principle 'from each according to his abilities, to each according to his needs' – or perhaps one should add the word 'deserts' to the second part of the formula) as well as various imported articles such as knives, scissors and looking glasses. They did not only work as farmers. Many of the missions had large *estancias* with many hundreds, and sometimes thousands, head of cattle, and on these the Indians worked as herdsmen and cowboys. Many of them were also taught to be craftsmen, in an astonishing variety of trades. They were builders, stone masons, sculptors or woodcarvers; they were weavers, tanners, tailors, hat-makers; coopers, cordage makers, boat builders, cartwrights and joiners; in some cases they manufactured the muskets and powder for the militia; the musical instruments used in the mass – including even the organs – and in the religious festivals were nearly all made by them; they produced carpets, astronomical spheres and beautiful illuminated manuscripts – and they learned how to print and bind books.

Most observers, however, give little credit to the Guaraníes for these achievements, apart from acknowledging their docility as pupils. Was this lack of initiative, together with the extreme docility, native to the Guaraníes, or was it the result of Jesuit indoctrination, of the iron hand in the velvet glove? Or to put it another way, was the typical Jesuit reduction a kind of religious Arcadia, or a disguised concentration camp controlled by a subtle form of brain-washing?

Few would deny that the Jesuits were paternalistic in their attitude. Southey, for example, who is at pains to point out that 'the sanctity of the end proposed and the heroism and perseverance with which it was pursued, deserve the highest admiration', says as well that 'never was there a more absolute depotism'. And Professor C. R. Boxer, one of our most distinguished contemporary historians of Latin America, writes:

> 'The Jesuit attitude towards their charges was indeed a paternal one, but it was the attitude of a father towards a backward boy who is never expected to grow up. Their neophytes were never trained to look after themselves, but to follow blindly in all things the orders and advice of their spiritual fathers. When they had become men, they had no chance of putting away childish things. They were thus inherently incapable of taking their place in the civilized society which was slowly developing around them.'[4]

On the other hand, Magnus Mörner, in his important study, makes two important points. In the first place, he suggests that at the time the Jesuits began their work, the Guaraníes were culturally at an in-between stage, one that made them particularly susceptible to colonization. They were, Mörner says, 'on the one hand the most culturally advanced people in the eastern part of the La Plata region, and on the other hand they lacked the cultural and religious traditions and the political consciousness of the Andean peoples'.[5] At that particular stage in their development they were, in other words, in a fluid state, and from the beginning the Jesuits were struck by their extreme tractability, their eagerness, almost, to be directed into a mould. One of the main reasons for the success of the Jesuits, in fact, was simply that the Guaraníes of the Alto Paraná region were more obedient than any of the other Indians; when the Jesuits tried, time after time during the seventeenth century, to establish similar missions among other Indian tribes, they seldom met with much success.

Secondly, Mörner also points out that the frequent migrations by the missions as the result of the Mameluco invasions, by breaking the ties with their own localities and thereby weakening their cultural traditions, inevitably increased the dependence of the Guaraníes on their Jesuit masters. In any case, one cannot help asking, would it have been of any use to the Guaraníes if they *had* been capable of further cultural advance? The fate of the Indians of the Andes or of Mexico hardly leads one to suppose so. Even if one does not accept 'the black legend' in its entirety, and even if one is sceptical of the romantic picture of a religious Arcadia of simplicity and bliss, there can surely be little doubt that the Indians' lot under the Jesuits was in most respects preferable to what it would have been outside the settlements.

For nearly two hundred years, in fact, whatever their failings, and however mistaken their good intentions may have been, the Jesuits were the protectors of their Indians from the worst of the physical ills that assailed those outside. In treating their charges like children they may have been, as happens so often in parent–child relationships, too confident in believing that they alone knew what was best for their welfare; but if they were stern fathers they were seldom cruel ones. And as far as the children were concerned, one thing at least was certain: whether or not life in the reductions resembled 'that happy garden state' which the poet Andrew Marvell ascribed to our first parents in the biblical Eden, it would not in this case be disobedience that would lead to the Fall.

A fall, indeed, was the last thing that seemed possible in 1641, after the victory on the Rio Mbororé. It is true that the Jesuits suffered a number of setbacks after the appointment, in 1642, of Don Bernardino de Cárdenas, a Franciscan, to the see of Paraguay, at a time when there was a good deal of rivalry between the Jesuit and Franciscan missionaries, but in the end the Jesuits triumphed.

Their privileges were fully confirmed by the Crown, and the years from the final departure of Cárdenas from Asunción in 1650 until about 1721 were in many respects their golden period. The prosperity of the reductions increased steadily. Between 1686 and 1697 new mission-towns were founded, though it was not until 1706–7 that the last two of the thirty townships which constituted the 'Jesuit State' were established; bringing the total population to about 100,000, a considerable figure by the standards of the day.

Nevertheless throughout this long period of consolidation, progress and prosperity, powerful factors were at work against the interests of the Jesuits. The Cárdenas affair had left its mark; his supporters in Madrid continued their intrigues against the Jesuits for a long time, and the latter gradually began to lose their high standing and influence at court. Human nature being what it is, there were also suspicions of the 'no smoke without fire' order; the rumours started by Cárdenas that the Jesuits had discovered valuable gold-mines, for example, persisted despite all the evidence to the contrary. What probably constituted the greatest single undermining factor in the Jesuits' position, as far as the colonists of Paraguay were concerned, however, was the fact that on two occasions the reduction Indians had been used against Cárdenas and his followers, after he had illegally seized the governorship. That on both occasions this had been at the request of the viceregal authorities in Lima made no difference at the purely emotional level. It was one thing to arm the reduction Guaraníes and send them against rebellious Indians of other tribes, or even against the Mamelucos; it was an altogether different matter to employ them against rebellious whites. The feeling of shock it produced was probably heightened by a rising in 1660 among the Guaraníes themselves (not, of course, those in the missions). It was the first for a long time; for by now, as Mörner points out, the Guaraníes were already to some extent a component part of the community in Paraguay and it was almost certainly caused by the more severe demands being made on the labour of the dwindling numbers of Indians held in *encomienda*. The two circumstances combined raised the spectre that haunts all colonists, that of a general native uprising.

The position of the Jesuits was further weakened when, in 1721, Paraguay entered upon another period of internal turmoil, as the result of Don José de Antequera's usurpation of the Governor-ship, even though with the defeat of the rebels in 1734 (with the help of the reduction Guaraníes) the Jesuits entered upon a further ten year period of development, during which they devoted much of their energies to trying to establish missions among the wild Indians of the Chaco and even farther afield, and even though in 1743 they received an important royal confirmation of their privileged status in Paraguay.

The train of events that eventually led to their expulsion started with the treaty signed in 1750 between Spain and Portugal, whereby the Portuguese agreed to exchange their settlement of Colonia do Sacramento (which threatened Spanish commercial interests and sovereignty in the area) for the seven Jesuit reductions on the river Uruguay, and at the same time to discuss a definition of the very vague boundaries. It was a particularly cynical piece of diplomatic horse-trading, entered into, of course, without any consideration for the inhabitants of the seven Jesuit townships concerned. When the Jesuits received instructions to prepare their Indians for an evacuation of the seven reductions, which they had themselves settled and held against the very Portuguese who were now to be allowed to dispossess them, and to march into the forests to search for suitable sites for new missions, the Indians, not surprisingly, refused to be shifted, and when the joint commission for marking out the boundaries between the two countries arrived in the area of the seven mission towns – they found themselves surrounded by a strong force of reduction Indians.

The 'Jesuit War', as the enemies of the Order called it, dragged on intermittently for eight years. The Indians, however, had no real chance of ultimate victory. There was never more than a small élite trained in the use of firearms, and the Indians were no match for the combined and fully equipped forces of Spain and Portugal. By 1757, serious resistance had petered out, and the commissioners at last set about their task – though by now the seven reductions were practically deserted.

To what extent, though, is the term 'Jesuit War' justified? There is no doubt that a few priests marched with the Indian rebels, though their actual commanders were in all cases *caciques*, but there is no evidence of planned military resistance on the part of the superiors of the Order.

The crowning irony to the whole tragic story is that after the death of Ferdinand VI of Spain in 1760 (and with the Spanish and Portuguese commissioners still arguing over the boundaries), the Jesuits succeeded in persuading his successor, Charles III, in

1761, to annul all that had been done, and to declare that the seven townships of the Uruguay would, after all, remain part of the dominions of the Spanish crown. But by now the tide was beginning to run against the Jesuits throughout Europe. The Marquis of Pombal, virtual ruler of Portugal, had banished the Order from the homeland and from Brazil in 1759, and Louis XV expelled them from France in 1764. After protracted intrigues, inquiries and deliberations in Madrid, the end suddenly came, too, for the Jesuits in Spain and the whole of her overseas empire, when on 27 February 1767, Charles III issued a decree of expulsion and confiscation.

The task of implementing the order in Paraguay was entrusted to Don Francisco de Paula Bucareli y Ursúa, the Viceroy of Buenos Aires (the administrative control of Paraguay had by now been transferred from Lima). There were a few cases of rioting on the part of the mission Indians, but the Jesuits themselves offered no resistance. As Bucareli and his soldiers advanced from town to town, they came out of their houses, peacefully handed over the keys and allowed themselves to be made prisoners. Seventy-eight Jesuits and their Provincials were sent back to Buenos Aires, and their missions handed over to priests from other Orders. The whole operation was over in a remarkably short time. And so, within the space of a few months, the two-hundred-year rule of the Jesuits in Paraguay was over.

What, then, of the charges that there was a 'Jesuit State' hidden in the wilds of Paraguay, and that this 'State' was part of a vast Jesuit conspiracy to seize power throughout the Catholic world, which were passionately advanced both at the time and since? Most objective historians would now probably agree with the summing-up of Magnus Mörner:

'Although the responsibility of individual missionaries remains uncertain, the rest of the questions can easily be denied today on the basis of historical documentation', though Mörner goes on to point out that it was more difficult for contemporary critics of the Jesuits 'to ascertain the truth, and the rumours emanating from Paraguay undoubtedly played an important part in creating universal suspicion of the Order'.[6]

There is also the question of Jesuit wealth in Paraguay. In most respects the rumours here were just as fantastic as those of the 'Jesuit State' and the 'world conspiracy'. Certainly it could hardly be said that the Jesuits had acquired anything impressive in the way of worldly goods for themselves. On their expulsion they were permitted to take their personal possessions away with them. In a letter dated 30 October 1768, Bucareli listed some of them. The first of the Jesuits on this list is recorded as having in his possession ten shirts, two pillow-cases, two sheets, three pocket handkerchiefs, two pairs of shoes, two pair of socks, and a pound and a half of snuff. The others were less richly endowed with shirts, though some had cloaks, and one a nightcap. (All of them, however, had their snuff.) A paper from their Provincial, which accompanied the list, testified that most of the clothes (and, of course, they had an arduous journey of several months ahead of them) had come from the common stock – and all the snuff.

The economic wealth of the missions, as the result of the years of sound organization and management, was certainly considerable. They were, for example, far ahead of their competitors among the colonists in the very profitable *yerba mate* trade – largely because, to the fury of the colonists, they had at their disposal a much greater labour force, and they owned a good deal of land, and in particular land for grazing cattle, mules and sheep. On the other hand, there is no evidence to support the charge that the profits from the reductions were used to any important extent to swell the income of the Order in Rome. By far the greater part of them was employed, in fact, within the reductions themselves to enhance the magnificence of the churches and of the religious ceremonies and festivals, in accordance with the well-known Jesuit motto: *Ad Maiorem Dei Gloriam*. One should, perhaps, add a postscript here: the fabled gold-mines were never discovered, frantically though Bucareli's agents searched for them.

There is also the very important question of whether the two hundred years Jesuit experiment had any lasting effect. Cunninghame-Graham uses a very telling image when he describes it as a 'sort of dropping down of a diving-bell in the flood of progress to keep alive a population which would otherwise soon have been suffocated in its muddy waves'. It was an experiment, he adds, in 'a half-Arcadian, half-monastic life, that was doomed to failure by the very nature of mankind'.

It is a view which has been widely held. George Pendle, for example, has stated that in spite of their sojourn in Paraguay 'the Jesuits exercised little or no permanent influence on the development of the Paraguayan people and character. Their purpose was merely to "domesticate" the Indians, not to develop Paraguayan civilization.'[7]

Certainly the Jesuit mission towns fell into decay. John Parrish Robertson, the young Scottish merchant who visited some of them in 1811, painted a depressing picture, oddly reminiscent of Goldsmith's *Deserted Village*:

'Sad, cheerless, desolate was the appearance (of the mission towns and their inhabitants). Everything was falling into decay – the church, the College, the huts. Many of the latter were in ruins; the men stood listless at their doors; weeds and briars were everywhere springing up; the population was dwindling away daily, and it was with difficulty the two curates in each town could scrape together enough from the labour of the whole community, scantily to feed, and badly to clothe, the members of it.'[8]

In Candelaria, which under the Jesuits had a population of over three thousand, and a splendid church, Robertson found only seven hundred Indians still hanging on, and these in a condition of apathy and listlessness.

A Spanish–American contemporary of Robertson's, Dr Gregorio Funes (he had been brought up in the Argentinian province of Tucumán) amply confirms the rapacity and incompetence of the missionaries appointed by Bucareli to succeed the Jesuits in the reductions. 'Ignorant of Guaraní, and without patience to acquire it, confusion reigned in the missions as in a tower of Babel' – and he goes on to say that before long 'a wall of hatred and contempt began to rise between the Indians and their masters'.[9]

On the other hand, Magnus Mörner maintains that 'it is an easily proved fact that the famous missions of "Paraguay" suffered only a gradual decline after the Jesuits had left in 1768', and he is surely right in saying that 'not all Guaraní Indians forgot the abilities they had acquired from their Jesuit masters but, thanks to these same qualities, were easily absorbed into colonial society'. There were indeed desertions from the mission towns which led to steady decline, but these desertions, far from being 'back to the jungle', constituted an important cultural fillip to the development of the Río de la Plata region.[10]

In other words, the two hundred years' Jesuit rule must be seen as an integral part of the history of this region of South America and the Indians trained by that rule as part of the area's political, social and cultural texture.

As far as Paraguay herself is concerned, there is no doubt that Guaraní behaviour patterns formed under the influence of the Jesuits (though they may also have been to some extent inherent) continued to play a considerable part in the life of the nation as a whole.

This really brings us back to the question of the 'docility' of the Guaraníes which was made so much of by anti-Paraguayan propagandists during the War of the Triple Alliance. Colonel George Thompson who had ample first-hand experience of the Guaraníes as soldiers (he was the only Englishman to receive a commission in the Paraguayan army of Francisco Solano López) certainly believed that it was the Jesuits who had brought them 'to a more than military state of discipline and obedience, under which they gradually abdicated reason and thought'.[11] This, of course, is an adverse view, but it is certainly arguable that the special qualities of the Paraguayan people, in war or peace, were in some degree the product of that blend of kindness and authoritarianism which was peculiar to Jesuit rule.

Among these qualities must also be included a conservatism and suspicion of foreigners reminiscent at times (as Burton and several other nineteenth-century writers suggested) of China or Japan before they reversed their traditional xenophobia (though they did not exclude innate instincts of friendliness and hospitality) and a conviction that a simple, pastoral way of life, based on an economic self-sufficiency such as prevailed in the Jesuit missions, was the law of nature.

Dr Pelham Horton Box, in his classic study of the causes leading up to the War of the Triple Alliance, came to the conclusion that it was the 'political and economic isolation and the long discipline of the Jesuits that had prepared the Guaraní people of the province of Paraguay for the assertion of independence of 1811'.[12]

The seeds of the movements of liberation from Spanish rule throughout Spanish America lay (though there were all sorts of other factors, including the influence of the French Revolution on young Spanish–American intellectuals) in the rivalries between the *peninsulares* (that is, Spaniards born in Spain and sent out as soldiers or colonial administrators) and the *criollos* (that is, descendants of the original colonists born and bred in Spanish America), rivalries which had been acute from quite an early date, and which became more so with the gradual decline of Spanish power, culminating in Napoleon Bonaparte's entry into Madrid in 1808.

These rivalries were particularly fierce in Paraguay, partly because of its isolation and the early emergence of a distinctive Paraguayan racial consciousness. The spirit of independence among the *criollos* grew as Asunción became increasingly remote from the rest of the Spanish–American empire, especially after 1617, when the Spanish government came to the conclusion that the hoped-for route across the Chaco to the mines of the Andes, which would have made Asunción of the utmost economic and strategic importance, was impracticable; and decided on the separation of Buenos Aires, originally founded from Asunción but now regarded as possessing far greater potential, from the province of Paraguay. From this date onwards, Spain really lost interest in Paraguay, except as an outpost of empire against the encroachments of Brazil, with the Jesuit reductions fulfilling some of the functions of frontier garrisons.

The later Governors of Paraguay tended to have a particularly stormy passage. Antequera's usurpation of the governorship in 1721, for example, had the ardent support of many of the *criollos* of Asunción, and the attempt by the Viceroy of Peru to reinstate Balmaceda, the legal Governor, led to what George Pendle describes as 'one of the earliest and most serious risings against Spanish authority to occur anywhere in the Spanish–American Empire'.

Ironically enough, though, it was actually through defending the king's authority that Paraguay finally asserted her independence. In 1776 the country had been incorporated into the Vice-royalty of the Río de la Plata. The Porteños – inhabitants, that is, of the port of Buenos Aires – were especially hated in Asunción, partly because they were seen as offspring who had grown too big for their boots, partly for solid commercial reasons in that it was they who controlled Paraguay's access to the sea. The idea of receiving orders from Buenos Aires was, therefore, anathema, and when in 1810 the *criollos* of Buenos Aires deposed the Viceroy, and set up a junta of patriots (in effect declaring their independence of Spain) and 'invited' Asunción to follow suit, the natural reaction was to refuse. Thus the Governor of Paraguay, Don Bernardo de Velasco, found that he had an army behind him pledged to fight for the Spanish crown, when the Argentines followed up their invitation with a more tangible argument in the shape of General Belgrano and an expeditionary force.

Belgrano was defeated at Paraguarí on the 19 January 1811, and again on 9 March, at Tacuarí. He was forced to withdraw, but after lengthy 'educative' talks with various Paraguayan officers, managed to insert a declaration of the Junta's policy into the actual articles of the armistice. 'The object of his expedition,' one of the paragraphs ran, 'had been to assist the natives of Paraguay in order that, supported by the forces of the Junta, they might recover their rights, and that they might appoint a deputy, who should take part in the deliberations of the General Congress on the common policy to be adopted.'[13]

This clause certainly does not sound like a recognition of Paraguay's right to independent action on the matter of Spain's sovereignty – and Buenos Aires did not intend it to be. Obviously it is of some importance in understanding the background to the War of the Triple Alliance, pointing as it does to the proprietary attitude Argentina tended to adopt towards Paraguay, and which lay behind the suspicions (even if they sometimes reached extravagant proportions) entertained by Paraguay's subsequent rulers towards Argentine intentions.

At the time, in fact, the Paraguayans were themselves doubtful as to which path they should follow. It did not take them long to come to the conclusion that Belgrano was right as far as Spanish suzerainty was concerned, and they deposed the Governor on whose behalf they had taken up arms against the Porteños (though he continued to live among them). But those who immediately succeeded him left the position undefined. In her state papers, Paraguay continued for some time to call herself a province and not a republic, and when a formal treaty was concluded with Buenos Aires, in the October, the options were left open on the question of whether or not Paraguay would join the proposed Argentine confederation.

Equally significant is another clause in the armistice agreement which expressed the pious hope that there should in future be 'peace, union, entire confidence, and free and liberal commerce in all the products of the province (Paraguay, that is) including that of tobacco, with the States of the Río de la Plata, and particularly that of Buenos Aires.'

Bartolomé Mitre – later President of the Argentine Confederation and commander-in-chief of the Allied armies invading the

Paraguay of Francisco Solano López – had a shrewd comment to make on this apparently minor matter of the 'free and liberal commerce' in tobacco:

'This was putting the finger on the wound. Tobacco was the monopoly of the Government in Paraguay, and the planters might not export or sell their crops until the needs of the monopoly had been satisfied. Anyone who infringed this regulation was punished as a smuggler. The factory established in Asunción was accustomed to pay two pesos for each arroba of tobacco selected by it, which it sold again for nine pesos two reales. Moreover, it would buy at the lowest prices those lots of tobacco which it had rejected in the first instance – prices which the planter found himself under the necessity of accepting.'

Now what we have here is an indication not simply of the clash of commercial interests, but in some measure a clash also between two utterly opposed economic systems. The revolution in Buenos Aires had been a predominantly middle-class one (like the French Revolution of 1789) directed against the effete Spanish aristocracy and the cumbersome colonial administrative machine, which had thwarted the energies of the native urban bourgeoisie. It was a 'liberal' revolution largely in the sense that it desired liberty from archaic economic restraints, and freedom to exploit the workings of *laissez-faire* capitalism. The commercial classes of Asunción (which included some of the leading *criollo* families) had much the same aspirations, and in this respect at any rate a good deal in common with their counterparts in Buenos Aires – especially if the latter could be induced to allow them free access to the sea. As the quotation from Bartolomé Mitre shows, however, there was also already established in Paraguay a tradition of state-control, almost certainly influenced by the example of the Jesuit reductions – though of course, also by other factors including the country's peculiar geographical position. And this system was to be greatly extended by Paraguay's dictators.

But before we examine this question any further, something must be said about the remarkable man who canalized the motives that had driven his countrymen to arms against the Porteños so completely that the Paraguayan nation is in effect his life-work and legacy.

The origins of Dr José Gaspar Rodríguez Francia are obscure. According to William Parrish Robertson (both brothers knew him personally) Dr Francia alleged that his father was a Frenchman. Burton, on the other hand, says that the family was 'of Paulista origin' and that their house was, in his time, still to be seen in São Paulo. Others claim that Francia's father was a Portuguese named Rodríguez who had lived in France, and expanded his name to demonstrate the fact. There seems no doubt, at any rate, that he moved to Paraguay, probably, as Burton tells us, as supervisor of a tobacco plantation at Yaguarón, and his famous son was born on Paraguayan soil – though the date, too, is doubtful; Burton puts it as early as 1757, others as late as 1766.

There is also uncertainty about Francia's earlier years – apart from the fact of his youthful distinction of intellect and personality. It seems certain, however, that he studied at the University of Córdoba (in Argentina) where he obtained the degrees of Master of Philosophy and Doctor of Theology – though according to some his doctorate was in Law. Certainly it was as a lawyer that he earned his living when he returned to Asunción, and he soon won a reputation for efficiency, hard work, incorruptibility, and for his aloof and austere way of life.

Even more significant was the fact that he took every opportunity to defend the legal rights of the Guaraníes, who addressed him as Carai (the Guaraní word for 'great chief') and for whom he became an object of reverence and awe – with the reputation of being a magician, because of his learning and his possession of a few simple scientific instruments.

His abilities won him several important appointments under Spanish rule. He played a prominent part in the events leading up to the assertion of independence, and he was one of the members of Paraguay's own revolutionary Junta elected by the country's first Congress; it was he, more than anybody else, who ensured that in rejecting the old master in Madrid Paraguay did not acquire a new one in Buenos Aires – and it is of the utmost importance, if we are to get the War of the Triple Alliance into its proper perspective, to realize that the possibility of absorption by Argentina remained a very real threat for some time to come, in spite of the defeat the Paraguayans had inflicted on Belgrano.

Less than three months after the formation of the Junta in Asunción Francia resigned from it, though he had by no means abandoned his ambitions. It was at this turning-point in Paraguay's history that John Parrish Robertson had his first meeting with him. The young Scot was a guest of an eccentric Paraguayan lady,

Doña Juana Ysquibel, whose country house was not far from the small cottage to which the enigmatic Dr Francia had retired:

'On one of those lovely evenings in Paraguay, after the south-west wind had both cleared and cooled the air, I was drawn, in my pursuit of game, into a peaceful valley, not far from Doña Juana's, and remarkable for its combination of all the striking features of the scenery of the country. Suddenly I came upon a neat and unpretending cottage. Up rose a partridge; I fired, and a bird came to the ground. A voice from behind called out "buen tiro" – a good shot. I turned round, and beheld a gentleman of about fifty years of age, dressed in a suit of black, with a large scarlet capote, or cloak, thrown over his shoulders. He had a mate-cup in one hand, a cigar in the other; and a little urchin of a Negro, with his arms crossed, was in attendance by the gentle-man's side. The stranger's countenance was dark, and his black eyes were very penetrating, while his jet hair, combed back from a bold forehead, and hanging in natural ringlets over his shoulders, gave him a dignified and striking air. He wore on his shoes large golden buckles, and at the knees of his breeches the same.

'I apologized for having fired so close to his house; but with great kindness and urbanity, the owner of it assured me there was no occasion for my offering the least excuse; and that his house and grounds were at my service, whenever I chose to amuse myself with my gun in that direction. In exercise of the primitive and simple hospitality common in the country, I was invited to sit down under the corridor, and to take a cigar and mate. A celestial globe, a large telescope, and a theodolite were under the little portico. . . .

'He introduced me to his library in a confined room, with a very small window, and that so shaded by the roof of the corridor as to admit the least portion of light necessary for study. The library was arranged on three rows of shelves, extending across the room, and might have consisted of three hundred volumes. There were many ponderous books on law; a few on the induc-tive sciences; some in French and some in Latin upon subjects of general literature, with Euclid's Elements, and some school-boy treatises on algebra. On a large table were heaps of law-papers and processes. Several folios bound in vellum were outspread upon it; a lighted candle (though placed there solely with a view to light cigars) lent its feeble aid to illumine the room, while a matecup and inkstand, both of silver, stood on another part of the table. There was neither carpet nor mat on the brick-floor; and the chairs were of such ancient fashion, size, and weight, that it required a considerable effort to move them from one spot to another. They were covered with old tanned ox-leather, indented with curious hieroglyphics, and, from long use, very brown and glossy. Their straight backs were conspicuously higher than the head of the party seated upon them, and to sit in a reclining posture was out of the question. The ground of the apartment was scattered over with thousands of pieces of torn letters, and untorn envelopes. An earthen jar for water and a jug stood upon a coarse wooden tripod in one corner, and the Doctor's horse-furniture in another. Slippers, boots, and shoes lay scattered about, and the room altogether had an air of confusion, darkness, and absence of comfort, the more striking that the cottage, though lowly, was perfectly neat outside, and so romantically placed, as to have all the air of an abode at once of beauty and of peace. . . .'

A little before this first meeting of Robertson with Dr Francia, Doña Juana had celebrated St John's Day with a large garden fête. In Robertson's description the scene emerges as an almost symbolic picture of Paraguayan society in this brief interim between the old colonialism and the new dictatorship that was soon to succeed it. We see an ancient but still sprightly hostess – she was in her eighty-fourth year but had not long before made a determined pass at young Robertson – decorating the image of the saint with jewellery lent for the occasion by her friends. Outside, the orange-groves on either side of the house are festooned with lamps. The tables are laid out under the trees. As the sun sets, a motley cavalcade begins to approach the house. A company of Franciscan friars, each of them carrying an umbrella and mounted on a sleek, gaily caparisoned horse, arrive first; they are in special demand because they bring with them the band of their convent, hired to assist in the festivities. Next to arrive is a huge, lumbering carriage nearly a hundred years old, bearing the wives of the members of the Junta, the husbands escorting them on horseback, dressed in ball-room costume with short knee-breeches and silk stockings with heavy sabres at their sides, and every now and then causing their mounts to prance in the special steps to which they have been trained. Other gentry arrive, from Asunción or from neighbouring country districts, some of them in what Robertson calls 'caravans' with awnings over them, and 'mattresses under the ladies to break the shock of the constant jolting', drawn by four oxen apiece, and moving at the rate of two miles an hour.

Groups of army officers in full dress are next on the scene, one of them bearing his 'favourite Dulcinea' riding pillion behind him. They are followed by the shop-keepers and the merchants. Last to arrive is General Velasco, the deposed Spanish Governor himself. When all the guests are assembled, the music strikes up and the dancing begins, both in the salons and on the lawns outside the house. Robertson goes on:

'The brilliancy of the light on the spot, and the chastened transparency of the country and atmosphere in the distance reminded me of the night gambols of fairies, in haunts not yet encroached upon by human beings. What added greatly to the romantic simplicity of the scene was that, ever and anon, little groups of Paraguayan peasantry, uninvited except by the report they had heard of the rejoicings that were to take place at Doña Juana's, came through the valley in different directions. They were escorted by one or two guitareros . . . who accompanied themselves on that instrument to some plaintive triste or national ballad. As they emerged from behind the copses, or came out from the surrounding dark woods, in their white dresses, they looked in the distance like inhabitants of another world; and as their simple harmonious music came undulating from different quarters upon the breeze, one might have fancied it a choral contribution of the shepherds of Arcadia.'

The imagery of Arcadia or Eden does indeed seem to attend the story of Paraguay. And meanwhile, Robertson tells us, the invited guests were dancing on the lawns or in the salons, the more active of the friars among them, as well as Don Fernando de la Mora, a member of the Junta who 'danced with the gout', and other members of the government. Not to be outdone, the octogenarian hostess sprang to her feet 'and danced a sarandîg, or heel-dance' and outside the house 'swains and their nymphs crowded the orange-grove, and each there wooed the lass he loved.' At the same time, the servants were collected in groups around the fires they had lit in the groves for cooking various dishes and 'every little singing company, as it came up, was accommodated with room, and entertained with good cheer; defiance seemed to be bidden to the ills of life; and, uncouth as was the music of the church choirs, and vociferous as was the din of the guests, yet the whole scene had an air thrown over it, of abundance, simplicity, and cordial hilarity, which I shall never forget.'

It all has a poignant, fin de siècle atmosphere to it, like that of a Russian novel on the eve of the Revolution – and as Robertson points out, the light and the music at Doña Juana's party must have reached Dr Francia's cottage. He tells us, too, that the old Spanish Governor, the amiable if somewhat ineffectual General Velasco, came up to him, and speaking with what afterwards struck him as 're- markable and foreboding emphasis', said: 'Ah, Mr Robertson, I am afraid this is the last scene of festivity we shall ever see in Paraguay.'

It was, perhaps, an exaggeration, but it was not far off the truth as far as General Velasco and his friends were concerned.

But this scene should be set beside another in Robertson's narrative which was equally significant. It took place after Francia had returned to the Junta, and to a position of much greater in- fluence, and after he had summoned another motley group of deputies to Asunción in October 1813,

Robertson describes for us a typical deputy – an Indian *Alcalde* 'with an antiquated three-cornered hat, and an old red or brown wig that had been worn under the said hat from its earliest days', decked out in all kinds of shabby finery, bearing in his hand his cane of office, attended by ragged and bare-footed servants, and mounted on a horse trained to 'dance' in the old Spanish tradition. His objective was invariably the front of Government House – and 'Carai' Francia:

> 'Increasing there the rigidity of his upright posture on horseback, with his eyes immoveably fixed on his horse's ears, he gave the Carai a horse-dance, a calabash tune, and finally made his reverential act of obeisance. All this he performed on horseback, and then took his departure in the same dancing though slow and measured solemnity of state in which he had arrived. . . .'

Robertson is laughing at his Indian *alcalde*, but he was the very symbol of Francia's future power; for it was he and his fellows who made Francia joint Consul with Don Fulgencio Yegros, an aristocratic but ignorant gaucho whom Francia easily dominated and who took his advice in refusing to send deputies to the Constituent Assembly in Buenos Aires, annulled the treaty of 1811, and reaffirmed the absolute independence of the republic of

Paraguay. It was he and his kind, too, who, in a third Congress which met in October 1814, made Francia Dictator for a term of five years – it was incidentally, characteristic of Francia's stern rectitude in such matters that he refused to accept more than a third of the salary assigned to the post, on the grounds that the resources of the country did not warrant it. And it was the *alcalde* and his kind who, with the summoning of yet another Congress, elected Francia in May 1816, at the age of sixty, perpetual dictator with the title of 'El Supremo'. It was indeed as the supreme ruler that Francia guided the destinies of Paraguay during the next twenty-four years; as Burton so rightly says, Francia 'was like Mirabeau, one of the few capable of guiding a revolution to its logical end. . .'.

Dr Francia has usually been presented to English readers as one of the monsters of history, largely on the authority of the Robertson brothers, though Thomas Carlyle, as early as 1843, expressed doubts as to the accuracy of their portrait, arguing that Francia's absolutism was a more intelligent response to the challenge of independence than the high-sounding theories about constitutionalism and democracy in other parts of Latin America – which served merely to shroud a state of anarchy, and which in any case did not touch the Indian population. For Carlyle, in fact, Francia was a 'true man in a bewildered Gaucho world'.[14] Burton, who takes a balanced view of Francia, as he does of Francisco Solano López, makes much the same point when he says that Francia was able to 'show to the world in the recluse kingdom of the Jesuits, the sole exception to republican anarchy . . .'.

Some at least of the denigration of Francia springs from an inability, within the nineteenth-century context, to understand what exactly he was at. That he was guilty of many acts of terror is not to be denied. His power was as absolute as that of any Roman emperor or eastern potentate, subject to the same temptations, and attended by the same whims and vagaries. He would not brook contradiction or disobedience, and those who attempted them were thrown into gaol and loaded with fetters. As time went by he became increasingly touchy, and subject to fits of unreasoning rage. He ordered that everyone should wear a hat of some sort – if needs be only a brim, he declared with grim humour – so that it could be doffed in his presence; and those who failed to do so with sufficient promptitude or respect likewise found themselves in his dungeons. If, when he was out riding, passers-by failed to get out of the way quickly enough, his guards would lay about them with the flats of their swords. Eventually, people were so terrified that they kept out of the way when he was abroad, and he rode through deserted streets, dressed in black, his head sunk on his breast in gloomy contemplation. He frequently ordered floggings and other tortures, for insignificant misdemeanours, and he made a habit of witnessing them himself. He had, too, the fantastic, largely paranoid attention to detail of the typical despot. As Richard Burton tells us: 'he knew exactly the cost of hoe or axe, and he used to count and measure the needles and thread necessary for a uniform'.

At the same time, the scale of Francia's cruelties seems to have been exaggerated by the Robertson brothers and other hostile critics. For one thing, they were in the main directed against a small section of the community, the aristrocrats, both 'old Spanish' and *criollo* (and also those merchants and traders who refused to obey the stringent regulations we shall come to shortly.) One of his earliest actions after assuming the supreme power was to have all the 'old Spaniards' (in whose hands, Robertson tells us, the trade of Paraguay was still mainly concentrated) assembled and warned as to their future conduct, and he further humiliated them by forbidding them to marry whites, and in his determination to crush also the power of the church, he decreed that he alone had the right to authorize marriages.

The persecution of the 'old Spaniards' and the upper-class Creoles only reached considerable proportions after 1820. In this year, the gaucho leader General Artigas, who had served the Banda Oriental (Uruguay) in much the same way as Dr Francia had served Paraguay, by rigidly maintaining his country's independence both of Argentina and of Brazil, was ousted by a rival, Don Francisco Ramírez. Granted asylum by Dr Francia, Artigas (who spent the rest of his life in Paraguay), was able to help his benefactor uncover a large-scale conspiracy in which the discontented Spanish upper class had been in touch with Ramírez with a view to his invading Paraguay from the south.

The classes hostile to Francia now indeed found themselves victims of a reign of terror. Hundreds of suspects were thrown into Francia's dungeons and tortured. Among the first to be executed was Francia's old colleague Fulgencio Yegros. For many days consecutively eight of those suspected of the conspiracy were executed, and the firing squads continued to be busy at intervals for some time after that. On 9 June 1821, Francia rounded up no fewer than three hundred 'old Spaniards' and only released those who survived eighteen months' confinement on payment of a large collective fine.

At the same time, the mass of the people remained firmly behind him, and the close links between him and the Guaraníes were never broken; even during his later years, when he suffered from dictator's paranoia – living alone, and continually shifting his bed in order to reduce the danger, actual or imaginary, of assassination – they usually had access to him. As Horton Box is at pains to emphasize: 'the Guaraní population was the veritable foundation of his dictatorship; the aristocracy and bourgeoisie, Spanish and native alike, were its only enemies'. Those whom he crushed so remorselessly, Box continues, 'were also the exploiters of the Guaraní peasantry. . . . His terrorism succeeded because, like all successful terrorisms, it was directed against a small though important section of the population. He was secure save against the few; hence the smallness of the military establishment he found necessary, and hence also his far-flung system of espionage.'

Box also stresses the point that many of the enemies of Francia had close contacts (inevitably, because of their class and commercial affiliations) with the Porteños, so that in his view what happened in Paraguay was a dual revolution: 'the vindication of Paraguayan independence' he says, 'was the complement of the social revolution within the new state. . . . The social and national revolutions are interwoven.' And by this social revolution he means 'the emergence of a new class, the Guaraní peasantry, whose organ Dr Francia is . . .'.

Perhaps Dr Box is over-confident in his conclusions; but there can be little real doubt that something of this sort did happen, and it is something that makes Paraguay different from all the other countries of Latin America which were achieving, or were about to achieve, their independence from Spanish colonial rule. For it was only in Paraguay that the nationalist revolution was accompanied, thanks largely to Francia, by a social revolution involving the indigenous population. All the other wars of independence were fought by white *criollos* against white *peninsulares*; the Indians might play their part as cannon-fodder, but they had no share in the results of victory.

In many respects, moreover, Francisco Solano López was the heir to Francia: the classes he feared were the same as those who opposed Francia; the masses he relied on, and whose representative he was, were the same Guaraní masses who formed the basis of Dr Francia's power.

The political and social revolution in Paraguay, was attended by – or perhaps 'supported by' would be the better term – a special economic system; and it is at this point that we return to the question of state control raised by Bartolomé Mitre's comments on the state monopoly in tobacco. For, as Horton Box points out, the kind of political system founded by Dr Francia and developed by his two successors must inevitably be characterized by '"paternalism" and the omnipotence of the State'.

Such monolithic systems exist primarily, in Dr Box's view, to prevent the growth of that complicated network of vested interests, produced by private enterprise, whose freedom of operation is basic to bourgeois regimes of the sort that were coming into being as the old colonial power of Spain crumbled; and particularly, of course, in that busy emporium and *entrepôt*, Buenos Aires. In other words, the only alternative to free enterprise as practised in Buenos Aires and aspired to by the merchants of Asunción, was state control and bureaucracy as exemplified by the partial monopoly on tobacco described by Bartolomé Mitre (and to be much extended by Francia's successor, Carlos Antonio López), the complete government monopoly of *yerba mate* instituted by Francia, and, in the 1850s, what was virtually a state monopoly of foreign trade.

Not that this was an economic revolution in any Marxist sense, of course. It was, rather, a return to a pattern that had already been established – and Horton Box is among those who recognize the 'Jesuit state' as an integral part of Paraguay's development, when in commenting on Dr Francia's economic measures, he says:

'The growth of an independent trading and commercial middle class was thus prevented and a fascinating social evolution begun in that land that had already witnessed the rise and progress of the Jesuit Communist Empire.'

Burton had made much the same point a good deal earlier when he described Francia's Paraguay as 'a reproduction, in somewhat a sterner mould, of the Jesuit Reduction system', which succeeded, he adds, 'because the popular mind was prepared for it'.

But Burton was one of the few nineteenth-century commentators on Paraguay capable of thinking in genuinely historical terms, and it was he who saw that the War of the Triple Alliance itself belonged to the same process: 'It is the Nemesis of Faith; the death-throe of a policy bequeathed by Jesuitism to South America.'

It was not only in its rigid control, however, that Francia's system resembled that of the Jesuit reductions, but also in its exclusiveness. To begin with, Francia hoped (while reducing commerce with Paraguay's neighbours to an absolute minimum) to develop her trade overseas – but Buenos Aires had no intention of allowing the freedom of the Río de la Plata and its great tributaries from duties and tolls, on which such plans depended. Francia decided, therefore, on quite another course – to seal his country off, as far as possible, from the outside world. Foreign merchants who were already in Asunción were expelled and forbidden to return – among them the brothers Robertson. It was this, of course, which particularly aroused their enmity against Francia, and as energetic representatives of the British merchant class of their period, they could hardly be expected to understand the logic that lay behind Francia's actions. There was a logic, nevertheless, given Paraguay's peculiar circumstances. Now that Spain's restrictions on trade and immigration had been removed, European pioneers and specula-tors were pouring into the liberated territories of Latin America, and Francia feared, not without reason, that foreigners entering Paraguay would exploit the country and undermine his own posi-tion and the implementation of his social and economic system. By an extension of his policy of exclusiveness, foreigners were, there-fore, now prohibited from entering the country, and those already domiciled forbidden to leave.

Diplomatic relations with foreign powers were practically brought to an end. In both 1824 and 1840, for example, Argentina despatched envoys, but Francia refused to receive them. At first he tried to make an exception in the case of Brazil, realizing with true statesmanlike insight (which his successors unfortunately lacked) that as far as Paraguay was concerned, Brazil formed the natural counterweight to Argentina. He was prompt to recognize Brazil's declaration of independence from the Portugese crown in 1822, under the Emperor Pedro I, and he entered into commercial relations with her, through the port of Itapuá on the Río Paraná. In 1824 he received a Brazilian envoy in Asunción, who two years later was raised from the rank of Consul to that of Minister.

In 1827 Brazil, now in open conflict with Argentina, tried to persuade Dr Francia to invade the Argentine province of Cor-rientes in collaboration with a Brazilian force, but he refused to do so. The defeat of Brazil at the battle of Itazaingó confirmed him in his determination to have no further diplomatic or commercial relations with Buenos Aires, but at the same time he resented the efforts of Brazilian diplomacy to involve Paraguay in the political maelstrom of the Río de la Plata. He insisted, though in a restrained and courteous manner, on the removal of the Brazilian agents, diplomatic as well as commercial, to Itapuá, which became the sole centre for what limited foreign trade was still permitted – a kind of South American Hong Kong.

By 1829 Paraguay was as effectively sealed off from the outside world as the 'Jesuit state' had ever been. But if Paraguay's external trade (apart from the trickle that came through Itapuá) was destroyed, Francia saw to it that the country developed and diversified her internal economy, and he achieved some quite astonishing results. In 1833, for example, there were bumper crops of maize, wheat, peanuts, sweet potatoes, vegetables of various kinds, and sugar; while cotton, which up to that date was still being imported from Corrientes, produced an enormous yield, with tobacco and *mate* not far behind. The trading loophole of Itapuá was nothing like big enough to absorb such a glut, but when Francia was urged by his Minister of Finance to relax his isolationist policy in order to dispose of it, Francia in reply gave this classical formulation of his policy:

'. . . he recognized the advantage the country would obtain by the exportation of such products as were surplus, but not yet had the germ of anarchy in the neighbouring states been extinguished; on the contrary, it was every day gathering greater energy through the purely personal struggles of the factions seeking power and continuing one and all to conspire against the independence of Paraguay which must be preserved at all costs; this was the reason that had decided him to continue his policy of non-intercourse, above all since Paraguay had no need of these countries and was self-supporting'.[15]

In order to ensure that she remained so, Francia devoted to agriculture all the attention to detail and all the ingenuity that went to all his other activities. It was he who decided what crops should be sown each year. When, in 1819, a plague of locusts descended and a serious famine threatened, he ordered the farmers to re-sow their devastated land with crops similar to those consumed by the locusts – and when fresh harvests sprang up, it was realized, probably for the first time, that the soil and climate of Paraguay were capable of producing more than one crop during the year. When Paraguayan cattle caught disease, he immediately ordered the infected herds to be shot, thus preventing the spread of the disease – and anticipating the kind of preventative measures used in more modern times.

In his last years Francia became increasingly morose, and solitary. He had no intimates; he never married, and even his amorous affairs, which were numerous but apparently devoid of any emotional attachment (he never acknowledged his illegitimate offspring), tailed off. He went in constant fear of assassination, and he was morbidly suspicious of everyone he met, even of his own bodyguard. But he never for a moment relaxed his iron control, and a measure of the awe in which he was held can be drawn from the fact that after his death in 1840, people still took off their hats and glanced anxiously about them at the mention of his name; while many, fearing to utter even that aloud, always referred to him in whispers as 'El Difunto' (the dead one) as if this were a title every bit as awe-inspiring as that of El Supremo which he had borne in life.

Nevertheless, it could be argued that he had served his country well. While most of the other Spanish American territories which had thrown off the yoke of Madrid were being torn apart by internal strife, so that even Simon Bolívar, the great 'Liberator', bitterly commented shortly before his death in 1830: 'America is ungovernable. He who serves a revolution ploughs the sea', Paraguay enjoyed twenty-eight years of a hermetically sealed peace, more absolute even than that of the Jesuit reductions, which were subject so often to the incursions of the dreaded Mamelucos.

An apt summing-up of Francia's career is that of the great Argentine jurist Juan Bautista Alberdi:

'America does not know the story of that land (i.e. Paraguay) save as it is related by its rivals. The silence of isolation has left calumny victorious. . . . Dr Francia proclaimed the independence of Paraguay of Spain and preserved it against her neighbours by isolation and despotism: two terrible means that necessity imposed on him in the service of a good end. . . .'[16]

'A good end . . .' – remembering the torture cells and the firing squads one is forced to wonder once again whether justifications of this sort are not turning one's normal judgments upside down. Yet without Francia it is doubtful whether Paraguay, in the ferocious, chaotic world of early nineteenth-century Latin America, would have survived as an independent nation. By continuing, in effect, the policy of the Jesuits he had also preserved an oddly distorted and macabre form of their self-contained and self-sufficient Eden – the reverse side of the coin, as it were. What is certain is that it was the reversal of his policy by his successors that drove the Paraguayan nation into the wilderness of power politics that eventually led to disaster and tragedy.

NOTES

[1] Ignatius Loyola, the founder of the Order, had died in 1556. Aquaviva died in 1605.
[2] *A Vanished Arcadia*, R. B. Cunninghame-Graham. London 1901.
[3] *History of Brazil*, Robert Southey. Vol. II. London 1817. Quotations from Southey are taken from this book.
[4] *Salvador de Sá and the Struggle for Brazil and Angola: 1602–1683*, C. R. Boxer. London 1952.
[5] *The Political and Economic Activities of the Jesuits in the La Plata Region*, Magnus Mörner. Stockholm 1953. Where not otherwise indicated, quotations from Mörner are taken from this book.
[6] Introduction to *The Expulsion of the Jesuits from Latin America*, ed. Magnus Mörner. New York 1965.
[7] *Paraguay: a riverside nation*, George Pendle. 3rd ed, London 1967. Quotations from Pendle are taken from this book.
[8] *Letters on Paraguay: comprising an account of a four years' residence in that republic under the government of the dictator Francia*, J. P. and W. P. Robertson. 3 vols, 2nd ed., London 1839.
[9] *Ensayo de la história civil del Paraguay, Buenos Aires y Tucumán*, Dr. (Dean) Gregorio Funes. Buenos Aires 1816. Book V, p. 133.
[10] See for example Los Guaraníes después de la expulsión de los Jesuítas, José M. Mariluz Urquijo, *Estudios americanas*, VI, 1953, p. 328.
[11] *The War in Paraguay: a historical sketch of the country and its people, and notes upon the military engineering of the War*, George Thompson. London 1869. Quotations from Thompson are taken from this book.
[12] *The Origins of the Paraguayan War*, Pelham Horton Box. 2 vols, Urbana, Ill. 1927. Quotations from Box are taken from this book.
[13] This and the following two extracts from the armistice agreement are quoted by Koebel in *Paraguay*, as is Bartolomé Mitre's comment on tobacco on p. 19.
[14] *Foreign and Quarterly Review*, No. 52, July 1843; reprinted in *Critical and Miscellaneous Essays*.
[15] Quoted by Box in *The Origins of the Paraguayan War*.
[16] *Las disensiones de las repúblicas de la Plata y las maquinaciones del Brasil*, Juan Bautista Alberdi. Paris 1865.

ACT TWO

Father and Son: Further Lessons in Autocracy

The enemies of Dr Francia prophesied a violent reaction on his death. In fact there seems to have been little disturbance. Francia's secretary, Policarpo Patiño, called upon the commanders of the army corps in the capital to form a junta, though this was driven from power by a rival group of officers – and Patiño hanged himself in gaol, presumably fearing that he would be cast in the role of scapegoat for El Difunto's tyrannies. On 12 March 1841, Congress assembled in Asunción, and elected two Consuls to wield the executive power of the state – one of whom was Carlos Antonio López, who had played a commanding part in the events following Francia's death. A general amnesty was proclaimed, and most of the political prisoners languishing in Francia's prisons were released; and Francia's isolationist policy was immediately put into reverse.

On 14 March 1844,[1] Congress ratified a new republican constitution, and elected Carlos Antonio López the first President of Paraguay, for a term of ten years in the first instance; this was later extended by three years, and in 1857 he was elected for a further term of ten years – and given the virtual right to nominate his successor.

There are a number of conflicting stories about the origins of Carlos Antonio López – including one that he was the nephew of Dr Francia himself, though there is no real evidence to support it. According to Cunninghame-Graham, his grandmother was half Negro, and his father half Guaraní[2] – though Masterman claims that the strongest admixture of Indian blood was the far less 'respectable' primitive Guaycurú, derived from his mother's family.[3]

He was born in 1787 at La Recoleta, a hamlet three miles or so from Asunción. His father (again according to Cunninghame-Graham) was a tailor, and he was one of eight children. Nevertheless,

33

he was educated at the College in Asunción, studying theology, philosophy, and jurisprudence. He practised law in Asunción long enough to acquire a reputation for efficiency and administrative ability. When, however, he suddenly married Juana, step-daughter of Don Lázaro Rojas, a rich and aristocratic landowner, he gave up his practice, withdrew from the capital and lived quietly and inconspicuously on his estates – realizing that it was safer to hide his light under a bushel while Dr Francia was still alive.

There was a rumour that this marriage had been hastily arranged in order to cover up the fact that Juana was with child by her step-father, and the rumour is of some importance because it was later seized upon with relish by the enemies of Francisco Solano López – Juana's first-born – and because it figured prominently in the alleged conspiracy of 1869.

There are a number of contemporary descriptions of the elder López at the time he assumed the Presidency, when he was forty-four years old. Most of them depict him as a man of extreme corpulency – 'with chops flapping over his cravat' Burton says, so that his face had 'a porcine appearance' remarkably reminiscent of the later George IV, though Burton hastens to add that this is by no means incompatible with high intellect.

Many of the contemporary accounts stress both the extent of his absolutism, and the extreme punctilio and seriousness with which he regarded the office he held. When the scientist, C. B. Mansfield, who was in Asunción in 1852 was received in audience by the President, he found, he tells us, the President seated, 'with his hat on, cocked a little to one side'.[4]

Masterman, too, draws attention to this practice. Burton suggests that Carlos Antonio sat down to conceal the fact that one leg was shorter than the other. But Masterman has a much more interesting, and convincing, explanation, relating it to the fact that the President 'always spoke of the supreme power of the Government as a vague but terrible abstraction, saying that he was not it, but only represented it.' In the same way, Masterman claims that the President never acknowledged a salute because in his view 'that sign of respect was not paid to him as an individual, but to *el gobierno supremo*, of which he was but the visible type'.

The same attitude is implicit in the term 'El Ciudadano' (the Citizen) which Carlos Antonio López liked to apply to himself – and it is an attitude which perhaps deserves to be taken rather more seriously than it has been by most foreign commentators.

Those of us who have been imbued since birth with democratic ideals and who have inherited an inbuilt conviction of their absolute rightness, find it extremely difficult to take an objective view of other political systems, or to accept that even those at the opposite pole to our own can be practised with varying degrees of integrity. The very idea of absolutism is so repugnant to us that it tends to make us dismiss professions such as those of Carlos Antonio López as hypocritical and dishonest. In fact, though, he was in this respect at any rate absolutely sincere. If it comes to that, in this specialized sense, so were his predecessor Dr Francia, and his son and successor, Francisco Solano López. However much they may have schemed and intrigued for their power, they were none of them mere opportunist dictators – though admittedly neither Carlos Antonio nor his son had the same high standards, as far as personal rewards were concerned, as had Dr Francia. Still, within their limits and those of the traditions they had inherited, they all took their sultan-like offices seriously, and genuinely regarded themselves as properly constituted embodiments of the State.

Among the older writers on Paraguay, only Burton seems to have appreciated this, and to have realized that the Paraguayan political system was really based on principles which had more in common with seventeenth century theories about the 'divine right of kings' than it did with those of either the French Revolution or nineteenth-century liberal democracy. Thus, pointing out that 'Paraguay was ever a repertory of old world ideas', Burton suggests in effect that political thought in the country had never advanced beyond 'the days of the Grand Monarque'. He argues, too, that Paraguay was not unique in this respect, but merely displaying an inherited Spanish characteristic: that is, 'a marvellous, Oriental, fatalistic patience under despotisms.' As far as Paraguay was concerned, the despotism was not an imposed solution, but one that seemed natural and inevitable to the vast majority of the population. It was a despotism, in other words, that evolved from within just as much as it was imposed from without; and one, moreover, that changed and developed, even if it was in directions of which we disapprove.

This raises the question of 'the people's consent'. All the writers on Paraguay from the brothers Robertson onwards speak of the various Paraguayan national assemblies with condescension, jocularity, or contempt. From our point of view, no doubt, they *were* pure farce. Their powers were practically non-existent, and their main function was to rubber-stamp the claims of those who had sufficient ability, will, and ruthlessness to drive to the forefront in the power-struggle (it has been known to happen outside Paraguay too). By these few, the assemblies were shamelessly manoeuvred, exploited and at times terrorized. Occasionally there were signs that some of the deputies had independent ideas, but these were always circumvented – and it was in any case very dangerous to express minority opinions.

On the other hand, there is no real evidence that any of these Congresses (and of course there was no official opposition) objected to the actual form of government; if some of the deputies favoured some other contender, it was only in order to confer upon him exactly the same despotic powers as those afforded to his successful rival.

To what extent, though, could these assemblies be called in any degree, 'representative'? The second Congress, which Francia summoned in October 1813, to vote himself and Yegros into the joint-Consulate, was so numerous (consisting of no less than a thousand chiefs of the various districts) that it could hardly fail, on a purely statistical basis, to be so to some extent at least.

The Third Congress (of 1844) set the pattern for subsequent ones, and Burton thus describes the pyramid of power:

> 'The Chief authority, Consul, Dictator or President, chooses the members by his right to appoint the President of Congress, the latter chooses the commandants of districts, and these again choose their delegates for each "partido" or arrondissement: thus all the citizens vote, and Congress chooses the Consul, Dictator, or President, who virtually chooses himself.'

This obviously, was an Alice-in-Wonderland version of the democratic process, standing the whole thing on its head. But one can't help wondering whether the sarcastic references of Robertson to these deputies were in part activated by the fact that they were mostly Indians who just did not *look* like Members of Parliament. One would like to know more about them, their place in their respective communities, their standing, their neighbours and so on. Until we do know a great deal more about these circumstances, it is impossible, though clearly enough these deputies were not 'representative' in our sense of the word, to be sure to what extent they were so in a looser sense. It is a subject which demands a good deal more research. It is at any rate likely that they were every bit as representative, and probably more so, than British Members of Parliament before the passing of the Reform Bill of 1832.

There is, too, no real evidence that there was ever any widespread popular resistance to any of Paraguay's dictators. Indeed, Burton is almost certainly right when he argues, in connection with the Paraguayan's loyalty to Francisco Solano López during the war, that 'the logic of facts' proves that 'the people were enthusiastic both for the system and its administration. . . . They were doubtless, and they still are, in a state of semi-barbarism, but they have given their lives rather than abandon the customs of their ancestors and betray what must be called their political creed.'

Whether we like it or not, we just have to accept that this was the way the vast majority of the Paraguayan people wanted it. And all the evidence is that the dictators they voted into power wanted their approval, no matter how much they bullied, cajoled and intrigued in order to get it. If they had been mere bloody tyrants, why go to all the trouble of convening Congresses, especially with a nation so notoriously 'docile', so accustomed by long years of practice and tradition to obedience? Again we have to accept, whether we like it or not, that the approval of the various Paraguayan Congresses, even if it was in effect no more than a rubberstamp, was something that was highly valued and respected both by those who conferred it and those who were its recipients. And it is important to step outside our own traditions and try to put ourselves inside the skins of the Paraguayans of the time, if we are to understand their heroic conduct during the long-drawn-out ordeal they were soon to endure.

As dictators go, in fact, Carlos Antonio López was a reasonably benevolent and enlightened one. He was guilty of a few acts of capricious tyranny – as when he ordered the execution of a merchant who in a fit of rage, on being told that the stamped paper he had bought in order to free some of his goods from the Customs house was not sufficient for the purpose, tore up the document and trampled on it – thus, in the eyes of Carlos Antonio, desecrating 'a symbol of the sacred State', that is himself.[5] His execution of the Decoud brothers for their share in an alleged plot against his life in 1859 (the so-called Canstatt conspiracy) attracted more attention than it might otherwise have done, because rumour had it that one of the brothers was a successful rival in love of the President's eldest son, Francisco Solano; though in fairness it should be added that the Decouds were one of those families with commercial interests in Buenos Aires which had provoked the special suspicions of Francia – and that the brothers' father, who had been acting as Carlos Antonio's agent in Buenos Aires for the sale of hides and *yerba mate*, had apparently, according to Cunninghame-Graham, embezzled more than a million dollars.

The elder López, however, was not as a rule a cruel man, and these were the only political executions during his 'reign'. He was responsible, moreover, for several liberal and humane pieces of legislation, and especially that of 24 November 1842, whereby slavery was abolished – twenty years in advance of the U.S.A., and forty-six of Brazil. (This, was to be accomplished in gradual stages. All children of slaves born after the promulgation of the edict were to become free, males at twenty-five and females at twenty-four.) He founded over four hundred public schools, catering for 24,000 pupils, and offered scholarships in chemistry, pharmacy, law and medicine (when sufficiently qualified candidates should become available) at universities abroad. In 1845 he founded Paraguay's first newspaper, *El Paraguayo Independiente* – a government organ, needless to say, which often contained the President's own very flowery perorations. He built roads, dockyards, and a cathedral. He persuaded foreign and especially British engineers, builders, mechanics and surgeons to settle in Paraguay (relaxing the strict regulations governing foreign residents) and started a hospital service. In 1858 he employed a British firm to begin the construction of one of the first railways in South America. Another Englishman, William Whytehead, constructed an arsenal at Asunción, with thirty English artisans and three hundred Paraguayans under him. Before Carlos Antonio's death, the construction of a telegraph line from Asunción to the fortress of Humaitá had also been started, and in all these respects Paraguay was considerably in advance of most of her neighbours.

The country undoubtedly prospered materially under him and to a large extent he continued the economic system initiated by Dr Francia. He, too, discouraged any large scale acquisition of land by private proprietors. Most of it was owned by the State and hired out for a ground rent in small plots to separate families, and in 1854 he issued a decree prohibiting the purchase of land by foreigners. Not only *yerba* and tobacco were state monopolies, but also (apart from a few exceptional concessions) timber, another important commodity in a country more than half covered with forests.

The President's handling of foreign affairs, though marked by a good deal of shrewdness, and – as he learned by experience – by an increasing caution, was by no means as happy in its results. He was anxious to break the isolationism Francia had imposed on the country, and to drag it into the nineteenth century, but he had little knowledge himself of the world beyond his frontiers, and he was steeped in that deep Paraguayan distrust of foreigners which Francia had done so much to intensify. He fell foul of the American Consul, Edward R. Hopkins, to whom he had granted a commercial monopoly, withdrawing his consular *exequatur*, and forcing him into bankruptcy. Hopkins appealed to his government, and after they had backed his claim to compensation, and finally sent a pair of gunboats to reinforce it, Carlos Antonio agreed to pay up, though he managed matters so dexterously that his own countrymen were convinced that he had scored an important diplomatic victory over their great North American neighbour.

The President also fell foul of Britain over the conspiracy of 1859. Among the suspects whom he arrested and condemned to death, was a merchant and adventurer named Santiago Canstatt, who claimed British nationality. C. A. Henderson, the British Consul in Asunción, demanded that he be released for a fair open trial. Carlos Antonio refused and though he was too wary to implement the death-sentence on Canstatt, kept him in prison. These, however, were the days when the British lion could roar effectively (not to say, arrogantly). The President's eldest son, Francisco Solano, was in Buenos Aires, and while there had bought and armed a steamer, which he named the *Tacuarí*, after a river in Paraguay, a tributary of the Alto Paraná. Edward Thornton, the British Minister in Buenos Aires, took what now seems the incredible step of seizing the *Tacuarí*, and holding her as hostage against the release of Canstatt. As Cunninghame-Graham so rightly says, this action 'quite in defiance of the law of nations' carried out in a neutral port 'was an act of war against the State of Paraguay, and a gross insult to the Argentine Confederation' – though he added that the authorities in Buenos Aires 'seem to have been rather pleased than otherwise, for it was known that Paraguay was building up a formidable military force, and arming steadily'.

Carlos Antonio was, therefore, forced to release Canstatt, so that his son could return home; and after further forceful actions by the

British government, to pay Canstatt an indemnity – though again he saved his face with his countrymen by persuading the British not to disclose the amount.

These incidents are worth relating because not surprisingly (and whatever the rights and wrongs concerned) they confirmed the ingrown Paraguayan suspicion of foreigners, and, again hardly surprisingly, served to exacerbate the highly-developed sense of *amour propre* that existed in Carlos Antonio – and even more so in his son. Far more significant as an indication for the future, however, was the kind of reaction in Buenos Aires. Carlos Antonio's quarrels with the United States and Britain were of the sort that could be solved without too much difficulty by diplomacy, and they did not seriously damage future relations. What was of the utmost importance were the difficulties inherent in Paraguay's relations with her immediate neighbours. When Carlos Antonio assumed the Presidency, the old disagreements between Paraguay and Argentina had by no means been resolved, although Dr Francia had succeeded by his policy of complete isolation in putting them, so to speak, into cold storage.

What must always be borne in mind is the way in which the countries of the La Plata region began to emerge into nationhood. In a very broad sense it could be said that Argentina, Uruguay, and Paraguay formed a geographical unit in that they all bordered the Plata estuary or its main tributaries – the Paraná–Paraguay river system. But there were tremendous differences between different areas, and the vast distances involved excluded any real unification. In the earlier days of the Spanish–American colonial empire, a division into regions more or less followed the dictates of geography. In the late eighteenth century, however, Spain extended the viceroyalty system, and Argentina, the Banda Oriental (Uruguay) and Paraguay were administratively united under one viceroy. The overthrow of Spanish rule led to a break-up of the viceregal delineation and a return to the regional pattern of the earlier colonial period. But Buenos Aires, as the capital of the old viceroyalty, regarded herself as the rightful heir of Spain, and believed, as Koebel puts it 'that Paraguay should in the natural order of affairs form an integral portion of the Argentine Confederation.' To some extent such an attitude was understandable; Argentina, Uruguay and Paraguay were, after all, all Spanish-speaking, and were at least united in their suspicions of Portuguese-speaking Brazil. It is for this reason that several Spanish–American historians tend to speak of the War of the Triple Alliance as having many of the attributes of a civil war.

In addition, Spain had never drawn up exact boundaries between her various administrative units – viceroyalties, captaincies-general, audiencias, and provinces – largely because the frontier regions were usually wild, sometimes unexplored, and often ranged by warlike tribes of nomadic Indians, so that the boundaries were inevitably fluid. Inevitably, too, this meant that when the various regions achieved independence from Spanish rule, they were faced with all kinds of boundary disputes with their neighbours.

As far as Paraguay was concerned, there were obvious natural frontiers to the east, west, and south, in the form of the rivers Paraná and Paraguay. But there was a problem to the west and another to the east of the common frontier between Argentina and Paraguay formed by the river Paraná. It is not necessary here to go into the very complicated geographical, administrative and legalistic factors. Briefly, the problem to the west concerned the sovereignty of the mysterious and still largely unexplored Gran Chaco (in which Brazil and Bolivia were also involved), and that to the east centred on the former Jesuit reductions, in the territory which is now the Argentine province of Misiones. A Royal Decree of 6 November 1726 had detached some of the *pueblos* (townships) concerned from the Paraguayan *Misiones*, and placed them under the jurisdiction of Buenos Aires. On the other hand, another royal ordinance of 24 March 1806, had appointed Don Bernardo de Velasco, the last Spanish Governor of Paraguay, to be governor also of the missions of the Uruguay and Paraná.

Various treaties (including that of 1811) appeared to recognize most of the Paraguayan claims in both the disputed areas, but some of the agreements were not ratified in Argentina, and the situation was still very much in the melting pot. For some time after the achievement of independence by the two countries, Argentina was in no position to bring pressure to bear on Paraguay. Unlike that country under the iron rule of Dr Francia, she was racked by internal dissensions brought about by the conflicting interests of Buenos Aires, which was gradually emerging as a great international seaport, and the interior which had made very little progress and was frequently at the mercy of various *caudillos* who controlled vast areas in a way reminiscent of medieval barons or Chinese war lords. The former wanted a closely-knit organization centred on Buenos Aires; the latter favoured a much looser form of federation which would leave the provinces more or less autonomous. The opposing tendencies coalesced round two main parties, the *Unitarios*, who by and large represented the interests of Buenos Aires, and the *Federales*, whose main strength lay in the provinces. It was a Federal, Juan Manuel de Rosas, who in 1829 put an end to twenty years of chaos, and dominated the Argentine Confederation until 1852. Rosas was a wealthy *estanciero*, and himself a typical *caudillo* of the pampas. Handsome in appearance and a brilliant performer at the rodeos, he was adored by the gauchos. He was even more ruthless than Dr Francia and ruled by the usual tyrant's weapons of spies, secret police, intimidation and murder. Schools were closed, the University disendowed, the press silenced. His portrait was displayed over the altars of the churches, engraved on domestic crockery and ladies' gloves, and no one who valued his life dared to be seen in public without the scarlet insignia of the Federal Party.

Rosas had been well-disposed towards Dr Francia, because of the latter's strict non-intervention policy and because, as a consequence of it, he refused to give asylum to the Argentine dictator's enemies. Less than a year after Francia's death, however, Carlos Antonio López and his fellow Consul (this was before López had established himself as sole ruler of Paraguay) – in their anxiety to break out of Francia's isolationism – signed a treaty with the Governor of the Argentine province of Corrientes, which was in revolt against Rosas. When, in the following year, the Paraguayan Congress (still apparently anxious about the country's status) issued a further declaration of independence, and the Consuls asked Rosas to recognize it, he replied in an ambiguous tone which was tantamount to a refusal. After various other exchanges, Carlos Antonio López (now President) extended his relationship with the rebel province of Corrientes and Rosas retaliated, in January 1845, by what was virtually a complete blockade of Paraguay's river traffic beyond her borders. Ironically enough, therefore, Paraguay's first attempts to break out of her isolation had ended in her being as completely cut off from the outside world as she had ever been, with trade once more reduced to the trickle over the Brazilian frontier which had been permitted by Dr Francia.

Rosas also protested to Brazil because she had responded to the Paraguayan 'second declaration of independence' by formal recognition, which was soon followed by a treaty between the two countries. Brazil, always anxious to check the growth of her most powerful neighbour, regarded Paraguay as a useful ally against Rosas. She used her good offices to secure for Paraguay recognitions of independence from Bolivia, Venezuela, and Austria (though even now the United States, Britain, and France declined the invitation). More important, she encouraged Carlos Antonio López to enter into an offensive and defensive alliance with Corrientes against the Argentine Confederation. In return for armed assistance, Corrientes promised to surrender to Paraguay the territory of Eastern Corrientes in the Misiones region. Corrientes, as a rebel province, had no legal right, of course to make such a deal; but it is important to bear this arrangement in mind, because it helps to explain the strong eeling against Paraguay in Buenos Aires, and the prominent part that Corrientes was to play in the earlier stages of the War of the Triple Alliance.

Carlos Antonio López issued his formal declaration of war against Rosas on 4 December 1845. It began with the words: 'Long live the Republic of Paraguay! Independence or Death!' Those last three words were part of an old Paraguayan motto: in a few years' time they were to be uttered in far more serious circumstances – and to go on being uttered in mounting tones of heroic despair. And the man who led the Paraguayan force of 5,000 men, which crossed the Paraná early in 1846 and entered Corrientes, was none other than Francisco Solano López, already a general at the ripe age of eighteen.

On this occasion, he was not to receive his baptism of fire. For after a period of confused operations, and disputes among the allies, the Paraguayan contingent re-crossed the Paraná without firing a shot, and Carlos Antonio López (partly at the instigation of the United States) decided to be neutral in the conflict – much to the annoyance of Brazil. The rebels were defeated at the battle of Vences in 1846, by General Justo José Urquiza, a gaucho chieftain almost as powerful as Rosas himself who, although owing allegiance to the Argentine Confederation, was practically king of the province of Entre Ríos; later he built a vast and magnificent palace at San José, with gardens, walks of finest sand imported at enormous expense, aviaries, piazzas, a grand entrance fronted by eight massive Corinthian columns, clock towers, the interior luxuriously furnished in Louis Quinze style, with thick curtains, heavy carpets and massive furniture, and decorated with frescoes depicting the various battles in which he had fought.

Rosas did not follow up Urquiza's victory at Vences by instructing him to cross the Paraná and invade Paraguay, as he might have done, mainly because he was at the time fully involved with England and France who, strongly objecting to his closing of the river-system, subjected Buenos Aires in its turn to a protracted blockade. But Rosas took every opportunity to impress upon Paraguay that he did not regard her as an independent state. Thus, in a message to the Congress of the Argentine Confederation on 27 December 1847, he said: 'the Government of the Province of Paraguay still cherishes the senseless design of separating itself from the Confederation . . .'.[6] Further, he sent orders in 1848 to the new Governor of Corrientes, installed after the battle of Vences, that if for any reason he communicated with Carlos Antonio López, he should address him as 'the Governor and Captain General of the Province of Paraguay'; and in a note to the Austrian government protesting against their recognition of Paraguay's independence, he argued that Paraguay never really intended to separate itself from the Argentine Republic, which in any case, he asserted, had 'always preserved its rights over the territory of Paraguay and regarded and regards it as one of the Argentine provinces'.[7]

The Paraguayan President, desperate to break the blockade, again sent an army under his eldest son's command, temporarily to occupy the left bank of the Paraná, in the hope of bringing pressure to bear on Rosas. On Christmas Day, 1850, he also entered into an alliance with Brazil, whereby both countries promised to help each other if either was attacked by the Argentine Confederation.

Only five days later, the whole situation was transformed. General Urquiza had decided to join the enemies of Rosas. He made an alliance with the Governor of Corrientes, and signed a treaty with Brazil and Uruguay for the destruction of the dictator. Paraguay was also invited to take part in the crusade, but the President, reluctant to embark on an adventure so far afield, and also suspicious of Urquiza's intentions, in effect did nothing. The 'ifs' of history force themselves upon us here; for if only Carlos Antonio had been more forthcoming with Brazil at this juncture, the War of the Triple Alliance would probably never have taken place – and if only he had secured General Urquiza as a firm friend, Paraguay would probably have won it.

On the other hand, as far as Brazil was concerned, he had ample cause for hesitation. There is little doubt that Brazil had been using Paraguay, with great skill, as a pawn in her policy of checking the growth of Argentina. Between Paraguay and Brazil, moreover, there were boundary difficulties every bit as acute, and as complicated, as those between Paraguay and Argentina. Again very briefly, these were in the main concerned with disagreements as to whether it was the river Apa or the river Blanco which formed the boundaries between Paraguay and the Brazilian state of Mato Grosso – the matter having been left extremely vague in the Treaty of Ildefonso which in 1777 had attempted to delineate the common frontiers of Spain and Portugal in the New World.

The first discussions between Brazil and Paraguay on this boundary question had taken place during the reign of Dr Francia, who had protested against encroachments by the Brazilian authorities in southern Mato Grosso on the northern limits of Paraguay. When the Brazilian envoy did not give him a satisfactory answer, Francia had ordered him to leave Asunción.

The Treaty of 7 October 1844, between Brazil and Paraguay, agreed to nominate commissioners to settle the boundary question, but nothing further was done, and the treaty was not in fact ratified by the Emperor of Brazil. In spite of the community of interest between the two countries in relation to Rosas, the Brazilians continued their policy of encroachment, and in 1850 established two posts in the disputed territory. Carlos Antonio promptly sent a force to disperse them. Brazil, deciding that first things must come first, swallowed her pride and acquiesced for the time being, entering into the alliance with Paraguay for the destruction of Rosas. At the same time, she let it be understood that she considered that Paraguay had taken a cynical advantage of her position – although it might seem that all López had done was to vindicate his country's sovereignty over territory that had always been regarded as Paraguayan. Further negotiations for a settlement of the boundary dispute, moreover, were frustrated because of Brazil's insistence on the line of the river Apa as her frontier.

But to return to the struggle with Rosas. General Urquiza began his series of brilliant operations by defeating Manuel Oribe, the Blanco Uruguayan general and ally of Rosas, who for the past nine years had been besieging Montevideo, the Uruguayan capital, which was in the hands of his political rivals, the Colorados. Urquiza then recrossed the Paraná with an allied army of 26,000 men, and on 3 February 1852, defeated Rosas' remaining forces at the battle of Monte Caseros, known as the 'crowning mercy'. The 'mercy' was, however, darkened by an appalling massacre. A regiment of Buenos Aireans which had declared themselves in Urquiza's favour at Montevideo had later deserted to Rosas. Urquiza ordered all members of this regiment captured at Monte Caseros to be put to death. Over a period of several days they were rounded up and shot in groups of ten or twenty. The Argentine historian, César Díaz, relates that the naked and bloody corpses were left in heaps along the sides of the main roads, or hung from the trees lining the broad avenue leading from Palermo to Buenos Aires.[8] Citizens who came out of their houses to welcome the man who had liberated them from the tyrant Rosas, were horror-stricken by the spectacle. It was widely believed that Urquiza had ordered the massacre because the victims were Porteños rather than because they were deserters. Buenos Aires never forgave Urquiza, and well before the year was out she had seceded from the Confederation, plunging Argentina into yet another round of civil war. As for Rosas, he took refuge in an English ship, the H.M.S. *Locust*, and spent the rest of his life (he died in 1877) as a peaceable but by no means wealthy farmer – unlike some dictators he had not lined his own pockets – at Swaythling, near Southampton.

Thanks to General Urquiza, Brazil had achieved her two main objectives: the prevention of a reconstructed viceroyalty of Buenos Aires, and freedom of navigation of the river Plate. In many respects, Paraguay, too, benefited from the overthrow of Rosas. With Brazil's influence now dominant in the Río de la Plata area, the Argentine Confederation, now under Urquiza's presidency, at last recognized the independence of Paraguay, on 17 July 1852; and it was in the same year that Britain, France, and the United States also sent their ministers to Asunción. It is sometimes considered, though, that from this point Brazil ceased to consider friendship with Paraguay to be of any value, and that Paraguay had really been left isolated in the interior of the continent. In spite of all the efforts of Carlos Antonio López to improve Paraguay's standing in the outside world, in fact, the country was in a weaker position than she had been under the isolationist policy of Francia. The intense national consciousness that Francia had so assiduously cultivated had not been allayed. A twentieth-century Paraguayan writer has aptly summed up the feelings of his fellow countrymen of the period:

'From the time of the defeat of Belgrano, the return of the invader to the attack was anticipated; the newspapers of Rosas scoffed at our independence, and this enraged even our women. They believed the enemy would behead the boys and violate the women; our parents may have been mistaken in part, but this was how they saw the situation, and the worst of it was that they were unable to look at it in any other way. Thus patriotism was even then the instinct of self-preservation'.[9]

At the same time, although there may have been a good deal of provincialism, morbidity, and even hysteria about this state of mind, what has been said about the relations of Paraguay with her two great neighbours surely makes it clear that she *was* in a distinctly insecure, if not perilous, position, with her independence still only recently, and on the whole grudgingly, acknowledged. It is difficult, indeed, to see how some writers can speak of the war that eventually broke out in 1864 as if it had no real political and diplomatic hinterland, as if it was entirely an act of diabolical will on the part of Francisco Solano López.

As the eldest son, Francisco Solano (who was born on 24 July 1826) lived the life of a crown prince: from an early age, his every whim was indulged, and he was encouraged to expect instant obedience from all about him; among these expectations, apparently was that of *droit de jambage* – like his youngest brother, Benigno, he was a great womanizer from his early teens onwards, and in this field of operations as in others he did not easily tolerate the thwarting of his plans. Masterman tells an appalling story in connection with the execution of Carlos Decoud (one of the two brothers executed after the alleged conspiracy of 1859) in which it is alleged that the naked corpse of Carlos was deposited at his mother's door, on the orders of Francisco Solano, his unsuccessful rival for the affections of a girl whom he, Francisco, had coveted for himself; and that the girl, discovering the corpse, was so shocked that she lost her reason. This is not the only story of the kind about Francisco Solano. The rumours, no doubt may contain part of the truth, but how much of it, and to what extent it has been distorted, it is now almost impossible to say.

The younger López had the best education available in the country. His tutor was Fidel Maiz, a tall handsome priest, only some nine or ten years his senior, who had himself been educated by the Jesuits of Córdoba, and who later achieved notoriety as Francisco Solano's 'grand inquisitor'. Francisco Solano proved especially apt at languages, and learned to speak French with considerable fluency. According to Barrett he was proficient, too, in German and Portuguese, and he had something more than a smattering of English.

There were some reports to the effect that Carlos Antonio López would really have preferred his youngest son Benigno (who was made Admiral of the Fleet) as his heir apparent. But there is certainly plenty of evidence that the elder López set out from the moment he achieved power to train his eldest son to succeed him. Thompson, for example, tells how 'from an early age, this young man was entrusted with a great deal of the executive power by his father, who used sometimes to pay him an official visit, on which occasion the folding-doors were all thrown wide open with a rush, as he used to take his son by surprise'.

By the time the President (eager to cement and if possible extend his country's international status) despatched the young man to Europe, he had created him not only General-in-Chief of the Paraguayan Army, but also Minister of War. Army life, it seems, always appealed to him, and it was apparently his tutor, Father Maiz, who aroused his hero-worship of Napoleon Bonaparte, and pointed out to him that Napoleon, too, was a man of small stature. In youth, he was apparently slim and active, and an excellent horseman, though later in life he developed a decidedly Napoleonic paunch, as well as bandy legs from early riding. His hands and feet were unusually small. This is an Indian characteristic, and apparently his complexion and cast of features also suggested an Indian ancestry. Burton tells us his thick black beard was cut in the style known as the Newgate frill.

His eyes caught the attention of many contemporary observers. In ordinary circumstances, they were said to be intelligent and kindly, and there are plenty of testimonies to his capacity for affection for those to whom he was closely attached. He could also be an excellent companion, both among his equals and with his troops, with whom he developed a chaffing, comradely relationship (provided they knew their place), and with whom, in spite of the harsh discipline to which they were subjected, he was very popular. Even Masterman acknowledges that 'his manners when he was pleased were remarkably gracious', and believed that there was good in him which could have been developed 'if he had only had but one trusted counsellor'. Several of the British and American naval officers who visited him during the war (he seems to have got on particularly well with naval men) commented enthusiastically on his charm. He was, however, subject to periods of sullen, intro-spective depression – and also to fits of violent anger, and then his eyes would grow bloodshot and bulge with terrifying effect.

His worst defects appear to have been a highly developed dis-trustfulness, derived no doubt from his father and from the era of El Supremo – and his inability to admit that he was wrong. At first, this was perhaps not much more than youthful arrogance: the Chilean writer, Federico de la Barra, who visited him in his campaign tent when the eighteen-year-old general was com-manding the Paraguayan contingent at Corrientes in 1845, related that in the course of a conversation he had with him, he had boasted:

'The military art has no secrets for me. General Paz cannot teach me, nor have I anything to learn of his science.'[10]

The one-armed General Paz, the commander of the Corrientes forces, was regarded as one of the best tacticians and military organizers of the day in Latin America.

As time went by, the suspiciousness, combined with the arro-gance, tended to harden into a dangerous pig-headedness. At the same time, there is little doubt that the younger López was a man of considerable ability, with an iron will and remarkable tenacity of purpose. His industriousness was often commented on; during the war he frequently sat up all night composing his own despatches, and there seems little doubt that, under his father's supervision, he became from an early age thoroughly conversant with the affairs of state.

This, then, was the young man of twenty-seven who, on 12 June 1853, set out for Europe (the first Paraguayan of any im-portance to do so); a young man who was neither the monster nor the ignorant and uncivilized barbarian of popular legend, but one whose character, upbringing and privileged position contained untold potentialities for good and for evil alike, and more than enough of the fatal flaws that lead to tragedy.

No one seems to know exactly how and where Francisco Solano met Elisa Alicia Lynch,[11] the woman who, in the view of many writers, played the part of Lady Macbeth in the tragedy. One rumour has it that she was introduced to him, on his arrival at the Gare du Nord, by Juan José Brizuela, a Paraguayan already resident in Paris (he was chargé d'affaires at the Paraguayan Legation, according to some accounts), acting more or less in the role of pimp. Another story has it that Elisa, after making careful enquiries of Brizuela, whom she had met at the home of a friend, and refusing to visit Francisco Solano in his apartment, invited him to visit her own salon.

It seems likely that Elisa was a member of the *demi-monde*, a fairly considerable and in some ways brilliant segment of Parisian society during the reign of the Emperor Napoleon III. But Elisa Lynch (Ella, as she was known to her intimates) was the victim of as many hysterical calumnies as Francisco Solano López himself; and later on anti-Paraguayan propagandists seized on her Parisian antecedents with a merciless glee. None of them seems to have reflected that she was still only nineteen when she first met her lover, and that her life had in many respects been a wretched one.

Her social origins were impeccable. In the *Exposición y protesta*, which she published in Buenos Aires after the war, in connection with her claims against the Argentine and Paraguayan governments, she gave the following details of her family background:

'I was born in Ireland in 1825 of honourable and worthy parents belonging to an Irish family which on my father's side included several bishops and over seventy magistrates; on my mother's side a vice-admiral in the British Navy who had the honour of fighting, with his four brothers, under Nelson at the Battles of the Nile and Trafalgar. All my uncles were British army or naval officers. My cousins and various others of my relatives now occupy high positions in Ireland'.[12]

These facts are certainly correct. But Elisa's girlhood had not been an easy one. Her two brothers and her sister (who married a French musician and went to live in Paris) were a good deal older, and she was in effect brought up as an only child. Both her father and her mother appear to have been charming, happy-go-lucky, improvident and impoverished. The Irish potato famine of 1845 further depleted the family's fortunes, and John Lynch decided to try his luck in Paris. But he was no more successful there; the family lived a hand-to-mouth existence, and Elisa, when she was still only fourteen, decided to accept the proposal of Jean Louis Armand de Quatrefages, a surgeon (some accounts say a veterinary surgeon) in the Algerian army. The marriage took place at Folkestone on 3 June 1850; Elisa was fifteen. For the next two years she lived with her husband both in France and Algiers. Then she left him. Some accounts say it was simply because she was bored with garrison life in a French colonial town; others that she had acquired a lover. Barrett maintains that the lover came on the scene only after Elisa's husband had consistently failed to protect her from the advances of the elderly colonel of his regiment. According to Hector Varela, the Argentine writer and biographer of Elisa, this lover was a Russian of title and rank, who within a fortnight of meeting her, had challenged the colonel to a duel and fatally wounded him.[13]

At this juncture her husband apparently took advantage of a loophole in French law which allowed him to discard his wife. There seems to be some doubt as to the exact nature of this loophole; some writers have said that it was connected with Elisa's age at the time of the marriage; Barrett says that although Elisa had married Quatrefages 'in the eyes of the Catholic Church and according to the laws of Great Britain,' French law 'did not recognize as legal the marriage of a French subject who failed to comply with the forms and the notices and the banns.' The cruelty of the situation as far as Elisa was concerned was that Quatrefages was now free to re-marry, while Elisa herself was not.

The seventeen-year-old girl fled to Paris to escape the scandal, only to find that her father was dead and that her mother had returned to Ireland. Her Russian lover followed her to Paris and apparently remained her protector until he was recalled to Russia. Then, in January 1854 (not long before she met Francisco Solano López) came the news that English and French squadrons had steamed into the Black Sea and that the Crimean War was imminent – so that Elisa's Russian lover would not be able to return to France.

Whether these circumstances influenced her decision to accept López as a new protector or not, there is no doubt of the depth of Elisa's affection for him or (as the end would show) of her unswerving loyalty. It was a loyalty and an affection, moreover which extended to the country of her adoption. As for the young Paraguayan who, in spite of his confident strut and his gaudy uniforms, was inwardly still a gauche provincial from a remote country which many Europeans had never even heard of, he was dazzled by the more youthful but very self-assured Parisienne. Not without reason, it would seem. There is no pen portrait of Elisa in her Paris days, but Hector Varela, who met her some two years later in Asunción, described her, in true Spanish romantic style as follows:

'She was tall and of a flexible and delicate figure with beautiful and seductive curves. Her skin was alabaster. Her eyes were of a blue that seemed borrowed from the very hues of heaven and had an expression of ineffable sweetness in whose depths of light Cupid was enthroned. Her beautiful lips were indescribably expressive of the voluptuous, moistened by an ethereal dew that God must have provided to lull the fires within her, a mouth that was like a cup of delight at the banquet table of ardent passion, Her hands were small with long fingers, the nails perfectly formed and delicately polished. She was, evidently, one of those women who make the care of their appearance a religion.'

Sober Englishmen could not be expected to equal this grandilo-quence, but Burton tells of an English officer who met Mme Lynch at a much later date, during the war, who was 'impressed most favourably' and compared her to Eugénie, the Empress of France, describing her as a tall 'belle-femme', handsome, with grey-blue eyes and hair 'châtain-clair', though by then 'somewhat sprinkled with grey'. And even Masterman, who hated her bitterly and believed she was her husband's evil genius, admitted that she was a remarkably handsome woman and declared that he could 'well believe the story that when she landed in Asunción the simple natives thought her charms were of more than earthly brilliancy, and her dress so sumptuous that they had no words to express the admiration they both excited.'

At what stage she made up her mind to accompany her new lover when he returned to Paraguay is not clear, but it is evident that from the start she set out to complete his education. She was well qualified to do so. Hector Varela believed that her talents and educational attainments surpassed even her beauty. General MacMahon, the American Minister who succeeded the egregious Washburn in 1869, found her a clever and cultured woman;[14] and there are many other testimonies to the same effect. As far as the social graces were concerned, she could certainly hold her own anywhere; and Masterman had to admit that she 'gave capital dinner parties, and could drink more champagne without being affected by it than anyone I have ever met with.'

It appears that she began her educating of Francisco by directing him to the best civilian tailors in Paris, and persuading him to lay aside the more gaudy of his uniforms – though he ordered others equally splendid, and distinctly Napoleonic in design, to take home with him. His appearance in his new Parisian clothes reminded some people of the English Crown Prince, who was to become King Edward VII.

It seems, too, that it was Elisa who, through her many contacts in high places, arranged for him to have a private audience with the Emperor and Empress of France. This was of considerable importance for his ego, for England (which he visited before he went to France) had, Burton says, 'treated him with her usual trick of neglect', and according to some stories Queen Victoria had snubbed him by refusing to receive him at Osborne; and when he had attended a large public audience of the French Emperor he had received scant attention. Now with Elisa's help it appears that he established the friendliest relations with both Napoleon III and the Empress Eugénie.

Elisa also accompanied her lover to Spain where he had an audience with Queen Isabella II and her Minister for Foreign Affairs; and to Italy where he was received at Caserta by the King of the Sicilies and invested with a splendid order. There was also a visit to Germany, but none of the more scholarly of the recent writers on the subject confirms the earlier story that Francisco and Elisa had also gone to the Crimea and watched the allied armies in action.

On the other hand, Francisco Solano certainly attended military reviews in France, and took careful notes of equipment and methods of military organization. There is an unsubstantiated story that on one occasion he astonished his hosts by skilfully putting a company of soldiers through their paces himself.

Although the social whirl and his passion for Mme Lynch took up a great deal of his time, Francisco Solano never forgot that he was his country's Minister Plenipotentiary. Even in inhospitable England he had not wasted his time. He had visited a number of large industrial plants, contracted for the building of steamers especially adapted for river navigation; contracted J. and A. Blyth and Company to act as Paraguay's purchasing and supply agent; and hired a number of British technicians who, when war came, were to play a vital part in the defence of Paraguay.

Rumour has it that his brother Benigno, who was in Paris with him, tried to persuade him not to allow Elisa to go to Paraguay, but when on 11 November 1854, he set sail from Bordeaux on the long journey home, the matter was settled between them. Elisa arrived in Buenos Aires on the packet boat following the one which had carried her lover; and she remained in Buenos Aires in order to bear her first child by him.

When she finally reached Asunción with her infant son, she found that her life was far from easy. Her lover was as devoted as ever (and in spite of his numerous mistresses, always remained so), but the President and his family refused to receive her.

Her unmarried status (in spite of repeated efforts she never succeeded in getting a divorce from Quatrefages) caused her much bitterness. Francisco Solano's former tutor, Father Maiz, insisted that he was prevented by Paraguayan law from christening their child in church, though a humble parish priest, named Father Manuel Antonio Palacios (later to become Bishop of Paraguay) was persuaded to perform the ceremony in his little church six miles outside Asunción. The child was named Francisco after his father, but was usually known in the family as Pancho.

Although, too, the simple folk of Asunción went in awe of the beautiful lady from Paris, the aristocratic families hated and despised her. 'I was struck,' Hector Varela wrote of his visit to Asunción, 'by the deep dislike and rancour that all the Paraguayan ladies showed towards Madame Lynch because of her handsome physique, superior education, modishness and elegance. Particularly did they resent, as mortifying and even humiliating to themselves, her role in Asunción. They hated to think of the even more prominent position she would occupy when López succeeded his father.'

The hostility of the ladies of the European colony was of a different order – the merciless censoriousness of a strait-laced and hypocritical period. All kinds of scandalous stories were invented about Elisa's past, and the fact that she was evidently living a life of exemplary propriety in Asunción, and carrying off her difficult position with outstanding tact and dignity only enraged her enemies the more. The sneering, condescending tone is well caught in these comments by Charles Ames Washburn, the American Minister, whose wife was one of those who refused to recognize Elisa when she arrived in Asunción:

'This imported teacher of morality (Madame Lynch), having suspected a man employed about her premises of too great intimacy with one of her maid servants, affected to be so greatly scandalized and shocked that any improprieties should be committed in her abode of virtue and purity that she sent the offender with a note to Colonel Barrios, then holding the office of Mayor of the Plaza. . . .'

The most virulent of Elisa's enemies appear to have been Madame Laurent Cochelet, wife of the French Consul, and Señora Barmejo – despite the fact that it was Elisa who had been largely instrumental in bringing the latter's husband, Ildefonso Barmejo, a noted Spanish novelist and playwright of the day, to Asunción in order to launch a Paraguayan National Theatre.

Whatever Elisa Lynch's faults may have been, and whatever crimes she may have later committed or connived at, one cannot help sympathizing with the situation in which this young woman, still in her early twenties, found herself – and hoping that the widely circulated story of the revenge she eventually took on the ladies of the European colony is indeed true. This is supposed to have taken place in May 1855, on the occasion of the official dedication of the French colony at Nueva Burdeos (now Villa Hayes) in the Chaco – one of the results of Francisco Solano's conferences with Napoleon III and his ministers. The President, now grown monstrously bulky and in poor health, declared a national holiday (although he was not happy about the scheme and the ultimate failure of the colony was largely due to his unco-operativeness). The members of the *corps diplomatique* and all high-ranking officials were invited to the function. The men were to travel on horse-back, the women by river-steamer. Madame Cochelet was the guest of honour – and Madame Lynch was to act as hostess.

On board the steamer Madame Cochelet pointedly ignored her hostess's presence beneath the canopy to the right of the gangplank and turning to the left, sought a spot on the deck as far away as possible. Not so far away, however, that Elisa could not overhear Señora Barmejo declare, 'it is an experience for a memoir to have been the honoured guest of an Irish courtesan'.

At midday Elisa ordered the servants to serve lunch, but when she approached Madame Cochelet's table, she found that no place had been left for her. She turned aside, and going over to her servants, whispered fresh instructions to them. A few moments later they appeared, each bearing a covered tray, approached the tables, then acting with almost military precision, turned aside and dumped the contents of their trays over the rail into the river.

Madame Lynch bowed stiffly and, the story goes, fixing her eyes unwaveringly on Madame Cochelet and Señora Barmejo, declared 'and it shall be written in my memoirs that I refused to serve cats at my table!'

By the time the ladies returned to Asunción after the ceremonies, they were extremely hungry; and Francisco Solano is said to have laughed uproariously when he heard the story. Apparently, according to Barrett, the social tide turned in Elisa's favour from this point onwards, especially among those who had not been invited on the excursion, and who now eagerly called on Madame Lynch to pay their respects. According to some observers, however, the episode hardened and embittered her.

Nevertheless, and in spite of all these vexations, Elisa had effected a cultural and social transformation in Asunción. The furnishing of her house in itself set an entirely new standard of elegance and sophistication. To quote from a report in a contemporary Buenos Aires newspaper:

'Although one of the finest houses in Asunción, the house of Madame Lynch would appear but ordinary in Buenos Aires. It is in the interior arrangements that it achieves distinction. The luxury, elegance, variety, and dignity of its furnishings makes its reputation as the rendezvous of foreign visitors understandable. Many of Madame Lynch's brasses and porcelains are museum pieces, and the French tapestries and Oriental rugs are distributed with excellent taste and in a manner to delight the eye. . . .'[15]

Elisa had seen to it, too, that her lover's house (while the old President was alive they maintained separate establishments) was furnished in the same impeccable taste. Another contemporary Buenos Aires newspaper describes it:

'The drawing-room furniture would be perfect in Paris. López has gilded furniture, silk curtains, chiffoniers and cabinets of exquisite workmanship inlaid with ivory, mirrors in Florentine frames, paintings of distinction, rare bronzes and porcelains. His is the residence of a well-travelled man with a taste for good living.'

In her personal presence as well Elisa contributed a touch of European *chic* to provincial Asunción; as another Buenos Aires correspondent writes:

'It is enough to see her ride by, gracefully and easily, firmly seated and handling her spirited horse with all the coolness of a woman who had overcome fear, to realize that she is like the woman riders of gay background, whom one has read about, who ride daily in Regents Park (*sic*) and the Bois de Boulogne.'

It was Elisa, too, who was largely responsible for encouraging her lover to set his recently-imported English architect (merely a stone-mason, in some accounts) Alonzo Taylor, to work on a number of important new building projects, including a new presidential palace and an opera house. In addition she stimulated an interest in music, organized tea-parties, costume balls and literary evenings, and apparently persuaded two French ladies to come to Asunción to establish an academy for young ladies along the lines of a French finishing school.

The project which was perhaps dearest to Elisa's heart was that of the Paraguayan National Theatre – despite the irritation of Señora Barmejo's presence. Hector Varela has left a vivid description of the scene on the opening night, notable both for the way in which it illustrates the patronizing tone of the Argentine press of the day towards anything connected with Paraguay, and for the thumbnail sketch of the ageing President:

'In the box of honour, the broad-faced and corpulent dictator sat with his wife and two daughters. In the next box sat General Francisco López and Colonel Venancio López, sons of the Dictator. Madame Elisa Lynch was seated in the centre box, gorgeously dressed and displaying many jewels. Even a famous courtesan like Cora Pearl, the most fashionable for a while in Paris, would fall short of awaking the jealous envy in the ladies of the Faubourg St Germain that Madame Lynch, more resplendent and enticing than I have ever seen her, awakened that night in the ladies of Asunción.

'The gentlemen all watched her with definitely respectful admiration. The ladies gave her hostile looks, the meaning of which was perfectly obvious.

'López I was really an imposing figure. One rarely sees a more impressive sight than this great tidal-wave of human flesh. He is a veritable mastodon, with a pear shaped face, narrow forehead, and heavy, pendulous jowls.

'During the entire performance, the President ostentatiously wore an enormous hat, quite appropriate to him and equally

suitable either for a museum of curiosities or for the Buenos
Aires carnival. The performance of the players can be dismissed
with a line. It was as ludicrous as López's hat.

'During the evening, I watched López I for a sign of any impression produced upon him, upon witnessing a play for the first
time in his life. It was like watching a stone in a field. He is the
master in the art of concealing emotion. At the end of the
tedious proceedings, without any display of either approval or
disapproval, the old monarch of the jungles rose and left,
ponderously followed by the soldiers of his Praetorian guard.'[16]

Carlos Antonio may not have known what to make of the
occasion, but his son and Elisa were both well aware it had not
been a success; according to some accounts this was the fault of the
old President, because he had refused to allow the importation of
professional actors from Spain; according to others, it was Elisa
who had insisted that if the new theatre was to be truly national,
then the play must be performed by Paraguayans; in any case it
appears she was able to put most of the blame on to the hated
Señora Barmejo.

Thus Francisco Solano López's eighteen-month sojourn in
Europe, besides bringing 'Ella' Lynch into his life, had important
social and cultural repercussions as well. What effects if any,
though, did it have upon political developments?

Ever since he had become Commander-in-Chief and Minister
of War, the younger López had been steadily building up the
strength of Paraguay's armed forces and one of the main objectives
of his European tour had been the purchase of equipment and the
hiring of technicians for his country's military programme. But
was he already considering the possibilities of war? There are
some who think he was, and suggest that Napoleon III, in the
course of their private interviews, encouraged his guest in both his
military and his imperial ambitions. Certainly there seems little
doubt that he conceived a tremendous admiration for the French
Emperor and for the kind of military despotism, based on the
support of the *petite bourgeoisie* and coloured by the Napoleonic
legend, which he practised. He was, of course, the heir of a long
tradition of despotism, but his contact with Napoleon III sharpened
his views on the subject. 'What do you mean by liberty?', he asked
Hector Varela in a conversation with him when he returned
from France – 'the kind you have in Buenos Aires? The liberty to

insult each other in the press, to kill each other in the district assemblies for the election of deputies, to keep the nation divided, for everyone to do what he fancies without respect for anyone else?'

In the same conversation, Varela reports in his book, Francisco Solano expressed his complete approval of the economic paternalism of his own country, represented in particular by the state monopoly of *yerba mate*, and pointed out that the tirades against it in the doctrinaire liberal papers of Buenos Aires, despite their profession of high-sounding principles, were basically a reflection of the views of those who would have liked to be exploiting the commodity themselves. Like his father and Francia before him, he had a profound distrust of the aims of the Porteños, the commercial free-for-all which they preached and practised, and the demagogy and anarchism which, he argued, attended it. In this connection it should be added that López felt himself directly menaced by the 'anarchism' of Buenos Aires because of the presence in that city of an emigré revolutionary committee of Liberal Paraguayans. These represented the class that in the normal circumstances of nineteenth-century capitalism would have been controlling the economic life of their country. As it was, the members of this class had been forced, from the time of Francia, either to accept a very limited and strictly supervised role within the state bureaucracy – or voluntary exile. A realization of this helps to explain, if not condone, the extremely harsh measures adopted during the war against the merchant class in Paraguay, both native and foreign. Looked at from the point of view of the political and economic *mores* which were dominant at the time, and seemed the only true and natural ones, such persecution seemed wicked and perverse. But, given the archaic political and economic system to which Paraguay had committed itself, there was obviously a logic behind it.

Holding such views as these, it was inevitable that López should regard the Liberals of Buenos Aires as his natural enemies – and the feudal chieftains of the Argentine provinces like Urquiza as potential allies. As Horton Box puts it:

'. . . between the Liberals of Buenos Aires and the strange and formidable Government of Paraguay there could in the end be no genuine appeasement; there was a fundamental conflict of principles. More and more the reactionaries of the Río de la

Plata came to look upon Paraguay as the last stronghold against the Liberal Revolution.'

It is the view of Hector Varela, in fact, that Francisco Solano was convinced of the inevitability of war as early as 1855. It can at least be said with some certainty that he was convinced that Paraguay could hold her own, both as regards this fundamental conflict of principles, and the border disputes with Argentina and Brazil, only by a show of armed might. Francia had avoided this necessity by his policy of isolation. Carlos Antonio López tried to follow a mixed policy, refusing to yield on any of the border issues, but at the same time practising as far as possible Francia's aloofness and caution. But clearly such a mixed policy was only possible if it had teeth to it, and the younger López, who did not shrink, as his father did, from the grim consequences that might follow, saw to it that it did, and from the moment of his return to Paraguay his influence over his father steadily increased.

At the same time, it must be said, he showed himself ready to explore the possibilities of negotiation, and did so with considerable skill and acumen. He showed, too, that he could play a peace-making role in the tangled affairs of the Argentine when, in 1859, his father sent him to act as mediator between Buenos Aires and General Urquiza.

Buenos Aires had again seceded from the Argentine Confederation in 1853, but on 23 October 1859, General Urquiza and his provincial army had defeated the forces of Buenos Aires, under General Bartolomé Mitre, at the battle of Cepeda.

Francisco Solano began his task of mediation by negotiating a truce between Urquiza and Mitre, and then persuaded the two parties to sign the Pact of San José de Flores. The statesmanship which he displayed in these negotiations has tended to be ignored or glossed over, but at the time his efforts were praised by both sides to the dispute. Thus a representative of the Buenos Aires Government addressed the younger López:

'The diplomatic action of Paraguay in bringing together the members of the same family and allaying difficulties which until now had appeared insurmountable, has contributed strongly to the solution, by peaceful means, of questions which could never have been resolved honourably for all through recourse to arms.

'It is a pleasure to inform your Excellency that the Government of Buenos Aires will cherish the agreeable impressions inspired in it by the distinguished person of the representative of Paraguay as a complement of the noble and successful mission which he has performed.'[17]

Similarly, the Vice-President of the Argentine Confederation offered a:

'Vote of gratitude to the Supreme Government of the Republic of Paraguay and to His Excellency Brigadier General and Minister Mediator D. Francisco Solano López, who with noble and generous effort, has employed his good and paternal offices to promote the union of the dissident parties of the Argentine Republic.'

Particularly enthusiastic were the citizens of Buenos Aires, who presented Francisco Solano with an album of signatures – among them that of Bartolomé Mitre – which contained this preamble:

'The people of Buenos Aires dedicate this token of gratitude and respect to his Excellency Brigadier General D. Francisco Solano López, Minister Plenipotentiary of the Republic of Paraguay, to whose friendly interposition is due the saving of the blood of their sons, the fortunate peace in which they now find themselves, and the long-sought union of the Argentine family. Our best wishes shall always accompany the illustrious mediator and His Excellency President Carlos Antonio López, and the Republic which they represent. Our gratitude for their valued assistance shall be eternal.'

It is difficult to believe, after reading these words, that less than six years later the name of the 'monster' Francisco Solano López would be greeted, by the same citizens, with howls of execration.

The most important of all the tributes, however, as far as Paraguay's political interests were concerned, was that of General Justo José de Urquiza, the great gaucho chieftain and at the time still President of the Argentine Confederation, who issued a manifesto addressed to 'the illustrious mediator of Paraguay', which declared that 'no demonstration of gratitude will be too much to honour his friendship'. Some weeks later General Urquiza followed up his manifesto with the gift of the sword he had worn at the battle of Cepeda.

'I wish to present Your Excellency' the general wrote in his accompanying letter, 'with a token of the appreciation which I entertain for your virtues, and I can find no more suitable object than the sword I wore at Cepeda. I present it to you as a modest token of friendship. Please accept it. I shall always look forward with pleasure to the occasion on which I can prove my friendship and gratitude to the Government of Paraguay and to you.'

If only, one cannot help once again reflecting, these words had been put into practice when the occasion did indeed present itself.

In reply, Francisco Solano wrote:

'Your Excellency's wishes for my personal prosperity are most cordially appreciated, and although the invaluable friendship of Your Excellency is the greatest token which you could offer me, it is my profound pleasure to accept the generous gift of the sword which you wielded at Cepeda with so much glory. When the occasion shall require that I unsheath it, I shall do my utmost to render it the honour it deserves.'

In this case, the words were indeed acted upon when the occasion required, though no one knows where the sword of Cepeda now lies.

In other words, at this stage in the career of Francisco Solano López, all occasions seemed to conspire in his favour, apart from the irritating circumstance of the dispute with Britain, and the high-handed action of her Minister in Buenos Aires in seizing the *Tacuari*.

But, as it has already been pointed out, the attitude of Buenos Aires towards Paraguay in connection with this incident was decidedly ambivalent. The results of Francisco Solano's skilful mediation were short-lived, and so, in consequence, were the emotions of gratitude and good-will towards him. In spite of its defeat at the battle of Cepeda, Buenos Aires was still secretly determined either to dominate the Argentine Republic, or to 'go it alone', and when General Urquiza was succeeded in the Presidency (when his term of office expired) by Santiago Derqui, with whom he was on bad terms, Buenos Aires, under her newly-elected Governor Bartolomé Mitre, once again seceded from the Confederation, and took the field against Derqui. This time the federal forces were defeated, on 17 September 1861, at the Battle of Pavón. General Urquiza in fact took part in the battle, with 4,000 of his men from Entre Ríos, but with no particular enthusiasm, and after the battle he withdrew his army and refused any further support to Derqui, who resigned from the Presidency and fled to Montevideo. A series of Liberal revolutions in many of the provinces in Mitre's favour followed. The Confederation dissolved, a new National Congress was summoned, and on 27 August 1862, Bartolomé Mitre was unanimously elected President of the Republic, now at last united under the Constitution of 1853 – with Buenos Aires as the capital. General Urquiza acquiesced in the situation, and the new President was content to leave him in control of his Entre Ríos territory, though for some years to come he was to remain something of an Achilles lurking in his tent.

As for Paraguay, she had derived little, if any, benefit from all these events. They had not, for example, in the least affected the situation as far as the boundary question was concerned. The Treaty of July, 1852, between Paraguay and the Argentine Confederation, had contained clauses which recognized Paraguayan sovereignty over the Gran Chaco north of the river Bermejo. But as Box says, the Argentine Congress had refused to ratify the treaty because of these clauses, and General Urquiza (who at that time was President of the Confederation) had ordered fresh negotiations. Incidentally, one of the main reasons for the foundation of the French Colony at Nueva Burdeos, on the Chaco side of the Río Paraguay, in May 1855 (when Elisa Lynch exacted her revenge on the foreign ladies of Asunción) was to consolidate Paraguayan claims in the area. A new treaty was eventually negotiated in 1856, but with the question of the boundaries between the two countries still left in abeyance.

Horton Box is of the opinion that Carlos Antonio López once again missed a golden opportunity, just as he had done at the time of the battle of Caseros, when in 1859 Urquiza endeavoured to obtain something more solid in the way of support in his struggle with Buenos Aires and Bartolomé Mitre than the offer of Francisco Solano as mediator, by insisting on a settlement of the boundary dispute as a pre-condition. Dr Box argues that Paraguay had a far better chance of eventually obtaining a settlement favourable to herself from a friendly-disposed General Urquiza, and a Confederation dominated by Provincials whom Paraguay understood, than from the Porteños who would almost certainly be adamant in their opposition to her claims.

Again one can say, if only – if only, that is, Paraguay had now reached a really close understanding with General Urquiza and the still powerful Provincial interests he represented in Argentina, the outcome of the War of the Triple Alliance might have been very different, and the history of both countries radically altered. On the other hand, with hindsight it is easy to see that it was Bartolomé Mitre and his Liberals who represented the forward-moving currents of history, while Paraguay and General Urquiza alike belonged to a way of life that was doomed, sooner or later, to be submerged.

Boundary difficulties with an Argentina still struggling to consolidate its unity were, however, a good deal less serious than those with a Brazil firmly united over a number of years under a determined and able Emperor – and in fact they nearly led to war as early as 1855. In that year Brazil reverted to her policy of encroachment on the northern frontier, by establishing a post at Salinas, on the right bank of the Rio Paraguay and north of Fort Olympo. Just as he had done five years earlier, the elder López promptly despatched a force to expel the garrison. But this time Brazil began to make open preparations for war, and the Paraguayan President adopted counter-measures.

Brazil, it should be added, was just as much concerned about the free navigation of the river Paraguay as she was about the border question, for the simple reason that without it her province of Mato Grosso was completely cut off from the rest of the nation. By the same token, Paraguay saw, in her control of the river routes to Mato Grosso, one of her most powerful bargaining counters.

Brazil now sent a naval squadron to Paraguayan waters, though it halted off Corrientes to see what effect the show of armed force would have. A despatch from the British Consul in Rio de Janeiro illustrates the mood in which Francisco Solano López had returned from Europe, and his increasing influence over his father:

'. . . the arrival of the Brazilian Squadron at Corrientes shook the determination of the President to attempt resistance, and he dispatched a Commissioner to parley with the Brazilian Admiral. General López, however, . . . overruled the President's fears, and caused the Commissioner to return'.[18]

And some months later, the British Consul in Asunción provided further evidence of Francisco Solano López's attitude, when he wrote home:

'Both the Industry and Trade of the Country, which have already been very seriously affected by the conduct of Brazil, would be unhesitatingly sacrificed (by him) to the cry of National Honour and Independence.'[19]

Nevertheless, this crisis too was surmounted, and largely by the efforts of the younger López himself who, put in charge of the negotiations by his father, signed a treaty with Pedro Ferreira de Oliveira, the Brazilian plenipotentiary who had been sent with the naval squadron – a treaty which, although again postponing the settlement of the boundary dispute, was decidedly in Paraguay's favour. So much so, in fact, that there was an outcry in Rio de Janeiro, and the Emperor refused to ratify it.

Further negotiations then took place, and eventually Carlos Antonio found himself obliged, very reluctantly, to concede freedom of navigation on the Upper Paraguay, although the settlement of the border question was once again shelved. By 1858 Brazilian steamers were plying at regular intervals between Rio de Janeiro and Cuiabá, the capital of Mato Grosso, and continued to do so for the next five years.

But the dispute over boundaries smouldered on, and flared up again in the summer of 1862. Again war was averted, but it was clear that the situation was deteriorating.

By mid-September it was clear, too, that Carlos Antonio López was dying. On his death-bed, and acting on the right conferred on him by Congress six years previously, he nominated his eldest son as Vice-President, empowered to fulfil all the duties of the Presidency until Congress met to choose a successor. Father Fidel Maiz had already administered Extreme Unction when the old man stirred and suddenly spoke to his eldest son, who was standing nearby:

'There are many problems waiting to be ventilated; but do not try to solve them by the sword but by the pen, *chiefly with Brazil*'.

These last three words, according to Father Maiz, were pronounced 'with emphasis' but, he goes on, 'the general remained silent; he did not answer his father, who also after he had finished speaking remained silent. . . . He was not long in breathing his last.'[20]

Did Francisco Solano remain silent out of grief, or because he had already made up his mind that war with Brazil was now inevitable? Certainly less than two months after his father's death he spoke to Washburn, the American Minister, of 'the difficulties impending between Paraguay and Brazil', and made some pointed inquiries about the use of the recently introduced Monitor in naval warfare. Washburn wrote home (he was at this stage well-disposed towards López):

> 'I assured him that if he wanted to whip Brazil, or any other of his neighbours, the Yankees would furnish him the tools to do it with greater dispatch, on more reasonable terms, giving at the same time a more efficient article than could other nations or peoples.'[21]

This, of course, is not conclusive evidence, and no one will ever know now what exactly was in Francisco Solano's mind at this juncture. Perhaps he really had returned from Europe with his decision already made. Perhaps he had been genuinely trying to see if negotiations could solve the various impasses with which his country was confronted, without loss of national honour. Perhaps he had merely been buying time in order to make his military preparations. And perhaps, too, the objectives of both Brazil and Buenos Aires were so firmly fixed that nothing he had done or failed to do would in the long run have altered the outcome. But all this lies in the realm of speculation.

As for Carlos Antonio López and his Paraguay – this passage from George Thompson is as good an epitaph as any:

> 'Notwithstanding all the selfishness of López I, his Government was comparatively a good one for Paraguay. Probably in no country in the world has life and property been so secure as all over Paraguay during his reign. Crime was almost unknown, and when committed, immediately detected and punished. The mass of the people were perhaps the happiest in existence. They had hardly to do any work to gain a livelihood. Each family had its house or hut in its own ground. They planted, in a few days, enough tobacco, maize, and mandioca for their own consumption, and the crop hardly wanted looking at till it was ready to be gathered. Having at every hut a grove of oranges, which form a considerable article of food in Paraguay, and also a few cows, they were almost throughout the year under little necessity of working. The higher classes, of course, lived more in the European way, many families being very well off and comfortable.
>
> 'Everybody was liable at any moment to have himself and his property pressed into the public service, without payment, at

the call of any judge of the peace; but this power was not generally abused in the old man's time. He would allow only his own family to tyrannize over the people to any great extent. As to most Paraguayans the idea of the sum of human happiness is to lie down all day on a "poncho" in the shade, and smoke and play the guitar, they may be considered to have been very happy, as they had little else to do.'

Granted that Thompson, looking back across the years of bloodshed, may have been tempted to romanticize the past a little, it is nevertheless clear that something of that 'happy garden state' which attracted travellers to Paraguay still survived when Carlos Antonio López died in 1862. It was an Indian summer. The garden was soon to become a graveyard.

NOTES

[1] 1845, according to both Masterman and Burton.

[2] *Portrait of a Dictator*, R. B. Cunninghame-Graham. London 1933. Quotations from Cunninghame-Graham are taken from this book, unless otherwise indicated.

[3] *Seven Eventful Years in Paraguay*, George F. Masterman. London 1869. Quotations from Masterman are taken from this book.

[4] *Paraguay, Brazil and the Plate*, C. B. Mansfield. Cambridge 1856.

[5] So Charles Ames Washburn, the American Ambassador, (who played such an ambiguous role in later events) alleged in his *History of Paraguay, with notes of personal observations and reminiscences of diplomacy under difficulties*. New York and Boston 1871. Quotations from Washburn are taken from this book.

[6] Cited in *La diplomacia oriental en el Paraguay. Correspondencia oficial privada del Doctor Juan José de Herrera, ministro de relaciones exteriores de los gobiernos de Berro y Aguirre*, ed. Luis Alberto de Herrera. 3 vols, Montevideo 1908–19.

[7] *ibid.*

[8] *Memorias inéditas del general oriental Don César Díaz*, publicadas por Adriano Díaz. Buenos Aires 1878.

[9] *Causas del heroísmo paraguayo*, Manuel Domínguez. Asunción 1903.

[10] Quoted by Box in *The Origins of the Paraguayan War*.

[11] There are several renderings of her name, but she used this one herself when she wrote her name in full in her claims against the Argentine and Paraguayan governments after the Paraguayan War.

[12] *Exposición y protesta que hace Elisa A. Lynch*, Elisa Lynch. Buenos Aires 1875. Quotations from Elisa Lynch are taken from this book.

[13] *Elisa Lynch*, Hector F. Varela (pseud. Orion). Buenos Aires 1870. Reprinted 1934. Quotations from Varela are taken from this book, unless otherwise indicated.

[14] Testimony of Martin T. MacMahon in U.S. House of Representatives Report No. 65, 41st Congress, Second Session.

[15] This and the following two extracts from contemporary newspaper accounts are quoted by Barrett in *Woman on Horseback*. Barrett apologises for having

failed to note the names and dates of the newspapers concerned, but is certain of the accuracy of his quotations.

[16] Also from a newspaper report quoted by Barrett.

[17] This and the following extracts are taken from *Solano López*, Arturo Bray. Buenos Aires 1945.

[18] Howard to Clarendon, Rio de Janeiro, 11 June 1855, F.O. 13.330, despatch no. 79.

[19] Consul Henderson to Clarendon, Asunción, 19 July 1855, F.O.59.12, despatch no. 17.

[20] F. Maiz to M. L. Olleros, Arroyos y esteros, 12 September 1905, text in *Alberdi a la luz de sus escritos en cuanto se refieren al Paraguay*, M. L. Olleros. Asunción 1905.

[21] Washburn to Seward, Asunción, 2 November 1862, State Department MSS, Paraguay Diplomatic 1.

ACT THREE

The Napoleon of South America?

Whether or not Francisco Solano López entertained ideas of making himself the Napoleon of South America, he had first to secure his own position as undisputed ruler of Paraguay. It was not as straight-forward as he might have imagined. On the death of his father, he took a number of precautions (as he was entitled to do as Vice-President) by doubling the guards round the Presidential Palace, sending strong patrols through the streets, taking possession of his father's state papers – and, according to some highly coloured accounts, of the state treasury as well. With great promptitude he also summoned a Council of State to whom he read his father's will appointing him Vice-President, and therefore Chief Magistrate, and sent out orders for the convening of a Congress.

Although the members of this congress were for the most part judges and chiefs of police, who were directly nominated by and dependent on the Government, a few brave spirits ventured to express their doubts as to the advisability of the hereditary principle. When it came to it, though, Francisco Solano (at the age of thirty-five) was elected to the Presidency by a unanimous vote, on 2 October 1862; but the British Chargé d'Affaires at Buenos Aires, who was in Asunción at the time, reported that:

> 'His Excellency was not free from anxiety, and in conversation expressed to me that his position was one surrounded with difficulties tho' he hoped to be able to silence his opponents. I heard from a confidential source that Don Benigno López, his youngest brother, was the leader of a party against the President who had opposed his election to the Presidency'.[1]

The opponents were indeed silenced. Among those arrested were Pedro Lescano, the Chief Justice, and the new President's former tutor, Father Fidel Maiz, on charges of conspiring against the constitution. They were found guilty and sentenced to terms of imprisonment. Benigno, who was reported to have Liberal ideas, was banished to one of the López family estates in the interior.

Many years later, when most of the principals in the case were dead, Father Maiz admitted that there had in fact been a plan to change the constitution, not necessarily in order to dispense with López himself, but certainly to limit his powers.[2]

This admission of Father Maiz is of some importance, in that it furnishes proof that Francisco Solano López was not, as many of his detractors insist, in a continuous state of paranoid obsession, forever suspecting conspiracies that existed only in his own imagination. When the evidence is impartially examined, indeed, it becomes clear that this supposition is nonsense; López was, it is true, morbidly suspicious and would brook not the slightest disagreement with his authority, but when he claimed that there was a conspiracy (in 1869 as much as in 1862) it seems pretty certain that, with his highly organized spy-system behind him, he had (to put it at its lowest) something to go on.

It was a sign, no doubt, that the new President had effectively silenced what opposition existed, and that he was considered to be firmly in the saddle, when (before the end of the year) a number of old Spanish families as well as well-informed foreigners, began to leave Asunción, mostly to go to Buenos Aires. Some of these, among them the Saguier brothers, had undoubtedly been involved in stock-piling and speculation on the expectation of an imminent war with Brazil. Other actual or would-be war profiteers were imprisoned. Actions such as these, and especially the seizure of the property of the Saguier brothers from the English merchant to whom they had assigned it when they left Asunción, were regarded by many (including the American Minister Washburn), as examples of a purely personal tyranny. So they were, from the point of view of the prevailing Liberal economic philosophy, but basically, the second López was merely continuing the economic policies that had been laid down by his father and Francia before him, with the added justification that something approaching a war emergency was already in existence.

Other economic measures taken by López in the first two years of his Presidency were of a similar nature, designed primarily to check both foreign merchants and native exporters whose financial interests were, inevitably to some extent, tied to Buenos Aires. Among these measures were the granting of government loans to native-born Paraguayans for 'enterprises of general utility'; exemption from import duties on all machinery and tools designed for the country's agriculture and industry; and a government subsidy to promote the cultivation of cotton, particularly necessary because the Civil War in the North American Republic had largely put an end to imports of cotton from the southern states.

López made other provisions for the benefit of the ordinary native Paraguayan, including an appropriation for the extension of the school system and another for setting up thirty scholarships annually for Paraguayan students to continue their studies in Europe – declaring that his ultimate aim was to make the country independent of foreign teachers and technicians.

What the educational measures introduced by father and son meant in practice it is difficult to ascertain with any certainty. Francia had not believed in educating the masses, and the country's long isolation made even those who had acquired some learning extraordinarily ignorant of the outside world. Masterman says, for example, that the Paraguayans 'had most singular ideas about geography'; many of them took Paraguay as the only standard for position and distance, so that to them all countries were either 'arriba o abajo de río' – that is, on one side or the other of the River Paraguay, which they believed extended to Europe 'and could never realize the existence of another continent with an ocean rolling between'. Even someone like Father Román (another of López's inquisitors in the later stages of the Paraguayan War) when found by Masterman reading a Spanish translation of the life of Cardinal Wiseman, asked him 'with a most puzzled expression of face, if Londres were in Inglaterra, or Inglaterra in Londres, and if the latter really adjoined France!'

Masterman also sneers at the Public Library in Asunción – another of Francisco Solano's innovations – saying that 'the books were nearly all theological' and that he had 'never heard of anyone reading there'. He adds the bizarre detail (also with a sneer) that during the war, when all kinds of materials were scarce, 'López found . . . a most characteristic use (for the books) . . . he had the ponderous tomes cut up for rocket and squib cases! I saw them one day serving thus a folio Hebrew Bible, with an interleaved Latin translation – a most South American mode of diffusing useful knowledge.'

But Masterman does also say that although it was rare to find a Paraguayan woman who could read or write, nearly all the men could do so: 'in each town and village, there was a primary school supported by the Government, where the boys were taught these simple accomplishments and the easier rules of arithmetic.' He was probably right in saying that this is about as far as most Paraguayans got in their education, apart from the wealthy aristocrats, and it is doubtful whether many ever reached a high enough standard to qualify for the scholarships abroad. But surely this elementary education was in itself a considerable achievement for a small country like Paraguay in a remote corner of the world, at a time when Britain's first compulsory elementary education system was still a good many years off. What other contemporary Latin American countries had anything at all comparable? If it comes to that, how many of them could equal it today? What is more, even at the height of the war, some level of literacy was insisted upon in the armed forces. Burton describes his visit to the scene of battle after the retreat from the fortress of Humaitá:

'. . . the miserable remains of personal property told eloquently of the heart which the little Republic had thrown into the struggle. The poor rags, ponchos of door-rug, were rotting like those that wore them; and amongst fragments of letters we picked up written instructions for loading heavy guns. All were in the same round hand . . . it is said that in Paraguay the writing drill is regular as any other.'

It is difficult to see how the Argentinians and Brazilians of the day, though admittedly their élites were probably better educated than that of Paraguay, could persist in regarding their opponents as savages and barbarians.

There are, of course, two ways of looking at the 'popular' measures of the younger López. Barrett sees them as genuine efforts for bettering the lot of the common people. Washburn, the American Minister on the spot at the time, suspected more demagogic motives. In a despatch to his Secretary of State he wrote:

'The lower classes have been indulged in a manner they never dreamed of before, and the fear among many is that this is but a stroke of policy on the part of the President to ingratiate himself with the masses preliminary to acts of severity against those who have in any way become obnoxious. . . . He evidently has an ambition to be something more than a petty despot and looks to find it gratified in the improvements he may introduce into the country. He evidently desires reputation abroad as well as at home and he must be aware that he can only get the respect of other people by using his power for the public advantage and prosperity.'³

It should also be borne in mind, though, that here too Francisco Solano López was, in some degree at any rate, merely following the policy of his father and Francia in ensuring that his power rested on the broad basis of popular support.

But Washburn was undoubtedly right in calling attention so shrewdly to Francisco Solano's desire to be something more than a petty despot, and to his anxiety for a reputation abroad as well as at home. A number of commentators, indeed, regard the President's character as the key to the whole situation. Masterman called the conflict in which Paraguay was embroiled 'essentially a personal war' and believed that its real origins could be traced to López's visit to France. And Cunninghame-Graham throughout his book more or less takes it for granted that Francisco Solano López was consumed by personal ambitions.

At this point perhaps we ought to look a little more closely into the question of whether these ambitions included that of becoming an emperor. Such aspirations, it has already been pointed out, were not unusual in Latin America; there was, after all, already one long-established Empire, that of Brazil. Indeed, as Burton says, the issue had been raised before in Paraguay itself, when in 1854 one obsequious deputy had proposed in Congress that Carlos Antonio should be created Emperor, with the crown hereditary in his family.

At any rate, in November, 1863, Washburn reported to his Secretary of State that Francisco Solano was conducting a voluminous correspondence with the Tuileries, and that he had reason to suspect that this was in order to secure the support of the French Emperor in the event of his becoming an emperor himself.⁴ This, incidentally, was not long before Maximilian of Austria left Europe under Napoleon III's sponsorship, to become Emperor of Mexico for a brief period.

The rumours continued to gain strength, and two months later the American Minister in Buenos Aires also wrote home:

'. . . I have just learned from what seems to be a reliable source that López intends to declare himself Emperor on the first of January and that he is going to be recognized by France and Brazil. . . .'⁵

The British Chargé d'Affaires in Buenos Aires had also heard the rumours:

> 'It has been reported to me that the President of the Republic of Paraguay has made application to the Governments of England, France, and Brazil to know if, in the event of his being called upon by the nation to assume the title of Emperor, and to accept for his family the hereditary succession to the throne, the three governments above mentioned would recognize him in his new position. I have further been informed that President General López has already received a favourable reply from the Brazilian Government. . . . From what I observed of His Excellency the President's character while at Asunción I am also led to believe the report is not without foundation. . . . I was informed General López is already assured of the support of the Emperor of the French.'[6]

It is noticeable that the despatches from the British and American Ministers in Buenos Aires suggest with some confidence that Brazil had given her support to López II's imperial plan – and indeed Washburn claims that López told him that the Emperor Pedro II of Brazil had himself actually urged him to convert Paraguay from a Republic into an Empire.

Now this lends colour to another intriguing rumour – that about the same time the Paraguayan President was conducting secret diplomatic negotiations to explore the possibilities of a marriage between himself and Princess Isabel, daughter of Dom Pedro. According to Barrett, he formally announced his intention to Madame Lynch, who received the news with great dignity but much inner bitterness, knowing that she could be dismissed far more easily than Josephine had been discarded by Napoleon Bonaparte, for the simple reason that she was still not married to the would-be Emperor Francisco I. In the event, she had no cause for concern, for by October 1864, Princess Isabel was married to the Conde d'Eu. Again according to Barrett, Dom Pedro II did not even bother to reply to Francisco Solano's inquiry as to the possibility of a betrothal, thereby further deepening the latter's hatred of Brazil.

There is little positive evidence to support this addition to the imperial theme. But the story of López's intention to turn himself into an emperor is rather more solidly supported. Burton records that when he was in Buenos Aires during the war, he was shown 'the plaster model of a crown, apparently that of the first Napoleon, which, stuck to a board, had been forwarded for any alterations which the Marshal-President might suggest' together with furniture and hangings of a decidedly imperial luxury – though Paraguayan historians later claimed that the plaster model was for a crown to adorn the statue of the Virgin in Asunción.[7]

There is one piece of evidence that might possibly discount the rumours: when he received the despatch from his Chargé d'Affaires in Buenos Aires (reporting that the Paraguayan President had been 'assured of the support of the Emperor of the French') Lord Russell, the British Foreign Secretary at the time, immediately forwarded it to Paris with a request for information; and was assured that the French Government had received no request from López of the kind suggested[8] – though this, admittedly, refers only to the report that the Paraguayan President had sought Napoleon III's endorsement of his plans.

On the whole, it is perhaps reasonable to assume that with his inordinate concern for prestige, both personal and national, the idea of creating himself emperor had, to put it at its lowest, at least occurred to López.

Horton Box sees him as a man obsessed with the idea of a 'forward policy' that would secure for his country a place in the sun among the nations of South America and beyond – a sounding board for the voice of Francisco Solano López; and he quotes a statement López had made in Buenos Aires at the time of his successful mediation in 1859, in which he declared he could foresee an eventual conflict in the Río de la Plata, which would inevitably involve Paraguay, 'called to be a weighty factor in the balance of power of these anarchical peoples'.

Horton Box sums up the significance of a declaration such as this:

'It is the revelation of a policy diametrically the opposite of that which had enabled Dr Francia to create Paraguay and Carlos Antonio López to consolidate the nation-state. It was, in a word, a policy of adventure, as all such claims to "a place in the sun", and a right to make one's voice heard and "national dignity" must be. The Greeks would have called it a policy of *Hubris*. It was not based on an exact appraisement of the national interest, but on a purely romantic, one might say Fascist, estimate of the national worth, the national power, the important position that so worthy a nation ought to occupy – an importance estimated in terms of the fear and deference of neighbours.'

At the same time, Horton Box (perhaps slightly contradicting himself) sets himself resolutely against any undue emphasis on purely personal factors. These might have helped to precipitate the crisis, but he insists:

'The origins of the Paraguayan War lie in the growth and establishment of the two states that are now fast qualifying for the rank of Great Powers – Argentina and Brazil. It may be regarded as an episode in the establishment or as a phase in the economic development of Brazil.'

And he describes Paraguay as 'the detonating point of the great explosion'.

In order to understand why and how this explosion came about, one must look now to the smallest of the countries in the Río de la Plata, for although Paraguay's border disputes with both Argentina and Brazil continued to be serious, from about the time of the accession to the Presidency of López II they tended to merge into the gradually developing crisis in the Banda Oriental del Uruguay (to give the country its full name, signifying the eastern bank of the River Uruguay).

Uruguay had long been a bone of contention between Argentina and Brazil. In 1825, a group of patriots known in Uruguayan legend as the 'Thirty-three Immortals', under the leadership of Juan Antonio Lavalleja, declared the independence of the country, at the same time also pledging its adherence to Buenos Aires; and when the latter accepted, Brazil declared war. The combined Argentine and Uruguayan forces won a decisive victory at the battle of Itazaingó in February, 1827, and a few months later the independence of Uruguay was formally recognized by both Argentina and Brazil, and thereafter the country became a highly valuable buffer-state between the two great rivals.

The newly-created republic was soon racked by international dissensions. These culminated in a civil war between the followers of President Manuel Oribe and those of the former President Fructuosa Rivera (both of them heroes of the war of independence). With the aid of the Argentine dictator Rosas, Oribe defeated his rival at the battle of Carpentería in 1836. In the battle Oribe's men carried white pennants and Rivera's red and in this lie the origins of the two great parties, the Blancos and the Colorados, who to this day dominate the politics of Uruguay.

In 1838, however, Rivera overthrew Oribe and was re-elected President. Oribe, again with the help of Rosas, once more defeated Rivera in 1843, and besieged the Colorados in Montevideo. The siege, which lasted until 1851, attracted world-wide attention, and Montevideo became the centre for most of the Argentine refugees from the dictatorship of Rosas.

The party divisions of Uruguay had therefore to a large extent become parallel to those of Argentina, with the Blancos of Oribe and the Federals of Rosas outside the walls of Montevideo, and the Colorados of Rivera and the refugee Argentine Unitarians (including Bartolomé Mitre) within.

The situation, however, was nothing like as straightforward as this would suggest. There were no real constants, and a number of permutations were possible between the two pairs of parties. There were men of vision on both sides who looked beyond party differences. It was General Urquiza, for instance, who was responsible for bringing about the fall of Rosas in spite of the fact that fundamentally his sympathies, too, were with the Federal party. There were, of course, various shades of opinion within the four parties, too, particularly among the Blancos and Colorados of Uruguay, each of whom had an extremist wing which was often in open conflict with the moderates, and in addition the opposing parties sometimes came together within coalition governments. But by and large the equation Blancos equals Federals and Colorados equals Unitarians holds good, with the former, on the whole, representing the provincial and more traditional interest, and the latter, on the whole, representing the interest of the Liberals and the commercial classes in the respective capital cities. From this it also follows that both the great provincial chiefs in the Argentine Provinces, among them General Urquiza, and the Paraguayan President would tend to sympathize with the Blancos rather than with the Colorados.

After the lifting of the siege of Montevideo, followed a year later by the overthrow of Rosas, Uruguay was governed by a coalition of Colorados and Blancos, but this soon broke up, largely owing to the intrigues of the Colorado Minister of War, General Venancio Flores. He drove out the Blancos from the government, and then, with the help of the Brazilians, got himself elected

President, only to be expelled in his turn by a coalition of discontented Colorado and Blanco moderates.

Flores and the extreme Colorados fled to Buenos Aires, and a
series of raids, emanating from either Buenos Aires or Montevideo,
took place – some of them of considerable proportions and many
of them marked by exceptional savagery. This was at a time when
Buenos Aires had seceded from the Argentine Confederation, and
following one of the most serious of the clashes, Montevideo
invoked the help of both General Urquiza (then President of the
Argentine Confederation) and Brazil, and even tried to form a
triple alliance for the crushing of Buenos Aires, which had obviously, if indirectly, been supporting the Colorado cause. Eventually, of course, the conflict between Buenos Aires and the
Provinces was resolved by the defeat of General Urquiza at the
battle of Pavón and Bartolomé Mitre became President of a shakily
united Argentina.

Now one of the main factors in General Urquiza's defeat had
been the energy and ability of the exiled Colorado President of
Uruguay, Venancio Flores, who was in any case an old friend of
Bartolomé Mitre. The new Argentine President, anxious to consolidate the country and his own power, proclaimed a policy
of strict neutrality towards the warring Uruguayan factions –
but at the same time he was conscious of the immense debt of
gratitude he owed to Flores. Whether he himself encouraged
his friend's intrigues is not really known for certain, but he
appears to have done little to check them and there is no doubt
that Flores received a good deal of unofficial support in Buenos
Aires.

Then, on the night of 16 April 1863, Venancio Flores with a
band of his Colorado comrades, set sail from Buenos Aires. Two
days later they landed on Uruguayan soil. With their arrival civil
war broke out again and, although few could have realized it at the
time, the whole tragic train of events had been set in motion, and a
general conflagration was only a matter of time.

It is now necessary to look again at Brazil's position in the
imbroglio. She had taken every opportunity of making her
presence felt in Uruguayan affairs, and she had by no means given
up her dream of eventually absorbing the little country, which
would neatly round off her province of Rio Grande do Sul and
make the River Plate her southern frontier. The deterrent, of
course, was Argentina who also coveted the country. The Brazilian

attitude at this time in relation to her chief neighbours was, in fact, basically a very simple one: opposition to Argentina, intervention in Uruguay, and encroachment on Paraguay.

On the face of it one would have assumed that Brazil would have encouraged the Blancos in Montevideo simply in order to counteract Argentine (or rather Buenos Airean) support of Flores, especially as she had helped Blanco governments in the past. But there were a number of factors that militated against this straightforward alignment.

The most potent of these was the intense rivalry that existed along the frontiers between Uruguay and the Brazilian province of Rio Grande do Sul. The country here is exactly the same both sides of the border; if it weren't for the simple rows of short posts marking the frontier, it would be impossible to tell which country one was in. There are the same interminable pampas, flat and uninteresting from a distance, teeming with bird life at closer range; in winter, the same chill wind, known as the *minuano*, whistles across them, necessitating the same thick walls of densely packed reed and mud to shelter the gauchos, the same heavy ponchos and the same *bombillas* of scalding *mate*; the same South American ostriches, their untidy feathers ruffled by the wind so that they look like great grey feather-dusters, wander both sides of the border – and so from time to time do the vast herds of cattle on ranches often as big as an English county.

At that time, before the introduction of wire fencing, the herds wandered even more freely – not always without encouragement, for it was typical cattle-rustling country. The mutual animosity that was inevitable in these circumstances was considerably heightened in this case by the fact that Brazilians and Uruguayans, along a frontier which more or less corresponded to the limits of expansion (in this direction) of the old Spanish and Portuguese South American colonial empires, inherited the traditional hatreds of the rival imperial powers. And the situation was further complicated by the presence within the Uruguayan border of some 50,000 Brazilian settlers, many of whom had bought large tracts of land and established well-stocked *estâncias*.

The savagery that prevailed in this area has already been referred to. General Urquiza's massacre of the defecting Porteño regiment after the battle of Caseros was typical of the gaucho temper. The same General (to introduce a bizarre note) after another battle in 1845 had his prisoners beheaded to music; in

1870 General Medina's head was used in a game of bowls. The vendetta was waged just as ferociously in times of peace, and year after year there were discussions between the Brazilian and Uruguayan governments about the ever-mounting list of atrocities committed by both Brazilians and Uruguayans, on both sides of the border.

At this time there were several outstanding personalities in Rio Grande do Sul, several of whom became generals during the Paraguayan War. These men were *caudillos* or feudal lords of the same type as General Urquiza, and many of the Brazilian *estâncias* over the Uruguayan border belonged to them. They wanted to export their cattle from these *estâncias* when and how they pleased. It was, therefore, very much in their interests to have a well-disposed government in Montevideo – and the present Blanco one had been displaying an increasing tendency to free itself from the influence of Brazil. When, therefore, Venancio Flores started his revolution in Uruguay, these Brazilian *caudillos* regarded him as a potential ally, especially as the local Uruguayan authorities, instead of trying to conciliate the large Brazilian element in its northern departments, stepped up their harassments. In addition, the Brazilian *caudillos* had nearly all been actively involved in a ten-year rebellion (one of many) of the Rio Grande do Sul against the central authorities, which had not ended until 1847, so that the Brazilian Government, knowing that the movement for independence was by no means dead (one still meets Rio Grandenses who are enthusiastically in favour of it) could not afford to ignore their complaints.

The greatest of the Brazilian *caudillos* was old General Felipe Netto, who had originally helped the Blancos to power in Montevideo but who now believed that a Colorado government under Flores would be far more favourable to his interests and those of his fellow *estâncieros*. In the winter of 1863-4, the old General went to Rio de Janeiro, to conduct a propaganda campaign on their behalf, backed up by banquets of oriental sumptuousness and a lavish scattering of largesse, and ably seconded by his spokesmen in Congress. The Brazilian Government had, in October 1863, tried to bring about a reconciliation between Argentina and Uruguay, only to be thwarted by the decision of the Blanco government in Montevideo to insist on Francisco Solano López as co-arbitrator with Dom Pedro II. Other efforts, too complicated to deal with here, had also failed; so that the Brazilian Emperor and his government were in no position to stand out for long against the rising tide of jingoistic fervour on behalf of the 'outlanders' provoked by General Netto and his supporters.

Dom Pedro, therefore, reluctantly yielded to popular clamour for a more positive policy towards Uruguay. He despatched José Antônio Saraiva, one of the country's most brilliant and likeable diplomats to Montevideo with a list of very forthright Brazilian demands, backed by a naval squadron. These demands Saraiva, with great skill, managed to temper, in the hope of keeping negotiations alive. Meantime, in a determined effort to preserve the peace, Rufino de Elizalde, representing President Mitre, and Edward Thornton, the British Minister in Buenos Aires, proceeded to Montevideo in a British warship (it would already have been too dangerous for an Argentinian ship to venture there) for further discussions with the Blanco Government, in co-operation with Saraiva.

They set out to achieve some sort of *rapprochement* between the Blanco President, Anastasio Cruz Aguirre, and General Flores. To begin with all went well. They managed to arrange a truce between the two sides, followed on 18 June 1864, by the Conference of Puntas del Rosario at which it appeared that a settlement had been reached, whereby the civil war in Uruguay would be brought to an end and either a non-partisan, or a coalition, government of both Colorados and Blancos, would be set up. But President Aguirre had by now been driven into a corner by the extreme Blancos, and at the last minute the whole plan collapsed. After further attempts by Saraiva to persuade the Blancos to see reason, and after another abortive attempt at mediation by the Italian Minister at Montevideo, Saraiva presented an ultimatum to President Aguirre on 4 August 1864. A Brazilian army massed at the Uruguayan frontier; the Brazilian naval squadron stood by in Uruguayan waters.

Saraiva had hoped that the Argentine President would agree to a joint intervention. Bartolomé Mitre, doubtful of the attitude of the still powerful General Urquiza (who was known to favour the Blancos in Montevideo), was unable to agree to this. But to all intents and purposes he gave his blessing to the Brazilian action. In other words, the Uruguayan crisis had brought the old enemies, Brazil and Argentina, closer together than they had ever been before. Thirty years later, indeed, Saraiva was to see the conferences that had taken place at Puntas del Rosario between the Argentine and Brazilian envoys and General Flores as the real foundation of the Triple Alliance.

Turning now to the part played in these chaotic affairs by Paraguay and by Francisco Solano López, there was one obvious and fundamental similarity between the situation of Paraguay and that of Uruguay. They were both small countries in constant danger of being ground between the upper and lower millstones of Brazil and Argentina. Even before the death of the first López, Blanco diplomacy in Asunción was directed to driving this point home and to urging the desirability of a closer relationship. The elder López, however, was by now distrustful of all alliances, and had no intention of allowing his country to become further entangled in the affairs of the Río de la Plata.

After the old President's death, therefore, Blanco diplomatic efforts were redoubled, and every argument was employed to stress the apparent community of interests between the two countries, and also Paraguay's own vulnerability in view of the fact that both Argentina and Brazil still refused to come to terms with her over the border disputes. After the landing of Venancio Flores in Uruguay and the outbreak of the Civil War in that country, Francisco Solano López was at last persuaded to take positive action. On 6 September 1863, he sent a demand to the Argentine Government for 'explanations' of its policy towards Uruguay, accompanied by copies of the Uruguayan Government's notes to himself in which they complained of the active co-operation of Argentina with Flores. As Horton Box rightly says, this note 'inaugurated that abandonment of the policy of isolation that was rapidly to draw Paraguay into the cockpit of the Río de la Plata'. President Mitre of Argentina side-stepped this, and subsequent demands for explanations, and at the same time counter-attacked by drawing Francisco Solano's attention to the still unsettled boundary questions between the two countries.

In February 1864, accordingly, López ordered a general con-scription throughout Paraguay. He established a large military camp at Cerro León, where (Thompson tells us) 30,000 men between the ages of sixteen and fifty were drilled; 17,000 were also drilled at Encarnación, 10,000 at Humaitá, 4,000 at Asunción and 3,000 at Concepción. Between March and August about 64,000 men received military training. This was a considerable, and rapid, expansion, for Thompson also reports that before this the total number of men under arms had been no more than 28,000. These preparations, it is important to note, were at this stage directed against Argentina, not Brazil, who had not yet delivered her final ultimatum to Uruguay; while López had not yet abandoned his hopes of obtaining Brazilian support to his assumption of imperial dignities.

It was in July 1864, at the time of the joint attempt by Saraiva, Elizalde and Thornton to bring about an understanding between the Blancos and General Flores, that Francisco Solano López offered to mediate in collaboration with the Emperor of Brazil – an offer which was declined by both Argentina and Brazil. Further offers of mediation by López were also rebuffed.

After the breakdown of negotiations following the Conference of Puntas del Rosario, the Blancos conducted an even more feverish diplomatic onslaught in Asunción, and although they were unable to obtain any definite commitments from the Paraguayan President, they were confident that if Brazil carried out her threat of an invasion of Uruguay they could count on Paraguay's intervention.

They were confirmed in these expectations when, following further abortive efforts to salvage the situation by Edward Thornton as well as Bartolomé Mitre, the Paraguayan Foreign Minister, José Berges, on orders from his President, presented the Brazilian Minister in Asunción with a formal note deploring the Brazilian ultimatum to President Aguirre of Uruguay, and disclaiming any responsibility on the part of Paraguay for consequences that might ensue. In his reply the Brazilian Minister declared that 'no consideration would impede the Imperial Government in carrying out the sacred mission which has devolved upon it of protecting the life, honour, and property of the subjects of His Majesty the Emperor'.[9]

To this Berges replied that if the Brazilians did indeed take the measures threatened, his Government would be under the painful necessity of making its protest effective. The news was greeted in Asunción by enthusiastic demonstrations, accompanied, according to Thompson, by 'dancing, drinking, and serenading – by order, of course.'

A further protest was handed to the Brazilian Minister on 14 September after the Brazilian Admiral Baron de Tamandaré had chased the *Villa del Salto*, a Uruguayan vessel carrying reinforcements to defend Mercedes (a port on the River Uruguay which was about to come under attack from the forces of General Flores) and forced it to seek refuge in Paysandú, a port higher up the river. Even now the moderates among the Blancos – and notably

Andrés Lamas, the Uruguayan Minister in Buenos Aires (and one of the country's great men) struggled to preserve the peace, but the Blanco extremists were now in control in Montevideo and at this late stage the situation could not be put into reverse. On 12 October a brigade of the Brazilian Imperial Army crossed the frontier between the two countries and shortly afterwards occupied Villa de Mello, capital of the Uruguayan Department of Cerro Largo.

Here, however, it is necessary to examine some of the implications of López's actions during this crisis. The most startling of these was the inclusion, along with his demand to Bartolomé Mitre for explanations, of the confidential Uruguayan despatches – a procedure contrary to all diplomatic precedent. Some historians have argued that this is a particularly gross instance of López's ineptitude and inexperience in international affairs. It is an argument which Horton Box, for one, insists will not bear the slightest examination. All the evidence, indeed, is that López kept himself thoroughly posted, by his many agents and correspondents in Montevideo and Buenos Aires, and that he knew perfectly well what he was doing. There seems little doubt that the gaffe, and others like it, were deliberately calculated. Their main purpose was to keep the pot boiling; and other actions of López during this period, including the rejection of several apparently quite genuine overtures from President Mitre, served the same end. He did not want the crisis to be solved, unless it was by himself; he wanted to keep Argentina and Uruguay embroiled so that he could emerge triumphantly in the role of successful mediator, as he had done in 1859, and so secure for himself respect tinged with fear, and for Paraguay an unchallenged place in the sun.

Personal vanity and ambition certainly played a part in all this. In the circumstances, too, 'keeping the pot boiling' was a highly dangerous policy, and one of its consequences, undoubtedly, was to nullify the efforts of Uruguayan moderates like Lamas and to bring the most extreme and intransigent of the Blancos to the fore – though they might very well have got there anyway. But, as Horton Box maintains, dangerous though this policy may have been, it was not intended to make war inevitable. Indeed, given the extraordinary touchiness of López's nature, it is surprising that he exercised as much restraint as he did. Even Masterman, critical as he usually was, praised his offers of mediation and considered that they were 'refused very curtly'; and Washburn described López's note to President Mitre, asking for explanations, as 'wise and timely'.[10] Masterman also criticized the unrestrained comments of the anti-López press outside Paraguay. He pointed out that López's protest to Brazil, after she had commenced operations against Uruguay, 'was received with shouts of laughter, and its author was recommended by the Colorados to attend to the state of his *tolderia* – his cluster of huts – and settle the squabbles of his half-naked squaws at home'. Thompson, too, drew attention to the extreme language of many of the Buenos Aires newspapers, telling us, for example, that the balls which accompanied the demonstrations in Asunción were referred to as St Vitus' dances.

Although, moreover, the efforts to preserve the peace by both Argentina and Brazil were genuine, aims of quite another kind lay not far below the surface. The frequent references by President Mitre to the unsettled boundary questions between his country and Paraguay, for instance, constituted (whether intentionally or not) a real threat. As Burton commented on López's expansion of his military forces, 'there is little doubt that he thought the proceeding one of self-preservation against his mortal enemies the Liberal party, which threatened incontinently to hem him in . . .'.

Moreover, when once it became clear that the ultra-Blancos in Montevideo would not tolerate a compromise, old appetites awoke in Brazil, and in spite of official disclaimers of any idea of the eventual incorporation of Uruguay, there were powerful elements in Brazil in favour of it, as this extract from a despatch from the American Minister in Rio de Janeiro would seem to confirm:

'. . . I was not a little surprised . . . when a few days since I was visited by a gentleman connected with the government, who manifestly came for no other purpose than to enquire of me what the Government of the United States would think of the conquest and annexation of Uruguay? I promptly replied that under no circumstances would the United States acquiesce in the absorption of the little Republic of Uruguay by the Kingdom of Brazil, and the extension thereby of the area of human slavery. He replied that that objection had been duly considered; that he himself was emancipationist; that if Brazil were permitted by the United States, England and France, to annex Uruguay, Brazil would consent to hold it as a *free* Province; and adjoining as it does, the Province of Rio Grande, where slavery is not profitable and which has been repeatedly in a state of insurrection, it would ultimately insure the abolishment of slavery in that Province, and thus become the entering wedge for general emancipation throughout Brazil. Of course, I gave no encouragement to any such idea as the conquest of Uruguay.'[11]

It is also worth noting Thompson's comment that 'Brazil openly joined Flores, without declaring war against the Banda Oriental.' In other words, though López may have exaggerated the threat, at the same time as he over-estimated his own country's strength and influence, he had good reason for suspecting Brazil's intentions towards Uruguay. It is also understandable, if regrettable, that he argued that if once Brazilian appetites were whetted by the acquisition of Uruguay, they might very well look in the direction of Paraguay for further satisfaction, especially as it was known that Brazil had for some time been building up munitions of war in Mato Grosso, from which she had in the past practised her encroachments on the northern limits of Paraguay.

On the whole, it seems likely that both those who see Francisco Solano López as a pure patriot concerned only with his country's security and independence, and those who regard him as an unmitigated self-seeker and opportunist are alike over-stating the case. It seems to me that the truth lies somewhere between these two extremes. The Paraguayan leader was genuinely concerned about his country's position and determined to assert it beyond any possibility of doubt; but at the same time he was not averse to exploiting the circumstances in order to further his own ambitions. A time was to come when the first aim inevitably took precedence, and Francisco Solano López and his country would both be fighting for their lives.

In fact, López did not plunge into war as soon as the opportunity offered. If the ultra-Blancos now in power in Montevideo had imagined that as soon as the Brazilian forces crossed the Uruguayan frontier a Paraguayan army would march to Uruguay's assistance, they must have been profoundly disappointed. López was by no means convinced of their wisdom or trustworthiness, and he had been careful not to enter into a formal alliance or to make any specific guarantees. He was not yet ready for war. Above all, he wanted to build up his fleet, and most observers are agreed that if he had been able to do so, the story of the Paraguayan War might have been very different. For, as it turned out, it was river-power that was to be the decisive factor.

It was perhaps symbolic, therefore, that the first real act of war on the part of Paraguay should take place on the river. On the day after the Brazilian action against the Uruguayan steamer *Villa del Salto*, López's chief agent in Montevideo wrote to him (possibly at the instigation of the Uruguayan Ambassador in Asunción)with the latest information, and the news that the *Marquez de Olinda*, one of the regular steamers plying between Rio de Janeiro and the far-away Mato Grosso, had left Montevideo with arms and ammunition as well as Colonel Federico Carneiro de Campos, the new Governor of Mato Grosso, on board. The *Marquez de Olinda* reached Asunción on 11 November 1864, and stopped there for re-coaling. It also seems likely that she carried among her mail the letter from López's agent in Montevideo. At any rate, travelling on the newly constructed railway, a messenger took this letter, together with the news of the Brazilian ship's arrival, to Cerro León where López was under canvas with his army. Thompson reported that when he had studied the despatch López exclaimed: 'If we do not strike now, we shall have to fight Brazil at some other time in the future which may be less convenient for us' – an assessment, incidentally, with which Thompson was in agreement. López therefore sent the messenger back to Asunción by special train with urgent orders for the Paraguayan war-steamer *Tacuari* to set off in pursuit of the *Marquez de Olinda* which, after re-coaling, had left early on the morning of 12 November. The faster Paraguayan vessel quickly overhauled the Brazilian steamer, and fired a shot across her bows as a signal to her to heave to. It was the opening gun of the Paraguayan War.

The Brazilian ship was brought back to Asunción on the morning of the 13th, and soon after converted into a gun-boat for the Paraguayan Navy. The rest of the crew and the passengers were sent to prison-camps in the interior. At a later stage in the war, the survivors were transferred – as potential bargaining counters – to a prisoners' stockade behind the Paraguayan lines, near Humaitá. Colonel Carneiro de Campos was never to take up his Governorship in Mato Grosso; he died in November 1867, from a combination of his privations and shock[12] at seeing a Brazilian standard captured at the second battle of Tuyutí. The flag of the *Marquez de Olinda* had been made into a rug for López's office in the presidential palace in Asunción.

On the same day that the *Marquez de Olinda* was brought back to Asunción, the Brazilian Minister received a note from Berges, the Paraguayan Foreign Secretary (dated the previous day) informing him that as Brazilian forces had invaded Uruguay, Paraguay must now implement the measures she had hinted at in her note of 30 August, that diplomatic relations between the two countries were now severed, and that the Río Paraguay was, in consequence, now closed to all Brazilian shipping. The Brazilian Minister lodged a formal protest at the seizure of the *Marquez de Olinda*, demanded his passports, and was eventually allowed to leave Asunción by river steamer. Washburn, the American Minister, also protested to López about the incident, declaring that as it had taken place without any declaration of war (though, if it comes to that, so had Brazil's invasion of Uruguay) it was an act of piracy. Washburn reported in his book that, after defending his action, López:

'. . . with more candour than discretion went on to say that the situation of Paraguay was such that only by a war could the attention and respect of the world be secured to her. Isolated as she was, and scarcely known beyond the South American states, so would she remain till by her feats of arms she could compel other nations to treat her with more consideration.'

This certainly makes the part that prestige played in López's calculations very evident. One other curious incident must be related in this connection. Amongst the booty taken from the *Marquez de Olinda* was a large sum of Brazilian dollars. López sent it down river to pay for a consignment of military supplies which was waiting for him in Montevideo. On the way the Paraguayan steamer passed two Brazilian warships which had not yet heard of the fate of the *Marquez de Olinda*. Oddly enough, no attempt was made to interfere with them, in spite of the fact that Paraguay now considered herself at war with Brazil.

Even now, though, López did not march to the aid of the hard-pressed Blancos in Uruguay. He had quite other plans. On 14 December 1864, a Paraguayan naval squadron with transports carrying 3,000 men and two field batteries, and with two flat-bottomed gunboats, each mounting an 8-inch gun, in tow, assembled off Asunción. The whole of the city gathered at the river-side, in a state of great excitement. The troops were among the best in the Paraguayan Army, and Thompson tells us that they 'had all new uniforms and looked very picturesque in their scarlet camisetas'. A rousing proclamation from the President was read out before the flotilla set sail. They were bound for Mato Grosso, some ten days' sailing distance away, and about eight weeks from Rio de Janeiro. Francisco Solano López had decided to settle the boundary dispute with Brazil at a blow.

The plans had been carefully laid, and the expedition was ably commanded by Colonel Vicente Barrios, brother-in-law of the President. It was to be a two-pronged invasion, with Colonel Francisco Isidoro Resquín in command of 2,500 cavalry, supported by a battalion of infantry advancing into Mato Grosso from the up-river port of Concepción, while Barrios and the rest of the expedition continued by river.

There was only a small Brazilian force in Mato Grosso scattered along a chain of forts, stretching back to Cuiabá the capital, the most important of which was Coimbra, situated on the River Paraguay close to the frontier on the spur of a mountain and commanding the river-entrance to the province. About forty feet above the river and built of stone, with scarps some fourteen feet high, it was assailable only from one side, so that the 400 men manning it constituted a reasonable defence-force, especially as they were commanded by the veteran Colonel Hermenegildo Portocarrero. It was at Coimbra that the only really considerable battle of the Mato Grosso campaign was fought. Barrios began the siege on 27 December. The first assault was repulsed. Just as the second was about to begin, on the following day, it was found that the fort was deserted, apart from two wounded Brazilian soldiers; the garrison had evacuated during the night, so silently that their movements had been unobserved. In Thompson's view they 'certainly ought to have held the place' in view of the fact that 'their communications were open, and that they had steamers.' As it was, all the guns were left behind unspiked and still mounted, all the powder, ammunition and military equipment, and, Masterman noted, 'some valuable private property, especially the most costly case of surgical instruments I have ever seen'. Portocarrero was placed under arrest by his superior officer and sent to Cuiabá to stand trial.

Barrios and his force pressed on northwards, spreading panic and destruction. He occupied the fort of Albuquerque and then Corumbá, the chief commercial town of the province; both of them were evacuated by their garrisons before the Paraguayans' arrival, leaving the inhabitants and the property to the the far from tender mercies of the victors. Two steamers were despatched up river in pursuit of the fleeing garrison of Corumbá. One of them, the *Yporá*, a light passenger-boat built of planks in Paraguay and carrying four small guns, outpaced her consort and in the San Lorenzo river sighted the *Añambay*, a Brazilian war-steamer, also small but properly constructed for its job by an English shipyard, and mounting six guns, 'the stern-chaser', Thompson comments, 'being a beautiful brass 32-pounder'. She was commanded by an Englishman, Captain Baker, who, as the *Yporá* came after her, kept up a running fire from this stern-chaser without any assistance at all from his panic-stricken crew. Eventually the Paraguayan craft succeeded in drawing alongside the *Añambay* and placing a boarding-party on her decks. Most of the Brazilians jumped into the water; the remainder were cut down without offering any resistance; Captain Baker managed to swim ashore and escape into the woods. The Paraguayans cut off the ears of the dead Brazilians, strung them together and hung them in the shrouds of the *Yporá*. When she returned to Asunción the ears were quickly removed on the President's orders.

There were plenty of other atrocity stories, true and false, to keep the Brazilian and Argentine newspapers busy. Colonel Resquín's force, which all this time had been advancing rapidly by land (he had crossed the river Apa, incidentally, on the same day that General Sherman began his famous march to the sea), meeting only the most tepid resistance from the garrisons of the various forts, apparently behaved with considerable brutality, sacking the houses, raping the women, and torturing landowners to make them reveal the whereabouts of buried valuables. The Barão de Villa Maria, the wealthiest man in the province, managed to escape with a bottle of diamonds in his pocket, and, accomplishing the overland journey to Rio de Janerio in the record time of forty-seven days, to bring to the Brazilian capital what was apparently its first news of the Paraguayan invasion. Among the valuables looted from his house was his Patent of Nobility, with the Emperor's seal and splendidly mounted in a gilt frame. It was presented to Elisa Lynch, who hung it in her anteroom.

It is probable that the savage behaviour of the invaders was in part a matter of deliberate policy. If so, it certainly achieved its purpose. On the one side, Cunninghame-Graham states, it created a legend of Paraguayan ferocity and invincibility that Brazilian commanders had great difficulty in counteracting. On the other side, it reinforced the profound contempt which the Paraguayans had always entertained for the fighting qualities of the Brazilians, even when events did not justify it (and there were to be many instances of Brazilian heroism later on in the war), an attitude which obviously stood them in good stead when they were faced by odds of four to one.

The Paraguayan advance in Mato Grosso did not reach as far as Cuiabá, the capital, because the waterways beyond the mouth of the River Cuiabá were too shallow for their steamers and transports. Garrisons were left in the various captured forts, and these remained until April, 1868. The rest of the expedition returned home, taking with it a large number of prisoners, great herds of cattle, and vast quantities of booty. Brazilian writers on the campaign have argued that Paraguay derived but slight benefit from the victorious campaign, and that the captured military supplies were not of any considerable importance. Thompson, however, insisted (and he was in a position to know what he was talking about) that Paraguay 'drew from Mato Grosso almost all the stores it consumed during the war'. Masterman, also close to events, reported that the captured supplies included 'seventy guns, three steamers . . . and an immense quantity of arms and ammunition.' For some years past in fact, the Brazilian Government had been concentrating military supplies – but not, unfortunately for them, reinforcements of troops – in Mato Grosso. Thompson reported that in one small village alone, Colonel Resquín's cavalry found '4 cannon, 500 muskets, 67 carbines, 131 pistols, 468 swords, 1,090 lances, and 9,847 cannon balls', and Resquín himself is said to have observed: 'It looks as if the Brazilian Government had been expecting to defend the frontier simply with racks of arms.'[13] And Washburn provided similar evidence of the rich haul.

As for the strategic implications, López, as well as occupying the disputed frontier areas, no doubt wanted to secure his flank from possible attack from Mato Grosso. He probably exaggerated the danger, in view of the province's isolation from the rest of Brazil, though in the summer of 1865 the Brazilians did send an expedition to the Mato Grosso District of Miranda, near the Paraguayan border, which took nearly two years to reach its destination and then met with disaster. In the view of Horton Box, however, by invading Mato Grosso López had merely frittered his time away. If, instead, he had launched an attack across the Misiones against the Brazilian province of Rio Grande do Sul, he might have saved the legally constituted Blanco government and altered the whole course of the war.

For, while the invasion of Mato Grosso had been taking place, Brazil's still undeclared war against Uruguay was moving towards its bloody climax. As soon as the Brazilian army (assembled on the frontiers between Rio Grande do Sul and Uruguay) was assured of the co-operation of Venancio Flores, it advanced into the country from the north; while Admiral Tamandaré sailed up the Río Uruguay to join forces with the army and with Flores' men in the investment of Paysandú.

The thirty-five day siege ranks high in South American annals. The city had no fortifications, and the defending force consisted of no more than 1,200 men (against 10,000 besiegers) with 15 cannon – but it had an outstanding commander in the brave and ruthless Colonel Leandro Gómez. The city was subjected to a terrific bombardment by Admiral Tamandaré's warships, until it was reduced to rubble and the clouds of smoke made it impossible to see more than a short distance. Most of the civilian population fled, but Gómez and his garrison savagely resisted the attacks of Flores and his Brazilian allies. Brutal atrocities were committed on both sides. In a gesture of defiance Gómez beheaded fifteen Brazilian prisoners and exposed the dripping heads above his trenches. When, on 2 January 1865, his garrison so reduced that the dead lay unburied in the streets, Gómez was forced to surrender to the Brazilians, he was, together with his chief officers, promptly handed over to Flores's men, taken into a small garden and shot. According to one report, the survivors of the garrison were then saved by the intervention of an Argentine colonel. Thompson claimed, though, that there was 'an indiscriminate massacre of the women and children of the place.' He also claimed that while Gómez was considering a demand to surrender the Brazilians 'treacherously entered the town, under cover of the flag of truce', and that they seized Gómez while he was still composing his reply to the ultimatum. 'The taking of Paysandú, with the atrocities committed there' Thompson declared 'form a revolting page in the history of Brazil'; though Kolinski suggests that Thompson was not in possession of the full facts, and that the Brazilians were justified in disclaiming responsibility for the death of Gómez.[14]

The heroic defence of Paysandú and its aftermath had widespread repercussions, arousing indignation as far afield as Chile,

Peru, and Bolivia, where López was now looked upon as the sole champion of Spanish America against Portuguese Brazil: indeed he retained the sympathies of these countries throughout the war, although the hopes he held of more material support were disappointed.

Far more important for López's prospects – if he could but have seen into the future – was the wave of anger that swept through the Argentine provinces adjacent to Uruguay. It was only in Buenos Aires, indeed, that Brazil's actions in Uruguay were defended. Feeling in General Urquiza's province of Entre Ríos ran so high that he had the greatest difficulty in preventing a general rising on behalf of the neighbouring republic. His own natural sympathies were with the Blancos, just as those of President Mitre were with Flores, and his son Colonel Waldino Urquiza had actually led a small expedition to their assistance. Urquiza himself, however, was rapidly assuming the stature of a major statesman and was working ever more closely with his President, Bartolomé Mitre, in the task of preserving the unity of the Argentine Republic, and he had assured Mitre of his support in the policy of neutrality that he was observing in relation both to the civil war in Uruguay and the war between Paraguay and Brazil. Nevertheless, the old instincts of a *caudillo* of the provinces could not be entirely obliterated, and Urquiza shared his fellow-provincials' bitter hatred of Brazil, a hatred which very much predisposed him in favour not only of the Uruguayan Blancos but also of the Paraguayans. There seems little doubt that he was hoping that López would march to the assistance of the Uruguayans, and he dropped several very broad hints to Mitre to the effect that although he would not tolerate any foreign presence in Entre Ríos or the neighbouring province of Corrientes, he would take a more tolerant view if either Paraguay or Brazil (he was sufficiently 'neutral' to mention both) moved their forces across the practically uninhabited province of Misiones (where the Jesuit reductions had once flourished). Mitre reiterated his belief in absolute neutrality but, bearing in mind the state of public opinion throughout Argentina (with the exception of Buenos Aires, and even there López had his defenders), it is difficult to see that Mitre could have done much about it if the Paraguayans, with Urquiza's tacit support, had indeed crossed Misiones. It seems very likely, in fact, that if Mitre had declared war against Paraguay on this particular issue, it would have resulted in a renewal of civil war in his own country – for there is some evidence to suggest that as far as Brazil was concerned, López had received definite encouragement from Urquiza.

And yet the Paraguayan leader, after first committing himself to the faraway Mato Grosso adventure, continued to stand by while Flores and the Brazilians, after crushing resistance at Paysandú, began their preparations for the siege of Montevideo itself. In the process, a number of events took place which could not fail to be inimical to the interest of Francisco Solano López. For one thing Flores, who from time to time suffered pangs of conscience over what could reasonably be called the traitor's part he was playing – in that the Blanco government was the legally constituted one and it was he who had brought in a foreign invader entertaining designs upon his country's independence – was induced by the very astute Brazilian diplomat, José Maria da Silva Paranhos, to sign a formal alliance. This contained the specific pledge that when the Blanco Government was finally liquidated, Uruguay would give to the Empire of Brazil 'all the co-operation in its power, regarding as a sacred task its alliance with Brazil in the war treacherously declared by the Paraguayan Government, whose interference in the internal affairs of the Uruguayan Republic is a bold and unjustifiable pretension.'[15]

It is difficult not to agree with Barrett's view that the making of this pledge and its acceptance by Brazil were 'indefensible acts. Francisco López had taken no armed action at any time during Uruguay's internal strife, either for or against either of the warring factions. There were no Paraguayans fighting for either side in Uruguay. . . .' Venancio Flores had, as Horton Box points out, tied his unhappy country to the war-chariot of Brazil. It could only escape civil war at the price of a foreign war.

Da Silva Paranhos devoted himself to the task of making sure that this price would indeed be exacted. He kept up a continuous pressure on Bartolomé Mitre in the hope of persuading him to abandon his declared policy of neutrality. He brought pressure to bear, too, on Flores and the Brazilian commanders in order to ensure that there would be no repetition of the horrors of Paysandú, with the danger of intervention by Britain or the U.S.A. which that might involve. Above all, he set himself to eliminate any possibility of a successful mediation either by Mitre or by the foreign ambassadors. Nothing less than the complete overthrow of the Blanco government by his collaborator Flores would provide Brazil with Uruguay as a military base against López.

All his efforts were, in the long run, successful. The foreign ministers in Montevideo, particularly the British and Italian, did in fact make strenuous attempts at bringing about a settlement, while Mitre (if reluctantly) agreed to act as one of the mediators if called upon; but it was not until the last moment, with Montevideo already under threat of bombardment from the Brazilian fleet, that the Uruguayan President turned to the Diplomatic Corps for help, in the form of a detachment of Marines, to secure his authority against the extremists in his own party, who were quite prepared to die amid the rubble of their capital. By an agreement of capitulation signed at Villa de la Unión on 20 February 1865, the virtual dictatorship of Venancio Flores was established, and all the principal members of the Blanco party, together with the senior officials of the regime, were forced to flee the country. The Blanco party was not to control the government of Uruguay again until 1958.

When it had become obvious that Montevideo was about to be besieged, the Blancos had once again appealed to López. His reply had been: 'Fall with the glory of Paysandú, and I shall soon reconquer your territory.'

Was this, then, the main reason behind his failure to come to their aid at a time when there were many circumstances in his favour – an overweening confidence, that is, in his ability to reverse the situation whenever he chose to do so? It certainly looks like it. López may have preferred to see the Blanco hot-heads go under, confident that the *macacos* (or monkeys, as the Paraguayans contemptuously referred to the Brazilians) could easily be disposed of, so that he could later impose upon Montevideo an administration more to his liking. Perhaps he really was planning to establish the hegemony of Paraguay over the whole of the La Plata territories. It is, at any rate, obvious that he was playing a waiting game, and it is most unlikely that this was the result of simple vacillation. Presumably his exact motives will never be known, but what evidence there is suggests that he was expecting developments in Argentina, even more favourable to himself. It is probable, in fact, that he expected General Urquiza to make common cause with him against the hated Brazilians. On the other hand, aware of the growing understanding between Urquiza (despite his natural sympathies) and Mitre, López may very well have been seeking to counteract it by reaching secret agreements with some of the other provincial leaders, with whom he was in correspondence. Little is known about the exact tenor of the intrigues with them, but they undoubtedly existed. Either way, it is very likely that López believed – – not without reason – that a rising of the Argentine provinces against Buenos Aires and President Mitre, led, if not by Urquiza, then by some other *caudillo*, was once again imminent. Dreams of territorial expansion at the expense of Argentina may also have entered into his calculations.

What does seem certain is that out of all these obscure calculations, expectations and intrigues emerged what most historians regard as López's greatest blunder. For on 14 January 1865, (just over a month before the capitulation of Montevideo) he had written to Mitre asking permission for a Paraguayan force to cross not the sparsely populated Misiones (on the borders of which he had already concentrated troops) but the comparatively populous province of Corrientes. It was a step that played straight into Mitre's hands. For if Urquiza might well have winked at a move across Misiones, in spite of Mitre's attitude, he was bound to oppose interference in a province next door to his own Entre Ríos. So López had pushed Urquiza into Mitre's arms. And thus assured of his most powerful rival's firm attachment to his cause, Mitre had no need to hesitate in rejecting the Paraguayan request, or even to fear that Urquiza could seriously oppose his entering into an alliance with Brazil, if he should decide to do so.

It is true that Paraguayan sources show that López and his ministers suspected the existence of a secret agreement between Argentina and Brazil dating from as far back as the early 1860s,[16] and there can be little doubt that the weight of evidence supports the supposition. On the other hand, Mitre, whatever his personal sympathies may have been, provided some proofs of his neutrality in the struggle between Brazil and Paraguay. On at least two occasions, for instance, he allowed ships carrying arms and munitions for Paraguay to proceed up-river from Buenos Aires without interference, or any demand that these supplies should be specified in the bills of lading; and he also refused to allow a Brazilian blockade of the Río Paraguay at Tres Bocas.

Urquiza did his best to avert the catastrophe he now foresaw, by sending his private secretary, Dr Julio Victorica, on a confidential mission to Asunción (with Mitre's knowledge), to assure López that he had nothing to fear from the Argentine President provided he avoided unnecessary complications; and Urquiza revealed his own partisan hopes when, in a letter to Victorica, he wrote: 'I believe that once this circumstance is averted, Paraguay will gain great advantages and place Brazil in a difficult position.'[17] But Victorica, though courteously received, found the Paraguayan President in an intractable and defiant mood. He expressed his indignation at Mitre's rejection of his request for transit across Corrientes in the most passionate terms, and then gave Victorica the broad hint that his master 'could count on him in making himself President by overthrowing General Mitre'. When it was made clear to him that such an offer could not be accepted by the man who was the 'Liberator of the Republic' from the tyrant Rosas and the founder of his country's constitution, Victorica reported that 'raising his voice', López declared 'If they provoke me I shall go straight ahead with everything.'

Even before Victorica's arrival, indeed, López had issued a decree convoking an extraordinary National Congress, and published it in the *Seminario*. The two hundred hand-picked delegates met on 5 March 1865. A special message from the President justified his actions as regards Brazil and explained the situation as far as Argentina was concerned. Congress then appointed a special commission to survey the whole situation, which reported back on 17 March. Its conclusions which, needless to say, supported all of the President's actions were approved by Congress the next day – and a declaration of war against Argentina was authorized. In addition Congress conferred upon the President the rank of Marshal and approved the constitution of the new Order of Merit he had drawn up.

And so the would-be Napoleon of South America had taken on yet another foe, and apparently with complete confidence in the outcome. Horton Box describes this further step towards the abyss as a 'fearful aberration' and even Carlos Pereyra, one of López's most ardent apologists, calls it 'the summit of political folly'.[18] One of the main explanations for such a terrible step may lie in the state of patriotic euphoria throughout the Paraguayan nation. This is well caught in this extract from a letter written by Berges, the Paraguayan Foreign Secretary, a few days before the declaration of war against Argentina:

'The troops are filled with enthusiasm. They are well disciplined and are on the best war footing. Every day numerous contingents of recruits arrive at the military camps to reinforce the ranks of the army. At this moment we can count on 50,000 resolute and enthusiastic men almost all young, impatient to distinguish themselves and to make known their daring and courage. With soldiers of this kind my people are invincible.

'Paraguay, with her present force, with the unity and enthusiasm of all her sons, is strong, and it will not be Brazil, whose flag is devoid of glory, nor the Argentine Government, which is impotent to curb the raids from the pampas, nor the rebel Flores, who has too much to see to in his own home-country, nor all these heterogeneous elements combined, who can fight Paraguay with any probability of success.'[19]

In fairness it must be remembered that behind such outpourings lay the long tradition of distrust of Argentine intentions, much of it with ample justification. It could also be argued, of course, that López was convinced that a passage across Corrientes was an absolute military necessity and that command of Corrientes itself was vital to his plans of frustrating a Brazilian blockade of the river. There was the added attraction that Paraguay and Corrientes had a good deal in common; not least the Guaraní language which the inhabitants nearly always spoke among themselves. Undoubtedly, too, López still believed (as Berges' reference to the raids from the pampas confirms) that the Argentine Republic was a rickety structure which would collapse at the first prod from Paraguayan bayonets. And as a matter of fact López did not have to wait long for evidence that must have convinced him that his arguments were correct.

It was on Good Friday, 13 April 1865, that five Paraguayan war steamers suddenly appeared without warning off the port of Corrientes. Two small and antiquated Argentine naval vessels, *25 de Mayo* and *Gualeguay*, were seized after a brief skirmish and towed away. Three thousand men, under the command of General Wenceslao Robles, disembarked on the beach outside the city, and waited until some of its citizens appeared. After assuring them that (to quote Thompson) 'they were come as brothers to free the Corrientinos from the despotism of Buenos Aires, and that they and their city would be respected', a garrison was left in Corrientes and Robles, having received reinforcements, began to move slowly south along the east bank of the Paraná. The Paraguayan Foreign Minister, Berges, took over the administration of the city, with the help of a group of carefully selected Paraguayan officials and three equally carefully chosen citizens of Corrientes.

López had delayed until 3 May the actual delivery to the Argentine President of the declaration of war, presumably in order to take Corrientes by surprise, to give his agent in Buenos Aires time to conclude various financial transactions, and in the hope of ensuring the arrival of expected military supplies from Europe – though in fact the news of the declaration leaked through to Mitre on 17 April, the day after he learned of the attack. The outburst of patriotic fervour in Buenos Aires was as passionate as it had been in Asunción. There was the same outpouring of speeches, the same fervent singing of national hymns. A great crowd assembled outside the Presidential Palace, where Mitre delivered a slogan which aroused particular enthusiasm:

'In twenty-four hours to the barracks;
In three weeks in the field;
In three months in Asunción'.

He was not the only military prophet, before or since, to have indulged in wishful thinking. For the moment, however, all was confidence. An urgent call was issued for men to serve in the newly formed Guardia Nacional, and according to Thompson the first battalions of troops had left Buenos Aires for Corrientes as early as 24 April. A Paraguayan Legion, recruited from dissident Paraguayans in Buenos Aires was formed – and, above all, General Urquiza promised President Mitre that he would support him with a large army. In his message to Congress, which authorized the official declaration of war, Mitre went out of his way to commend Urquiza for his loyalty, accompanied him to the pier where he was to embark en route for his own province, and shook him by the hand with the words 'Hurry yourself, General'.

Back in Entre Ríos, Urquiza took less than a month to assemble an army of 10,000 men. He set out to join Mitre, who by now was also in the field. At Basualdo, on the frontier of Entre Ríos, he went on ahead, intending to joint Mitre in discussions at Concordia. What happened then was exactly what López had been hoping and praying for.

Before he reached his destination, Urquiza was overtaken by a messenger, with the news that almost the whole of his army had broken up. Urquiza returned immediately and gave the rest of his army leave of absence for a month. He then wrote an account of the affair to President Mitre, reassuring him that he would have reassembled 12,000 men under arms within the month. But three months went by, and he had succeeded only in collecting a few thousand. With these he set out once again to join Mitre – and again the greater part of his army broke up and Urquiza was once more obliged to give them leave of absence and to return himself to Entre Ríos. The rest of the story as far as Urquiza is concerned is well summarized by Thompson:

> 'When the Allies invaded Paraguay next year, he sent a few hundred men, who mutined on board the steamers, and were ultimately disbanded. He also sent a few old guns, which he had formerly taken from Buenos Aires. He was not heard of again during this war, except as selling large quantities of cattle and horses to the Allies, and thus amassing immense wealth. His name was often used during the war by López to enliven his troops, who were told that Urquiza was on the march to help them.'

It is worth anticipating events here, in order to underline the fact that López was indeed not without justification in assuming that the Argentine nation was by no means united behind President Mitre. The truth of the matter was that Urquiza in his desire to co-operate with Mitre in preserving the Argentine Republic (whether or not Thompson is right in suggesting that he was also not averse to becoming a war profiteer) had placed himself in an impossible position. For, in order to maintain his purpose, he had to go against not only his natural inclinations but also against his fundamental interests, which were bound up with those of the old feudal elements in the provinces, upon whose support his own power rested – and in fact he ultimately met his end by assassination at their hands.

By now, as Thompson's references to the Allies indicate, Argentina, Brazil, and Uruguay under Venancio Flores had made common cause against Paraguay. The attack on Corrientes had speeded up negotiations and the famous Treaty of the Triple Alliance was signed on 1 May 1865, and the ratifications exchanged on 12 June and 13. The terms were supposed to be secret, but they soon leaked out; H. G. Lettsom, the British Minister at Montevideo succeeded, indeed, in obtaining a full copy of the 'secret' treaty, and transmitting it to England, where it was published in a parliamentary blue book early in 1866.

To begin with, the revelation of the terms of the Triple Alliance worked very much in López's favour. For although the Allies declared that the war was directed solely against him, it was evident that they had granted each other the full extent of their territorial aspirations against Paraguay. Startling evidence of the far-reaching nature of these aspirations as far as Argentina was concerned, is provided by a report from Thornton, still British Minister in Buenos Aires, written while the negotiations for the Triple Alliance were still in progress. In this report Thornton explained that he had noted an evident coolness between the Brazilian Minister on the one hand and Mitre and Elizalde (his Foreign Secretary) on the other. Thornton then goes on:

'I can only attribute it to the stipulation demanded by the former that both parties should declare that they would respect the independence of the Republic of Paraguay. Both President Mitre and Señor Elizalde have at different times declared to me that for the present they wished Paraguay to be independent, that it would not suit them to annex Paraguay even if the Paraguayans should wish it, but that they were unwilling to make any engagement to that effect with Brazil; for they did not conceal from me that whatever were their present views on this point, circumstances might change them hereafter, and Señor Elizalde . . . said to me one day though in mere conversation that "he hoped he should live to see Bolivia, Paraguay, Uruguay, and the Argentine Republic united in one Confederation, and forming a powerful Republic in South America."[20]

The British Government decided to publish this despatch and did so on 30 June 1865, so its contents were publicly known. It is strange that so few of the writers on the Paraguayan War have quoted it, for here, surely, is the clearest proof imaginable that Francisco Solano was right in suspecting that the traditional Argentine ambitions of reconstituting the Spanish Viceroyalty (including the old myth that the Paraguayans themselves really wanted to be re-absorbed) were by no means dead.

The British Government's action in publishing both the terms of the Treaty of the Triple Alliance and Thornton's despatch, is a measure of its disapproval, and indeed that of Europe in general. In the neutral republics of South America there was, as might be expected, even more widespread indignation. In July 1866, the Peruvian government issued a strong protest, acting not only for

Peru but also for Bolivia, Ecuador and Chile. It was addressed to Brazil, Argentina and Uruguay, and published in *El Peruano* on 11 July. It tartly suggested that there was nothing to choose between the conduct of Brazil and that of France in Mexico, or of Spain in the Pacific and in Santo Domingo. A copy of the protest reached the *Illustrated London News* which, in its issue of 6 October 1866, reported:

'The document, drawn up with the most consummate ability, attacks the pretensions of the allies to force upon the Paraguayans a new form of government.'

Even in Buenos Aires itself some of the newspapers criticized the Treaty, while there is little doubt that it was one of the reasons behind the disaffection of Urquiza's troops.

The effect of the publication of the text of the Treaty in Paraguay can well be imagined. López was in the position of being able to say 'I told you so'. It was not difficult for Paraguayans to calculate by reference to the maps that the Allies coveted, at the least, some 150,000 square kilometres of what the Paraguayans regarded as national territory. It was evidently, they contended, not a *guerra contra López* but a *guerra contra el Paraguay*, and even those who secretly had been lukewarm towards the Marshal-President and his policies, were now enthusiastic in his support. The Treaty, indeed, goes a long way towards explaining the really desperate resistance of Paraguay, whose people felt that their whole national existence was at stake. And López not unnaturally, became the personification of their fight. Even some of the foreigners living in Paraguay at the time were affected. George Thompson, for instance, declared 'when the Secret Treaty was published, it gave me a further zest to fight for Paraguay, as I believed, from the terms of the Protocol, that she must either fight or be absorbed.'

The Treaty was in part, of course, a measure of the fear which López inspired in the Allies. To what extent was this fear justified, in terms of the comparative strengths, actual and potential, of the contestants?

It was at one time common to find historians writing of Paraguay as a small country surrounded by enemies, but possessing a large and efficient military machine equipped with the most up-to-date armaments. Comparisons with the Prussia of Frederick the Great, or the Germany of the Kaiser Wilhelm II were frequent – Koebel equates Paraguay's actions in the first year of the war with those of Germany in Belgium in 1914. It is true that at the commencement of the war, Paraguay did have a larger army than any of her rivals, and one possessed of an infinitely superior fighting spirit. Nevertheless, a number of more recent historians, including Arturo Bray, after a careful examination of contemporary records, have come to the conclusion that Paraguay's military strength has been greatly exaggerated.

Estimates vary as to the actual size of the Paraguayan army at the beginning of the war. In his letter of 5 March 1865, (previously quoted) Berges speaks of 50,000 men ready for combat. According to Masterman, the army totalled 100,000 at the beginning of that year. Thompson put the figure in the summer of 1864 at 64,000, rising by the following spring to 80,000. Kolinski is probably close to the mark when he suggests a total of about 57,000 men under arms, comprising 50,000 infantry, 5,000 cavalry and artillerymen, and 2,000 sailors. When it is remembered that in 1857 the Paraguayan standing army had been no more then 18,000, and had not passed the 28,000 mark by the end of Francisco Solano López's first year in the presidency, this represents a truly remarkable rate of expansion.

The crux of the matter, though, as in all such cases, lay in the reservoir of manpower available. Burton put this at 150,000 males between the age of twelve and sixty, on the basis of a total population of 450,000. It is evident, therefore, that López did not have inexhaustible reserves to draw upon, and he made his man-power situation worse by frequently squandering his troops on unnecessary enterprises. In addition, the withdrawal of so many able-bodied men from essential occupations, especially agriculture, was a serious handicap; and some military historians believe that Paraguay might have stood the war better with a smaller army that would not have upset the economic balance of the country so drastically. An important sidelight on this neglect of agriculture is provided by Masterman (in his capacity as Chief Military Apothecary). Although, he points out, there were, in the earlier stages of the war, plentiful supplies of beef, the Paraguayans, unlike the Argentines and Uruguayans, were not accustomed to eating much meat (especially those living in the interior), 'consuming in preference maize, mandioc, and oranges.' When they were sent to Humaitá (the main fortress on the river Paraguay) which was, Masterman went on:

'a damp, malarious place, where they could get scarcely a particle of vegetable food, and during a cold, wet winter (the result was) as might have been predicted, a most intractable form of diarrhoea; pneumonia; and enteric fever. The wretched sheds of hospitals were crowded, and soon became themselves *foci* of disease; and that fine army melted rapidly and ingloriously away: the grave-digger was soon more active than the drill-sergeant.'

And Thompson pointed to another essential item of diet which was neglected because of the shortage of labour:

'During the war, salt was very scarce, and the want of it was felt more than the lack of anything else, costing Paraguay thousands of lives . . .'.

To turn now to the military situation of the Allies, of whom by far the richest and most powerful, of course, was the Empire of Brazil. At the outbreak of the war, her standing army numbered only 16,834, less than a third, that is, of the number that López had mobilized; though Thompson reported that it had been brought up to 25,000 for the operations against Uruguay. On the other hand, this small regular army had much more military experience, on active service, and was led by officers who had been trained at the Escola Militar in Rio de Janeiro, considered the finest of its kind in Latin America, while Paraguay possessed no such training establishment. But more to the point, Brazil had a *Guarda Nacional*, scattered among the various provinces, and constituting a reserve of at least 200,000 men. Even more important, though, was the fact that Brazil's population of about nine million in 1864 (nearly two million of them were then Negro slaves) provided an almost inexhaustible reservoir of replacements. Kolinski claims that by April 1866, and until the end of the war, in spite of vast problems of communications and logistics, Brazil was able to maintain an average of 40,000 fit men on campaign in Paraguay, a figure which by then Paraguay could come nowhere near equalling.

The main weakness of the Brazilian army (apart from a very fine élite) lay in its lack of fighting spirit, at any rate in the earlier stages of the war. Not that this should be a matter of surprise, in view of the methods of recruitment in use at the time, which were reminiscent of those practised by Falstaff in Shakespeare's *Henry IV*. Officers were given a bonus for every 'recruit' they were able to bring in; and no questions asked as to the methods employed. The 'recruit', however, could buy himself out by paying a tax and sending a slave in his place. The infantry battalions in consequence were composed almost entirely either of men (mostly mulattoes) too poor to obtain exemption, or of Negro slaves – and there was no reason why they should feel particularly patriotic. Undoubtedly, though, as the long war progressed a strong *esprit de corps* did gradually emerge, in large sections of the Brazilian army.

General Mitre, who was appointed to the supreme command of the allied armies, had military problems of a different kind. The total number of soldiers in Argentina in 1864 has been put as high as 30,000.[21] But this is taking into account the armed forces in the provinces, and they were not always available to the central government, as we have seen. It was only in the city and province of Buenos Aires that Mitre could look for really reliable troops. In 1864, these provided a nucleus of some 8,000 men. A year later this force had been expanded to about 15,000[22] by recruitment and conscription in Buenos Aires and the provinces. About 4,000 of these, however, usually had to be held back from the Paraguayan campaign to deal with Indian attacks in the pampas (which reached a peak during the 1860s), and with disturbances in the provinces which, according to Pereyra, were almost continuous as the war progressed. It is not surprising, in consequence, that Mitre had great difficulties in obtaining recruits from the provinces. In 1868 Hutchinson, the British Consul in Rosario, saw a contingent of 'volunteers' arrive at Rosario handcuffed and fettered, and he reported the story of a letter reputedly sent by the Argentine Minister of War to one of the provincial potentates asking for another batch of 'volunteers' for the Paraguayan War, to which the reply was:

> 'that a large troupe would be sent down as soon as the minister would remit back the fetters and handcuffs that had been ornamenting the first contingent forwarded.'[23]

The backing of the great commercial seaport of Buenos Aires, though, which in 1864 had some 150,000 out of a total national population of about a million and a half, with its access to European trade routes and banking facilities, was a considerable factor in itself.

As for Uruguay, she had been torn apart for so long by civil war, and was still in such a disturbed condition, that she could hardly be expected to contribute very materially to the allied war effort. The Uruguayan contingent which General Flores took with him to the Paraguayan War numbered, according to Kolinsky, no more than 1,500, of whom only 500 survived, though Masterman put the number at 4,000.

What, though, of the vast technical superiority which some historians have attributed to Paraguay? It is true that López had introduced a number of innovations considerably in advance of his neighbours, notably the steam locomotive and also the telegraph. After the successful conclusion of the Mato Grosso campaign he extended the railway line to Paraguarí, and the telegraph line, operated and maintained by a very able German engineer named Fischer von Treuenfeldt, southward beyond Villeta to the River Tebicuary, and on to the fortress of Humaitá. Hutchinson also drew attention to '"telegrafos ambulantes", or movable telegraphs, comprising batteries, wires and poles, sufficient to embrace a circuit of five leagues'.

The Marshal President made great use of this telegraphic system, and there is no doubt that it proved a considerable tactical asset. He was responsible, too, for a number of other technical experiments, some of which paid dividends. An American inventor of German origin, named Krüger, devised both rivermines and torpedoes, and the latter were to have at least one notable success. According to Barroso, another German named Wilhelm Wagner, a professional armourer whom López brought into his service at the beginning of 1864, developed a multiple Congrève rocket-launcher, apparently of advanced design and efficiency. In the later stages of the war, when supplies of all kinds became scarce, both López and his advisers continued to show the greatest ingenuity and resourcefulness in finding substitutes for basic materials and inventing new devices.

Of the utmost importance to the Paraguayan war effort was the newly-completed arsenal, directed with great efficiency (until his death during the first year of the war) by the English engineer William Whytehead. This arsenal, with its supporting iron foundry, was able to manufacture a variety of pieces, including three heavy siege guns, which played a prominent part in the defence of several key positions. One of these guns was known as *El Cristiano*, because (according to Thompson) it was cast in 1866 'from bells contributed by all the churches in the country'. Another, the *Criollo*, was made from church bells supplemented by 'all the copper boilers and saucepans in the country'. It was a ten ton gun 'bored and rifled to fit Whitworth's 150 pounder shot, of which some thousands were collected which had been thrown away by the enemy'.

Colonel Thompson himself was not the least of Paraguay's assets. Although he was a former British Army officer, he had had no previous training or experience in military engineering before he joined the Paraguayan Army, though he had apparently worked as an engineer on railways. He became a specialist, however, in fortifications and entrenchments, and was himself something of an inventor. Among the output of the arsenal were, he reported, 'three batteries of rifled howitzers, with a peculiar kind of shrapnel shell . . . made from my designs.'

However many strategic blunders López may have made as a general, in fact – and his record was no worse and probably a good deal better than that of the Allied commanders – his ideas as to what was needed to make his army the most formidable in South America, were sound and up-to-date. But, despite the myths to the contrary, he never succeeded in fully implementing them. In spite of all his able and energetic preparations, the limited time at his disposal (when once he had decided that Brazilian action in Uruguay must not go unchallenged) combined with the inaccessibility of the country to fresh supplies, all made it impossible. If he had delayed hostilities for even another year, it would probably have been a very different story. As Burton considered:

'The war . . . was altogether premature: had the cuirassed ships and the Whitworths ordered by the Marshal-President begun the campaign, he might now have supplied the place of Mexico with a third great Latin empire.'

In spite of all the efforts of his arsenal, for instance, and the capture of some of the best of the Allied guns in raids carefully directed to that purpose, López never succeeded in acquiring any really significant park of up-to-date artillery. Paraguay began the war with between 300 to 400 guns of all calibres, but many of them were antiquated if not antiques. At Uruguiana in September, 1865, the Conde d'Eu (son-in-law of the Emperor and later commander-in-chief of the Brazilian forces) reported that of the five captured Paraguayan cannon one had been cast at Douai in 1790, another at Barcelona in 1788, and a third at Seville in 1679.[24] After the fall of Humaitá in July 1868, Burton noted among the captured

Paraguayan guns: 'sundry quaint old tubes bearing the arms of Spain; two hailed from Seville, the *San Gabriel* (A.D. 1671) and the *San Juan de Dios* (1684)'.

And Thompson reported that 'the greater part of the Paraguayan artillery consisted of old honeycombed iron guns, probably taken by ships for ballast and bought by Paraguay. They were like the guns which do duty as posts on Woolwich Common.' In spite of this, López had to depend heavily on his artillery all through the war, partly because much of the fighting was defensive and partly because his infantry were never fully armed.

According to Max von Versen (a major in the Prussian Army who was sent as an observer to Paraguay, and managed to get through the Allied lines in July, 1867) López was among the first soldiers outside Europe to recognize the value of the new needle rifle, forerunner of the breech-loading, bolt-action Mauser repeating rifle. The Marshal-President was unable, however, to obtain supplies of this weapon for himself; and his efforts to buy weapons of the Minié type, single-shot muzzle-loaders, rifled for greater range and flatter trajectory (similar to the Springfields and Enfields used by Union and Confederate troops in the American Civil War) also failed. The best he had been able to do was to obtain a single shipment of Wittons rifles, sufficient to arm three infantry battalions, including his personal escort battalion, and a consignment of Turner's breech-loading rifled carbines for the 250 men of the Government Escort. An additional three or perhaps four battalions were armed with percussion-lock rifles, but all the rest had to make do, Thompson stated, 'with the old flint-lock "Brown Besses" with the Tower of London mark upon them', while von Versen saw many old-style German muskets, bearing the marks of Potsdam, Suhl, and Danzig. Paraguayan soldiers carried no side-arms except for bayonets without scabbards, and no one in the ranks wore shoes.

Linked with Paraguayan fire-power is the subject of the various fortifications that loomed so large in the war – and in particular, Humaitá. Burton, who made a detailed examination of the latter after its fall, could see no reason for such a grand name as 'the Sebastopol of South America' which was commonly applied to it:

'Can these poor barbettes, this entrenched camp sans citadel . . . be the same that resisted 40,000 men, not to speak of ironclads and gunboats, and that endured a siege of two years and a half? . . . Humaitá was a monstrous "hum" . . . with the rest of the public, I had been led into believing the weakest point of the Paraguayan campaign to be the strongest.'

Thompson also spoke of 'the weakness of the place, which consisted in 15,000 yards of trench garrisoned by less than 3,000 men'. He himself did his best, with the inadequate materials at his disposal, to make good the deficiencies of some of the other fortresses. He was notably successful with his systems of trenches, in a struggle where trench-warfare played such an important part, perhaps for the first time on such a scale. This is one of the factors that sometimes gives this faraway war an eerie kind of modernity.

At the beginning of the war, of course, there were quite a number of old flintlocks still in use in the Allied forces too. But the Brazilian army had received its first shipment of 1,200 rifles and 1,000 carbines of the Minié type from Belgium as early as 1855. By 1864 these were being supplemented, on a fairly large scale, by the newer Minié rifles and by Enfields, of both British and Belgian make. As the war progressed, moreover, both Prussian needle rifles (the Dreise model of 1857) and American breach-loading carbines made their appearance. A Brazilian military historian also claims that a Brazilian purchasing commission went to the United States late in the war, and obtained 5,000 Roberts-type rifles and 2,000 Spencer repeating carbines.[25] Bayonets, short swords, pistols and revolvers were also used. In 1864 many of Brazil's guns, too, were antiquated, but most artillery units had been provided with some modern La Hitte, Paixhans, or Whitworth rifled muzzle-loaders of calibres from 90 to 120 mm. The most effective of these, with the longest range by far, were the 32-pounder Belgian made rifled Whitworths.

On the whole this looks a far more formidable array than Paraguay's 'motley armature', as Burton called it. Some of the advantages were offset by frequent failures on the part of the Brazilian War Department to match up ammunition and weapons, and by inefficient control of both on the battlefield. The Brazilians were in the habit of blazing away indiscriminately, and as a high proportion of their very miscellaneous projectiles failed to explode, the Paraguayans made regular forays after a bombardment to replenish their own restricted supplies of ammunition.

Most contemporary observers, however, seemed to agree that

the Paraguayans were more adept with their comparatively primitive weapons than the Brazilians were with their more sophisticated
ones. Thompson added an interesting detail in making this point:

> 'Neither the riflemen nor the artillerymen of Paraguay were ever
> taught the use of the graduated sights of their arms, but they
> elevated their guns by pointing them so many yards above the
> mark, according to its distance. They nevertheless made much
> better practice than their enemies, who understood the use of
> sights.'

Hutchinson visited the Brazilian fleet at Paso de la Patria (on the
Paraná, slightly north-west of Corrientes – now an anglers'
paradise for *dorado* fishing) after it had passed into Allied hands;
and he declared that within three days:

> 'I could distinguish without going out of my cabin, between a
> shot from a Brazilian monitor, and one from the fort at Itapirú,
> the latter having invariably that sharp ringing crack which tells
> of good gunnery.'

Commander A. J. Kennedy, who took H.M. gunboat *Spider* along
the Paraná about the same time, also commented on the superior
qualities of the Paraguayan artillerymen.[26]

Nevertheless, the fact remains that the sheer weight of armament
was bound to tell in the Allies' favour as the war progressed. The
Allies also had the advantage in another respect which, at that date,
was of the utmost importance – the availability of good horses for
gun-carriages and cavalrymen alike. Thompson explained the
position as far as Paraguay was concerned:

> 'There were at this time, in the whole of Paraguay, perhaps
> 100,000 horses, only half of which could gallop two or three
> miles. The Paraguayan horses were never good, and a terrible
> disease in the spine had latterly carried off the greater part of
> them, attacking generally the best animals.'

By contrast, for the Allies there was nearly always a large reservoir
of sound animals to draw upon. The cavalrymen of both sides,
incidentally, carried lances.

Where the Brazilians possessed a really overwhelming superiority was in their navy. It was by far the largest and most powerful
in South America – that of Argentina being negligible at the time.
At the outbreak of war the Brazilian Navy consisted of 45 vessels,

33 of them steamers and the rest sailing ships, all of them comparatively well-equipped, and with experienced officers and crews. Among the ships were a number of gun-boats, which had been specially constructed for river use in 1857–8, at the time of Brazil's earlier quarrel with Carlos Antonio López. The existence of these craft more than offset the fact that some of the other ocean-going ships were not adaptable to river operations.

Probably the most important single factor in the whole war, however, was the acquisition by the Brazilian Navy, from the end of 1865 onwards, of a number of ironclads.

It must have been a bitter pill for López to swallow, for (as in the case of the needle rifles) it was probably he who had first realized their potentialities, and for at least a year past he had entertained hopes that it would be possible to have ironclads constructed in Europe for his own navy. He had, moreover, picked on an especially formidable model, a monitor-type ironclad equipped with two turrets and mounting heavy Krupp cannon – a model which, if it had been constructed, would have produced a sensation in La Plata. But he had been unable to raise the necessary finances, and it was Brazil who bought ironclads. The first of them, the *Brasil*, arrived on the scene of operations in December, 1865. By the summer of 1867, Commander Kennedy reported that the Brazilian fleet 'had now, from the arrival of successive reinforcements, assumed most formidable dimensions.' He listed, in addition to lighter wooden ships, no less than fourteen ironclads of varying sizes in operation at this date below Humaitá – two of them Monitor types, though he claimed the *Lima Barros* and the *Bahia* as the most efficient:

> 'These vessels were built by Messrs. Laird, of Birkenhead, and fitted on Captain Cole's principle, the former with two turrets and the latter with one, each turret being armed with two 150-pounders (Whitworths).'

Kennedy strikingly illustrated Brazil's growing naval power and her own ship-building potential when he reported:

> 'The different large ship-building firms of England and France received orders to prepare ships of the most approved form and armament, at any cost, and send them out as soon as possible to the seat of war. The imperial arsenals were worked night and day, building and completing for sea the vessels designed in

Brazil, and the constant arrival of heavy rifled guns from England enabled them to be armed directly they were finished, and sent off to Paraguay.'

It is almost laughable to turn from all this to Paraguay's navy of seventeen small steamers, all of them converted passenger boats, with the exception of two gunboats, the *Tacuari*, and the *Añambay* (captured from the Brazilians in Mato Grosso), supported by flat-bottomed barges and rafts; all of them armed with smooth-bore guns, from 4 to 32-pounders, except for the *Jejuí*, which mounted a 12-pounder rifled breech-loader. This so-called navy had never been tested under combat conditions, and Captain Pedro Ignacio Mesa, its commander in 1864, had also had no previous experience in naval warfare. López was rightly proud of his arsenal and ship-yards, which could turn out ships of up to 280 feet in length, but they could hardly compare with the facilities available to Brazil.

To sum up: it was only in the initial stages of the war that Paraguay had any material advantage. For the rest of it, Burton was not far off the mark when he described the war as one:

'waged by hundreds against thousands; a battle of Brown Bess and poor old flint muskets against the Spencer and Enfield rifles; of honey-combed carronades, long and short, against Whitworths and Lahittes; of punts and canoes against ironclads.'

The miracle, indeed, was that the war lasted as long as it did; and this is where that intangible element of morale comes in, that strange upsurge of spirit which can offset so many material dis-advantages – within limits. Burton put it this way:

'The war brings before us an anthropological type which, like the England of a past generation, holds every Paraguayan boy-man equal, single-handed, to at least any half-dozen of his enemies.'

And eye-witness accounts are full of tales that support this sugges-tion. Typical of these is the story which Hutchinson related of Sergeant González:

'A Paraguayan, who fought alone against ten Brazilian soldiers; but at last surrendered by force of persuasion. And when asked why he fought against such unequal odds, and without hope, answered: "I fought because I am valiant, as are all Para-guayans!"'

Paraguayan morale was in large part a matter of great courage and fierce patriotism. To some extent, too, it may have been a product of that docility inculcated by the Jesuits and by the dictatorships that succeeded them. But there is, as well, something sombre and atavistic about the desperate courage and obstinacy of both the Paraguayan people and their Marshal-President. There is about the Paraguayan War a kind of twilit, *Götterdämmerung* atmosphere, as of the death-throes of a race bound to an outmoded principle of being.

NOTES

[1] Doria to Russell, Asunción, 18 October 1862, F.O. 6.241, despatch no. 30.
[2] *Etapas de mi vida. Contestación á las imposturas de Juan Silvano Godoy*, Fidel Maiz. Asunción 1919.
[3] Washburn to Seward, 5 August 1863, State Department MSS, Paraguay Diplomatic 1.
[4] Washburn to Seward, Asunción, 21st November, 1863, State Department MSS, Paraguay Diplomatic 1; and Washburn to Seward, 3 November 1863.
[5] Kirk to Seward, Buenos Aires, 12 December 1863, State Department MSS, Argentine Republic Diplomatic 14.
[6] Doria to Russell, Buenos Aires, 12 October 1863, F.O. 6.246, despatch no. 96.
[7] See for example *Francisco Solano López y la Guerra del Paraguay*, Carlos Pereyra, Buenos Aires 1945; and *Madame Lynch*, María Concepción de L. Chaves, Buenos Aires 1957. Quotations from Pereyra are taken from this book.
[8] Russell to Thornton, 30 December 1863, F.O. 6.224.
[9] Quoted by Box in *The Origins of the Paraguayan War*.
[10] Washburn to Seward, Asunción, 27 October 1863, State Department MSS, Paraguayan Diplomatic 1.
[11] J. Watson Webb to Seward, Petropolis, 19 September 1864, State Department MSS, Brazil Diplomatic 30, no. 92.
[12] *A guerra do López*, Gustavo Barroso. 3rd ed. São Paulo 1929.
[13] *Memórias do Visconde de Taunay*, Alfredo d'Escragnolle Taunay. Quotations from Taunay are taken from this book unless otherwise indicated.
[14] *Independence or Death : the story of the Paraguayan War*, Charles J. Kolinsky. Gainesville 1965. Quotations from Kolinsky are taken from this book.
[15] Flores to Silva Paranhos, Colorado, 18 January 1865, *Relatorio*, Annexo I, 1865.
[16] See, for example, *La declaración de guerra de la república del Paraguay a la república Argentina : Misión Luis Caminos, Misión Cipriano Ayala, declaración de Isidora Ayala*, Arturo Rebaudi. Buenos Aires 1924.
[17] *Urquiza y Mitre. Contribución al estudio histórico de la organización nacional*, Julio Victorica. Buenos Aires 1906.
[18] *Francisco Solano López y la guerra del Paraguay*, Pereyra, *op. cit.*
[19] Berges to Bareiro, Asunción, 15 March 1865. Quoted by Rebaudi in *La declaración*.

[20] Thornton to Russell, Buenos Aires 24 April 1865. *Correspondence Respecting Hostilities in the River Plata*, Part III, no. 19.
[21] *Invasão paraguaia no Brasil*, Walter A. Spalding. São Paulo 1940. Introduction.
[22] História da Guerra do Paraguaï, von Versen, *op. cit.*
[23] *The Paraná, with incidents of the Paraguayan War, and South American recollections from 1861 to 1868*, Thomas T. Hutchinson London 1868. Quotations from Hutchinson are taken from this book.
[24] *Viagem militar a Rio Grande do Sul*, Gaston d'Orléans (Conde d'Eu). São Paulo 1936.
[25] *Brasil militar*, José de Lima Figueiredo. Rio de Janeiro 1944.
[26] *La Plata, Brazil and Paraguay, during the present war*, Commander A. J. Kennedy, R. N. London 1869.

ACT FOUR
Offensive and Defensive

So far the war had gone almost entirely in Paraguay's favour. It was not until 25 May, 1865 (one of Argentina's independence days) that the Allies launched their first major offensive move. It was to be a diversionary attack on Corrientes, aimed at halting the Paraguayan invading force of General Robles, which had now advanced south of Corrientes, meeting only scattered resistance, occupying Bella Vista on 20 May and heading along the east bank of the River Paraná in the direction of Santa Lucía and Goya, where eight Brazilian war-steamers had arrived some three weeks earlier. Argentine complaints about the sluggishness of the Brazilian fleet, which were to grow in volume and bitterness as the war progressed, had already begun; and the Brazilian fleet, leaving Buenos Aires on 3 April 1864, had in fact taken just a year to reach the nearest point to Paraguay.

For the attack on Corrientes, the Brazilian Admiral Francisco Manoel Barroso da Silva, had taken on board a force of 4,000 troops, which included a small Brazilian contingent of 350 men, commanded by the Argentine General Wenceslao Paunero and had sailed down the river Paraná, arriving opposite Corrientes.

General Robles had made the mistake of leaving behind in Corrientes only 1,500 men, under Major Martínez, with two small guns, to garrison the city, and while the Brazilian fleet (supplemented by two Argentine war-steamers) kept up a heavy bombardment, a force composed of crack Buenos Aires units and a few Brazilians, amounting in all to 2,000 men, were landed just outside the town. In the fierce hand-to-hand fighting, the 'greatest gallantry was shown on both sides' according to Thompson.

The Paraguayans retreated to a stone bridge which led into the city, where they put up ferocious resistance, under constant bombardment from the fleet. It was here, Thompson sarcastically reported, that the Brazilians:

'first showed a peculiarity in their tactics, which consists in firing whenever they have any guns to fire with, no matter whether they kill friend or foe, or both together . . . or whether they see or do not see what they are firing at.'

Eventually, with the bridge riddled with shot from the fleet, and both sides having left many dead on the spot, the Paraguayans retreated. Their losses were about 400 dead (against 350 of the Allies), their three guns and their battle flag.

Then, fearing the possible arrival of reinforcements from Robles, Admiral Barroso re-embarked his men the following day and, taking on board those citizens of Corrientes who wished to leave, sailed back down the river. Berges and his mixed Paraguayans and Corrientino administration, who had left the city before the attack, promptly reinstated themselves.

This setback for the Paraguayans at Corrientes, slight though it was in itself, had consequences which were of the most far-reaching significance. López's grand plan of campaign was to synchronize an invasion of the northern part of the Brazilian province of Rio Grande do Sul by Robles and his army, with another invasion by 12,000 men under Colonel Antonio de la Cruz Estigarribia, which was already encamped in the old Misiones district, his ultimate aim being to free Uruguay and invade Argentina as well. But the success of the Allies at Corrientes had made it only too clear that Robles' advance southwards could be continually hampered as long as the Brazilian fleet had command of the Paraná. López resolved, therefore, to challenge the Brazilians with his own tiny fleet.

First, though, he reviewed his troops in Asunción, including the newly-formed 40th battalion composed entirely of Asunción men, commanded by José Díaz, formerly a police officer and later López's favourite and most dashing general. Thompson was an eye-witness at this review, and according to him this battalion (which was more often in action than any other, and 'was five times almost completely annihilated and as many times reorganized') performed 'very creditably'; as did the horse-artillery, which Lieutenant-Colonel José Maria Bruguez had got 'into very good trim'. It was on the same day that the American inventor Krüger first demonstrated his torpedo, by blowing up a raft of palm trees when he was about six yards only from the point of explosion.

On 2 June 1865, López announced that he had decided to take personal command of his forces in the field, and he boarded the

Tacuarí leaving Elisa behind as Regent and apparently taking with him several chests of gold coin from the treasury (the first of several such appropriations), though it is not known whether this was for payment of his troops, which was in fact very irregular, for bribes, or to be buried in a safe place.

As the *Tacuarí* steamed out of Asunción, the sailors on the other ships were formed up along the bulwarks, while the British gunboat *Dotterel*, which had arrived on an official visit (and had been accidentally fired on by a Paraguayan ship on the way) manned her yards. When López arrived at Humaitá, he at once began to discuss his plan of attack against the Allied fleet with Captain Pedro Ignacio Mesa and with his own brother Benigno, who had by now been restored to favour and to his post of High Admiral.

The enemy squadron, still commanded by Admiral Barroso, was now carrying out a blockade a few miles below Corrientes, off a small tributary of the Paraná called the Riachuelo. The Brazilian ships had not tried to enter the mouth of the Paraguay itself, although its sole protection was the small fort of Itapirú, mounting only three 32-pounders. The Brazilian squadron consisted of nine large ships – so large that they towered above any of the Paraguayan vessels. All of them were war-steamers, eight of them were screw-propelled – a tremendous advantage for river manoeuvres. They all carried infantry as well as their crews and Masterman noted that they 'had strong and lofty nettings stretched as a precaution against boarding'. Their total armament amounted to 59 guns, some of them up-to-date 120 and 150-pounder Whitworths.

Against this formidable river force, The Paraguayans had the same number of ships, but the *Tacuarí* (the flag-ship) was still the only authentic warship, and only one other, the *Paraguarí*, had iron platings. The rest were converted merchantmen or passenger-ships (including the ill-fated *Marquez de Olinda*) with their boilers unprotected and far above the water-line. Only four of them were screw-propelled, and of these, the *Yiberá* was unable to take part in the action because the key of her screw fell out; the remainder were paddle-wheelers. Four of the ships were from 300 to 600 tons each, but the others were, in Masterman's picturesque description 'about the size and build of the passenger boats running between London Bridge and Westminster'. The flotilla carried a total of 30 guns, only two of them 32-pounders, the rest mostly 14-pounders.

One of López's characteristically ingenious make-shifts came into

play here, however, for the Paraguayan fleet was to tow into battle
six flat-bottomed boats, called *chatas*, each mounting an eight-inch
cannon. As these *chatas* were to prove a considerable bug-bear to
the Allies for some time to come – Barroso says that one Brazilian
admiral called them 'monitores de madeira' (wooden monitors) it is
worth while turning to Hutchinson, who made a detailed inspection
of one of them after the battle:

> 'In construction, the shape resembled an English canal barge,
> except that it is more gracefully tapering at the ends and not so
> long, whilst at each extremity is a rudder. . . . The top of its
> bulwark is only 18 inches over the water. Being flat-bottomed, it
> must have a very shallow draught of water. In its centre, the
> deck has a depression of a foot in depth, within a circle, that
> permits a brass swivel, whereon a . . . gun is turned to any point
> of the compass which the commander may desire. The whole
> length of the craft is but 18 feet, and there is no protection for the
> crew.'

Hutchinson himself witnessed one of these *chatas* in action,
manned only by ten men, and attacking two large Brazilian monitors. It managed to fire a shot through a port-hole of one of the
monitors 'killing four officers and wounding fourteen or fifteen
men.' He adds the gruesome detail that one of the officers 'was cut
right in the middle, as if he had been sliced in two with a scythe'
as a result of the port-hole being blocked with chains which 'thus
smashed into small bits, served as so much canister or grapeshot
in their deadly effects'.

According to Washburn, many of the details of López's battle-
plan for the Riachuelo encounter were suggested to him by John
Watts, one of the English chief-engineers of the Paraguayan
squadron who was said to have served earlier in the Brazilian Navy.
After the battle was over, López made him Knight of the Order of
Merit – though three years later he became a victim of one of the
Marshal-President's purges.

The plan was for the Paraguayan ships to sail at dawn right past
the Brazilian squadron – the river Paraná near Corrientes is over
two miles wide and spreads out to nearly nine miles at Riachuelo –
then to turn short round, and come back alongside the Brazilian
ships, discharging their broadsides and boarding them. For
López's aim was not only to regain command of the Paraná, but
also if possible to capture the whole of the Brazilian squadron. In

order to seal off its escape up-river, a small land-force under Colonel Bruguez, together with a battery of rifled 12-pounders, was to go ahead to a point on the river banks some miles the other side of Riachuelo.

On the evening of 15 June, the five hundred picked men who were to form the boarding-parties were marched down to the waiting steamers. Before they embarked, López himself arrived on horseback and addressed them in the familiar chaffing way he often adopted to his troops. 'They were all in a great state of enthusiasm' Thompson reported 'and promised to bring back the Brazilian fleet.' When it was dark they set sail. But it was now that things began to go wrong. Owing to the breakdown of the *Yiberá* (whose captain, Thompson wrote, 'was so vexed at not being able to go, that he absolutely cried'), and to the fact that the towing of the *chatas* necessarily slowed down progress, the fleet reached the scene of action far later than planned.

The element of surprise, therefore, was largely lost. Even so, Masterman declared, the Brazilians were in a state of 'desperate panic [because] they were amazed to see the little vessels going steadily on after receiving their fire'. Thompson criticized this plan of first sailing past the Brazilian squadron, on the grounds that it gave the latter too much time to weigh anchor and so to be on the move by the time the Paraguayans had completed their manoeuvre. By leaving a gap of about a mile between the two flotillas, the superior fire-power of the Brazilians was immediately brought into play, and in fact one of the Paraguayan steamers – the *Jejuí* – was soon shot through the boiler and put out of action.

The remaining seven ships completed the manoeuvre successfully, turned round and came back to close with the Brazilian ships, now coming up river to meet them, while the little guns of Bruguez joined in the action with a lively fire from the river bank.

The English engineer of Captain Mesa's flag-ship told Masterman afterwards that the 'poor old man . . . lost his head completely as soon as the firing began' (though he did not lack personal courage) 'and did not issue a single order afterwards'. Most of the other Paraguayan officers, according to Masterman, were drunk – though being Paraguayans that would mean fighting-drunk – so that the movements of the vessels were really directed by the English engineers on board. Thompson, on the other hand, reported that the Brazilian Admiral Barroso panicked so completely that it was the Corrientino pilot on his ship who was 'for the time the real commander of the fleet'.

The greatest blow that the Paraguayans suffered from the dereliction of their high command revealed itself, however, when they set out to fulfil the second part of their instructions, to run alongside the enemy ships and board them. It was found that someone had blundered with a vengeance – there were no grappling-irons aboard. Although, therefore, the Paraguayans succeeded a number of times in getting close to their towering opponents, they could not stay there; except in the case of the *Paraíba* which, after several abortive attempts, was boarded by thirty Paraguayans. These went into action with their usual ferocity. Those Brazilians who did not jump overboard – to be killed, if they succeeded in swimming ashore, by the Paraguayan land units – made for the companion-ways, and according to Masterman the boarding-party were doubled up with laughter at the way 'the terrified *cambas* [Brazilian negro troops] tumbled over each other in their eagerness to get below'.

It looked as if the Paraguayans had captured one great prize at least for their Marshal-President. They hauled down the Brazilian flag and began to steer the ship. Unfortunately, they had failed to secure the hatches, wasting time applauding their sergeant who, in his delight, was marching up and down the deck, beating the reveille on a drum which he had found there. The delay enabled the Brazilian flag-ship, the *Amazonas*, to come alongside, with another of the Brazilian squadron, and to sweep the decks of the captured ship with grape, mowing down three-quarters of the boarding-party. At this a group of Brazilian Marines, with fixed bayonets, came charging up the open hatchways. The few surviving Paraguayans (including the sergeant) were forced to jump overboard and swim ashore.

Although this was the closest the Paraguayans came to fulfilling the grand plan of capturing the Brazilian fleet, they made other determined boarding attempts, and their heavy gunfire at close range did considerable damage. The *Paraíba* was reported to have as many as thirteen holes in her, at or near the water-line. The *Belmonte* was riddled with holes, several of them below the water-line, and had to be run aground. The *Yequitinhonha* ran into range of Bruguez's shore-battery and went aground on a sand-bank where, Thompson reported:

'she stuck fast, firing all day long till the afternoon, when she was abandoned, after an effort had been made with two steamers to tow her off.'

Thompson also paid tribute to the 'great bravery' shown by the Paraguayans throughout the battle, telling the story of one Paraguayan who, having managed to leap across the gap between his small craft and the Brazilian ship it was trying to board, 'split an officer's head through to the neck with his cutlass when, finding himself alone, he jumped through the opposite porthole and escaped.' Kennedy reported that Paraguayans who succeeded in boarding enemy vessels 'would frequently drag their adversary overboard with them, when both would be lost,' while the wounded commander of the *Marquez de Olinda*, who was taken aboard the *Amazonas* after the battle, and had an arm amputated: 'tore off the bandages and died, saying he preferred death to being taken prisoner.'

Hutchinson was on board the British gunboat *Dotterel* when she passed through Rosario a few weeks later. The gunboat had taken on board a number of Paraguayans wounded in the battle, including some from the *Marquez de Olinda*. He told of one Paraguayan whose abdomen had been pierced by a rifle-ball and who was suffering agonies from peritonitis. As the man lay groaning while preparations for an operation were being made (Hutchinson, himself a surgeon, was to assist) the Paraguayan sergeant approached the bedside:

'One word uttered by the sergeant stopped the complaints. The same official pronounced a harangue in Guaraní, and which the pilot on board translated for me as follows: "Dog of a bad Paraguayan! are you not ashamed to let the enemies of your country hear you complain; and give them reason to laugh at you? The glory of having been wounded fighting for that country does not appear sufficient without crying for sympathy in your sufferings! Do not let me hear another groan from you, or I shall report you to the highest power' – meaning, of course, Field-Marshal López. From that moment the poor sufferer never uttered a moan, although he died four hours afterwards, evidently in dreadful torture.

'Some Argentines who were on board – no doubt those described as "enemies of his country" – called this "Paraguayan stolidity or stupidity"; but to me it seemed the perfection of discipline, joined to the highest class of moral and physical bravery.'

Unfortunately, this kind of spirit was not sufficient to bring the Paraguayans victory at the battle of Riachuelo. The superior height, tonnage, fire-power and manoeuvrability of the Brazilian ships, combined with that ghastly blunder of the Paraguayan command in failing to bring grappling-irons with them, constituted odds that courage alone could not surmount. The *Marquez de Olinda* had been shot through the boilers, and drifted out of action on to a sandbank, with, Thompson wrote, 'many of her crew scalded to death and nearly all of them killed or wounded.' The *Salto*, too, had her boiler knocked to pieces, and with most of her crew also dead or wounded, drifted out of action, close to the *Marquez de Olinda*. The *Paraguari* was rammed by the big Brazilian flagship, the *Amazonas*, and also driven on to a sandbank. She kept up her fire, until most of her men were killed. The remainder swam to the Chaco side of the river to avoid being taken prisoner, where they were joined by survivors of the other stranded ships. The *Jejui*, which had been put out of action at the beginning of the battle, was sent to the bottom by gunfire. Two of the *chatas* were sunk, and the other four took refuge in the Riachuelo. Of the four ships that limped back to Humaitá, the *Ygurey* had lost one of her boilers and could only go very slowly; the *Tacuari*, which hung back in order to protect her, had had a remarkable escape, a 68-pounder shot skimming her boiler without, in fact, damaging it at all. All four ships had holes in their hulls, and their funnels were riddled with shot. All the guns were dismounted, either from incessant firing or because they had been hit. Captain Mesa came back mortally wounded by a rifle bullet from the high bulwarks of one of the Brazilian ships. He died a few days later, and Thompson was probably right in saying that if he had recovered López would have had him shot for incompetence.

The four surviving ships were soon repaired, and determined efforts were made to salvage some of the others. The Brazilians had set fire to the *Paraguari*, but as she was one of the Paraguayans' two ironclads, only the interior had burned, and they were able to tow her back to Asunción. To López's bitter disappointment, it proved impossible to restore her, though her plates and machinery were later put to good use. Nothing could be done with the stranded Brazilian vessel, the *Yequitinhonha*. She was stripped of her contents, including two 68-pounders and, according to Thompson, 'four beautiful 32-pounder iron guns'; several smaller guns; a quantity of books, swords, clothing, watches and instruments – and her main-yard which, Thompson reported, 'was taken to Humaitá, and made the centre column of a dancing rotunda.' For the worse the news became the more López insisted on 'spontaneous' balls, festivals and other jollifications.

As soon as the river was free of the enemy, the men who had escaped into the Chaco also made their painful way back to Humaitá, after a three days march and crossing the river Paraná. Among them, Thompson recorded, 'Messrs. Gibson, Bagster, Spivey and other English engineers, the last two badly scalded'.

Two of these engineers died a few days later, and López had an English cemetery made at Humaitá, 'with a decent wall round it, and an ornamental gate.'

The Brazilians did not pursue the retreating Paraguayan ships, though in Thompson's view in any other country Admiral Barroso would have been tried by court-martial for not trying to stop them. Instead Dom Pedro created him Baron Amazonas. In fact the Brazilian squadron retreated along the Paraná; and were soon driven back further still, for Bruguez, after receiving reinforcements, made a lightning forced march past them to Bella Vista, where he set up his batteries on the fifty-foot high cliffs overlooking the river. The Brazilians ran Bruguez's gauntlet, but their infantry massed on the decks and in the tops to return the enemy's fire, suffered heavy losses from the Paraguayan guns. They anchored six miles further down the river; but Bruguez made another forced march and by the next morning had again placed his batteries beyond the Brazilian ships, at Cuevas. This time the Brazilians ran the gauntlet with their men below decks; though, according to Thompson, the crew of an Argentine steamer forming part of the Allied fleet stayed on deck and 'behaved gallantly . . . returning the fire all the time'. This was on 12 August, and thereafter the Allied fleet remained downstream, not to be seen in action again for eight months.

Most historians, including Brazilian ones, are in agreement with Thompson's verdict that, in spite of the overwhelming odds against the Paraguayans, the battle of Riachuelo had been very much a matter of touch and go. In Thompson's opinion the Paraguayans would very likely have taken the Brazilian squadron had they gone alongside at once instead of going past it first. Nevertheless the fact remained that despite their curious behaviour after the battle, it was the Brazilians who now had real command of the river; and whereas Paraguay could not replace her naval losses, Brazil could do so without much difficulty.

The battle of Riachuelo is often looked on as a minor incident in the war. In the roll of the world's great naval actions, it is no doubt a mere miniature. But its ultimate consequences for Francisco Solano López were just as serious as the French defeat at Trafalgar had been for Napoleon Bonaparte. One of the dreadful fascinations of the Paraguayan War, indeed, is the way in which it repeats, on a miniscule scale, so many of the elements of those 'great' wars which are supposed to have shaped the destinies of mankind, and which have acquired a remarkable aura of 'glory' only because the canvas on which they were projected was so much vaster.

It was Masterman who probably saw most clearly the true significance of the battle of Riachuelo, when he declared that:

> 'It is not too much to say that that battle of four hours and a half really decided the war.'

It was not so much the loss to the Paraguayans of their four ships, Masterman pointed out, but:

> 'the loss of an opportunity which could never occur again, of capturing five vessels and heavy guns, which made the defeat of Riachuelo so serious.'

If López had succeeded, Masterman was convinced he would have appeared before Buenos Aires or Montevideo, threatened a bombardment, and forced them to make terms. And with the fall of either of these ports, of course, the Brazilians would have lost their precious command of the river. As it was, the return of the shattered Paraguayan squadron to Humaitá in the dense fog of a cold dawn seemed to Masterman to signify 'the sun of López setting amid storm and tempest for ever'.

López himself, however, certainly did not regard his failure at Riachuelo as more than a temporary setback, and it did not cause him to abandon his grand overall strategy. While he had been planning the naval action, the army which had been massed in the old Jesuit mission areas of Corrientes had leaped into action, driving eastward across the province against slight resistance. This army consisted of 12,000 men under Colonel Antonio de la Cruz Estigarribia, and on 10 June, the eve of the battle of Riachuelo, it reached the river Uruguay, crossed it with canoes (carried in carts for the purpose) and quickly and efficiently established a bridge-head on the other side, at São Borja, in Rio Grande do Sul itself. At the very moment, therefore, that the Paraguayan fleet was being defeated, a Paraguayan army was on Brazilian soil. According to some reports, the Paraguayan officers told the citizens of São Borja that they were shortly expecting General Urquiza to march to their aid from Entre Ríos and that they would then divide their forces for a simultaneous drive on Pôrto Alegre, the main port and capital of Rio Grande do Sul, and on Montevideo. It is difficult to know whether this was merely a piece of propaganda, or an indica-tion of something more tangible; though Thompson pointed out that agents were continually coming and going between Urquiza and López.

What, though, of General Robles and his army? It too had been advancing through the province of Corrientes, though separated from Estigarribia's force by nearly two hundred miles across an immense and impassable morass. But all was not well as far as General Robles was concerned. After the brief Allied incursion at Corrientes, he had again advanced southwards, reaching Goya on 3 June. On the day of the battle of Riachuelo, however he began to retreat – probably, Thompson thought, because he heard the gun-fire and did not know what it portended. He reached Empedrado some thirty-six miles below Corrientes, halted and appeared to be curiously reluctant to stir himself again.

Shortly after, Resquín (who had been recalled from Mato Grosso and promoted to the rank of brigadier-general) joined him, ostensibly as his second-in-command, taking Colonel Alén, his Chief of Staff, with him. Their secret instructions were to keep a close watch on General Robles. Then, on 23 July, General Barrios, the Minister of War, arrived. Robles came out of his tent, and Barrios handed him a letter from the Marshal-President. When he had read it, Robles took off his sword and handed it to Barrios. He had been relieved of his command, pending investigation of re-ports that he had been in communication with the enemy. He was taken under guard to Humaitá. His papers were confiscated by Barrios and sent direct to López.

Most references to this episode either deal with it very briefly or, following Cunninghame-Graham, take it for granted that the accusations of treachery against General Robles were without foundation, and merely symptomatic of López's alleged paranoia.

Masterman's opinion (and he was certainly no friend to López) that the suspicions of Robles were 'perhaps on good grounds', seems to have been largely overlooked. He declared that Robles 'was a bad, cruel man, and bribes were the weapons the Brazilians were most used to fighting with', though he was doubtful of the story, current at the time, that letters from the Brazilians to Robles had been discovered, presumably by Resquín or Alén, under flat stones near Robles' quarters. Barrett, however, thinks that the defeat at Riachuelo had convinced Robles that Paraguay had little chance of ultimate victory, and that the story was true – though Barrett's book, admittedly, is a romantic one which does not hesitate to make use of hearsay.

The story as Barrett tells it involves Elisa Lynch. Left alone with her children in Asunción, she had found herself still kept at arm's length by the President's family. Increasingly embittered by her experiences, and grown devious and ruthless in her determination to fight for the father of her children by all means in her power, she had organized an efficient spy service of her own. She had long realized that many of the aristocrats and merchants, with business connections in Buenos Aires, were secretly opposed to the war; but now she had suspicions of a far more serious nature. According to Barrett:

'She had a dozen tales of secret information that went through spies to the old lady of Asunción – to the mother of the President. Madame Lynch could take the evidence trail as far as the door of the old lady's house. She could take it no farther. Men, known and proved to be in the service of Brazil, had hired and instructed foolish or frightened dupes to divulge information; and had then given them that address to which they could carry more news. The Brazilian spies under torture had known no more than that they were so instructed themselves in advices from the headquarters. She could not get behind those despatches.'

López's mother was apparently a rather foolish and talkative woman, with little understanding of politics. She did not like the war because it was beginning to make life inconvenient and denying her a number of luxuries to which she was accustomed. As in the case of many other members of the ruling classes in South America at the time, the concepts of nation-hood and patriotism meant little to her. The same was true in many parts of the northern provinces of Argentina, especially among older people. To them López seemed like a local caudillo hardly different from the many heroes they had championed themselves. To such people, the conflict was predominantly a personal war, as between rival caudillos, to be supported or opposed for equally personal reasons.

It was well-known that Doña Juana's favourite among her children was her youngest son, Benigno – and it was the latter who, Elisa Lynch suspected, was the real moving spirit in any dealings with the Brazilians that might be taking place. According to Barrett, Brazilian agents would come to old Señora López's house, ostensibly for a friendly chat. She enjoyed listening to what they had to say, though without really understanding what it was all about. Meanwhile Benigno would be sitting in an adjoining room listening carefully for any messages that might be embedded in the flow of chatter. If he had anything to communicate himself, he would enter the room and address it to his somewhat bewildered mother. 'It was like speaking through a translator,' Barrett explained, 'but safer.'

This, if Barrett was right, was Elisa Lynch's information. But she had as yet obtained no definite proof. In Paraguay no one, not even Elisa herself, dared to utter a word against the López family unless he was very sure indeed of his ground. So Elisa decided to bide her time, while urging her spies (actuated in part, no doubt, by personal resentment) to redouble their efforts. But in the course of her enquiries she *had*, according to this account, collected evidence that seemed also to implicate General Robles. These suspicions, at any rate, she felt it safe and proper to communicate to López. She resolved, therefore, to go to Humaitá in person.

First, though, she delivered a rousing patriotic speech to the women of Asunción, at the end of which she appealed to each of them to contribute one fifteenth of her personal jewels towards the cost of the war. According to some accounts, the jewels went into Elisa's own coffers, though Barrett indignantly denies the rumour.

Twenty-four hours later Elisa presented herself to López in Humaitá – dressed (in Barrett's romantic version) in riding breeches, with a white shirt open at the throat – and told of her suspicions of General Robles. López, it appeared, was reluctant to listen to her, but sent Resquín and Alén to investigate.

It must once again be emphasized that much of the foregoing

rests on hearsay, but it is of some importance because it shows that there was already a background of rumours and suspicions of conspiracy, involving many highly placed personages, including members of López's own family. When this is borne in mind, López's later behaviour towards his family, though undeniably cruel (if all the reports are true) cannot be regarded as the sudden aberration of a monster with a persecution mania. In this connection, it is significant that, as Thompson noted, not long after this López sent for his brothers, Venancio and Benigno, to come down to Humaitá, to have them under his eye.

In the case of Robles' suspected treachery, in fact, there were none of the summary executions that were to become a feature of the later desperate stages of the war. Robles and several of his officers were kept in close confinement at Humaitá for several months, while further evidence was collected. They were then brought to trial on charges of treason, and condemned to death. It was not until 8 January 1866, however, that General Robles was taken out, mounted on his horse, together with a number of his officers in carts, and shot in the presence of the assembled army at Paso de la Patria.

Robles' command was temporarily assumed by General Barrios, and then transferred to General Resquín – one of the few Paraguayan generals, incidentally, to survive the war and record their impressions afterwards – and he advanced the army once more to Bella Vista. There it halted to wait news of Estigarribia's column, inactive apart from a few skirmishes and a great deal of looting; among the booty, Thompson reported, were, 'immense stores of wine, liquors and beer', and a fine new piano, which was sent as a present to Mrs Lynch.

When Estigarribia had crossed the River Uruguay opposite São Borja, he had split his army for an advance south along the river, leaving 2,500 men, under Major Duarte, on the right bank (that is, on the Corrientes side), while he himself marched along the left or Rio Grande do Sul bank. The two columns marched more or less abreast and in sight of each other, communicating by means of canoes. Although the Brazilians had 30,000 troops in the area, the Paraguayans met with little resistance. General David Canavarro, the Brazilian commander in Rio Grande do Sul, kept (in Thompson's view) a prudent distance – he was afterwards courtmartialled, but the proceedings were suspended. Nevertheless, the Paraguayan advance was a slow one. Estigarribia had too small a cavalry force to keep an adequate watch on enemy movements or to forage efficiently for supplies. Much time was also wasted in pillaging nearby towns and villages. The line of communications back to Itapuá, on the upper Paraná, grew daily longer, and finally all contact was lost with Robles' (later Resquín's) army on the Paraná throughout the whole advance. Estigarribia received only one reinforcement of 400 men from Paraguay. According to Brazilian sources, a further complication was a river patrol formed by the brilliant young Brazilian Floriano Peixoto, and manned by members of the crack Negro unit from Bahia – the Zuavos Bahianos – which hampered contact between Estigarribia and Duarte. Eventually, however, the Paraguayans reached Uruguaiana, to which General Canavarro had retreated, and which he had fortified – before once again retreating.

In the meantime, the Allies had been making preparations, though hampered by rivalries between their commanders. The port of Concordia, on the river Uruguay between Paysandú and Uruguiana, was the rallying point. There, the Brazilian General Manoel Luíz Osório assembled his troops; he was joined by Bartolomé Mitre, Commander-in-Chief of the Allied Armies (though not, it was sharply pointed out to him, while he was on Brazilian soil) who had left the government of the Argentine Confederation in the hands of his Vice-President; and by General Flores, who was named General in Chief of the Vanguard and despatched along the right bank of the river Uruguay to meet the advancing Paraguayans.

On 6 August, Estigarribia entered Uruguaiana, while Duarte encamped on the other side of the river at a small place called Yataí (the name of a palm tree, which has an edible and most appetizing heart). The former had 8,000 men, the latter, 2,500. The remainder of the original force of 12,400 men (including the 400 reinforcements) had been sent back sick, or had died of illness or in the few skirmishes en route.

Duarte's scouts now brought Estigarribia the news that General Flores, with a force of no less than 13,000 men, was marching rapidly towards Yataí. Duarte sent to Estigarribia asking for reinforcements, which were refused. Nevertheless, when on 17 August Flores called on him to surrender in face of the overwhelming odds, Duarte refused. Posting his line behind a row of houses, and with his rear secured by the river, he waited the onslaught. The first wave of Flores' troops were met with a devastating fire from the Paraguayans, who then charged with their scanty cavalry, cutting down many of the attackers. The weight of numbers, however, soon had its effect, and Duarte's line was broken, though the Paraguayans continued to keep up a fierce fire from small groups and as individuals, until (according to Thompson) 'they were absolutely cut down, for they would accept no quarter. Not a man escaped.' The only surviving officer seems to have been Major Duarte himself; less than 400 prisoners were taken. Thompson reported:

> 'Officers of the allied army wrote from the field of battle that the carnage had been something frightful, as no human power could make the Paraguayans surrender, and that even single individuals would rather fight on, with certain death before them.'

Flores' men had suffered heavy losses too – about 2,500 killed and wounded. The Paraguayan prisoners were given new clothing, as their own was by now worn out and most of them were practically naked; then, it appears, they were immediately drafted into the Allied Army. This practice was to give rise to a good deal of controversy. The Allies argued that Paraguayan prisoners of war voluntarily entered their ranks, glad to strike a blow against the 'tyrant'. López himself accused the Allies of giving prisoners no choice. There were, of course, a number of genuine defections, as there are in all wars, but it is notable how often Paraguayan prisoners escaped, or if they had been drafted into the Allied ranks, deserted as soon as they had the opportunity, even when the war situation was at its most desperate for Paraguay. Burton asserted that far from reviling their leader 'the Paraguayan prisoners are rarely if ever known to utter a word against him'.

As for Major Duarte, he was sent to Buenos Aires and treated with every courtesy, though Thompson felt that this clemency was somewhat marred by the Buenos Aires press which day after day harped upon it, and on the gift of clothing to the Paraguayan prisoners. As he drily observed of the latter:

> 'They were probably astonished at the moderation of the Allies in having left any prisoners alive, such an event being almost unknown in the annals of South-American warfare – the custom being to cut prisoners' throats after a battle.'

With the right bank of the Uruguay cleared of the invaders, the Allies turned their attention to Estigarribia in Uruguaiana. General

Mitre arrived on 25 August with the rest of the Allied army. Estimates vary widely as to the eventual total of this army, though Thompson, who was rarely mistaken in these matters, put the figure as high as 30,000.

But what is certain is that Estigarribia's situation was hopeless, and the Allies confidently expected him to capitulate at once. He rejected the first summons to surrender, however, and the Allies made preparations for a huge, long-distance bombardment. Estigarribia began to make rafts, with the idea of escaping across the river, but realized it was impossible. By now his provisions were nearly exhausted, and finally, on 18 September after further parleys and an exchange of long and highly rhetorical letters, he agreed to the Allies' terms of surrender, whereby his men (reduced now to some 5,000) were to become prisoners of war and his officers were to be free to reside wherever they wished, outside Paraguay.

The humane nature of these terms, were, no doubt, due in part to the presence of the Emperor of Brazil himself, who had arrived at the front with his two sons-in-law – the party had at one point been mistaken by the startled Rio Grandenses for invading Paraguayans.[1] It was in the presence of the Emperor that Estigarribia handed over his sword, which was later placed in Brazil's National Historical Museum. Dom Pedro was shocked at the wretched condition of the prisoners (Thompson reported that for some time they had had nothing to eat but a ration of lump sugar, of which there happened to be a stock in Uruguiana) and at their poor equipment. According to Barroso, all of them carried old flint-lock muskets, and writing to his friend the Condessa de Barral about it the Emperor commented: 'o inimigo era indigno de ser batido – que gente!' – 'the enemy was not worthy of being defeated – what a people!'

According to Thompson, these prisoners too were drafted into the Allied armies 'excepting a few hundred, who were sent to the different countries of the Allies to be stared at.' A large number of prisoners, in fact, managed to escape and eventually made their way back to Paraguay. Estigarribia himself went to live in Rio de Janeiro.

The news of his surrender came as a profound shock to López. For a time his mood was so savage that no one dared to approach him, not even Pancho, his eldest son by Elisa Lynch, to whom he was devoted. He summoned all the officers at Humaitá, and denounced Estigarribia as a traitor, declaring that he had sold the garrison of Uruguiana to the enemy. Masterman was at Humaitá shortly after the disaster, and attended a levée at which Bishop Palacios (the one-time poor parish priest who had christened Pancho) delivered a speech in which he mentioned the traitors Robles and Estigarribia. At this, Masterman recorded, the Marshal-President

> 'burst out in a torrent of invective and passionate complaint, concluding in a loud tone, very different from his ordinary delivery: "I am working for my country, for the good and honour of you all, and none help me. I stand alone – I have confidence in none of you – I cannot trust one amongst you". And then striding forward, and raising his clenched hand, white with tension, he cried, "Cuidado! But take care! Hitherto I have pardoned offences, taken pleasure in pardoning, but now, from this day, I pardon no one". And the expression of his face gave double power to his words. As I looked round the room on the wide circle of officers bowing low as he left the room, I saw many a blanched face amongst them, for they knew he would keep his word'.

It was now, according to Masterman, that López began a system of punishing the relatives of all real or supposed deserters, and it seems clear that from this point on he became increasingly harsh and ruthless in his methods of exacting unquestioning adherence.

There was certainly ample reason for López to feel dismayed. For one thing, the surrender at Uruguiana (in marked contrast to Major Duarte's heroic action at Yataí) had been a severe blow to Paraguayan pride – López's pride, for he had boasted that all Paraguayans were prepared to fight to the last man rather than lay down their arms. More materially, he had lost between 15,000 to 20,000 of his best fighting men – a truly gigantic loss considering the limited manpower at his disposal. Above all, this disaster combined with that of Riachuelo (and indeed the one followed inevitably from the other) meant that his grand design for a rapid invasion to the south, and a quick victory, had been utterly destroyed. The offensive phase of the war, as far as Paraguay was concerned, was over.

López himself was well aware of the seriousness of the situation, and as soon as he had recovered from the blow, he issued orders for the total evacuation of Corrientes province. General Resquín carried them out with skill and despatch. He embarked the Paraguayan artillery at Cuevas in captured steamers, deployed his army in a long arc from the river towards the east, and marched northwards, sweeping before him all the cattle and horses. The Brazilian fleet ventured into Cuevas after the Paraguayans had evacuated it, and then proceeded along the river towards Corrientes – at a safe distance.

The passage of the Paraná to Itapirú began on 31 October. Five Brazilian warships now came practically within cannon-shot of the two small steamers and lighters which were busy transporting the Paraguayan troops and the captured cattle. Thompson commented:

> 'People who saw this, of course, gave up the army as lost, thinking that the Brazilians would never allow it to cross the river, and that it would soon be overtaken and destroyed by the allied armies.'

The Brazilian ships, however, fearful of the possible existence of Paraguayan masked batteries (for which they had had a wholesome respect ever since the exploits of Bruguez and his gunners) withdrew without firing a shot. By 3 November 1865, Resquín had passed his last man and gun over the river, as well as 100,000 head of cattle.

According to Thompson, the men were delighted to be back in Paraguay. They were, however, terribly fatigued, and many of them were sick. He calculated that about 8,500 men had died during the Corrientes campaign – bringing up the total loss to 21,000 men; and that since the war began no less than 40,000 men had already perished. As for the vast haul of cattle, which at first elated López's commissariat, most of them died either from exhaustion and inadequate pasturage on the Paraguayan side of the river, or from eating a poisonous herb, so common in the south of Paraguay that native cattle had learned to avoid it, but which was fatal to animals which had not hitherto encountered it.

The Paraguayans were given plenty of time to get ready for the invasion that was now inevitable. It took the Allied armies nearly five months, in fact, to reach Corrientes, partly because of heavy winter rains, and partly because of sickness and desertions. Many of the latter were of men from the Argentine provinces, recruited by General Urquiza, who was still caught in the cleft stick of partiality to López and reluctance to disrupt the unity of Argentina which he himself had done so much to create. His hatred of the Brazilians had indeed nearly prevailed, and when Burton visited him in 1868, he 'openly declared that had not Marshal-President López invaded Corrientes, which he looked upon as a portion of his Mesopotamia, he would have aided him with 15,000 men against the Macacos . . .'.

López himself was still keeping up the spirit of his troops with assurances that Urquiza would soon be coming to their aid, and agents were still passing to and fro between them. It was also rumoured that Bolivia was about to enter into an alliance with Paraguay, and that 12,000 Bolivian troops were on the march to Mato Grosso. Some substance was lent to this rumour when López had a rough road constructed between a point near Corumbá (in the part of Mato Grosso still in Paraguayan occupation) and Santo Corazón, in Bolivia. No Bolivian troops, however, traversed it, though for a long time the Allies supposed that the Paraguayans were receiving stores and also ammunition along it. Thompson thought that this also would be quite impossible, because of the roughness of the track and the fact that there were no bridges nor even proper boats, to cross the numerous rivers and streams. He insisted, in fact that this route was only used three or four times, and that all that was ever carried along it 'was a little sugar and coffee, which might all be placed on an armchair'.

Among the allied sick were several cases of smallpox. Two of their deserters who crossed the Paraná to join the Paraguayans, took the disease with them; López was convinced that they had been sent deliberately, in order to infect his troops, and according to Thompson he had them flogged to death.

López had a few deserters of his own to contend with at this time, when morale was at a low ebb following the disasters of Riachuelo and Uruguiana. Their families were forced to publish denunciations of them in the official papers. He also now took up the question of the treatment of Paraguayan prisoners of war direct with General Mitre. In a letter addressed to him on 20 November, after accusing the Allies of various atrocities and claiming that his own troops had throughout the campaign behaved in the most exemplary manner, he protested that many of the Paraguayan prisoners of war had been forced against their wills to take up arms against their country, and, asserting that the great part of the remainder had been 'taken and reduced to slavery in Brazil', apart from those who 'from the colour of their skin, were even less suitable for sale', and had been sent to forced labour in Uruguay or Argentina. He ended his letter with a threat of the most vigorous reprisals against any Allied citizens in Paraguay whether prisoners of war or not, if he did not receive a satisfactory reply.[2]

In his answer of 25 November, Mitre (besides making some counter-charges of his own) refuted all López's complaints. He declared that all Paraguayan prisoners of war had been treated 'not only with humanity, but with benevolence – many having been placed completely at liberty, many others having been sent to the towns, and part destined to passive service in the Allied armies, especially in the hospitals in which their own companions were being treated'. As for those who had entered the Allied armies, he insisted that it had been 'by their own free will and because they desired it, which favour could not be denied them, when their countrymen who were refugees in the territory of the allied nations had spontaneously requested to be armed, and it had been conceded to them'.

López had anticipated Mitre's reply, by having all the Allied citizens in Paraguay brought to Humaitá, where they were kept under close arrest, and subsequently exposed to the bombardment of the Brazilian ironclads. It was claimed by Allied sources that all who survived were, with one exception, eventually shot or tortured to death.

Who was right on this issue of forced recruitment? Hutchinson was not the only one to be convinced that López had very real cause for complaint. He asserted that at least 1,500 Paraguayan prisoners were drafted into General Flores' army after Uruguaiana. He scoffed at Mitre's claim that Paraguayan prisoners of war were joining the Allied armies at their own request, and quoted as proof of their unwillingness to do so a number of extracts from a diary kept by Colonel Pallejas, who acted as war correspondent in Flores' army:

'Dec. 7th. On our muster we found seven Paraguayans missing, whilst eight of our infantry and artillery had also deserted. . . .
Dec. 8th. Three more Paraguayans have escaped in the woods. . . .
Dec. 10th. Two Paraguayans cleared out last night; two more deserted this evening. . . .
Dec. 15th. Three more Paraguayans deserted this morning. . . .
Dec. 16th. Three serjeants and five Paraguayans escaped before dawn. . . .'

Hutchinson went on to claim that there was so much resistance among the Paraguayans to their enrolment in Flores' army that eventually the general was obliged to disarm them and treat them as authentic prisoners of war – though this did not by any means stop the desertions. Masterman declared that the Allies 'shot many who did not "volunteer" to fight against their own people'.

There was one other accusation in López's letter to Mitre (also contemptuously dismissed) which deserves comment. It was to the effect that a Paraguayan deserter named Juan González had been secretly sent to Paraguay in order to assassinate him. Whether he had grounds or not, López became increasingly fearful of attempts on his life; he was convinced that the Allies were seeking to eliminate him as a short-cut to ending the war.

Both López's letter and Mitre's reply were published in the *Seminario*. The next time the two men came into contact was to be in very different circumstances.

While the Allies were slowly advancing through Corrientes and making their preparations to carry the war into Paraguay itself, López was working out his defensive strategy – while still cherishing the hope, even now, that the day would come when he would take the offensive again himself. Various batteries were hidden at points where it was thought the Allies might make their crossing of the river Paraná, and on the bank of the river Paraguay, about a mile above the confluence of the two rivers – and Thompson made a 'trigonometrical survey' of the ground between the Paraná and Humaitá, the first ever to be made. By means of a vigorous recruiting campaign, López managed to scrape together an army of 30,000 men, though from now on the new recruits tended increasingly to be either boys in their early teens (and even younger in the later stages of the war) and older men. Most of the surviving veterans were now cavalrymen, and several thousand of them were drafted into the infantry. Privately owned horses were confiscated in order to mount the rest.

López, now in personal command of his army, had established his headquarters at the village of Paso de la Patria, on the banks of the Upper Paraná, eastwards from its fall into the river Paraguay at Tres Bocas, throwing up, Burton reported, 'a fine work, with redans and curtains, resting on two lagoons and impassable carrisal, and mounting thirty field guns', as well as many smaller pieces.

The army rapidly built huts for themselves and large fields of

Indian corn were cultivated. On Sundays López and his officers went to church to the accompaniment of his favourite march. 'Some of the Paraguayan bands of music played beautifully', Thompson declared, and after mass the troops would crowd round López and he would address them in Guaraní, assuring them that they would easily beat the *cambas* when they arrived, and 'always mixing in a little chaff, which pleased the soldiers more than anything.' When foreign visitors came to his camp, with Madame Lynch and his eldest son, Pancho, he entertained them to splendid dinners. His spirits had risen, and his army was once again full of confidence. Perhaps their morale had received a fillip when the men who had escaped after being taken prisoner at Uruguaiana, came swimming across the Paraná in groups of two to a dozen at a time; and although at first López regarded them with suspicion and kept them in a separate camp, he soon distributed them among the various corps, glad to have this small, unexpected reinforcement.

The high spirits of López and his men found vent in a series of daring raids, which went on almost daily during the next three months. One to two hundred Paraguayans would cross the Paraná in full sight of the enemy and standing up to paddle their canoes (according to the usual Paraguayan custom). When they reached the other side, they would fling themselves at the enemy sector in front of them in a ferocious assault, drive them half a mile or so inland, and then return the way they had come, taking with them their killed and wounded and any booty they could lay hands on. The Paraguayans treated these raids as holidays, and there was such fierce competition to take part in them, that López had to share out the places among the different battalions. They would set out for the river-side accompanied by the women and a band; Elisa Lynch usually went too, to speed them on their way, giving each man a small package containing gifts of cigars, tobacco and sweets.

The most considerable of these raids took place on 31 January 1866. The party of 400 men was commanded by the dashing José Díaz (according to Kolinski; Thompson, however, reported that it was commanded by Lieutenant Viveros). They landed at Corrales, opposite Paso de la Patria (where the river is usually forded) and attacked the vanguard of the Allied army, composed of Argentine units, which was encamped nearby. Thompson reported: 'these 400 Paraguayans were absolutely fighting with 7,200 of the allied troops'.

After four hours of fighting, the Paraguayans retired to the river bank where they had left their canoes, and spent the night there. During the night 400 fresh troops joined them, and the following morning the party made further attacks on the Argentine army, then returned to Paso de la Patria. The Paraguayan casualties amounted to 170 killed or wounded in this raid, but the Allies lost 900, and no less than 50 officers, among them four colonels.

A larger action took place on 19 February, when three of the remaining Paraguayan steamers sailed round from Humaitá to Paso de la Patria, took on board 1,000 men, and after sailing along the Paraná, landed them at Itatí, a village in Corrientes where the Uruguayan army, under General Suarez and numbering some 5,000 were encamped. They immediately withdrew, with the Paraguayans shouting after them 'Where are the heroes of Yataí?', and retired to a position eight miles inland. So precipitate was the retreat that the General left his papers and his gold watch and chain. After setting fire to the camp and the village of Itatí, the Paraguayans returned, taking with them stores and provisions and a number of cattle and horses.

The smaller raids also continued, the Paraguayans always making a point of bringing back some trophy or other to present to their leader. On one occasion a negro sergeant brought back nine allied soldiers' heads in a bag, and piled them at López's door. The sergeant was promoted to ensign, thus becoming the only black officer in the Paraguayan army, Thompson's very pertinent comment on these raids was: 'It appears incredible that the Allies should have permitted these men always to return instead of cutting them off'.

It is equally pertinent to ask what the Brazilian navy was doing all this time. With the virtual destruction of Paraguay's own river-squadron at Riachuelo, and the withdrawal of Bruguez's dreaded batteries, the Brazilian ships were free to operate without obstacle as far as Tres Bocas. But although they were within hearing of the musket fire during all these Paraguayan raids, they took no action, arguing – much to the disgust of their Uruguayan and Argentine Allies – that they must not risk the fleet against the possibility of concealed Paraguayan guns, until they were completely ready for full-scale invasion. Their Admiral, Tamandaré, did not join the fleet until 26 February 1866 (according to Thompson, he had been spending his time in Buenos Aires 'flirting'). He then publicly announced the precise date on which he would lead his fleet into Asunción harbour – 25 March.

He was presumably emboldened to make this optimistic forecast by the arrival of new, heavily armoured and plated ironclads, including one named after himself (the *Tamandaré*); and at last the Allied fleet steamed up from Corrientes and anchored, in line of battle, from Corrales to the mouth of the Paraguay. The fleet consisted of 18 steam gunboats of six to eight guns each, and four ironclads, one of which, the *Bahia*, was a monitor, with a revolving turrett and two 150-pounder Whitworth guns. In all, the squadron carried 125 guns. This formidable fleet began operations by bombarding the old Paraguayan river fort of Itapirú, one side of which had already fallen down, and which was in any case only rivetted with brickwork.

They were also engaged in battle with the little *Gualeguay*, the former Argentine naval steamer which the Paraguanyans had captured when they occupied Corrientes, and which carried only 12-pounder guns.

The forays of the *Gualeguay* produced as much excitement among the Paraguayans as had the exploits of their raiding parties. López himself would sit in the reinforced corridor of his house at Paso de la Patria and watch the proceedings through a telescope. Every afternoon, Thompson reported, the little steamer went out to a point off Itapirú :

'. . . and defied the Allied fleet, firing her 12-pounders, which were answered by the whole fleet, with every kind of projectile, from an 8-pounder to a 150-pounder. These used to fall round her like hail, throwing up immense water-spouts into the air. She used to retire a little before sunset. She did this every day for three weeks, without being hit, except by one ball, which passed through her funnel.'

At other times it would be one of the wooden barges or *chatas* which, single-handed, took on the whole of the enemy fleet. On one occasion the *Gualeguay* towed out one of the *chatas*, and left her close to the shore, half a mile below Itapirú. It opened fire on the fleet, putting four balls into the Brazilian flag-ship. Three ironclads advanced on the *chata*, which kept up an accurate fire until they were less than a hundred yards away. The crew then jumped overboard and swam or waded ashore. The Brazilians sent out boats to bring in the *chata* – only to run into the withering fire of 100 Paraguayans hidden in the woods lining the river bank.

Five days later, on 25 March, a *chata* was towed to the same spot and again opened fire on the Allied fleet, which again sent ironclads to surround it. Most of the 68-pounder balls from the *chata's* guns which found their mark were shattered into fragments when they struck the armoured plating of the ironclads. But one of them hit the edge of a gun-port on the *Tamandaré*, and its flying pieces entered, killing and wounding nearly all the occupants of the casement. Among them was the commander, who had to have both legs amputated without chloroform, and who died, like General Dan Sickles at Gettysburg, smoking a cigar. His second-in-command, three other officers and eighteen sailors were also killed, and another fifteen wounded.

Another *chata* succeeded in putting four shots through the plates of another Brazilian ironclad, the *Barroso*, which also had one of her Whitworth 120-pounder guns shot in two. Most of the ironclads, in fact, received damage of some kind, while the *chatas* lay so low in the water that it was extremely difficult to score hits on them.

The successes of the *Gualeguay* and of the *chatas* further raised the morale of the Paraguayans, and they awaited the Allied onslaught in an almost festive spirit. López was at pains to maintain their high spirits by providing various entertainments for his troops during their off-duty hours. Masterman wrote an amusing account of one of the more unusual diversions, which took place during his three months' spell of duty as an assistant surgeon at Humaitá. López had obtained from Paris, before the Allied blockade of the river had taken effect, a peep-show and a 'phantasmagoria lantern'. Unfortunately, the printed instructions had been mislaid, and López detailed Masterman and Thompson to see if they could set up the apparatus, which they succeeded in doing.

After they had inspected the peep-show display, López with the bishop and several generals and with the troops agog in the background, waited for the magic-lantern show to begin. It was a great success, in spite of the fact that most of the slides represented scenes from the recent Franco-Italian campaign. But the highlight was the showing of the comic slides, which nearly brought the house down. The unsophisticated Bishop Palacios had difficulty in preserving his episcopal decorum, according to Masterman:

'There was light enough reflected from the screen to see him distinctly, and his contortions, as he tried with his handkerchief stuffed into his mouth to stifle his laughter, were excruciatingly diverting. He dared not laugh out, yet his delight at the figures, especially at one, where the nose of a dwarf gradually reached portentous dimensions, was utterly beyond his control.'

Eventually, the time of waiting was over. The raids, by land and water, had delayed the Allied build-up, but they could not disrupt it. By now there were 62,000 men[3] assembled in readiness to make the crossing of the Paraná, with well over a hundred guns. The point that was finally chosen, after a good deal of heated discussion between the Allied commanders, was between Itapirú and Paso de la Patria. About two-thirds of the way across the river, and not far from Itapirú, there was a large, recently-formed sandbank, covered with long grass, known (among other names) as the Banco de Itapirú (a few years later some shift in the currents of the river caused it to disappear completely – a common enough phenomenon in South America). The Allies decided to begin their invasion by occupying this island during the night of 5 April 1866. Protected by the ironclads, the landing party made trenches and batteries, and mounted a number of guns. It was garrisoned with 2,000 Brazilian troops, and a further bombardment of Itapirú began.

The commander of the small fort of Itapirú was Lieutenant-Colonel Díaz. He organized a force composed of two divisions of 400 men each[4] equipped with canoes – these canoe-men were soon after formed into a special corps, the *cuerpo de bogovantes*. On 10 April under cover of darkness, they landed on the island unseen and, after firing a volley, charged the Brazilian trenches and guns. In a savage battle these changed hands several times. But the Brazilian artillery, aided by the guns of the ironclads, caused terrible destruction among the Paraguayans, who were eventually forced to withdraw. They left 500 killed, wounded, and prisoners behind them. So many of the survivors were wounded that they had difficulty in manning the canoes. Those who were wounded in the legs, Thompson says, 'sat down and paddled, and those who had still one arm paddled with it.'

It was a most perilous return journey to Itapirú, as it was now daylight, and the wounded canoeists had to contend with a fierce current and a heavy fire of grape and canister at close quarters from the Brazilian ships. Fifteen of the twenty-six canoes arrived safely at Itapirú, carrying 300 wounded men.

The Brazilians on the island had lost heavily too – about 1,000 wounded and killed – and they suffered further casualties in the immediate aftermath of the attack, when the guns at Itapirú scored a number of hits. One of these killed the commander of the Brazilian forces on the island, together with two of his officers, at the very moment when he was writing his report of the action. Other shots sank a Brazilian steam-launch and forced the Brazilian warship *Enrique Martínez* to run aground, while yet another shattered a Brazilian brass rifled 32-pounder on shore.

But while the Allies could stand these losses, the Paraguayans could not. Burton described the Paraguayan attack on the Banco de Itapirú (or the Ilha da Redencão as the Brazilians called it) as 'the first of the many reckless actions in which Marshal-President López frittered away his devoted forces.'

With the island in their possession, the Allies now began their crossing of the Paraná, while 4,000 Paraguayans, hidden in the woods lining the road between Itapirú and Paso de la Patria made ready to harass them. General Manoel Luíz Osório, perhaps the bravest and most able of all the Brazilian commanders, was the first to land on Paraguayan soil, with 10,000 men, on 16 April, 1866. The Paraguayans immediately attacked, but were driven back by sheer weight of numbers, and the landings continued. Fearing himself outflanked, López decided to abandon both Itapirú and Paso de la Patria. The gallant little *Gualeguay* was sunk in order to block one of the channels of the river. Both Burton and Thompson criticized this decision. Burton believed that López might have held the trenches of Itapirú and Paso de la Patria 'for months if not years', and Thompson (who had himself devised many of the trench-works) argued that if López:

> 'had defended the trenches of Paso de la Patria, he would have cut up perhaps eight or ten thousand of the Allies, with hardly any loss on his own side, and probably they would never have been able to take the trenches.'

Thompson was, however, among the few at that date who properly appreciated the potentialities of trench warfare, and in any case, López was himself one of the victims of the myth of the impregnability of Humaitá, higher up the river, against which he believed any invading force must eventually come to grief.

The departure of López himself from Paso de la Patria certainly deserves Burton's use of the word 'precipitate'. Thompson reported that he left at daybreak, insisting on riding alone, with his aides de camp some distance behind, in order to avoid the possibility of being identified by the Allies and fired on. It was a constant preoccupation. Wherever he stopped with the army, formidable shell-proof shelters had to be built for him, and he did his utmost to keep out of enemy range. López's enemies made great play of these precautions, frequently taunting him with cowardice. Washburn succeeded in contrasting López's behaviour in this respect with that of Elisa Lynch, to the detriment of both:

'Madame Lynch, for some purpose of her own, was always trying to increase the natural cowardice of López. She had an abundance of that courage of which he was so greatly in want and in time of battle would expose herself where the danger was greatest . . .'.

There were, indeed, a number of legends current at the time about Elisa Lynch's bravery, and one in particular which was repeated in the American *History of Nations* (edited by no less a personage than Henry Cabot Lodge):

'At that period the war was carried on by skirmishes, almost always adverse to the enemy, in which a young Englishwoman named Elisa Lynch, took a very active part, at the head of some battalions of Amazons . . .'.

This is almost certainly a romantic invention, and the evidence as to the existence of the 'Amazons' is contradictory. Thompson, for example, declared that all that happened was that in 1868, a deputation of women applied to the Vice-President for permission to take up arms, but that the offer was quite definitely declined. The nearest approach to an army of Amazons was when 'some twenty girls . . . belonging to the village of Areguá, got lances and white dresses with tricolour bands, and a sort of Scotch cap, designed by Mrs Lynch', and the only offensive action they were allowed to take was 'to go about Asunción singing patriotic hymns'. Masterman, on the other hand, was just as definite that at the beginning of 1868 several regiments of women were actually formed, and that he could 'vouch for the truth of it' having before him 'a printed list of names, sixty in number', and knowing personally the *capitana* of one of the companies. He added, however, that after the women's companies had been drilled for a few weeks, the idea of sending them to the front 'was given up'. However, in one of the last battles of the war the Allies claimed that many among the dead were either very young boys – or women. Young sub-lieutenant Dionísio Cerqueira, who was with the Brazilian forces at this particular battle, was much moved to find a mother and her young son lying dead at the entrance of a church, apparently killed by the same bullet.[5] And Hutchinson quoted an Argentine newspaper report which declared that after the engagement of 8 May 1867, in the Chaco, an old woman was found, dressed in a man's uniform

> 'shot by the side of a young man also killed, whose head she was holding in her withered hands, and who was probably her own son. The latter was clutching his musket with one arm, and the other twined round the neck of the old woman.'

According to Barrett, Elisa Lynch was in action on several occasions: during the battle of Villeta, in September 1868, for example, he declared that she rounded up all the women of the camp, mounted them on horses and led them in a charge to relieve General Díaz, who was surrounded by the enemy, and at the battle of Pikysyry in the December of the same year, he described her rescuing a Paraguayan flag from the hands of a dying boy-soldier.

There is, perhaps, a certain 'Angels of Mons' ring to some of these stories, but there is certainly ample evidence from trustworthy eye-witnesses of the quite extraordinary coolness in the face of danger displayed by Elisa Lynch. We know, too, from the sober Thompson, that large numbers of women, organized on military lines and with their own sergeants, were attached to all the Paraguayan camps. These women undertook all kinds of vital auxiliary work, including helping in the hospitals, keeping the camps clean and as free from infection as possible, and (most important of all) sowing seed and collecting crops to feed the armies. In performing these tasks they were, of course, in as much danger as the men from enemy attacks and bombardments. Elisa Lynch made these women's corps one of her special concerns. She also worked fearlessly in the camp hospitals, often during enemy shelling – and Barrett was probably right in saying that from time to time she used to wear a colonel's uniform.

If no one has ever doubted Elisa Lynch's courage, however, it does not necessarily follow that Washburn was justified in questioning that of her consort. It is true that Thompson maintained that

López possessed a peculiar kind of courage in that 'when out of range of fire, even though completely surrounded by the enemy, he was always in high spirits, but he could not endure the whistle of a ball'. On the other hand, Burton (writing in 1869) while ironically admitting that López 'has certainly never headed a charge, and he has rarely been reported to have fallen captive', also pointed out 'but there is no need for the President to act soldier; *l'état c'est lui.* If he falls the cause of Paraguay – and she has a cause – is sheer lost; whilst he lives, she has hope. He has always been able to escape; his enemies are ever ready to build for him a bridge of gold, and the best conditions are at his service; he has manfully rejected them all.' And it is difficult to see how López's long drawn-out resistance, not to mention the circumstances of his end, can be called anything but courage, peculiar or otherwise.

After the retreat from Paso de la Patria, the Paraguayans took up fresh positions at Estero Bellaco. The Bellaco is a pair of parallel streams, about three miles apart, and separated by a dense forest of palms, which flow into the river Paraguay near Laguna (lake) Pirís, and into the Paraná about 100 miles to the east. The word *estero* denotes the kind of marshland that is thus created. As Thompson had probably studied this terrain more thoroughly than anybody else his description is of importance in understanding the events that followed. After explaining that all the *esteros* were full of a species of rush growing to a height of between five and nine feet above the level of the water, he goes on:

'These rushes grow about two inches apart only, and are consequently almost impassable in themselves. The bottom they grow on is always a very deep mud, and the water over this mud is from 3 to 6 feet deep. The "esteros" are consequently impassable excepting at the passes, which are places where the rushes have been torn out by the roots, and sand gradually substituted for the mud at the bottom. In these passes, as in the rest of the "esteros", the depth of the water to be waded through is from 3 to 6 feet. In some places, one or even two or three persons, on very strong horses, can pass through the rushes; but after one horse has passed, the mud is very much worse on account of the holes made by the first horse's feet. These "esteros" formed the principal defence of the Paraguayans'.

This area, in extreme southern Paraguay, which even today is without roads and practically uninhabited, was the scene of some of the hardest fought battles of the war. As Burton observed, 'a glance at any map will explain to you how it was that two years were spent in battling over nine square miles of ground'.

By now the whole of the Allied armies had crossed into Paraguay. At Itapirú they had assembled 54 large steamers, 11 small ones, and 48 sailing vessels, by far the largest flotilla ever seen in these waters. Large bases were established both at Itapirú and at Paso de la Patria, while the Paraguayans were deployed along various points of the Bellaco.

On 2 May, López sent a force of 5,000 men, led by Díaz (1,000 of them were cavalry) on a surprise attack against the Allied vanguard, which was commanded by General Flores. They fell upon the enemy so suddenly that their artillery only had time to fire a few shots before the Paraguayans were swarming over the guns. Flores' own tent was taken and he himself nearly captured. He and his officers behaved with exemplary courage and their troops were inspired by their example. But they lost 1,600 men and 31 officers in the fighting, as well as most of their guns – including four 9-pounder rifled brass Lahittes (known thereafter as 'Flores' guns', they served the Paraguayans well during the rest of the war) together with their ammunition-waggons. General Osorio, who came to Flores' rescue, lost practically a whole battalion.

Not content with cutting the vanguard to pieces, however, Díaz made the mistake of continuing the battle, although the whole Allied army was now on the move. He was quickly outflanked and forced to make a hasty retreat, losing a large number of his men, and many of the captured guns. It is difficult, therefore, to decide whether the battle of Estero Bellaco should be rated as a Paraguayan or an Allied success. It is instructive, though, to look at the letter which General Flores wrote to his wife the day after the battle, indicative as it is both of the Allied estimate of the action, and of conditions, tension, and attitudes of mind in the Allied camp:

'My Dear Wife, – Good news as well as bad should always be calmly received. Yesterday the vanguard, under my orders, sustained a considerable defeat, the Oriental Division being almost completely lost. . . . I comprehended the bad position of our encampment. Some days before the event, Marshal Osório and myself went in person to the General-in-Chief, to show him the advantage of removing the camp, but Mitre answered us thus: "Don't alarm yourself, General Flores; the aggression of the barbarians is nil, for the hour of their extermination has sounded". If, therefore, anyone is responsible for the occurrence of May 2, General Mitre is the man.

'I can assure you, with all my heart, that during the whole of my campaign against the tyrant Berro,[6] I did not suffer so many annoyances as I have done in the short period we have been on Paraguayan soil. What is passing here does not suit my temper at all. Everything is done by mathematical calculations, and the most precious time is lost in making plans, measuring distances, drawing lines, and looking at the sky; only fancy, the principal operations of the war have been executed on a chessboard.

'Meanwhile some of the corps have had nothing to eat for three days. I don't know what will become of us; and if to the critical situation we are in, you add the constant apathy of General Mitre, it may very well happen that going to seek for wool we ourselves may be shorn.

'Everything is left for tomorrow, and the most important movements are postponed. I have seen activity displayed only on levée-days. Then there is plenty of it – regiments, bands of music, compliments, and felicitations everywhere; uniforms and rich swords are shown off. And this happens frequently; for one day is the Emperor's birthday, another the Princess Leopoldina's; tomorrow is the anniversary of the Independence of Brazil; and so on continually.

'In the future my vanguard will be composed of Argentines. There are no horses or mules for the trains, and no oxen to eat. If we remain here a month longer, we shall have to repass the Paraná and go into winter-quarters at Corrientes. In this case I shall have the pleasure of seeing you and my friends. I hardly think it worth while to tell you that the Brazilians turned tail in a swinish manner and there was a battalion which would not charge. . . .'

The Paraguayan President could have derived more than a grain of comfort from that letter. It would have gone far to vindicate his argument that internal tensions would eventually cause the Triple Alliance to fall apart. It would have gone equally far in justifying his confidence that, though his country had been invaded, the position was not irreversible – and that although he had been forced on to the defensive, he was by no means beaten.

General Flores concluded his letter in words which bring the

fierce old gaucho very close and which are a timely reminder that
the protagonists in this tragedy were human beings after all; it is a
reminder that is often necessary in the case of the Paraguayan War,
as it is perhaps in that of most wars of its kind:

'My tent was sacked by the Paraguayans. Send me a portman-
teau with a few clothes, a large cloth poncho, a straw hat, and
two pairs of boots. I enclose letters from our son Fortunato. A
kiss to my daughter Agapita, and you, my beloved María,
receive the whole heart of your impassioned old
Venancio Flores'

But in his postscript, Flores returned to the subject that was
obviously vexing him most, and which makes it evident that among
the casualties of the war must be included the old friendship
between the architect of modern Argentina and the man who had
done so much to help him:

'P.S. I recommend you, María, to send me nothing but camp
clothes – no finery or dress-coats. Curious to say, they have
lately been even wanting to order me how to dress. Did not
General Mitre, very politely, tell me that it would be convenient
for me to take more care of my person? At first I thought he
alluded to the individual, but he afterwards asked me why I did
not dispose of a uniform from the Commisariat in order to keep
up the dignity of my position. I assure you I do not know how I
found patience to hear him. I turned round and left him with the
words in his mouth.'[7]

Two other points should be made about the battle of Estero
Bellaco: several Paraguayans of good family (not all of them
officers – as in the French army of the day, all promotion was from
the ranks) who were out of favour at the time, took the opportunity
to desert to the Allies. These desertions increased López's suspicions of the Paraguayan aristocracy and confirmed him in his
conviction that (apart from a few exceptions) it was only upon his
faithful Guaraníes that he could rely with absolute confidence. He
also made sure that, in future, desertions, for whatever reason,
would be extremely difficult. The Paraguayan army was made up
in units of six. Each six was led by a man instructed to shoot anyone
in his command who faltered in the face of the enemy. Each man of
the six had another man whom he was detailed to watch – and in
addition each six had another six under observation. Paraguayan

soldiers must have felt that it was almost safer to charge into the enemies' guns than to risk a shot in the back for a moment's hesitation. It was no doubt one of the reasons that made them such ferocious opponents, though it was only Allied propaganda that could succeed in making it the only motivation – and possibly the whole story was an Allied fabrication.

On the other hand the desertions at Estero Bellaco had not been one way. Seven hundred of the Paraguayans who had been captured at Uruguaiana and pressed into the Allied army, went over the moment they caught sight of the Paraguayan flag.

As a matter of fact, at this stage of the war, with the Allies still struggling to consolidate their bridgehead on Paraguayan soil, the options between the defensive and the offensive roles were not yet completely closed to López. The battle of Estero Bellaco had fully demonstrated this, and three weeks later the issue arose again, in a confrontation between Díaz and Flores.

A further recruiting drive had brought the Paraguayan army up to 25,000 men. It was entrenched behind the northern stream of the Bellaco – protected by the lagoons and marshes. The vanguard which, since the battle of 2 May had been stationed on the southern Bellaco about four miles from the main body, were given orders not to dispute the passes of the Bellaco. When, therefore, on 20 May, the Allied army, its vanguard under Flores, crossed the Bellaco, the Paraguayan vanguard under Díaz retreated in good order to their prepared positions.

The Allied force, numbering some 45,000 men, with 150 guns, was disposed along a front of about three miles, with Flores' vanguard in the centre, the Brazilian army under General Osório on the left, and the Argentine units on the right. An important feature of the Brazilian position was a deep ditch, dug on Osório's orders, by Emilio Mallet's men, in front of the regiment's 28 Whitworth and La Hitte guns.[8] The freshly dug earth of this ditch (later called the *fôsso de Mallet*) was carefully scattered, so that the trench became a kind of sunken road.

Thompson's detailed description of the Paraguayan dispositions, with the Bellaco in front of them more than six feet deep at this point, and their flanks protected by dense forests or marshes, make it clear that it was a very strong position indeed. It was further strengthened by trenches guarding the few passes across the streams and swamps.

The original plan was to allow the Allies to waste themselves in an attack in which they would inevitably have suffered tremendous losses, and then to throw 10,000 men at their rear, by way of a rough road already secretly cut through the jungle on their right flank. Thompson believed that if this plan had been adhered to 'the whole of the Allied army might have been cut up'. On 23 May, however, López changed his mind, and decided to launch a surprise attack which would, he hoped, drive the Allies back to the Paraná.

The battle of First Tuyutí as it is called (after a small area situated on slightly higher ground) was one of the most bloody battles in South American history. On the eve of the battle, López went round among his various units, addressing the men, who were, Thompson reported 'in great spirits, and said they only wanted the order to go, and that they would finish up the Allies wherever he sent them'.

López spent most of the night briefing his commanders. The plan itself was well-conceived. General Barrios was to attack the enemy's left, with 8,000 infantry and 1,000 cavalry; General Resquín, with 7,000 cavalry and 2,000 infantry, the enemy's right; Colonel Díaz was to take the centre, with 5,000 infantry and four howitzers. These attacks were to be simultaneous. Resquín and Díaz were to wait until Barrios and his men had passed through the rough road through the jungle. The signal for the concerted attack was to be the firing of a Congrève rocket. Díaz was to get his force as close as he could to the enemy without being discovered, and at the signal to rush their centre. The cavalry of Barrios and Resquín were then to sweep round the Allies and link up behind them.

Barrios, however, took longer than expected to get his army through the jungle, so that the rocket signalling the beginning of the battle was not fired until nearly noon of 24 May, several hours later than planned; and as luck would have it, General Mitre had chosen that day for a reconnaisance in force of the Paraguayan positions, so that his soldiers were all under arms by the time the Paraguayans struck. In addition, it must be remembered that on this occasion it was the Allies who had the prepared positions, the advantage of being able to make use of their artillery, and a superiority in numbers of two to one. By now, too, Thompson said the Allied soldiers were probably without exception equipped with modern firearms, while nearly all the Paraguayans had flint-lock muskets.

The battle lasted four hours, and was so hotly contested that Thompson declared that the sounds of firing were continuous throughout the whole period. In the centre, Díaz and his men, though they had followed their orders to get as close as possible to Flores and the Allied vanguard, still had to cross a deep morass under the fire of Flores' guns, before they could come to close quarters. Thompson said that this morass was soon 'literally filled with dead'. Nevertheless, the Paraguayans launched a furious assault, and came close to breaking the Allied lines. On the left flank of the Allies, the battle swayed backwards and forwards, with Barrios and his infantry driving the Brazilians down to the Bellaco, to be driven back into the woods, there to re-group and charge again; while the Paraguayan cavalry and the Brazilian artillery alike 'made great havoc'.

The *fôsso de Mallet* proved an impassable obstacle to the infantry of both Barrios and Díaz. Barroso relates that Mallet's guns, protected by the ditch in front of them, fired shrapnel with fuses cut to six seconds at such speed that the Brazilians nick-named them *artilharia revólver* (repeating cannon). The Brazilian 3rd Division, commanded by General Antônio Sampaio, which was supporting Mallet, fought off seemingly endless charges by the close-packed, red-shirted infantrymen of Díaz and Barrios. It alone had 1,033 casualties, and General Sampaio himself was mortally wounded.

Meanwhile, General Resquín's cavalry force of 7,000 men on the left (directed, that is, against the right flank of the Allies) carried all before them at their first assault, putting to flight the Corrientino cavalry. They then charged right up to the enemy guns, losing half their numbers on the way. They had taken twenty enemy guns and were turning them round to take away, when reserves of Argentine troops came into action, and cut down the Paraguayans.

Resquín's supporting infantry, too, were almost totally destroyed. But he now sent his cavalry reserves round the enemy's right, in order to link up with the cavalry of Barrios, and thus implement the encircling movement that had been planned. The Argentines, however, were able to form a front against him. The remnants of one Paraguayan cavalry regiment, under Major Olabarrieta, did succeed in breaking through; and after fighting every inch of the way and losing many more men, twenty of them reached the agreed rendezvous – only to find that there was no one to meet them, for by now Barrios had been completely routed. They had to turn and fight their way back through the enemy; when Olabarrieta reached the Paraguayan lines, badly wounded, he had only two or three men with him.

There was so much smoke over the battlefield, and the difficulties of communication in this kind of terrain were so great, that it was not until the next day that either side could properly assess their casualties. Only then was the extent of the carnage realized. The Allies had been victorious, but Thompson calculated that they had lost over 8,000 killed and wounded. But the Paraguayan losses, too, were enormous. They left 6,000 dead on the battlefield, 7,000 wounded were taken into the Paraguayan hospitals, and in addition there were many with minor wounds who were not hospitalized at all. Only 350 were taken prisoner, all of them badly wounded. 'This,' Thompson says, 'was because the Paraguayans would never surrender, but when wounded, fought on till they were killed.' Most of the Paraguayan wounded were in the woods, and it took three days for all of them to crawl back to the Paraguayan lines. The Allies buried most of their own dead, but, Thompson says, they 'heaped up the Paraguayan corpses in alternate layers with wood, in piles of from 50 to 100 and burnt them', complaining apparently, that the Paraguayans 'were so lean that they would not burn'. Burton, who visited the scene of the battle over two years later, reported that it still 'smells of death'.

Strangely enough, only one field officer was among the Paraguayan dead, 'an old major' according to Thompson 'so fat he could hardly walk'. But nearly all of the Paraguayan officers who had taken part in the action were wounded.

There were many acts of heroism on both sides. Hutchinson paid tribute to General Mitre's bravery in the battle; he was constantly under fire – and one of his officers, Captain Fitzsimmons, an Englishman serving in the Argentine army, was shot in the shoulder while standing next to him. Most of the Allied soldiers had acquitted themselves well – including the Brazilians whose fighting qualities, once they were thoroughly committed to an action, have so often been under-estimated by Spanish Americans. The Paraguayans, it almost goes without saying, fought with their usual dogged bravery. Allied sources claimed that López had made his men drunk before sending them into action by giving them a mixture of spirits and gunpowder. Thompson, however, refuted this rumour, and declared that, 'on the contrary, the Paraguayans, through bad management, had to fight on an empty stomach; as, on days when an engagement was expected, the men were not allowed to go and kill the beef.'

Among the many individual acts of Paraguayan heroism was that (reported in an Argentine newspaper) of a sergeant, mortally wounded and unable to use his hands, who tore the flag he was carrying to shreds with his teeth in his last moments,[9] in order to prevent its capture by Allied troops who were searching the battlefield. The Brazilian General Osório sent this flag as a present to Admiral Tamandaré – perhaps to remind him that it was about time the fleet was in action again.

But acts of heroism alone could bring little comfort to Marshal-President López. On the evening after the battle he ordered the military bands to play all night in order to convince his men that they had gained the day, and the battle was announced in the *Seminario* as a great Paraguayan victory. The truth, as Thompson wrote, was that the Paraguayans 'had been completely defeated, and their army destroyed.'

According to Masterman:

'That battle of Tuyutí . . . may be said to have annihilated the Spanish race in Paraguay. In the front ranks were the males of all the best families in the country, and they were killed almost to a man; hundreds of families, in the capital especially, had not a husband, father, son, or brother left.'

As for the Allies:

'. . . they seemed to have accepted this victory with trembling gratitude; they made no attempt to follow up their success, only too thankful that they had not been swept into the Paraná . . .'.

And, incredible though it may seem, the victory had not been decisive. It had done no more than establish the Allies firmly on Paraguayan territory, but they were so exhausted after it that, still fearful of the Paraguayan system of fortifications centred on Humaitá that lay before them, they took over three months to recover. For one thing, sickness, largely brought on by exhaustion, swept through the Allied camp. Commander Kennedy reported that:

'The new, and very young recruits, which, by the great efforts of the Brazilian government, were being continually raised and hurried off to the front, died almost as soon as they joined their regiments. . . . This fatal epidemic affected the animals also to such a degree that the cavalry and artillery were nearly unhorsed.'

To make matters worse, while many of the Allied soldiers were still weakened by sickness, a sudden rise in the river turned the rivulets of the Bellaco into swollen torrents, which overflowed large segments of the Allied positions, drowning many men, and sweeping away large numbers of horses and cattle. Most contemporary accounts are agreed that as a result of all these disasters, following the heavy losses at the battle of First Tuyutí, the Allied forces were reduced to 30,000 men. No wonder that Thompson said that at this time the Allies' 'ardour for the war was spent', and that 'peace was talked of and wished for in their army'.

Nevertheless, it is difficult to understand the hesitation of the Allies after the battle of Tuyutí. Such was the Paraguayan disarray that they could almost certainly have marched round the left of the Paraguayans with hardly any losses, as by doing so they would have avoided their artillery – and so might have taken Humaitá and the river batteries from the rear. Particularly difficult to comprehend is the timidity of the Allied fleet. On 20 May a squadron of sixteen gunboats and corvettes, attended by four ironclads, had at last entered the river Paraguay but made no attempt to advance. Its inactivity, Kennedy said, caused 'the greatest impatience', even in Rio de Janeiro.

In the breathing-space thus afforded him, López managed somehow to get together an army again. The losses at Tuyutí had been so heavy that several battalions and regiments had to be amalgamated, and the whole army in consequence reorganized. According to Thompson, he collected most of the male slaves still remaining in the country, numbering about 6,000, and distributed them among the various units. He must have been most reluctant to take this step in view of the fact that one of his most telling propaganda points against Brazil was that it made large-scale use of slaves in its armies, whereas Paraguay had long since emancipated its slaves. This was indeed substantially true, but as the original decree of abolition passed by Carlos Antonio López in 1842 liberated only those slaves born after that date, the females at twenty-four and the males at twenty-five, there were still some who had not yet been liberated (between 40,000 and 50,000 according to G. Z. Gould, the official from the British Embassy in Buenos Aires who was in Paraguay later in this year).[10] The slaves drafted into the army, however, were immediately emancipated – as was now happening also in the Brazilian army.

Thompson tells how two hundred Payaguá Indians (a small tribe, many of them living in shanties on the beach at Asunción) who had volunteered to serve, were drafted into the heavy artillery; the Payaguás (a few still survive) were noted for their extreme taciturnity and aloofness; they were racially quite distinct from the Guaraníes and spoke an entirely different language, but in the army they earned a reputation for their honesty and truthfulness. The Allies, incidentally, also recruited 200 Indians – members of the Guaycurú tribe, from the Chaco – but they proved most unreliable allies.

By the end of June, López had succeded in bringing up his army to 20,000 – though, according to Thompson, 'half of them were boys and old men and soldiers recovered from their wounds'.

While he had been building up this army, he had concealed the true state of his forces from the enemy by keeping as many men as possible in his advanced guards, pushing them up close to the Allied lines, and harassing them by continuous attacks on their outposts, sniping at any Allied soldier in sight, especially the officers, and kidnapping the sentries; while roving bands of cavalry conducted lightning raids through the palm forests on the enemy's right, usually returning with prisoners, cattle, horses and other booty.

Harassments of another sort were carried out on the river, in order further to discourage the Allied fleet. Stakes were driven into some of the channels and three small ships were sunk in the channel between the island of Curuzú and the Chaco, though the water was so deep at this point that they would not have proved a serious obstacle. River mines were also laid – and the torpedoes which the American engineer Krüger had devised were brought into use. Both fakes and authentic ones were launched. The construction was still faulty, and the torpedoes did little actual damage, but their presence increased the nervousness of the Allied fleet, and when fire-rafts were also sent among them, they were more reluctant than ever to probe the Paraguayan defences. Unfortunately, both Krüger and his Paraguayan assistant were blown up in an accidental explosion of one of these torpedoes. Another of Krüger's assistants, a Polish refugee named Mischkovsky, who had settled in Paraguay and married a cousin of the President, carried on Krüger's work, taking the torpedoes down river by canoe, and propelling them in the direction of the Allied ships. On several occasions, indeed, the Paraguayans swam with them under cover of darkness and attached them to the rudders.

Mischkovsky was later arrested on suspicion of wanting to desert (one of his Paraguayan assistants had already done so), deprived of his captain's rank and sent to the front as a private, to be soon afterwards killed in action. But, to anticipate events somewhat, the project eventually justified itself in a more material way, for on 2 September, the Brazilian ironclad *Rio de Janeiro*, while bombarding the new Paraguayan river defences, struck one of the floating torpedoes, blew up, and sank with all hands. Thereafter, the Paraguayans were even more lavish in their use of the torpedoes, and Admiral Tamandaré ever more cautious in the handling of his fleet.

At the same time, the work of strengthening the area below Humaitá was conducted at a feverish pace. A fortified line was constructed, the right flank resting on a stretch of cliffs lining a bend of the river Paraguay known as Curupaíty (or tree plantation). Here Thompson made a sunken battery, along the whole length of the cliff, to be manned by both artillery and infantry. He also constructed a small gabion battery, armed with an 8-inch gun and two 32-pounders, at the southern end of the cliff, with fourteen small field-pieces placed in reserve at a point known as Curuzú (meaning a cross) by the island of the same name. Trenches, too, were frantically dug. The one in the centre was soon bristling with guns, brought from Asunción and Humaitá, and mounted at the parapets. Thompson wrote:

'In this short line of trench, being on the highroad, thirty-seven pieces of artillery were crowded, of every imaginable shape and size. All sorts of old honey-combed carronades, 18-pounders and 24-pounders – everything which by a stretch of courtesy could be called a gun – were made to do good service by the Paraguayans'.

Following the enemy's example, the Paraguayans also erected watch-towers from 50 to 60 feet high all along the lines (balloons had not yet made their appearance) in order to observe the movements of the enemy. Telegraphs were laid from López's new headquarters at Paso Pucu to all sections of his army, and kept working all day; López insisted on every detail being reported to him, and an officer was specially appointed to carry the messages to him. There were not enough of the morse-code writing instruments available for this complex system, but Thompson reported that 'an instrument was devised which was merely a knocker, the messages being received by listening to the succession of knocks, representing the dashes and dots of the morse hieroglyph', and apparently the Paraguayan clerks were 'very clever at this.'

By the end of the first week of July, incredible though it may seem, López was seeking to provoke the Allies to a general attack, convinced that if he could set them on the move again, he could inflict a heavy defeat on them, perhaps even exterminate them, and so be in a position to take up the offensive again himself – and this in spite of the fact that Manoel Marquez de Souza, Barão de Pôrto Alegre (one of Brazil's most famous commanders) had recently arrived at the Allied camp with 14,000 fresh troops and 50 guns and numerous excellent horses.

López, therefore, sent out several attacking parties, which would strike quickly, then appear to beat a hasty retreat in the hope of luring the Allies to follow. When this failed to produce the desired result, he decided to attack in greater force. On 11 July, he directed five battalions of troops, taking with them two rocket-stands and two regiments of cavalry in reserve, against the Argentine troops stationed on the northern side of one of the passes over the *esteros*. This time, the Allies were prepared for the attack, and a considerable clash took place, known as the battle of Yataity Corá. The Paraguayans found themselves opposed by five battalions of Allied troops under Colonel (later General) Rivas, who were soon obliged to bring up reserves. The Congrève rockets of the Paraguayans (which, according to Thompson 'did much execution') set fire to the long grass, however, and both sides had to withdraw. But as soon as the fire was extinguished, the action was joined again. Rivas had to bring in five more battalions, and General Mitre himself led two further battalions into action.

After a good deal more firing and a considerable artillery barrage from both sides, the action was broken off. This time both the Allies and the Paraguayans were justified in following their usual practice of claiming victory. The Argentines had been tempted into committing a larger proportion of their forces, and had suffered 500 casualties, including three field-officers, in the process. But López had not succeeded in getting the whole Allied army on the move, and he had lost 400 killed and wounded, which he could ill afford. The Paraguayans had retired, but this was according to plan and neither side really could be said to have won the day. Honours were just about even.

López now struck on another plan to force the Allies to launch a general attack. He sent a party of men under Thompson to reconnoitre the possibilities of digging a trench from a point near Potrero Sauce to the jungle of Potrero Pirís, in order to threaten the left flank and the rear of the enemy positions. The woods between Sauce and Pirís had not been occupied by either army, and as Thompson and his men made their way through them, making as little noise as possible, they came upon grim reminders of the battle of First Tuyutí. The unburied bodies, Thompson wrote, 'were not decomposed, but completely mummified, the skin having dried on the bones, and the bodies looking tawny and thin'. The ground all around was littered with bullets, cannon-balls, swords, lances, cartouche-boxes and other debris of battle, and some of the trees, Thompson noticed, were riddled with holes from rifle-fire.

They went through the woods, (passing a Brazilian mounted scout on the way, who did not, however, see them) until they were only 500 yards from the Brazilian trenches. The party then returned safely and Thompson reported to López that the trench was practicable. Seven hundred spades, shovels and picks were collected, and that same night the party returned, together with two battalions of sappers (who had already made the earthworks of the railway, and the large trench before Humaitá.)

Thompson marked out the line of the trench by a lantern placed at the far end, shaded from the view of the enemy by a hide, the sappers then dressing in line to it. They then laid down their muskets, and began digging a trench a yard wide and about the same in depth, throwing the earth forward in order to provide protection as quickly as possible. They were under strict orders to make as little noise as they could. While they worked, a hundred riflemen were posted in skirmishing order to give them cover if it were needed, lying flat on their stomachs. In some places, Thompson relates, 'they were so mixed up with the corpses, that it was impossible to tell which was which in the dark'. The Paraguayans were so close to the Brazilians that they could hear their sentries' challenges, and even the laughing and coughing in their camp. In spite of all the precautions, one of the spades or picks would occasionally strike a stone, but the enemy heard nothing.

Suddenly there was a tremendous explosion; the earth shook –

and the whole sky lit up. One of the biggest of the Paraguayan torpedoes, containing 1,500 pounds of powder, had gone off in the river; its reverberations were felt in Corrientes, some forty miles away, causing a panic among the inhabitants. By some miracle, the Brazilians still did not see the Paraguayan sappers, picked out in the vivid flash of light. When daybreak came, the trench, in two segments, had been completed.

The enemy artillery was then directed against it, but it was not until the morning of 16 July, that their troops went into action. The Paraguayans retreated from the smaller segment of the trench into the woods behind, from where they directed a galling musket fire which lasted, Thompson wrote, for nearly sixteen hours, in the course of which the Brazilians lost no less than 2,000 men killed and wounded, including seven field-officers. The artillery continued to fire all that night and all the next day. On the next morning, the Allies started another heavy bombardment, during which two Paraguayan powder-waggons were blown up, and followed up with an advance of their infantry. The Paraguayans retired in good order, taking their guns with them. As the Allied columns advanced, General Bruguez (whose prowess as an artillery commander the Brazilians in particular had good reason to remember) opened a devastating fire which caused them, so Thompson wrote, immense losses.

General Flores attacked another part of the trench, came close to it, and was driven back by a terrible enfilade fire from the Paraguayan artillery. Colonel Aquino, who commanded the Paraguayans in this sector, followed up the retreating enemy, riding ahead of his infantry with great daring, and attacking their rear alone. He was, however, badly wounded and the Paraguayans gave up the pursuit. Aquino was taken back to headquarters, where López promoted him to General. Two days later he died of his wounds.

General Flores, checking the flight of his troops, immediately ordered another assault. Half the Paraguayan guns were now dismounted because of the rapid firing; and though the remaining guns and the musketry caused such havoc among Flores' columns that the trench was soon filled with their dead, they succeeded in taking it, killing nearly all of the Paraguayan defenders and planting the Argentine standard on the parapet. As they were doing so, reinforcements were coming through the woods for the Paraguayans. Seeing the Argentine flag, the 200 cavalry-men in front dismounted, drew their swords, and charging on to the trench on foot, drove the enemy back out and recaptured the guns. As the Paraguayan infantry came hurrying up through the woods, the enemy retreated.

This was the end of the battle of Sauce. The Paraguayans had lost 2,500 killed and wounded. Colonel Aquino was the only senior officer lost. Lieutenant-Colonel Ximénez, whom Thompson considered one of the bravest of the Paraguayan commanders, was shot through the foot but continued fighting until the battle was over. Colonel Roa, a commander of artillery, was cut off alone and surrounded. In defending himself, his sword broke in two, but he refused to surrender. Two of the enemy officers rushed forward to overpower him, but (according to Thompson's narrative) 'he threw a handful of dust in their eyes and blinded them. He escaped from the very midst of them back to his people, without a scratch.'

As for the Allies, they had over 5,000 casualties, including a number of senior officers, the Brazilian General Victorino among them. It was they, moreover, who had broken off the action. Their plans had been disrupted, and they were filled with renewed respect for the fighting qualities of the Paraguayans. This time Marshal-President López was fully justified in claiming a Paraguayan victory; though it was not, of course, a decisive one.

Recriminations now broke out in the Allied camp between the commanders of the army, who reproached the navy for not advancing up the river to take Curupaíty, and Admiral Tamandaré who, in his turn, reproached his critics for not attacking Curupaíty by land. Barroso states that there were also disagreements – the first of many – between Tamandaré and Pôrto Alegre as to who had the seniority of command.[11] It was, at any rate realized that the Paraguayan right flank at Curupáity was a weak point, and that this should be the next major Allied objective.

But López realized it too, and was given ample time to remedy the defects. On 16 July, the Allied fleet had steamed up to within sight of Curupaíty, then turned round and steamed back again, without a shot being fired on either side – though this excursion was hailed in the Allied press as a great victory. The Allies took no further action of any note, and López brought in more guns to Curupaíty, strengthened the fortifications there and at Curuzú, and dug fresh trenches. He also recalled his 10th Battalion of 700 troops from Corumbá in Mato Grosso, where they had been on

DON FRANCISCO S. LOPEZ
Général de Division et Président
de la République du Paraguay.

1 Francisco Solano López

2 Elisa Lynch

3 Landing of Brazilian and Argentinian troops in Corrientes, 25 May 1865, when the Allies launched their first major offensive

4 Argentinian troops outside their quarters in Paraguay in 1866, after the Allies had crossed into Paraguay

5 The battle of Tuyutí, 1866, one of the fiercest battles in the war. A contemporary observer believed that it "may be said to have annihilated the Spanish race in Paraguay" (p. 153)

6 An Argentinian artist's impression of Paraguayan prisoners after the battle of Tuyutí. In reality there were few prisoners taken, for most Paraguayan soldiers preferred to fight to the death rather than surrender (p. 152)

7 General Mitre (right) at his headquarters at Tuyutí

8. The conference at Yataity Corá between López and Bartolomé Mitre (pp. 164–7), when they failed to reach any peace settlement

9 The Allied attack on Curupaíty, September 1866. In their over-whelming defeat of the Allies, the Paraguayans had fought in almost festive mood, and it seemed as though Paraguay might still win the war (pp. 168–71)

10 Curupaíty: Sarmiento's son and Lieutenant Paz are carried dead from the battlefield (p. 170)

garrison duty, replacing them by other troops. All the inhabitants of the town were also brought down by steamer, to endure a miserable existence in Asunción. These were not the only civilians to suffer in this way: when the Allies had landed at Paso de la Patria López had initiated his 'scorched earth' policy, expelling the local inhabitants to Misiones or areas north of the Arroyo Hondo, where many of them died of starvation.

It was not until the beginning of September that the Allies began to implement their plans against Curupaíty, the capture of which would enable them to take the Paraguayan army in the rear, and probably exterminate it. First, though, they had to dispose of the little fortress of Curuzú, which guarded the approach to Curupaíty. Their fleet began to bombard Curuzú on 1 September. The next day, Pôrto Alegre's corps of 14,000 men embarked at Itapirú, landed at a place called Palmas, under the protection of seven gunboats, marched along the river bank, and encamped opposite Curuzú. A terrific cannonade, meanwhile, was being exchanged between the Allied fleet and the Paraguayan batteries. It was in this action that the ironclad *Rio de Janeiro* was struck and sunk by a torpedo – after she had already had her four-inch plates twice pierced. Another ship, the *Ivahy*, had her boilers shot through, and all of the attacking ships were repeatedly hit by the one 8-inch gun and the two 32-pounders which formed the battery of Curuzú.

On 3 September, after a further bombardment from the fleet, Pôrto Alegre ordered a general assault on the Paraguayan positions. He and his men, with great gallantry, marched through the enfilade fire from the trench which the Paraguayans had dug at Curuzú, in order to turn its left flank, which involved wading through four feet of water. They lost 2,000 men in the process, but the Paraguayan 10th Battalion, which López had brought from Corumbá and which had never been in action before, took to flight (with the exception of their commander, who was killed). The rest of the defenders engaged in hand-to-hand fighting; eye-witnesses described how a Brazilian and a Paraguayan charged each other so fiercely that they were transfixed by each other's bayonets. But the Paraguayans were driven out, leaving 700 dead behind them, though they succeeded in carrying away their 1,800 wounded. One of them, a Captain Montiel, was left for dead. He recovered consciousness some hours later, to find himself in the rear of the enemy who, having secured Curuzú, were pursuing the retreating

Paraguayans in the direction of Curupaíty. Badly wounded, Montiel managed to crawl back to his regiment through the enemy lines.

It was the kind of conduct that López expected of a Paraguayan. That of the 10th Battalion was not; they had fled in the face of the enemy, almost certainly the only time during the war that such a thing had happened in the Paraguayan army. Accordingly, the survivors were lined up, and every tenth man was shot. The officers drew lots; those who drew the longest pieces of grass were also shot; the rest were reduced to the ranks. The battalion was then disbanded and its surviving members divided among the other corps of the division.

It was, of course, an exceedingly harsh measure – but not, by any means, the only example of its kind in similar circumstances, when it has been considered that national survival was dependent on the maintenance of discipline and morale. López has too often been judged on such matters by standards appropriate only to times of peace, and by those who apparently forget that in wars of this kind most of the normal moral values of civilized humanity no longer apply. Perhaps this is true of all wars; there is a certain type of war, of which the Paraguayan War over a hundred years ago and, indeed, others in our own times are outstanding examples, which tend to make pacifists of us all.

It would certainly be difficult to overestimate the seriousness of the crisis that confronted the Paraguayans with the fall of Curuzú. Had Pôrto Alegre, instead of withdrawing his army after a short pursuit of the retreating garrison, advanced immediately, he might very well have taken Curupaíty (whose defences were still incomplete) at once, in the same forward rush, thus taking López in the rear. And if Mitre and Flores had then attacked in front, the Allies would, to quote Thompson, 'almost inevitably have taken the whole of the Paraguayan positions that day, and destroyed their army'.

The Paraguayans made good use of Pôrto Alegre's hesitation. They worked frantically on the defences of Curupaíty and its approaches, and in particular on a 2,000 yard long trench round the battery, recommended to López by Thompson. Even so, the situation was alarming. It was doubtful if there would be time to finish the trench or the other defences before the enemy attacked again; and after the news reached him that several Argentine divisions were embarking at Itapirú to join Pôrto Alegre, López confessed to Thompson, 'things could not look more diabolical than they do.' Thompson was convinced that López was 'quite persuaded that the Allies were about to give him the coup de grâce'.

It was at this juncture that, under a flag of truce, López sent a letter to Bartolomé Mitre, as Commander in Chief of the Allied forces, proposing a conference to discuss the possibilities of peace negotiations.

Some sources consider that this was only a ruse, in order to gain time for the defences of Curupaíty to be completed. Burton, for one, spoke of it as a 'notable expedient' and a 'trap'. Thompson, too, was doubtful as to López's real motives. Most other commentators, including Cunninghame-Graham, tend to treat the approach as genuine.

In many respects it was a most propitious moment for it. The Paraguayans, it is true, were in a very serious position, but they had demonstrated more than once that they could fight superior forces to a standstill. It was about this time that the full terms of the Treaty of the Triple Alliance had been made public, and the indignant protest of the west coast republics, sponsored by Peru, addressed to the Allied governments. There was also the possibility of intervention by the European powers. In addition, there was mounting evidence that the war was becoming unpopular in the Allied countries. Hutchinson, for example, wrote of 'public anxiety' and declared:

'In Rio de Janeiro, in Montevideo, in Buenos Aires – amongst the army, as well as the commercial circles, and all classes of residents in the River Plate countries, a general desire for the conclusion of the war was felt. It was seen that a year and a half had gone by since the first passage of arms – with little progress made, save in the shedding of human blood, and the enormous outlay of money.'

This feeling was particularly strong in Argentina. In Buenos Aires, the only newspapers still in favour of a continuation of the war were *La Nación Argentina*, and *La Tribuna*. In favour of a negotiated peace were *El Nacional, El Pueblo, El Correo Mercantil, La Palabra de Mayo* – and *La América*. The last-named paper openly defended López, attacked Mitre as incompetent, and even reproduced articles from the official Paraguayan weekly, *El Seminario*. And in the Argentine provinces it was rumoured that the cry 'No queremos la guerra con López' ('we don't want war with López') was being raised with ominous frequency. López himself, of course, was aware of most of these circumstances.

Mitre, at any rate, agreed to López's suggestion, and the conference was arranged to take place at Yataíty Corá, on 12 September. The Marshal-President dressed carefully for the occasion. He put on a new képi and a new uniform frock-coat, and over it his favourite poncho, which was made of scarlet cloth lined with vicuña, with a fringe of gold round the border and a magnificently embroidered gold collar. He wore, too, his 'Napoleonic' grenadier boots with long spurs, and white gloves.

He set out, in a four-wheeled carriage, then changed over half way to his white horse. He had difficulty these days in mounting it. He had become almost as fat as his father, the pear-shaped Carlos Antonio, and his legs had become more bandy. He was in ill health at the time, and though barely forty looked many years older; his hair was thinning on top, and his teeth had grown black from decay and the almost continuous smoking of cigars. The strain of the last months was clearly visible.

He was accompanied by General Barrios, his brothers Venancio (sometimes spelt Benancio) and Benigno, and a large staff. He took a roundabout route, in order to conceal from the Allies the new roads which the Paraguayans had been making in the area. As a precaution against any attempt by the Allies to detain him, he had a rifle battalion hidden near the pass which led from the Paraguayan lines into Yataíty Corá. He also took with him an escort of his cavalry guard.

The Allied Commander in Chief appeared with his staff and an escort of lancers. Bartolomé Mitre was notorious (despite his lectures to General Flores on the subject of his personal appearance) for his eccentricities of dress. Thompson described him as 'dressed in a frock-coat and white sword-belt, wearing an old breakdown wideawake hat, which gave him quite a Quixotic appearance.'

The escorts halted, and the two Presidents rode forward. They saluted each other, and got off their horses, which were taken away by their orderlies.

The conference began on a sour note, with the arrival of a message from General Polidoro da Fonseca Quintanilha Jordão, acting commander at the time of the Brazilian army (whom Mitre had asked to attend) to the effect that it was impossible for him to come because he had no instructions to do so. General Flores, however, arrived but departed shortly after; it is said that López accused him in very forthright terms of being the real cause of the war, by bringing the Brazilians into Uruguay.

Eventually the two Presidents were left alone. They conferred for five whole hours, alternately walking up and down or sitting at a table which had been provided, with writing materials laid upon it.

No one knows exactly what the two men talked about all that time. All that emerged at the end of it was a memorandum to the effect that the Marshal-President of Paraguay had, to quote Thompson (who wrote by far the best and probably the most accurate account of the conference), 'invited President Mitre to consider whether the blood already spilled in the war was not sufficient to wipe out their mutual grievances', while President Mitre 'had limited his reply to saying that he would place the subject before the Allied Governments, which alone could determine the matter'.

The general drift of the discussion, however, is fairly clear from the publication later of the various relevant documents. One of the most interesting of these is a letter from Mitre to his Vice-President, Marcos Paz, dated 'Head-quarters at Curuzú, 13 September, 1866' – the very day after the conference, that is – which was published in the Buenos Aires papers the following June. It contains the following illuminating statement:

'In the course of our interview General López declared himself ready to treat on all questions, that may have led to the present war, or may affect our tranquillity for the future, so as to satisfy (as he says) the legitimate demands of the Allies, including a definitive arrangement of frontiers, without accepting any imposition, and least of all his retirement from command in the Republic of Paraguay. In this sense he manifested his readiness to arrange on bases, and even make a treaty – which amounting to a negotiation not in harmony with the stipulations and objects of the Triple Alliance, I neither could nor ought to accept same – but confined myself to hearing what he had to say, so as to communicate it to the Allies as is expressed in the attached memorandum.'[12]

And later in his letter Mitre recorded that at the conference he told López that he considered it

'Very difficult, if not impossible, to arrive at any arrangements, unless based on the conditions of the Triple Alliance treaty, since the antecedents of the quarrel induced the allied people to believe that no solid guarantees of future peace could be found outside of such conditions'.

Here, as Hutchinson said, 'we have it on the *ipsissima verba* of the President of the Argentine Republic himself' that López made proposals for peace, which on the face of it did not seem unreasonable, and that Mitre was adamant in sticking to the exact letter of the Triple Alliance – including the insistence on López's abdication and departure from the country. Even Cunninghame-Graham, perhaps the most hostile to López of all his biographers, commented:

'This certainly was a hard condition to impose upon a man who was still at the head of a considerable army, and between whose capital and the forces of the Allies, there lay two formidable fortresses[13] that must be taken before they could advance.'

Cunninghame-Graham claims that López offered Mitre a compromise on this issue, by suggesting that he should retire to Europe for a period of two years. Some of the other contemporary accounts confirm this, though Thompson does not mention it – and we know for certain that the proposal was made in later peace discussions. Cunninghame-Graham's opinion of the rejection of the offer (assuming it to have been made on this occasion) is that it was 'most unwisely rejected by the Allies'.

López, of course, was well aware of the terms of the Triple Alliance, but not unreasonably, he had assumed that they were negotiable. He had not reckoned with either Mitre's complete subservience to Brazil or Brazil's intractable, not to say intransigent, attitude.

The war, in fact, had become a matter of national honour for the Emperor of Brazil and his government. On 9 October 1866, Dom Pedro wrote to the Condessa de Barral:

'Peace is being spoken of in Río de la Plata; but I shall not make peace with López, and public opinion is with me; there is therefore no need for you to be worried over the honourable success of the campaign for Brazil. I fear some possible intervention from Europe, but we shall know how to conduct ourselves with polish and energy.'[14]

The 'public opinion' the Emperor referred to, however, was almost certainly that of the ruling classes alone. It is said, for example, that when Doña Rosa Maria Paulina da Fonseca heard that peace negotiations were taking place, she exclaimed that she would rather have her sons, who were at the front, buried on the battlefields of Paraguay than see her country accept a shameful peace.

In other words, the Brazilian General Polidoro's pointed absence from the Conference of Yataíty Corá had been symptomatic. At the end of it, the two Presidents, related Thompson, 'had some brandy and water together, and exchanged their riding whips in remembrance of the day'. López, Thompson added, 'looked very black' as he rode away.

He might well have done so. It had been made abundantly clear that the Allies were still determined upon a course (as laid out in the Treaty of the Triple Alliance) which involved not only his own disappearance from the scene, but also the satisfaction of the maximum territorial claims of both Brazil and Argentina, the disbanding of the Paraguayan army, the razing to the ground of all Paraguay's frontier and river fortifications, complete freedom of navigation for the Allies on the river Paraguay, and the imposition of an entirely different form of government upon the country.

It was evident, then, that if he himself went into exile it would not mean a return to the pre-war *status quo* for his country. Kolinsky is no doubt right in saying that López argued to himself that:

> 'Paraguay in 1866 was López, and Francisco Solano López was Paraguay. . . . So long as he lived, Paraguay would live; the war waged by the Paraguay of Francisco Solano López against its enemies thus became one of "Independencia o Muerte".'

It may be true that there were many respects in which López was a tyrant, and that he became a worse one as the war progressed. But in a sense this issue had become almost irrelevant, for the Allies by their own actions had turned him into a patriot.

After the failure of the conference at Yataíty Corá, the Paraguayans threw themselves into the task of preparing the defences of Curupaíty with redoubled energy. Working day and night under Thompson's direction, the Paraguayans (with the women helping in the digging) constructed a trench 2,000 yards long, six feet deep, and eleven wide. All the nearby trees were felled to provide protection for the gun positions, and, along the front of the trench, were sharpened stakes and branches, pointing outwards – a fore-runner of barbed-wire entanglements. The great trench stretched from the river on the right to the lake on the left – great care being taken to make it impossible for the enemy to march round this end through the water, as they had done at Curuzú.

Forty-nine guns were placed in position, thirteen in the river-battery, the rest in the trench – where 'Flores's guns' had pride of place, being, Thompson says, the only rifled artillery the Para-guayans possessed. These guns were arranged in order to give the most effective enfilading fire possible. Eight 8-inch 68-pounder guns were to play exclusively on the land front and four exclusively on the river. These could fire charges of grapeshot capable of decimating an entire platoon with a single round. In the trench were also placed the two rocket-stands, and 5,000 infantry. Díaz, now a full general, was put in over-all command. On the evening of 21 September, López sent Thompson to inspect the defences. He reported that the work was all finished, and that in his view the position was now a very strong one indeed.

The Allies had sent two Argentine regiments from Itapirú to Curuzú, in readiness for the attack on Curupaíty on 12 September – on the same evening of the day on which the conference of Yataíty Corá had taken place. After a meeting of the Allied high command, attended once again by much bitter controversy, it was agreed that General Mitre should direct the attack on Curupaíty, which was not expected to present much difficulty.

It began on 22 September, with a bombardment by the Allied fleet – now containing no less than eight ironclads. It did little harm, owing to the height of the cliff. The Paraguayan battery, on the other hand, caused considerable damage. A number of the plates of the ironclads were broken and many of their bolts shot off, while the timber backing to many of the plates was badly shattered. Two 68-pounders on the *Barroso* were dismounted by Paraguayan fire, and many balls entered the portholes of the attacking ships. The ironclad *Brasil* was so badly damaged that she had to be sent back to Rio de Janeiro for repairs. There were many casualties, one ironclad alone losing twenty-seven men.

This bombardment, however, was only a preliminary to the main land assault. At twelve noon 11,000 Brazilians and 7,000 Argentines moved forward, so confident of the result that, as well as fascines made of rushes and canes for filling the trench and fifteen foot scaling ladders, they also carried their saucepans and other cooking-utensils, with the intention of having their supper at Humaitá. They advanced in four columns; one against the Paraguayan left, two against the centre, and the fourth towards the right, along the bank of the river.

Firing at close quarters, the Paraguayan artillery wrought the most terrible destruction. The column attacking the right had a good firm road, but was subjected to an enfilading fire the whole way along it and then, when close to the trench, they came under the fire of the guns massed there, and in particular the huge canisters of the 8-inch guns. Only a few succeeded in reaching the trench.

In the centre, some of the Argentine officers, riding with great bravery through what was quite literally a hail of lead, reached the edge of the trench, urging on their men, a handful of whom managed to join them; but they were nearly all killed. On the left, the whole column was mowed down before they came anywhere near the trench. The Allies kept up a steady rifle-fire as they advanced, but killed only a few of the gunners, as the Paraguayan infantry were kept well down behind the parapet of the trench until, Thompson reported, 'the Allies came within range of their poor old flint muskets, when they got up and opened fire'.

General Mitre, standing on the parapet of the former Paraguayan trench at Curuzú to direct the attack, was appalled by the dreadful carnage, and ordered a retreat. His troops retired in good order. Legend has it that the crack Argentine 6th Infantry battalion marched backward from the trench in order not to show their backs to the enemy.[15]

But nothing could alter the fact that the Allies had suffered an overwhelming defeat. Estimates of Allied casualties differ, but all are agreed that they were very heavy. Thompson, who was, after all, an eye-witness, confidently asserted that more than 5,000 were left on the field of battle or in Paraguayan hands, and that a further 1,000, together with 104 field officers, were admitted to the Allied military hospital at Corrientes alone. He put the total figure at a good 9,000 killed and wounded, and in addition there were the casualties on the Allied battleships. By contrast, all sources are agreed that Paraguayan losses were remarkably light – 'incredibly small', according to Thompson, who put the figure as low as 54 killed and wounded.

A considerable amount of equipment was also abandoned, including more than 3,000 new model Liège Enfields – a very welcome addition to the Paraguayan armoury – and a large number of gold sovereigns, as the Allied troops had just received their pay. The bodies of the dead were stripped of clothing, which was becoming increasingly scarce in Paraguay, and Thompson noted later that several battalions were dressed in Argentine or Brazilian uniforms, with Paraguayan insignia added. It is said that the wounded who could not walk were shot.

The Paraguayans had again fought in almost festive mood. General Díaz was on horseback throughout and in high spirits, ordering music and reveilles to be played.

He was, indeed, the hero of the hour, and that night he was entertained by his Marshal-President to a champagne supper. Not unnaturally, López himself was, as Thompson put it, 'quite elevated by what he drank, and made a great noise, the only time this happened'. Meanwhile, the Paraguayan troops celebrated their great victory with a dance round the mast of the former Brazilian battleship, the *Yequitinhonha*, relic of the battle of Riachuelo.

In the Allied camp, on the other hand, all was despondency. Masterman had been right in claiming that the flower of the Paraguayan Spanish aristocracy had fallen at the first battle of Tuyutí; the same might be said of the battle of Curupaíty as far as the Argentine aristocracy was concerned. Among the bodies retrieved from the marshes or the lagoon were those of the twenty-one year old only son of Domingo Sarmiento, Argentine Minister to the United States, (and Mitre's eventual successor in the presidency) and young Francisco Paz, son of the Vice-President of Argentina.

The Argentine army itself, moreover, had suffered so badly in the defeat that the survivors were embarked at Curuzú and taken back to Tuyutí, leaving only the Brazilians under Pôrto Alegre, now reduced to about 8,000 sound men (though they had not suffered as heavily as the Argentines) to hold the Allied lines at Curuzú – if they could.

The news of the defeat produced the deepest despondency in the allied countries. There were demonstrations against the war both in Buenos Aires and Rio de Janeiro, accompanied by a clamour for scapegoats. It was the lowest ebb in the Allies' fortunes, and it was to be fourteen months before they were again in a position to attempt a major offensive. For Francisco Solano López it was, perhaps, a tide that might lead on to fortune.

Curupaíty had proved that Paraguay, in spite of all the losses she had suffered, could still fight a defensive war – and still might win it.

NOTES

[1] *Abrindo um Cofre*, Alcindo Sodre. Rio de Janeiro 1956. Quotations from Sodre are taken from this book.

[2] The extracts from this correspondence between López and Mitre are translated by Thompson in *The War in Paraguay*.

[3] According to Thompson. Kolinsky puts the figure at 50,000.

[4] Again there is a discrepancy between this figure of Thompson's and that of Kolinsky who puts the total raiding force at 1,300. On the whole, perhaps Thompson's estimates are to be preferred, as those of an eye-witness and participant.

[5] *Reminescências da campanha do Paraguaï*, Dionísio Cerqueira. Rio de Janeiro n.d. Quotations from Cerqueira are taken from this book.

[6] Bernardo P. Berro was a Blanco leader and former president of Uruguay.

[7] This letter was published in the newspapers of Buenos Aires. The translation is Thompson's. The letter was dated 3rd May – the day after the battle of Estero Bellaco.

[8] *Grandes soldados do Brasil*, José de Lima Figueiredo. Rio de Janeiro 1944. Quotations from de Lima Figueiredo are taken from this book. See also *Guerra do López*, Barroso.

[9] *La Nación Argentina*, 12 June 1866.

[10] Quoted by Masterman.

[11] *História militar do Brasil*, Gustavo Barroso. São Paulo 1938.

[12] Cited by Hutchinson.

[13] Curupaíty and Humaitá.

[14] Quoted by Sodre in *Abrindo um cofre*.

[15] *Humaitá*, Manuel Gálvez. Buenos Aires n.d.

Interlude

If the Paraguayan leader had been able to leave the shelter of his fortifications after the battle of Curupaíty, in fact, he might well have driven the Allies back over the Paraná. But the truth was that with an army now numbering not much more than 20,000 it was impossible, and whether he liked it or not, he was obliged to continue the defensive role. The victory of Curupaíty had, indeed, demonstrated in dramatic fashion how effective this could be as far as Paraguay was concerned. If it had been interpreted even more drastically, it might have been even more effective. Burton was undoubtedly right when he wrote that:

'The great strategical error committed by the Paraguayans was that of the Confederate States – an attempt to fight long extended lines. Instead of holding along the stream of a succession of outposts, which were all lost by direct attack or by evacuation, they should have concentrated themselves at fewer places, and should have rendered them doubly and trebly strong.'

From this point of view, the defensive system which the Paraguayans now set out to perfect, in the long interval before the Allies again ventured a head-on collision, may have been too ambitious, though it was thoroughly thought out and executed.

It consisted of a series of trenches and strong points running along the crests of the few small slopes in the area, and covering all the openings and passes through the swamps of the Bellaco, which in effect sealed in the whole of the Paraguayan army. Owing to its shape on the maps, this system was known among the Allied armies, and by their military historians, as the *quadrilátero*. It hinged upon the fortress of Humaitá, which commanded a sharp horse-shoe bend in the river Paraguay and which was regarded with excessive respect by Allies and Paraguayans alike. The only ways in which the Allies could take the *quadrilátero*, therefore, other than by direct frontal assault – and the risk of another rebuff similar to that of Curupaíty – was either for the fleet to force the passage of the river, or for the land forces to attempt an extensive and dangerous flanking movement to the east, through the difficult and largely unknown Gran Chaco.

Other measures taken by the Paraguayans to strengthen the *quadrilátero* included widening and deepening the great trench at Curupaíty, as well as mounting more guns (brought down from Humaitá) in the battery itself; the cutting of various roads and tracks through the woods to facilitate communications; deepening some of the channels in the marshland by constructing dams; erecting sluice-gates, so that large areas could be flooded at a moment's notice; and building parapets in front of López's beloved telegraph stations. It was at this period that new guns were cast from the metal of church bells.

Paraguayan morale was at its peak and it received a further fillip from the news, first that General Flores had been called back to Montevideo to deal with growing disturbances there, then that Mitre had been obliged to send General Paunero and 4,000 of his troops to quell an insurrection in the Andean provinces of the Argentine Confederation – and later (in February 1867) that Mitre had to go himself to supervise the arrangements for dealing with similar disturbances.

It was significant that a unit in one of the Argentine rebel armies defeated by the Argentine Government troops was called the 'Batallón Urquiza', and that one of the captured flags bore these slogans: 'Federación o muerte. Viva la unión americana. Viva el ilustre Capitán General Urquiza. Abajo los negreros Brasileños!'[1]

All these rebel movements were in fact defeated, and General Urquiza himself did not stir from his own satrapy of Entre Ríos, but naturally such evidence of continuing unrest in the Argentine provinces was bound to encourage López and his army to believe that help from the provinces – and eventually, perhaps, even from the cagey Urquiza himself – might still be forthcoming. As Mitre himself said, in a letter of 24 January 1867, to Vice-President Paz: 'Quién no sabe que los traidores alentaron al Paraguay a declararnos la guerra?' (Who doesn't know that by declaring war upon us the traitors have given new heart to Paraguay?).

López was at pains to maintain strict discipline during this long interim period, and also to bring as much military colour and pomp into camp life as possible. Acts of outstanding heroism were rewarded by promotion, special medals and (in the case of officers) appointment to one of the orders of merit that had been established at the beginning of the war – all attended by impressive ceremonies. Large celebrations, with banquets, dances and other entertainments were held on various feast days, such as Christmas – and above all, on the President's birthday (24 July) and the anniversary of his election to the presidency (16 October).

On these occasions there would be special levées, with the officers in full-dress, a laudatory address from the Bishop to López – and a long reply from López (he was, in Thompson's view, a very good speaker). Afterwards, champagne, beer and other drinks would be served under the orange-trees, and hundreds of toasts would be addressed to the Marshal-President.

On this particular 16 October, 1866, the ladies of Asunción (acting, according to Thompson, on a hint from Elisa Lynch) presented their President with a Paraguayan flag, embroidered in gold, diamonds and rubies, together with an album bound in solid gold and inset with precious stones, in a box also of gold and with an equestrian statue in gold attached to it.

On a later occasion the gifts were even more splendid. López's favourite sword was re-mounted; the hilt was decorated with a design of St George and the dragon, inset with jewels; the new sheath was of solid gold, chased with arabesques, and the whole, Thompson related, was 'encased in another telescopic sheath, also of pure gold, with a golden statue on top, and made so that when the telescopic part was shut up, the part which contained the hilt alone was visible, thus making a beautiful ornament on a table'. The sword of honour was accompanied by a crown of laurel leaves, also of solid gold. These magnificent objects were presented (on a huge silver salver) by a special commission which came down from Asunción for the purpose, and was headed by Don Saturnino Bedoya, the treasurer-general and López's brother-in-law – who, after he and all the other members of the commision had made their speeches, was promptly placed under arrest, under circumstances which will emerge later.

In addition to these diversions which must have provided splendid spectacle for the onlookers (and considerable pleasure to the recipient) several new newspapers, of special interest to the soldiers, were launched – one of them from a printing press at the front. Several of these papers contained articles in Guaraní, and two of them were entirely in Guaraní. One of these, the *Cabichui* (the name of a species of savage wasp) was a special favourite, and was illustrated with woodcuts, cut with penknives from their own drawings by some of the soldiers.

This was despite the fact that paper was now in very short supply. Von Treuenfeldt, however, the founder of López's beloved telegraph system, found a way of making good paper from cotton and other vegetable fibres. The fly-leaves of all the Government archives were also torn out and used for writing. Pieces of cowhide were scraped and treated until their surfaces were white, and were then bound up in volumes, for the keeping of journals and official records. Parchment was made – with great success – from sheepskin, and reserved for the commissions of officers. A way was found of making ink by extracting with ashes the colouring matter of a species of black beans.

Not the least of the Paraguayan activities at this time, in fact, was the search for alternative sources of supply, or substitutes for a number of essential commodities. Every army division, for example, manufactured its own soap by boiling together fat meat and the ashes of a particular species of jungle tree. The shortage of salt (which was growing increasingly serious) was in part met by the use of an extract obtained by boiling the leaves of another species of tree, with very thick leaves, which grew in the Chaco. The sulphur for manufacturing gunpowder was easy enough to obtain from iron-pyrites, which are abundant in Paraguay – and the saltpetre was made from urine and decomposed animal substances.

Every division had its own tannery, but clothing materials other than leather were in desperately short supply. The spinning and weaving of cotton had been revived but, as few women could be spared from agriculture and other occupations to attend to them, they came nowhere near meeting the demand. Hides, therefore, were stretched on large square frames, scraped until they reached the consistency of wash-leather, and then made up into trousers and other garments – though the soldiers complained that when these got wet in the rain, and then dried suddenly in wind or sun, they became stiff and painful to wear, and almost impossible to walk in. At the same time, all the ballrooms, hotels and clubs in Asunción, as well as the waiting rooms at the railway terminus, were stripped of their carpeting, which was cut up into ponchos – but these, too, were so stiff, Thompson declared, 'that they stood out like advertising boards'.

In the Allied Camp, meanwhile, in order to restore some semblance of morale after the recent disaster, a story was being spread that a revolution had broken out in Paraguay. More effective, perhaps, was the news that the demand in Rio de Janeiro that heads should roll had been listened to by the Emperor. Field-Marshal Luíz Alves de Lima e Silva, Marquês de Caxias, the most distinguished Brazilian soldier of the day, arrived to take over command not only of the Brazilian forces, but also (after the temporary departure of General Mitre to crush the Argentine revolts) of the whole Allied army. And in the December, the pompous and dilatory old Admiral Tamandaré handed over command of the naval squadrons to José Joaquim Ignacio – though this change can hardly be said to have noticeably speeded up operations on the river.

As might be expected from the swampy nature of the ground surrounding their camp, there was a good deal of malaria among the Allied soldiers, and one particularly severe bout of malaria was followed, early in 1867, by the arrival of cholera. Within three days, it had spread through the whole army. At Curuzú alone 4,000 men went down with it, and 2,400 of them, including 87 officers, died; fifty men were busy, day and night, digging graves. By the beginning of May, 13,000 Brazilians alone were in hospital, and admissions quickly rose to 280 a day. Fortunately, for the Allies, the Paraguayans were in no position to take advantage of the situation, as the outbreak soon spread to their own lines. Deaths in the army, on Thompson's testimony, averaged fifty a day 'for a long time'. A number of important officers were among the victims, and at one time Generals Resquín and Bruguez as well as Dr Skinner, one of López's English doctors, were ill with it at the same time, but all recovered. López himself, still in bad health, became convinced that he had caught the disease. Thompson reported that he felt keenly 'his utter impotence to contend personally with such a terrible scourge', and became 'almost mad, charging his doctors with an intention to poison him'. The camp was fumigated with burning laurel leaves and grass, and Thompson found that it was hardly possible to breathe at headquarters because of the dense smoke.

It was at this time that López had one of his accesses of religious fervour, which grew increasingly frequent as the war progressed. His former tutor, Father Fidel Maiz, was released from prison, and marked the occasion by writing an article in the *Seminario* in which he compared his former pupil to the Saviour. The *Seminario* itself compared him to the Almighty; and July, the month of the

President's birth, was described as 'the month of Christian López'. When he recovered, however, López 'contented himself', Thompson ironically observed, with being called 'the unconquered Marshal', which was, indeed, accurate enough.

Although the cholera spread through most of the country, killing many thousands of civilians, it gradually subsided in both the Paraguayan and the Allied camps.

The great difference, of course, was that whereas López could not replace his losses, a steady flow of new recruits was reaching Caxias. As the Brazilian commander had comparatively few supply difficulties to contend with, he was gradually able to restore the health of his men. Burton, who visited the Allied camp at a somewhat later date, found the Allied soldiers well fed and clothed – though he was shocked to find, too, that many of them were begging, because most of their pay took the form of rations. He was equally shocked by the large numbers of camp-followers – 4,000 of them, he was told – most of them, 'mounted *en Amazone*, and made conspicuous by mushroom straw hats, with the usual profusion of beads and blossoms.'

By this time, the army base at Paso de la Patria (now called Itapirú by the Allies) had become a sizeable town, with billiard halls, dance halls, a theatre, barber's and other shops, photographic studios – and innumerable brothels. There was even a branch of the Banco Maua.

A bizarre feature of the camp was the vast number of dogs – and when the bulk of the army eventually left to resume its offensive and the dogs' food supply was cut off, their howling became so oppressive that the remaining soldiers were forced to slaughter the starving animals in their thousands.

Ominously for the Paraguayans, it was not only supplies of food, clothing and new recruits that were arriving at the Allied camp, but new weapons and equipment as well. When he was in Corrientes, Burton met 'a Belgian of Scotch descent' named Edouard Peterkin, who had been given the rank of Captain by the Allies and the title of Inspector of Arms, and who was in effect a contractor for supplying Belgian Enfield rifles and Whitworth guns. Most of the Allied troops, in fact, were now armed with Enfields. Even more up-to-date weapons were also arriving; by the end of 1867 several infantry units had been issued with the new German needle rifles, and many of the cavalry units had been issued with Spencer re-peating carbines. The artillery were acquiring not only Whitworths and La Hittes, but also a certain number of Krupp guns. And the older ships in the Allied navy were being replaced by monitor-type ironclads.

Although, however, there were no major battles during this fourteen months' interlude, and Thompson related that 'people in the River Plate . . . lost all interest in the war, and it was almost forgotten', there was almost continuous warlike activity of one kind or another. For one thing, there was no slackening off of the bombardment of Curupaíty; that from the river, indeed, was re-doubled – the only result, Thompson caustically commented, of the change in command from Tamandaré to Ignacio.

The bombardment was so regular an occurrence that General Díaz, the *Vencedor de Curupaíty*, called it, according to Gálvez, the 'fiesta diaria de los Negros' (the daily fiesta of the Negroes). The Allied fleet, according to Thompson, thought nothing of 'throwing 2,000 shells before breakfast'. Occasionally they would be silent by day, only to break out into a furious bombardment after dark when, Thompson declared, 'it was very beautiful to watch the trajectory of the shells by their fuses.' Not that all the projectiles were conventional shells; the Brazilians, Thompson reported, 'put all sorts of things into their guns besides the shot – such as firebars, pieces of chain, etc. and once they sent a piece of 2-inch square iron, two feet long'. Throughout the whole of May 1867, the bombardment was non-stop by both day and night – 'wasting,' Thompson added, 'immense quantities of ammunition'.

The Allied marksmanship was so bad, in fact, that little damage was done; apart from the fact that the health of the Paraguayans suffered from being kept behind the parapets, where huts had been constructed. The Paraguayans were in no position to respond on the same lavish scale, but they made good use of what ammunition they had. In February 1867, the commanders of two of the new ironclads were both killed, and a Paraguayan ball went right through the side of another. A Brazilian gunboat was also set on fire, and most of the other ships in the fleet received some damage.

The land batteries of General Bruguez also harassed the Allies whenever suitable targets presented themselves. Their fire was so accurate that one of Caxias' first actions on assuming command was to prohibit his officers from wearing distinctive uniforms or accoutrements of any kind, because the Paraguayan gunners were picking them off whenever they assembled in groups.

Like the citizens of London during the Second World War blitz, every Paraguayan had his favourite bomb story. One of these concerned a soldier who was trundling a wheel-barrow when a percussion-shell struck his leather morion, blowing it several yards away; he himself was miraculously unhurt, apart from singed hairs and a scorched forehead, and immediately retrieved his battered hat, put it on again – 'with redoubled vigour, to the great delight of his companions, who set up a yell of pleasure', Thompson tells us.

On another occasion, a group of cavalrymen found an unexploded 9-pounder shell without realizing what it was, and used it to prop up their cooking pot. In the heat of the fire, the shell of course exploded, scattering the contents of the pot in all directions – to the joy of the onlookers. Thompson declared:

'If a Paraguayan in the midst of his comrades was blown to pieces by a shell, they would yell with delight, thinking it a capital joke, in which they would have been joined by the victim himself had he been capable.'

Many of the Allied guns and projectiles were given nick-names; the high-velocity shells of the Whitworths, for example, were called 'phews!' from the noise they made as they hurtled through the air.

The Allied bombardments, in fact, were 'a source of pleasure' to all concerned, according to Thompson:

'The Allies liked the noise, and thought they were doing immense execution. The Paraguayan soldiers liked them, as they got a mugful of Indian corn for every shell or heap of splinters they collected. López liked them, as he got large supplies of different kinds of shot and shell, and quantities of iron, which was sent to Asunción and cast into shot etc. The small splinters were made into canister-shot.'

The Paraguayans also gave vent to their frustration at not being able always to reply in kind to the bombardments, and their contempt for their enemies' marksmanship, by blowing on curious horns known as *túrútútús*, from the peculiarly derisive note they emitted. After each enemy salvo these horns would be blown from one end of the Paraguayan lines to the other. The mocking cacophony is said to have infuriated Caxias, and later in the war the Brazilians themselves adopted this strange device.

But the Paraguayans' contempt for the Allied bombardments had tragic consequences for one man whom they could ill afford to lose. General Díaz was already in the habit of riding about the camp during the heaviest bombardments. Then, towards the end of January 1867, he decided on an even more daring gesture of contempt. He went out with some of his aides-de-camp in a canoe – and calmly began fishing in full view of the Allied fleet. A shell burst over the top of the canoe, capsizing it, and nearly severing General Díaz's leg. His companions succeeded in swimming ashore with him. Dr Skinner was quickly on the scene, and amputated the leg. A telegraph message was sent to López, and Elisa Lynch arrived shortly after in her carriage, and had the wounded general taken back to López's headquarters. There López visited him every day and, to keep up his spirits, presented him with the amputated leg soldered in a little coffin of its own – following the precedent, perhaps, of the Mexican President General Antonio López de Santa Anna, whose amputated leg had been buried with full military honours in 1838. But whereas Santa Anna survived, Díaz never recovered from his wounds. His body was sent to Asunción, and the funeral was attended by the whole population.

The death of General Díaz was a great blow to López personally, as well as to Paraguay. In the book he wrote after the war, Father Fidel Maiz was to say:

'Those two men were friends and intimates. López was the idol of Díaz and Díaz was the right arm of López. Their two per- sonalities complemented each other; creating a unity of senti- ment, a singleness of patriotic aspiration. Both were, say what you will, brave and intrepid geniuses of warfare, worshippers of their fatherland. The death of Díaz was the only blow that made López exhibit his emotion publicly; this he never did, even when he suffered his greatest disillusionments and defeats.'²

One of Caxias' problems in preparing for his offensive (which everybody knew must come sooner or later) was his lack of precise knowledge both of the Paraguayan positions, and of the terrain as a whole. In part this difficulty was solved by the work of R. A. Chodasiewicz, a former Polish army officer who had deserted from the Russian army in 1853, worked for the British Secret Service during the Crimean War, and was now, after all kinds of further adventures, a lieutenant-colonel of engineers in the Brazilian army. Chodasiewicz was invaluable to the Allies because he made a

number of important maps and surveys of the Paraguayan fortifications for them.

But he was also involved in a more spectacular project. Early in
1867, Caxias had started experimenting with balloons. The first
of these experiments was carried out by a French aeronaut,
named Doyen. It was a failure; according to Thompson it caught
fire and was burnt just before the attempted ascent, though
Burton (who got his information from an ex-British officer serving
in the Brazilian army) said it 'was utterly spoilt by being burnt in
varnishing'. A rumour reported by Thompson had it that Doyen
had really been plotting to set fire to the Brazilian powder-
magazines before escaping in his balloon. Thompson also declared
that he was tried by court-martial and sentenced to death, though
the sentence was never carried out.

Caxias now had two new balloons brought from Rio de Janeiro
(purchased in the U.S.A.) and procured the services of two
American brothers named Allen, who had been assistants to the
famous American inventor, Professor Thaddeus S. C. Lowe. In
spite of difficulties in finding the right kind of materials on the
spot to produce the hydrogen gas needed for filling the balloons,
the two Americans were successful. On 24 June 1867, James Allen
took the balloon to a height of 270 feet. He was accompanied by
Chodasiewicz, who was delighted by the survey possibilities it
opened up. On a second ascent, on 8 July, (which lasted three
hours) a Paraguayan exile who was acting as a guide to the Allied
armies and who knew the area, accompanied them. Chodasiewicz,
Burton related, 'could easily discern that Marshal-President
López had about 200 guns in position and 100 field-pieces.' He
drew a map of the area of the Paraguayan left flank, previously
unknown to the Allies, while the Paraguayan scout, Kolinski says,
searched for trails through the marshes and thickets.

The balloon (which was of the fixed type) made between twelve
and fourteen ascents. At first it had produced a sensation among
the Paraguayans. Bishop Palacios, seeing it disappear behind a
cloud, came to the conclusion that it had the power to make itself
invisible. López feared that it might be used to bombard his positions, but was soon reassured. Thompson was able to measure its
diameter and the heights of its ascents. Its usefulness to the Allies
soon came to an end when the Paraguayans made smoke-screens in
front of their positions. López also made propaganda capital out of
the balloons by spreading rumours – of a kind only too familiar in

our own times – that they contained poisonous substances designed to spread diseases among his troops.

During the period of stalemate a number of foreigners succeeded in getting through the Allied lines and into Paraguay – no mean feat, in view of the strict blockade imposed by the Allies. The case of the Prussian officer, von Versen, who reached the Paraguayan lines in July 1867, has already been mentioned. He was treated by López with great suspicion, partly because a photograph of one of the Argentine commanders was found in his pockets, and his movements were considerably restricted, though he was not actually put in prison except for a very brief period on his arrival – probably because the fact that he had been imprisoned several times by the Allies during his adventurous journey to the Paraguayan lines spoke in his favour. He survived the war, to write what is probably the best contemporary account of it, next to Thompson's.

Another traveller, who arrived in August 1867,[3] was James Manlove; described by Masterman as a 'late Confederate major of cavalry', he was said by Washburn to have been with General Nathan Bedford Forrest's force at the massacre of Fort Pillow. According to Masterman, Manlove presented 'an ingenious scheme' to López, which 'might even then have changed very materially the aspect of the war'. This was a proposal that he should be granted letters of marque and a commission to fit out two privateers (which he claimed to have already available) in order to prey upon Allied shipping on the high seas. López refused what might have been a golden opportunity – and one which according to Barrett, Elisa Lynch urged him to accept. Masterman's story is that López had read an article in a Buenos Aires newspaper (apparently he had no difficulty in getting Allied newspapers, presumably through agents in the Allied camp) which claimed that Major Manlove 'was a crack shot in the Argentine service, who was going to pick off Paraguayan officers'.

The story was almost certainly apocryphal, but in order to be on the safe side, López first had Manlove imprisoned, then sent to Asunción. López paid him a salary for a time, but in 1868, during the great conspiracy scare, he fell foul of the police and was shot, in company with John Watts, the British ship's engineer who had advised López on the eve of the Battle of Riachuelo.

Charles Ames Washburn, United States Minister to Paraguay may have had almost as much difficulty as Manlove and von Versen in getting through the Allied lines – though a large part of the difficulty was of his own making. He had left Asunción early in 1865, on leave of absence – an odd time to choose for it, perhaps, with Paraguay already at war and the danger of a blockade of the river already imminent.

On his return journey, Washburn went first to Rio de Janeiro, where he was entertained to lavish dinners by the Brazilians, at which, with his usual volubility and indiscretion, he discoursed about the war in Paraguay. The subject of his return to his post in Asunción was treated by his hosts with courteous evasiveness. On 1 November 1865, he arrived in Buenos Aires – and met with the same evasiveness when he applied for permission to pass the blockade in order to return to Asunción. He therefore proceeded upstream as far as Corrientes, where he was again received with great hospitality, made much the same kind of speeches – but received no encouragement at all from General Mitre.

Returning to Buenos Aires, therefore, he imperiously ordered Rear-Admiral S. W. Godon, of the U.S. South Atlantic Fleet to convey him back to Paraguay in a gunboat. The testy admiral refused, for various reasons, and an undignified squabble, lasting many months, broke out between the two men, attended by a voluminous correspondence, not only between the protagonists but with almost anybody else who might be remotely implicated, much to the amusement of the citizens of Buenos Aires.

Eventually the U.S. Navy Department categorically ordered Admiral Godon to comply with Washburn's request. Astonishingly, Washburn gave an interview to the press about it – and the headlines in the Buenos Aires newspapers included:

'War with the Argentine Government; Mr Washburn's Instructions to Demand Gunboat to Take Him up the Paraguay; Admiral Godon Has Been Instructed to Take Him to Paraguay.'[4]

Swallowing his anger at this public disclosure of his instructions, Admiral Godon detailed Captain Pierce Crosby of the U.S. gunboat *Shamokin* to take Washburn and his family through the Allied blockade. After a further squabble, caused by Washburn's complaint that Godon should have supplied him with a more modern and comfortable ship, the *Shamokin* set sail.

When she reached the Allied fleet, Captain Crosby was told, politely but firmly, that he could not be allowed through the blockade, and that he must turn back. He presented his papers and the official authority for his errand, approved in Rio de

Janeiro. But it was not until he ordered the decks to be cleared for action that the *Shamokin* was permitted to pass through the Allied Fleet. She proceeded to Curuzú, where, on 4 November 1866, Washburn went ashore, and accompanied by a number of Brazilian officers under a flag of truce, presented himself at the Paraguayan outposts at Curupaíty. Formal permission from López having been received, and a Paraguayan flag of truce having also been hoisted, the American minister, his family and luggage, were finally landed.

It seems likely that the Paraguayan President, who had all along hoped that the U.S.A. would eventually intervene in the war, and who had regarded Washburn as a champion of the Paraguayan cause, derived a good deal of encouragement from the episode, believing that it must strain relations between the U.S.A. and the Allies – though the reports that had reached him from Buenos Aires of the bickerings between Washburn and Godon had caused him a certain amount of bewilderment. According to Barrett, López entertained Washburn to dinner that night at Humaitá, before sending him on to Asunción under military escort. In the course of the dinner, Barrett says Washburn tactlessly boasted of the far more splendid dinner Caxias had given him behind the Allied lines, and – even more tactlessly – showed López a set of sketches of the Paraguayan lines which had been given to him by Chodasiewicz. Whether there is any substance in this story or not, it seems that from the moment of the American Minister's return, López began to lose hope as to the possibility of an American intervention.

Nevertheless, the U.S.A. did make several attempts to bring about peace negotiations about this time, and López apparently welcomed them. Thus on 1 January 1867, General Asboth, U.S. Minister in Buenos Aires, acting on instructions from Washington, offered through Elizalde, the Argentine Minister of Foreign Affairs, his country's mediation in the conflict. He received no answer. On 26 January, he wrote to Elizalde again, enclosing a copy of his previous letter. This time he received a reply, curtly declining the offer.

Apparently Asboth was joined in these efforts both by General Webb, the U.S. Minister in Rio de Janeiro, and by Washburn from Asunción. On 11 March, indeed, Washburn, with López's approval, visited Caxias in the Allied camp, and stayed there three days, but returned without having accomplished anything. Thompson maintained that Washburn continued to be 'a staunch supporter' of López until he began his 'wholesale atrocities' in the middle of 1868, but that 'from the time Mr Washburn's mediation failed, López disliked him and annoyed him'.

Certainly Washburn's skill as a negotiator is, to put it mildly, open to doubt.[5] But a similar effort by Webb later on, in spite of the fact that it was strongly supported by several Buenos Aires newspapers, was no more successful, though Burton inferred that Webb, whose critics accused him of a passion for ultimatums, was not much more tactful than his colleague in Asunción.

But the real stumbling block to all these American efforts was the attitude of the Emperor of Brazil. On 23 March 1867, Sodre tells us, he wrote to the Condessa de Barral that 'the good offices of the United States do not give me reason for concern, and everybody knows the nature of my resolution'. And on 2 May: 'Above all we must go on and finish the war with honour. It is a question of honour and I will not compromise'.

There was, too, a British attempt (conducted in an equally clumsy manner) at bringing about a peace settlement. In August 1867, G. Z. Gould, Secretary at the British legation in Buenos Aires, arrived behind the Paraguayan lines on board the British gunboat *Dotterel*, in order to request the release of British subjects in Paraguay. He was in no position to make demands, for he was not, Thompson said, 'armed with proper credentials'. As Luis Caminos, the Paraguayan Foreign Secretary, pointed out to him, the new British Minister in Buenos Aires (G. Buckley Mathew) had not yet been accredited. Under these circumstances, it does seem less than courteous to have sent a subordinate official without a word of explanation – and one, moreover, who was, according to Burton who had often talked to him in Buenos Aires, 'wholly Brazilian in sympathy'.

Caminos also reminded Gould that his request for the release of British subjects was particularly inopportune:

'at a moment when the enemy of our country enlists British subjects amongst its troops, provides itself in England with all the war material it requires, and obtains money by public loans in order to be enabled to carry on the war against the friendly people of Paraguay'.[6]

Burton considered that López was quite justified in complaining that Britain 'should be more strict in enforcing the laws of neutrality', pointing out that not only was Brazil 'allowed to buy ironclads in England as well as in France', but that 'British and other foreign craft crowded the river, affording every possible assistance to the Allies', while López's letters from Europe were detained in the British Consular Post Office in Buenos Aires.

On the main purpose of his mission, Gould reported to Buckley Mathew from López's headquarters at Paso Pucu (10 September) that all the British subjects, with one exception, were in the Paraguayan service, that their contracts had been made in England, and afterwards renewed in Paraguay, but that 'most of these contracts have been expired since the beginning of the war. . . . These British subjects have in general been very well treated by the President, and their salaries are regularly paid even now.'[7]

Caminos argued, in reply to Gould's request, that none of the British subjects had ever expressed the slightest desire to leave Paraguay. According to Thompson, López housed Gould: 'in a little room in the middle of a long hut, the partitions being only made of rushes, through which anyone from the two adjoining rooms could easily hear and see what went on in his room', but added that: 'The Englishmen in the camp were allowed freely to visit him, and they made him thoroughly acquainted with the position of all the English residents in Paraguay'.

The outcome was that López would only agree to the release of a few widows and their children. He was strongly criticized for his actions, though Burton was of the opinion that 'it was hardly reasonable to expect that the Marshal-President should dismiss a score of men – of whom sundry were in his confidence and knew every detail which it was most important to conceal from the enemy' – and he claimed that, in fact, 'by a regrettable accident' the British widows and children who eventually left on the *Dotterel* with Gould: 'were allowed to land at Montevideo and to tell all they knew'.

Before he left, however, Gould was involved in a further attempt at peace negotiations. There is some mystery as to how this came about. Thompson declared that Gould drafted the proposals himself, probably at López's suggestion. Hutchinson, on the other hand, thought that the terms 'proceeded from the Brazilian Minister in Buenos Aires, and were approved of by President Mitre, as well as by the Marquês de Caxias, Commander-in-Chief of the Brazilian forces in the Allied camp'. And Burton suggested that Gould was deceived into drawing up the peace proposals: '. . . by a noted intriguer, whose sole object was evidently to ascertain the animus of the political visitor.'

The most important of the proposals drawn up by Gould were that the integrity and independence of Paraguay should be recognized by the Allies; that both sides should retire from any territory belonging to each other which they had occupied, leaving frontier questions for later negotiation or settlement by arbitration; that the Allied fleet should be withdrawn from Paraguayan waters; that no indemnity for the expenses of the war should be demanded of Paraguay; that prisoners of war on both sides should be set at liberty; that the forces of Paraguay would be disbanded apart from those needed for internal security – and last though certainly not least, that López should retire to Europe for a period of two years,[8] leaving the government in the hands of the Vice-President.

There seems to be some uncertainty, however, as to what exactly happened to these proposals. Both Hutchinson and Burton wrote as if Paraguay summarily rejected them – because, of course, of the demand for López's abdication. But Thompson was quite positive that López formally accepted them, through Caminos, and on the understanding that Gould would take them to the Allied camp.

He did so on 11 September, where, Thompson reported:

'they were favourably received, and referred to the respective Governments, and Colonel Fonseca (Chief of the Brazilian Staff) was immediately despatched in a special steamer to Rio, to receive the approbation of the Emperor'.

What happened next, if this version is correct (and there is no real reason why Thompson's word should be doubted) was that when Gould returned after two days in the Allied camp, he received a letter from Caminos declaring that the crucial article in the proposal – that relating to López's abdication – could not possibly be considered and had never been contemplated. In Thompson's opinion, López had changed his mind because, while Gould was in the Allied camp, he had received news of the second and more serious outbreak of revolts in the Argentine provinces which necessitated Mitre's temporary absence, and which López 'expected would force the Allies to make peace with him on any terms'.

Somehow, though, in spite of Thompson's confident statements, a certain air of unreality surrounds the Gould peace overtures.

During this long interval of virtual stalemate, the war did flare up in one area; but it was far removed from the main theatre and for some mysterious reason of his own López kept it a secret in spite of the fact that the outcome was in Paraguay's favour.

The Paraguayan invasion of Mato Grosso had been a severe blow to Brazilian pride, and the fact that Paraguayans were still on Brazilian soil was a constant source of distress to Dom Pedro – though by now in fact they held only the line of the river, having evacuated many of their garrisons – including the ill-fated 10th Battalion. But the Brazilians hoped to drive them out completely, and in the process launch an invasion of northern Paraguay itself.

Early in 1865 it was decided that a diversionary effort at least should be attempted, in order to relieve Paraguayan pressure in the south. Accordingly an expedition was organized, and on 1 April its advance party – which included young Alfredo D'Escragnolle Taunay, later one of Brazil's most distinguished writers and author of a classic account of the expedition *(The Retreat from Laguna)*[9] – left Rio de Janeiro under the command of Colonel Manoel Pedro Drago. It took nearly four months to travel about 280 miles, by which time it was already depleted by smallpox, malaria, beriberi and desertions.

On 18 October Drago was relieved of his command and the expedition advanced, under a new commander, to Villa de Miranda, near the Paraguayan border, which it reached in September 1866. It had taken nearly two years to get there and had suffered all kinds of disasters and lost at least a third of its members on the way.

It stayed at Miranda over three months. Another commander had died and the President of Mato Grosso appointed in his stead Colonel Carlos de Morais Camisão. He had been an officer in the garrison which had so precipitately evacuated Corumbá when the Paraguayans attacked it in December 1864, and was burning to vindicate his honour and to avenge himself on the Paraguayans, who were fond of making uncomplimentary jests about his bald head.

On 25 February 1867, Camisão began to march towards the borders of Paraguay. The expedition had now been reduced from 3,000 to 1,600 men. Camisão tried to supplement it by recruiting the Indians of the province, but instead of fighting with their rifles, Thompson tells us, the new recruits used them to shoot their game. Camisão also had four La Hitte rifled cannon, drawn by oxen, but both food and ammunition were short and there were no cavalry.

Although misfortune still dogged the expedition, it reached the river Apa, the line claimed by Brazil as its southern frontier, late in April. The river was crossed – and Camisão proudly headed his reports with the words 'Forces in Operation in North Paraguay', while his men, asserting Brazilian sovereignty over the area, headed their letters home 'Empire of Brazil'.

Camisão's plan was to push through North Paraguay to the river port of Concepción, where his guns would threaten Paraguayan traffic on the river. But desperately short by now of supplies, he made a détour to a nearby estate called Laguna (it was said to belong to President López) where he had been told large herds of cattle were to be found.

So far there had been little evidence of the Paraguayans, apart from an occasional glimpse of their cavalry patrols – and a number of insulting messages (making great play of Camisão's bald head) nailed on to trees. At Laguna there was another taunting message – but no cattle.

By now López had despatched a regiment of cavalry and two companies of infantry to the area to link up with the scanty local garrisons. The first major action took place on 8 May. Brazilian sources refer to this action as the Battle of Baiende, and claim it as a victory. Thompson, however, says that there was no real engagement, but that the Paraguayans simply surrounded the Brazilians on their march 'cutting off all supplies and taking what little cattle they had'.

There followed the epic retreat from Laguna, described so vividly in Taunay's book. For thirty-five days the Brazilians slowly fell back, harassed by continuous attacks from the Paraguayan cavalry, unable through their own lack of cavalry to forage for food (they were reduced to living on green oranges and the heads of palm trees) and finally stricken by cholera. Camisão, his second-in-command, and many other officers and men died and were buried along the path of the retreat – which had now become even more of a nightmare because the Paraguayans were setting fire to the tinder-dry surrounding bush.

Nearly a thousand Brazilians perished by battle, starvation, disease, and fire, and only 700 emaciated survivors eventually reached safety.

On 13 July 1867, another small Brazilian force embarked in

two steamers at Cuiabá and proceeded down stream to make a lightning raid on Corumbá. But they lost one of the steamers in the process, and when the Paraguayans did finally withdraw from Mato Grosso, it was of their own volition and as a result of crisis in the main area of conflict.

NOTES

[1] Quoted by Kolinsky.

[2] *Etapas de mi vida*, Fidel Maiz, *op. cit.* The translation here is Barrett's.

[3] August, 1866, according to Kolinsky.

[4] Investigation into the conduct of the late American Minister to Paraguay and of the officers commanding the South Atlantic Squadron since the breaking out of the Paraguayan War, commenced in Washington D.C., on 30 March 1869 – Report No. 65, U.S. House of Representatives, 41st Congress, 2nd Session, p. 49.

[5] See for example 'Efforts of the United States to mediate in the Paraguayan War,' Harold F. Peterson, *Hispanic American Historical Review*, XII, February 1932.

[6] Quoted by Hutchinson.

[7] Parliamentary Paper, River Plate, no. 1 (1868), *Correspondence Respecting Hostilities in the River Plate.*

[8] Thompson does not mention any time limit, but most other contemporary accounts refer to the two year period.

[9] *A retirada de Laguna*, Alfredo d'Escragnolle Taunay. 14th ed. São Paulo 1957.

ACT FIVE

The Long Retreat

Although the Paraguayans were still defiant within their *quadrilát-ero* the odds during the period of comparative calm had been steadily mounting against them. The contrasts between the two sides which emerge in G. Z. Gould's report on his mission of August 1867 make this abundantly clear. He put the Allied army at that date at 48,000 men on active service and from 5,000 to 6,000 in hospital – of whom 45,000 were Brazilians, 7,000 to 8,000 Argentinians, and about 1,000 Uruguayans.[1] The Brazilian government, moreover, had 'engaged to send 2,000 men per month to keep up the army to its present strength', while fresh horses were Thanks to the efforts of Chodasiewicz and his assistants, the 'daily coming in large numbers', so that the Allied cavalry numbered at least 8,000 'well mounted men'.

This large force, Gould noted, was 'fully supplied with every requisite for a campaign' – while the Allied fleet, in addition to its numerous wooden ships now contained ten modern ironclads.

The Paraguayan forces, on the other hand, Gould reported, 'amounted to about 20,000 men; of these 10,000 or 12,000 at most are good troops, the rest mere boys from twelve to fourteen years of age, old men and cripples, besides from 4,000 to 3,000 sick and wounded'.[2] The Paraguayan soldiers, Gould continued, were 'worn out with exposure, fatigue and privations . . . actually dropping down from inanition,' and many of them were 'in a state bordering on nudity, having only a piece of tanned leather round their loins, a ragged shirt and a poncho made of vegetable fibre'. There was, moreover, 'absolutely nothing for sale in the Paraguayan camp' and a 'great scarcity of drugs and medicines, if not a total want of them, for the sick, whose number is rapidly increasing.' Most of the horses had died and the few hundreds which remained were 'so weak and emaciated they can scarcely carry their riders'.

Gould was certainly mistaken in assuming from all this that Paraguayan resistance must soon come to an end. As Hutchinson reported, the Paraguayans themselves 'laughed such an idea to scorn', and he pointed out that a Paraguayan soldier needed 'nothing for his subsistence but mate tea and mandioca. A red shirt serves even a general, when on service, for clothing'. Nevertheless Gould and other observers were right in assuming that with such great inferiority in men and resources the Paraguayan positions, however strong and bravely defended, were in danger of being enveloped by sheer weight of numbers and armaments.

Thanks to the efforts of Chodasiewicz and his assistants, the Allies now had a reasonably accurate knowledge of the terrain before them, and their plan was to encircle the *quadrilátero*, outflanking it on the land side by advancing across the swamps, and on the river side by sending the fleet past the Paraguayan batteries at Curupaíty and Humaitá.

Their long awaited offensive began on 22 July 1867. It was directed by the Marquês de Caxias; General Mitre in fact returned to the front, having put down the revolts in the Argentine provinces, five days later; but though still officially Commander-in-chief he tended increasingly from now on to take a back seat, possibly because he felt that his own plan for the reduction of Humaitá had either been overruled or nullified by the extreme caution of the Brazilian naval commanders.

Commanded by General Manoel Luíz Osório and General Alexandre Gomes de Argolo some 30,000 Allied troops, advancing through swamps, often up to their waists in water, crossed the Bellaco and by nightfall reached an area known as San Solano, where the advance guards reported that it was in sight of the shattered church at Humaitá, which, as the only landmark in the area, had been repeatedly shelled by the ironclads. A further 13,000 men remained at Tuyutí, now a strongly fortified Allied base, under Porto Alegre's command.

Moving very slowly the Allied army advanced to a small village named Tuicué, where they dug themselves in and set up batteries which included a number of Whitworth guns. They were now able to send their cavalry patrols on to the highway leading to Asunción itself – though Paraguayan steamers could still use the river. In order to preserve his communications to the north, López sent an exploring party into the Chaco on the other side of the river Paraguay, and then had a road built from Timbó, about 9 miles above Humaitá, to Monte Lindo, some six miles above the mouth of the river Tebicuary. This road, 54 miles long, had to be laid through forests and swamps, crossing both the river Bermejo and five other deep streams. Together with its new telegraph line it was the last communications link between the *quadrilátero* and Asunción, and it must be reckoned as one of the most astonishing of all the Paraguayan feats. At the same time López continued his policy of presenting the invaders with a desert – 'making every abandoned place a small Moscow', as Burton puts it – by ordering all the civilian inhabitants of the area, now in danger of complete encirclement, to move north of the river Tebicuary, where many of them died of starvation.

In the meantime the Allied fleet was slowly advancing along the river to attempt its part of the plan of encirclement. On 15 August, it approached Curupaíty. There it suffered considerable damage from the Paraguayan batteries, but succeeded in sailing past them – and Thompson thinks that it was now that the Paraguayans began at last to realize that no matter how good their marksmanship 'they could do nothing against ironclads with their small artillery'.

On the testimony of Thompson, in fact, there were hardly any guns at all in Humaitá at the time, so that the Allied fleet could easily have carried on from Curupaíty and passed Humaitá in a single operation. Such was their caution, however, that they allowed the Paraguayans ample time to move all the big guns that Curupaíty possessed into Humaitá, where other heavy artillery was also rapidly concentrated.

The Paraguayans, of course, were doing their best meanwhile to frustrate the encircling movement. Patrols and raiding parties continuously harassed the Allied supply routes from Tuyutí to their forward positions at Tuicué. At the least these helped to replenish the depleted Paraguayan stores. On one occasion, for example, a cartload of paper was seized by a small party operating some distance inside the Allied lines. It was impossible to take the cart back by daylight, so the paper was hidden in the woods, and every night for a week a few reams were smuggled back through the Allied patrols. On another occasion a Paraguayan raiding party captured an enemy watch-tower and removed it bodily under cover of darkness back to their own lines. Some of these raids were on a larger scale. On 24 September, for example, a feigned attack was made on an Allied convoy in order to tempt the supporting troops into a pursuit, while a small Paraguayan force lay in ambush. In the sharp encounter which followed the Allies lost over two hundred men. The Brazilian cavalry, Thompson tells us, were splendidly mounted, while the Paraguayan horsemen had to remain in line waiting for the charge because their 'miserable, haggard mounts could hardly move', until, at the last moment they managed to spur them into a canter, whereupon the Brazilians turned tail and galloped away.

On 3 October, a Paraguayan cavalry force, 1,000 strong, under the command of major (soon general) Bernardino Caballero were victorious in another action, but on the 21 of the same month the Paraguayans were, in their turn, ambushed, losing over 500 men. Caballero and the survivors were completely surrounded for the whole three miles back to the protection of the guns at Humaitá, and had to fight hand to hand every inch of the way.

Gradually the weight of superior numbers and equipment began to have their effect, and on 2 November Brazilian troops overwhelmed the Paraguayan garrison at Tayí, a small fortified position on the east bank of the river Paraguay, about 15 miles to the north of Humaitá, and with the fall of Tayí the allied flanking movement had achieved its objective: the *quadrilátero* was surrounded, with the exception of the single escape route at Timbó on the other side of the river from Humaitá. Two of the remaining Paraguayan war steamers, moreover, had been sunk in the action, while trying to put the strong concentration of Brazilian artillery on the river bank out of action.

The Brazilian force, numbering 6,000 men, quickly entrenched themselves at Tayí, while a further 10,000 men were kept in support a short distance away. At the same time the Allied positions at Tuiucué at the other end of the line (on the left of the Paraguayan trenches) were also strengthened and the batteries there poured a continuous fire into the *quadrilátero*.

But before the Allied grip tightened, López, astonishingly, was able to hit back. He had for some time been contemplating a surprise attack on the enemy base at Tuyutí, with a view to relieving pressure at Tuicué – and also in the hope of capturing one of the Whitworth heavy guns. Accordingly he ordered Thompson to prepare a map of the enemy fortifications, and by using his theodolite from the tops of the Paraguayan watch towers and by interviewing prisoners, the Englishman was able to accomplish his task 'with tolerable success'.

López then assembled a force of 8,000 men, consisting of four brigades of infantry and two of cavalry. On 2 November he held a long briefing session with General Barrios and the other commanders he had selected for the operation, at which Thompson's map was studied in detail. The plan – as at the first battle of Tuyutí – was to get the army as close as possible to the enemy positions during the night; at dawn the infantry were to rush the enemy trenches, while Caballero's cavalry were to charge the Brazilian redoubts at the right. They were then to advance rapidly to Tuyutí, sending any captured guns back to the Paraguayan lines as fast as they were taken. With a force of this size López did not expect to be able to hold Tuyutí, but he gave orders that when they had entered it the troops were to be allowed to break formation and ransack the place – an order which provoked from Thompson the harsh comment: 'When a General can give such an order he deserves every reverse that may happen to him'.

The element of surprise, which had failed so dismally at the first battle of Tuyutí, succeeded brilliantly this time. Advancing silently and at the double the Paraguayan infantry reached the first line of enemy trenches at Tuyutí at daybreak on 3 November. They took them in a rush, setting fire to the whole camp and blowing up the powder magazines. They captured the second line of trenches with equal ease. The Brazilian troops then panicked and fled, accompanied by the camp sutlers and merchants, back to Itapirú, where, Thompson relates, 'Ferry-boat fares rose to such an extent that 100l. was paid for a passage across the river, and 10l. to be taken a little way from the shore.'

Beyond the second line of trenches the Paraguayans found themselves in the main commercial area of the camp – and the looting began in earnest. The folly of López's orders in this respect soon became apparent, for the Paraguayans disbanded without bothering to take the inner fortress. There Pôrto Alegre, who behaved with great gallantry, having two horses shot under him and his uniform perforated in several places by bullets,[3] succeeded in rallying some of his troops. They opened a devastating fire on the Paraguayans, who were wandering about in all directions, loading themselves with booty, and, Thompson tells us, 'drinking, and eating handfuls of sugar, of which they were very fond'. Pôrto Alegre, white beard streaming and waving his sword, now led a counter-attack. The Paraguayans retreated, losing many men on the way, but refusing to let go of their spoils – even the wounded staggered or crawled along still clutching their burdens.

In the meantime, Caballero's cavalry had also surprised the enemy trenches at the redoubts ('turning the garrison out in their shirts', Thompson tells us), and had then dismounted, captured all the positions and set the barracks on fire. When strong Allied reinforcements arrived from Tuicué, the Paraguayans charged through them time after time, and then after more than an hour of vicious hand-to-hand fighting, retired in accordance with their instructions.

The whole of the enemy camp at Tuyutí was now, Thompson says, 'from the centre to the right . . . a mass of fire and smoke, occasionally relieved by the explosion of a powder magazine'.

But who had won the battle? Up to the time they broke ranks the Paraguayans had carried all before them and their losses had been minimal. Nearly all their casualties occurred after they had collected their booty, and in the event they left 1,200 on the field, most of them dead: about the same number of wounded returned, so that of the original 8,000 nearly a third were put out of action. On the side of the Allies casualties were about the same, and as it was they who remained in occupation of the field, they claimed the victory. On the other hand López, it must be remembered, had no intention of holding Tuyutí. He simply did not have the men for it, and the most he had hoped for was to break the Allies' stranglehold on the *quadrilátero* and temporarily disrupt their offensive plans. If he had not allowed his men to scatter for booty (and, in fairness, for supplies of which he was desperately in need) they might, admittedly, have occupied Tuyutí and driven the Allies a good deal further back, until they regrouped and deployed their large resources – but that is all.

An ironic comment on the Brazilian claim that it was they who had won the battle occurs in the report from J. J. Pakenham, secretary to the British legation in Rio de Janeiro:

'A curious incident connected with the recent engagement . . . is, that the vanquished seized and were able to carry off, several pieces of artillery belonging to the victors; a proceeding unusual, I believe, in modern military annals.'[4]

Among the 'several pieces of artillery' were a Krupp 12-pounder rifled steel breechloader (which was taken loaded) and fourteen other guns of varying calibres.

But what of the Whitworth López had set his heart on? A fine 32-pounder specimen had indeed been captured, but on the way back it sank above the naves of the wheels in the mud of the *estero*, and its captors had to abandon it, within rifle-fire of the Allied trenches. It was a case of 'so near and yet so far'.

When the news was brought to López, the redoubtable General Bruguez was with him, and begged for permission to try and recover the gun. López agreed and Bruguez set out with a small force and twelve yoke of oxen. When he reached the gun, he found the Brazilians, too, were on the scene with teams of oxen. They returned to their trenches, and directed a terrible fire on the Paraguayans as they struggled waist deep in mud to get the gun moving. The latter suffered many casualties, but after a desperate struggle managed to free it and take it back to their lines – only to find that it was damaged and would not fire.

Nevertheless López set his men to collecting abandoned or unexploded enemy ammunition for the gun, and before long news was brought to him that the long coveted 'Phew' had been repaired. It was installed first at Curupaíty (still in Paraguayan hands, though the Brazilian ironclads had sailed past it), where it scored thirty-four direct hits on the wooden ships of the Brazilian fleet in a single afternoon, and then at Espinillo, facing the Brazilian positions at Tuicué, where it also did great execution. It became one of López's favourite after dinner pastimes at his headquarters at Paso Pucu to order his beloved Whitworth to bombard the Allied lines. The gunners had a number of large letters painted on hides to represent the different targets – T. for Tuicué, C. for Caxias's headquarters, and so on. One of these would be hoisted just before the gun was fired and officers posted with telescopes on top of the earthworks surrounding López's casements would immediately report the target to him, and then the result of the shot.

In addition to the guns, the spoil taken by the Paraguayans at Tuyutí is described as 'immense' by Thompson, who goes on to give a list of bizarre diversity, including artichokes (the first he had seen in Paraguay), General Mitre's recently delivered mail together with a chest containing, tea, cheese, coffee, and a pair of boots; brand new officers' uniforms; 'Crimean' shirts; a tripod telescope; large quantities of gold watches, sovereigns and dollars – and parasols, long dresses and crinolines.

Whether all this really spelt a victory for the Paraguayans or not, it is certain that it served as a considerable boost to their morale, while it provided the Allies with a sharp reminder that their enemies were by no means a spent force. As the very pro-allied Commander Kennedy put it:

'This action, in which a force of Paraguayans had been able to attack and completely rout a body of the Allies twice their number, capture their cannon, burn their camp, and destroy the reserve stores of the whole army, was viewed with the greatest astonishment'.

The Allied cause received a set-back of another kind in January 1868, when Marcos Paz, the vice-president of Argentina died. When on the 11th López saw flags flying at half mast in the Allied camp, he jumped to the conclusion that it was General Mitre who had died, and there was great jubilation among the Paraguayans, who believed that this would mean an early end to the war. As it was, General Mitre was forced to hand over his supreme command to Caxias and to return to Buenos Aires, in order to take control of the government – and to cope with further uprisings in the Argentine provinces, especially in Santa Fe. According to Thompson he was not sorry to go, 'as he could make nothing of the Brazilians' and had found that every time he put forward a strategic plan of his own 'Caxias said it was impossible' – but his departure was 'much to the sorrow of all the Argentines'. They continued to play an important part in the war, but from now on received few reinforcements. As for the Uruguayans, they were reduced after the battle of Second Tuyutí to a mere handful. Venancio Flores had already returned to Montevideo, where his old enemies the Blancos were once again stirring up trouble (a further fillip to López's hopes). On 19 February Flores' stormy career came to an end when he was assassinated when driving in his carriage – a fate which, Burton observes, 'curiously resembled that of Abraham Lincoln'.

In reality none of these events contained much comfort for Paraguay. The Triple Alliance might be showing signs of disintegration, and the war might be becoming more and more a struggle with Brazil alone – but Brazil was more determined than ever, and her potential was increasing daily. It soon became clear, moreover, that the destruction of the base at Tuyutí had not seriously affected the Allies' grip on the *quadrilátero*, and they still held their positions at Tuicué and Tayí. It could only be a matter of time before Caxias once more tightened the squeeze. López therefore decided to withdraw his troops into a smaller compass and to strengthen yet further the fortifications of Humaitá.

The morale of the Paraguayans nevertheless remained high.

They were not in the least intimidated when, after Mitre's departure, Caxias made what Thompson calls 'a military promenade' along his line in order to impress the Paraguayans with the size of his forces. 'The more their enemies,' Thompson says, 'the more the Paraguayans would laugh'. In addition to their 'gamesmanship' with the captured Whitworth they continued to make daring raids into the enemy lines, capturing cattle, stores and sentries. On one occasion fifty naked cavalry men, armed only with their swords, swam across the *estero* and fell upon the rear of a Brazilian battalion. On another, an Argentine reconnoitering force was ambushed and cut to pieces. At night, Thompson tells us, the Paraguayans used to play all sorts of pranks with the Brazilian guards, such as 'shooting at them with bows and arrows, and with *bodoques* – balls of clay shot from two-stringed bows, used by Paraguay boys to shoot at parrots'.

At the same time López had a redoubt constructed at La Cierva, some two miles to the north of Humaitá on the Arroyo Hondo (a tributary of the Paraguay), garrisoned by 500 men under Major Olabarrieta – largely, Thompson claims, to mystify the enemy, while he sent Thompson himself across the river to prepare a battery at Timbó. In public, of course, he would not for a moment admit that Humaitá was in any danger, but he was guarding against such an eventuality. It is an instance of the quite remarkable military prescience which López often displayed, side by side with such ill-judged orders as that given to his troops at Tuyutí to break ranks and loot the enemy camp.

The new battery at Timbó in fact proved more effective than those at Humaitá, because it was on lower ground, when, on 18 January, the allied fleet at last attempted the passage of the river, having first run past Curupaíty, where a few guns were still in position, without receiving any damage. Two of the new Brazilian monitors and the *Tamandaré*, one of the big older ironclads, were damaged by the guns at Timbó. The fire at Humaitá, too, was 'well sustained and true', Thompson reports, though most of the balls 'flew in pieces on the plates of the ironclads, and with an exceptionally high water-level in their favour the fleet steamed on past both Humaitá and Timbó, heading for Asunción itself.

López had been aware for some time of the threat to his capital. As soon as he learned that the ironclads had definitely decided on an attempt to pass Humaitá, he sent Elisa Lynch to Asunción to collect all their valuables and to remove them, secretly and at night, to a safe hiding place in the country. According to Barrett she found that not only the wealthy merchants but also some of the members of the diplomatic corps were taking advantage of the shortage of supplies to make large fortunes for themselves, and that many of the wealthy families were selling land in order to acquire ready cash. Elisa herself later claimed that López's brother Benigno was among these.

Barrett also says that it was now that Elisa Lynch discovered for the first time that Washburn had all this time been living in the huge barrack-like American legation without paying the owner any rent – a point which Masterman confirms, and which apparently increased the friction between the American Minister and López. This deterioration in their relations had been growing ever since Washburn had taken Masterman on to his staff following the latter's release from prison, where he had been sent by the Paraguayan authorities on suspicion of having been in communication with the Brazilians. Washburn also employed a young American historian named Porter Bliss, who was under contract to López.

Shortly after, orders arrived from López for the evacuation of the civilian population, and the transfer of the government to Luque, a village on the railway line about nine miles inland from Asunción (and now one of its suburbs). Washburn, however, refused to move, arguing that the Legation in Asunción was part of United States territory. 'I hardly think', Burton comments, 'that such a proceeding would have been adopted by European diplomats. Asunción had been proved dangerous; it might have been attacked at any moment by a squadron of ironclads, and the Marshal-President of the Republic was to a certain extent answerable for the lives of foreign agents accredited to him.'

Rumours were already current in Asunción that Washburn had been in secret correspondence with Caxias ever since his peace mission to the allied camp, and inevitably his refusal to transfer to the new provisional capital lent colour to them, especially as he foolishly allowed a number of people to deposit with him valuables and documents before they left Asunción, as well as giving harbour to several foreigners known to be under suspicion, and a group of English mechanics who did not wish to renew their contracts with the Paraguayans and who (encouraged by Washburn) expected to get away as soon as the allied fleet reached Asunción.

The ironclads arrived off the capital on 24 February and Masterman describes how with Washburn he eagerly watched them from the roof of the American legation 'expecting that they would take up a position in front of the city, for the battery . . . had only one heavy gun and a few field pieces. But they stopped and engaged this work at almost the verge of their range. The shots flew far wide of their mark; the greater number flew harmlessly into the river and a few into the city, the only damage being the destruction of a balcony of the President's palace, a slice off the front of a house, and the demolition of a couple of dogs in the market-place.'

The heavy gun to which Masterman refers was the *Criollo*, cast in the arsenal at Asunción, which was still working at full pressure. This gun threw three shots at the ironclads, which all missed, but were sufficient, apparently, to cause the Brazilian squadron to retreat. The operation was hailed in the allied capitals as a great victory, and there was dancing and cheering in the streets.

There was no cheering from Washburn. He found himself in an extremely awkward position. Convinced that the allies were about to occupy Asunción and thus bring the war to an end, he was aware of the extent to which he had stretched his diplomatic privileges. In addition he now found himself with a houseful of unwanted guests, among them several who were known to be under suspicion as spies or traitors, as well as the English mechanics who had incurred López's anger by refusing to go on working at the arsenal, where they were badly needed, and who, Masterman observes, 'had made a most unfortunate mistake in entering the Legation'. Indeed Washburn later admitted as much himself, excusing himself on the grounds that Dr Stewart (López's chief military surgeon) had informed him that when once the allies had taken Asunción a British ship would be sent to take the mechanics home.

In Barrett's view Washburn now had two alternatives open to him. He could either attempt to undo what had been done by apologizing to the Paraguayan government for refusing to move to the new capital and admitting that he had been indiscreet in offering sanctuary to refugees without consulting the authorities who had ordered their evacuation – or 'he could take the stand before his own country and before the world that the Paraguayan Government was unworthy of diplomatic representation and that the people whom he crowded into the legation were in danger of their lives' – as many of them undoubtedly were.

Whether a choice was available to him or not, it appears that not long after Washburn decided to send a letter of resignation to Washington, with a request for a gunboat to be sent as soon as possible to remove him and his family.

In the meantime a curious half-life went on in Asunción, deserted now except for police officers, those engaged in various kinds of war work (mostly at the arsenal), the small garrison, a few women and children – and Washburn's motley guests, many of them under police surveillance and frightened to venture beyond the compound of the American Legation, quarrelling among themselves and with their protector.

The bulk of the civilian population had scattered among the villages to the north-east of Asunción, where they lived in the most wretched conditions. The houses of these villages were crammed with refugees, but even so could only acommodate a quarter of them. The majority of the evacuees, therefore, had to camp in the open: it was the season of the heavy rains and large numbers died of disease or starvation.

When they had left the city they had for the most part taken their dogs with them, but not their cats. Within a few days these were starving, and, Masterman tells us, 'made descents upon us like wolves. At first the chickens were taken, and only at night; but at length, made desperate by hunger, they carried off large fowls in broad daylight.' Masterman and the American, Manlove (they were sharing a house within the precincts of the American Embassy) were forced to set traps for the marauders. They also adopted nine tame parrots which had been abandoned by their owners. One of these, during a visit from Washburn, created a minor sensation by croaking out 'Viva Pedro Segundo' (i.e. the Emperor of Brazil). Masterman tells the story:

'"*Hullo!*" cried Mr Washburn, looking around in amazement, "what's that?" "Viva Pedro Segundo!" repeated the parrot, turning her head on one side to look at him. "Wring the bird's neck directly!" said he to Mr Meinke, his secretary, "or we shall all get into trouble" . . . and in truth it was perilous enough.'

Masterman was not exaggerating; there were spies in the American Legation and the words of the unfortunate parrot were reported back to the Paraguayan authorities, to assume, in that highly-charged and highly-strung atmosphere, so reminiscent of that in Europe during the Kaiser's war, a grossly inflated importance.

Far more serious was a report which had reached López, according to Father Fidel Maiz, to the effect that certain officials in Asunción had hesitated about using the city's guns against the Brazilian fleet. The air was thick with rumours of treachery and conspiracy.

On the same day that the fleet had sailed past Humaitá, the Brazilian infantry had also attacked the redoubt at La Cierva. Major Olabarrieta and his small band of defenders beat back the first four assaults (in spite of the fact that one column of the attackers were armed with the new needle-rifles) inflicting well over a thousand casualties, until their ammunition gave out and they retreated on board the *Tacuarí* and *Ygurei*, which took them down the Arroyo Hondo and back to Humaitá.

Faced with a situation which was hourly becoming more desperate, López decided once more to make a canoe sortie into the Allied fleet, knowing, Thompson says, 'that if he could get only one ironclad, and man it with his own men, it would be sufficient to chase the whole of the Brazilian fleet out of the river.'

Seven of the ironclads had been left between Curupaíty and Humaitá and two of them, the *Herbal* and the *Cabral*, were stationed some distance above the others as a vanguard. On the night of 18 March, therefore, the famous *bogovantes* set out in twenty four canoes, each containing 12 men, armed with sabres and hand grenades, and commanded by Captain Ignacio Genés, one of López's aides-de-camp.

Some of the canoes were swept beyond their objectives by the very strong current, but in the pitch darkness the others came alongside the *Herbal* and *Cabral* and succeeded in boarding them. The Paraguayans quickly disposed of those who were on the decks, but the rest of the crew had retreated below and closed the steel hatches. Desperately the Paraguayans tried to prise them open, and to make use of their hand grenades, but the crew kept up a deadly fire of canister from the turrets and two more ironclads came to the rescue, sweeping the decks with grapeshopt. Nevertheless it was touch and go as far as the *Cabral* was concerned. The Paraguayans were just beginning to get inside her when nearly all of them were killed by the fire of the other ironclads. Over a hundred corpses were left on the decks of the two ironclads, and the same number in the water. Only a handful succeeded in getting back to their lines, among them Captain Genés, who had lost an eye in the action.

This attempt having failed, López on the following day left his headquarters at Paso Pucu for Humaitá. On the same night he, Elisa Lynch (who had returned from Asunción) and his suite embarked in boats and canoes, and rowed up the river and over to Timbó, practically under the noses of the Brazilian squadron. From there he proceeded through the Chaco to Monte Lindo. He had decided to evacuate the bulk of his army (now reduced to 10,000 men) across the river Paraguay into the Chaco, leaving behind only a small holding-force within the confines of the Humaitá fortifications.

The operation, as Masterman rightly says, 'was an extraordinary feat, and was most admirably planned and carried out'. So expertly carried out indeed that it was some time before the Allies realized what was happening. It was not until 22 March, for example that they ventured into Curupaíty, to find, in the words of Hutchinson, 'a battery composed of forty sham guns made of the trunks of palm trees, covered with hides and mounted on old cart wheels' while 'the troops in garrison consisted of some thirty or forty effigies, made of straw stuffed into hides, who were placed as sentinels in such positions as to be visible to the storming party'. Curupaíty had in fact been deserted for over a month.

Effective use of sham or 'quaker' guns was also made along the quadrilátero, while the few remaining Paraguayan soldiers continually fired what weapons remained to them in order to keep up the deception. They were also massed at intervals at various strategic points, with a great show of bustle and preparation, to make the enemy believe that attacks in force were imminent.

Meanwhile, unopposed by the Brazilian fleet, the Tacuarí and Ygurei (the only war steamers remaining to the Paraguayans) had transported the army, and its baggage, supplies and artillery (including, of course, the precious Whitworth) across the river into the Chaco. The army then set out on an extraordinary march through swamps and thickets that was to entail the crossing of the river Bermejo, and eventually a re-crossing of the River Paraguay, to take up new positions on the north bank of the River Tebicuary.

Even the laconic Thompson conveys something of the heroic nature of this march. He tells us, for example, how he and his Paraguayan comrades had to cross the two hundred yards of the swift-flowing Bermejo, red from the clay at the bottom, 'by swimming their horses on each side of a canoe'; how they had to ride 'through a league of wood, in mud three feet deep'; and how at one point his own skinny mount stuck so that he had to struggle on foot through another mile of mud to the next posthouse. He describes the building of bridges across streams to take López's carriage, the men 'in and out of the water all night in the greatest good humour'; and then the hauling of the carriage across by hand while the horses swam and López himself chaffed the men when they had difficulty in dragging the guns across the rough, swaying bridges, so that, 'greatly delighted', they 'pulled with a will, taking the guns over in a very short time'.

Eventually, they reached Seibo, where López set up his head-quarters with his army encamped around him, well concealed in the woods, while a battery was set up at Monte Lindo.

Thompson thinks that there was some possibility that at the time López had the idea of marching through the Chaco to Bolivia, and thence making his way to Europe. He offers as evidence the facts that López did not immediately send men across the Paraguay to defend the line of the river Tebicuary; and that he had fresh horses brought to Seibo as well as five cartloads of silver dollars.

If that were the case, López must have quickly changed his mind, for he gave orders to Thompson a few days later for the removal of the battery at Monte Lindo to the island of Fortín, near the mouth of the river Tebicuary (where it joins the Paraguay) and for the construction of other positions along the Tebicuary. Working his men in shifts Thompson had most of the guns mounted within three days. 'I had not shut my eyes the whole time', he tells us, 'and they felt like dead boards.' López established his new headquarters at San Fernando, four miles from Fortín, on a spot of dry ground some thirty square yards. At first the army had to encamp in the surrounding mud, until the ground had been drained. Huts were then quickly built for the troops, and a large house for López and his family. One of the Englishmen was brought from the arsenal in Asunción to establish workshops, and San Fernando soon took on the appearance of a thriving town.

Before he left Seibo, the Marshal-President had his brother Benigno brought down from Asunción in irons and put under guard. Saturnino Bedoya, the Treasurer (López's brother-in-law) and José Berges, the Minister of Foreign Affairs were also at Seibo, under a cloud, though Benges was not yet under arrest.

While he was busy with his batteries on the Tebicuary, however, Thompson heard 'whisperings' to the effect that 'something extraordinary was happening at San Fernando, and that many people were in irons there'. The period of the great conspiracy had begun.

The Brazilian ironclads came up to investigate the new batteries but after sustaining considerable damage, retired. This encouraged López to make yet another attempt to capture one of the ironclads.

At the beginning of July only two of them lay above Timbó – the *Barroso* and the *Rio Grande* – though they were protected by the allied shore batteries at Tayí. Accordingly, on the night of the 9th twenty-four canoes, divided into two divisions, paddled towards the ironclads. One of the divisions failed to contact its target, but the other succeeded in boarding the *Rio Grande*. The Captain and part of the crew remained below their steel hatches, while both the guns from Tayí and those of the *Barroso* which had steamed alongside, played upon the decks of the *Rio Grande* until the boarding party were nearly all killed, and the rest were taken prisoner. Nevertheless, the Paraguayans had once again come within an ace of capturing an ironclad – and the whole allied fleet was thrown into a state of great nervousness.

One of the reasons for the attempt, Thompson says, was López's growing anxiety about Humaitá – and we must now turn to the events that had been taking place there.

When López had taken his army across the river into the Chaco he had left behind a garrison of 3,000 men commanded by Colonel Paulino Alén, with Colonel Francisco Martínez (a favourite of Lopez, his wife was one of Elisa Lynch's closest friends) as his second-in-command, and with nearly 200 guns. To begin with there were ample stores and it was possible to send a certain number of cattle across the river from the Chaco. This became increasingly difficult when the ironclads controlled the stretch of river between Timbó and Humaitá, and the only remaining track across country was also soon threatened. In addition the *Tacuarí*, Lopez's best warship of which he had been so proud, was no more. At least she had not gone down before enemy gunfire, for the Paraguayans themselves sank her after she had landed the last of the shipment of guns on the Chaco side of the river. The *Ygurei*, however, was sunk by the ironclads, though her crew escaped through the Chaco.

For some time Alén and his small garrison, were able to deceive the enemy by the same means (including 'quaker' guns) as those which had been adopted by the holding-parties at other points in the *quadrilátero*, and it was not until 11 April that Caxias attempted a reconnaissance in force, but says Thompson 'discovered nothing of the weakness of the place, which consisted of 15,000 yards of trench garrisoned by less than 3,000 men.' In Thompson's view 'it might easily have been taken in a night attack.'

It was over three months before the grand assault took place. In the meantime, however, in spite of a number of brilliant sorties by the garrison, Humaitá had become all but isolated. The Argentine General, Antonio Rivas, had succeeded in establishing a force in the Chaco between Timbó and Humaitá, thus cutting off the last supply route. Gradually the stores in Humaitá were exhausted and the garrison faced death by starvation. The allies, Thompson claims, sent several letters to the commanders in Humaitá urging them to surrender, but received no reply.

As the situation within the beleaguered fortress grew steadily worse, Colonel Alén in despair attempted to commit suicide, but the shot misfired; he was badly wounded but survived.

The command now passed to Martínez who employed one last notable stratagem. He made a great show of activity on the river, with boats and canoes full of men passing to and fro, and ordered the gunners inside the fortress to stop firing, thereby persuading the Allies that he had evacuated the fortress. The ironclads, therefore, approached Humaitá on 15 July and bombarded it. The guns within the fortress were still silent, and on the following morning General Osório advanced on Humaitá at the head of 12,000 men, expecting to march into deserted batteries as they had done at Curupaíty. The foremost of the attackers broke into a run in order to be the first to enter when, in Masterman's version, 'a yell of "*muerto a los cambas*"', rose above the noise of the exalting throng, the loaded guns were run into the embrasures and a moment afterwards poured a storm of grape and shell into the disordered crowd'. And on Thompson's testimony the attacking force lost at least 2,000 men, while Osório had his horse shot from under him and three of his aides-de-camp killed at his side.

But Martínez and his garrison (as well as a number of women and children who were with them) were by now reduced to cutting up the hides of slaughtered cattle into strips and boiling them for food. According to Masterman, Martínez managed to get a message through to López explaining the situation, and received a reply telling him to hold out for five more days and then to retreat. Masterman is hardly fair, though, in claiming that López had made no attempt to relieve the garrison. Quite apart from the attack of the *bogavantes* the Paraguayans had, as Thompson testifies, been making a number of attempts to dislodge General Rivas from his positions in the Chaco.

The evacuation of Humaitá, however, was now inevitable. On the night of 23 July, the women and the wounded (among them Colonel Alén) were taken across the river to the Chaco without being detected. The 24th was López's birthday and the band in Humaitá (its instruments now badly battered) played music all day in order to deceive the enemy. When night fell, the rest of the garrison safely crossed the river. The band was the last to leave, playing to the end. It was not until the middle of the following day that the Allies became suspicious, and after a cautious reconnoitre entered the abandoned fortress.

The sufferings of the 2,500 survivors of the garrison were by no means over. Their rear was temporarily protected by a small battery on the Chaco side of the river opposite Humaitá, but they could not take the road alongside the river because it was occupied by the army and fortifications of General Rivas, and between them and the safety of Timbó lay woods, marshes and a wide lake called Laguna Verá. The Allies, moreover, as soon as they realized what had happened, reinforced General Rivas, increasing his force to 10,000 men, and in additon sent 60 boats, some of them with guns, into Laguna Verá itself, while their ironclads were placed at a point in the river where they, too, could send their fire across the lake.

The Paraguayans succeeded in carrying their canoes to the shores of the lake, and began sending their women and wounded across. They had to run the gauntlet of a terrible fire. 'Day and night,' Thompson relates, 'by regular reliefs, eleven guns and 2,000 rifles played incessantly, from all quarters, on the Paraguayans'.

At the same time the Allied boats on the lake attacked continuously, so that a hand to hand fight between the boats and the canoes took place every time they crossed.

As soon as the paddlers reached the other side of the lake, and the protection of the guardboats which General Caballero (who was in command at Timbó) had stationed there, they 'would give a yell of delight', Thompson tells us, 'and having landed their passengers, return through the same terrible fire to fetch more'.

Over a period of a week, Thompson calculates, 10,000 shells were thrown at them, quite apart from the non-stop rifle fire, but incredibly, over 1,000 were transported to the other side, though many of them were wounded in the process. Colonel Alén had been carried across on a stretcher in one of the first of the canoes. He was carried to San Fernando – where he was placed under arrest.

The situation for Martínez and the remainder of the Paraguayans was becoming increasingly desperate. The small rations of food they had brought from Humaitá had long since been exhausted. Nevertheless on 28 July they savagely repulsed an attack by Brazilian troops. Martínez had brought a few 3-pound rifled guns with him from Humaitá, and when the ammunition for them was exhausted he broke up the muskets of the dead Paraguayans and used the locks and fittings for grapeshot.

By now, however, all the canoes had been sunk or captured, so that the only way to Timbó was through the enemy positions. On 2 August General Rivas sent Martínez an invitation to surrender; the flag of truce was met with a defiant hail of bullets. Martínez was contemplating a desperate do-or-die attempt to break through the large army facing him, but he and his men were in no condition to undertake the exploit. On the 4th Rivas sent another invitation to surrender. This time Martínez agreed to an interview which took place on the following day, and ended with the surrender of the surviving Paraguayans, the officers being allowed to keep their swords. Martínez was so weak that he had difficulty in speaking. 200 of his men had laid down around him to die of hunger. Nearly all of them had been completely without food for four days.

On the other side of Laguna Verá General Caballero still waited. Then when he was sure that the last survivor from Humaitá who could manage it had got across, he turned and marched back, eventually (after receiving orders to evacuate Timbó and Monte Lindo) to leave the Chaco and rejoin López on the Tebicuary.

And so 'the Allies were left alone in the vicinity of Humaitá, where they rested for three months, having required thirteen months siege to reduce the weakest position of any the Paraguayans had held.'

That, at least, was Thompson's view. In the allied countries, however, the fall of Humaitá was the occasion for tremendous celebrations. Dom Pedro always looked back upon it as one of the happiest days of his life.[5] With the end of the long campaign, which according to some estimates had cost 100,000 lives, it was universally believed that the war was as good as over. But as

Kolinski says, the fall of Humaitá 'proved . . . to be no more indicative of the war's early end than had the final collapse of Vicksburg in the American Civil War.'

Meanwhile, at San Fernando, López announced that the fall of Humaitá did not materially affect his strategic plans. Nevertheless his anger apparently found vent in a particularly savage act of revenge against Martínez for surrendering. He ordered his wife, Juliana Ynsfran, to be arrested, flogged and finally executed, 'for no other apparent reason,' Kolinsky says, 'than her connection with the Colonel'.

There are some accounts, however, which suggest that Juliana had been receiving letters from relations in Buenos Aires, via Masterman, which though innocent in themselves López construed as treasonable correspondence with the enemy.[6] According, too, to Barrett, Colonel Martínez had been in correspondence with the Allies while he was in Humaitá, and this was one of the reasons for Colonel Alén's attempted suicide, though Barrett produces no evidence in support of these claims. Kolinsky points out that Juliana Ynsfran was on a list, reported to have been captured by the Allies, of people executed for complicity in the alleged conspiracy plot.

The question as to whether or not there really was a conspiracy in 1868 has never been satisfactorily settled. Most of those accused of complicity did not live to tell the tale, and the relevant papers disappeared with them. The contemporary accounts that did survive were either by men like Father Maiz and General Resquín, fanatical supporters of the Marshal-President, directly responsible for conducting many of the investigations or carrying out the executions, and therefore at pains to stress their conviction that a conspiracy really did exist; or foreigners like Masterman, Porter Bliss and Washburn, who were involved in the accusations and who sought to exonerate themselves in writing of their Paraguayan experiences. These latter stoutly denied the reality of the conspiracy, but all three obviously had something to hide. Both parties, therefore, had a vested interest in the attitudes they adopted.

Thompson is in a somewhat different category. He was one of López's most trusted soldiers, and in that capacity he served him loyally to the end. He was among the specially favoured officers who, when they were at headquarters, always dined with the Marshal-President and Madame Lynch. He admits that while he was actually in Paraguay he did not give much credit to stories of

López's atrocities, because the President's manner 'was such as entirely to dispel and throw discredit on any whispers which might be uttered against him'.

After he had left Paraguay, he received, he says in the preface to his book, 'overwhelming corroborations' to justify him in now regarding López as a 'monster without parallel', whose actions he can view 'only with the greatest horror and aversion'. This preface, however, makes it quite clear that by the time Thompson came to write his book he was uneasy about the important part he had played in helping López to wage the war, so that his book, too, (though not in the same sense as the accounts by Masterman, Porter Bliss and Washburn) was in some degree an apologia.

As for the 'overwhelming corroborations', Burton at any rate seems to suspect that Thompson may have been a victim of the barrage of propaganda directed against him from Allied sources as soon as he left the theatre of war. Referring for example to some of the 'windy notes' Washburn, after he had left Paraguay, directed against López, Burton writes, 'I regret to say that Lieutenant Colonel Thompson had largely quoted from a document which breathes in every line a spirit of fierce hatred against a quondam friend.' As for Washburn's document, Burton roundly declares that it 'savours of want of truth'.

Burton himself is inclined to accept the existence of the conspiracy:

'It would appear that shortly after 22 February 1868, when the Brazilian ironclads had fired into Asunción, many Paraguayans began to despair of the cause. General Bruguez, . . . others say the Minister of Foreign Affairs, was deputed by the citizens to perform the pleasant operation which is popularly called "belling the cat".'

On the whole the genuinely neutral observers took the conspiracy as an accepted fact.

On the whole, too, Barrett is right when he says that Washburn, Masterman, and Porter Bliss (who was almost certainly responsible for many of the Hallet and Breen anti-López propaganda pamphlets, which gave highly lurid accounts of López's alleged atrocities) 'supply strong evidence' – if of an indirect kind – 'that a conspiracy did exist' in the very books in which they vehemently denied it.

Kolinski, to turn to one of the most recent students of the

Paraguayan war, probably gives the most balanced summing-up
that is possible in the absence of any conclusive evidence one way
or the other. Pointing out that after March 1868, the best of
Paraguay's fighting men had been lost in battle or by disease; that
the remaining army of some 10,000 men consisted largely of boys;
that supplies, including foodstuffs, were practically non-existent;
that most of the artillery had been captured at Humaitá and that
the Brazilian fleet had virtually complete control of the River
Paraguay – he concludes that 'there may have been some among
the élite of Paraguay . . . who felt that further resistance was
useless.'

He justifies his use of the word 'élite' with the surely incontro-
vertible argument that an anti-López faction could hardly have
developed among the common people of Paraguay, conditioned
as they were against anything in the nature of popular, spontaneous
political demonstrations through their years of rigid obedience to
Dr Francia and the two Lópezes, and who appeared to accept the
leadership of the President without question; or among the troops,
whose fanatical loyalty was also above suspicion. Kolinski suggests,
therefore, that 'the sector which stood to lose most by continued
allegiance to Francisco Solano López in the face of impending Allied
victory may have been comprised by the Marshal's own family
members, some among the middle and merchant classes, and
some in high government posts.'

The most specific references to the existence of treason and
conspiracy are contained in the memoirs of General Resquín.
According to them several members of López's family were
directly implicated. Resquín claims, for example, that Benigno
wrote to the Marquês de Caxias giving him information about the
Paraguayan river torpedoes and of the removal of guns from
Curupaíty to Humaitá, and that towards the end of March 1868,
a letter was found in Benigno's handwriting addressed to Caxias
on behalf of himself and his accomplices, giving full details of the
Paraguayan military situation, and implicating Bishop Palacios,
Dean Bogardo, and Generals Barrios and Bruguez and more than
eighty other people.[7] Towards the middle of March López also
received letters from his vice-president, Francisco Sánchez,
informing him of the meetings that had taken place at Asunción
when the Brazilian ironclads had appeared, and when the strange
question as to whether the city's guns should engage the enemy
had been discussed.

Father Fidel Maiz was also convinced of Benigno's guilt – and there is a report in the second volume of Washburn's *History of Paraguay* (most of which he wrote while he was in the country) of a conversation between himself and Benigno which shows that Benigno was, at the least, aware that his name was being discussed as a possible successor to his brother:

> 'He spoke to me quite freely of the suspicion that his brother had in regard to him and professed to be ignorant of the cause. I told him he had been imprudent in talking to the French Consul, M. Cuberville, who was at best a fool, and not always sober; that he had told me of a conversation they had held together, in which he had asked Benigno who was the most suitable man to put at the head of a government in case Francisco Solano should not be able to maintain himself and that Benigno had suggested the name of his brother-in-law, Bedoya, as the most eligible and proper person. I told him that if Cuberville himself had said so to me, he had probably said the same to others, and probably to Madame Lynch. Benigno denied that he had ever said anything of the kind; that Cuberville[8] himself had suggested something of the sort, but that for himself, he had not indulged in any such calculations.'

Naturally, Benigno would make such a denial, but it is difficult to see how any government, at a time of war crisis, could fail to take action if it came to hear of such a conversation or others like it – and it is difficult, too, to see how Washburn could write that passage and yet at the same time so definitely assert that there was not, and could not possibly be, any conspiracy against López.

In his memoirs Resquín states that the Foreign Minister José Berges eventually confessed that a revolution had been planned for 24 July, while Father Fidel Maiz says that Juan Esteban Molina, another suspect, declared, in a separate deposition, that the chief conspirators were Benigno, Berges and Bedoya – and that the date fixed for the revolution was 24 July.

There are plenty of ghastly accounts by Masterman and others of the methods employed by the investigators. The validity of confessions obtained under torture is obviously suspect – though Kolinski points out that 'not all the confessions of those arrested were obtained through duress', and he draws attention to an account by Juan C. Centurión, contained in the memoirs of Fidel Maiz, which says that the confession of Venancio López was a case in point, and insists that many of the prisoners made statements without the use of torture.

In this connection Thompson relates a series of curious circumstances which seem to contradict his conviction, after the event (though, of course, he had not seen any of the depositions, and the memoirs of Resquín and Father Maiz were published much later) that there was no conspiracy. 'For about a fortnight before 24 July,' he relates, 'López continually told me that the ironclads would force the batteries on that day, which they really did.'

Furthermore, he tells us that as one of the ironclads, the *Bahia*, passed his batteries (at Fortín and other positions on the River Tebicuary) 'three people put their heads out of the turret . . . and one of them waved a handkerchief, and shouted something.'

As soon as the ironclads had passed (receiving considerable damage from the Paraguayan batteries as they did so) Thompson telegraphed López at his headquarters informing him of the number of ironclads. He was sitting down to write a detailed report, when he himself received a telegram from López asking him, 'What signal did the first ironclad make on passing the battery?'

Thompson continues: 'I then wrote and told him all about it, and that the men said it was the Paraguayan Recalde, who had formerly deserted from López. Hereupon he wrote me a terrible anathema against traitors, wondering that they had been allowed to pass in silence, and to open their polluted mouths to honest patriots fighting for their country. I wrote back that they had been well abused by all, which was a fact; he then wrote back that he was now "satisfied with my explanation".'

From all this it seems clear that López was in possession of information, or at any rate strong suspicions, which caused him to attach a peculiar importance to the occurrences of 24 July. Kolinski also observes, in this connection:

'More strangely still, 24 July was the birthday of the Paraguayan Marshal President as well as the date of the final evacuation of Humaitá by the Paraguayan garrison.' And Thompson reports the widely held belief 'that the conspirators were to have been joined by the enemy, both with his army and his ironclads, on 24 July, which accounts for López's despatches to me on that date'.

If there was indeed a conspiracy, was the American Minister implicated in it? In Resquín's view he was at the very centre of the web. He believed that Washburn had originally discussed the secret plan with the Marquês de Caxias on the occasion of his two 'peace missions' to the Allied camp in 1866 and early 1867, and he positively states that there was evidence that Washburn was a member of a group conspiring for a revolutionary movement, which included Benigno and Venancio López as well as José Berges and Generals Barrios and Bruguez.

As we have seen, Washburn had landed himself in an extremely awkward situation by harbouring refugees and their property in the expectation of the arrival of the Allies in Asunción. As Barrett points out:

'Inevitably, if there were arrests for treason in Paraguay, they would be of people in a group that conspired to welcome the Allies to Asunción and who arranged to check their property into the hands of the Allies. It was not surprising when arrests were made that some of those people were involved; the surprising thing is that they were not all involved.'

Washburn realized his predicament when, after the departure of the Brazilian ironclads, a number of his former 'guests' who had been arrested wrote (presumably at the dictation of the authorities) demanding the return of their property. He had no legal right to keep it, but if he let it go and it was found to contain incriminating documents, then obviously he had – whether wittingly or un-wittingly – made himself a party to conspiracy by having agreed to take charge of such material.

He therefore tried to stall by conducting an interminable correspondence, first with Gumesindo Benítez, successor as Secretary for Foreign Affairs to Berges, and then (at even greater length) with Luis Caminos, who succeeded Benítez after the latter had himself been arrested, a correspondence in which the American Ambassador, to quote Barrett, 'disputed every hair-splitting point that he could think of, made quotations from every law book in his library and evaded every concrete issue which the Paraguayan Government raised'.

The two main subjects of discussion were the Paraguayan Government's demands for the expulsion from the American legation of a number of suspects, including Masterman (who was said to have passed treasonable letters) and Porter Bliss (who was accused of fraud in addition to treason) – and of course the trunks and boxes of the arrested suspects.

Some of the letters written by the suspects and forwarded to Washburn by Caminos, described in detail the objects they had deposited at the American legation, but as Washburn now did not dare to admit having in his possession anything that might give the authorities the legal excuse for demanding a search of his premises, he denied ever having seen these objects – and thereby fell into a trap. For several people who were not under arrest but who had lodged with him at the time of the brief appearance of the Brazilian ironclads, and who could also give an exact account of the property they had deposited with him, arrived in person at the American legation and took this property away. The Paraguayan Foreign Minister, therefore, politely pointed out to Washburn that if he had been 'mistaken' in some instances he might also be mistaken in his other denials.

According to Masterman one of the reasons for Washburn's extreme reluctance to allow Paraguayan officials to make a search of the legation was that he did not want them to find the manuscript of his *History of Paraguay*, which, as earlier quotations have illustrated, was by no means friendly in its references to López. But fear also played its part – for Washburn's request for his *Exequatur* had been ignored by Caminos who continued to remind him that his own requests in relation to the expulsion of suspects and of the release of their property had not been met. This in fact was Washburn's own explanation when eventually the whole affair (including the quarrels between Washburn and the American Naval Commanders) was investigated by the U.S. House of Representatives (first in Washington, and then in New York, and later back in Washington). In his statement Washburn stated that he had dragged out the exchange of notes because he feared for his life and was playing for time. 'I considered after much reflection,' he declared, 'that it was my duty to forget, to a certain extent, the dignity of my position and prolong the correspondence until a gunboat should come to our rescue . . .'[9]

Washburn was now informed, still in the most correct diplomatic language, that many of the arrested suspects, including José Berges, had made statements to the effect that there had definitely been a conspiracy against the life of Francisco Solano López – and that it had been discussed and planned in detail at the American Legation. He was again asked to co-operate with the Paraguayan

Government by handing over suspects and by giving access to the suspects' property and to documents which, it was alleged, included incriminating papers given to Washburn by Berges. The Foreign Minister called upon Washburn in person urging him to 'confess', and so apparently, in a more informal capacity, did Elisa Lynch. As Masterman says, Washburn now 'made the great mistake of replying *seriatim* to these charges' and 'argued the points' with his accusers.

It was about this time that he also decided to visit the President himself at his headquarters at San Fernando, presumably to sound him on his own attitude. According to Thompson 'he was not well received', though Washburn himself claims that he was entertained by López and Elisa Lynch and after dinner played whist with Elisa and Colonels Thompson and Wisner von Morgenstern (the Hungarian engineering officer who was López's chief military adviser, but who was incapacitated by illness during most of the war).

According to Barrett, Caminos also visited López after Washburn left and told him that the American Minister had agreed, on receipt of his passports, not to insist on taking Masterman and Bliss away with him, and that López commented that this was tantamount to an admission by Washburn that he had been wrong in claiming them as members of his staff.

However that may be, both Masterman and Bliss were left to their fates when eventually the U.S. gunboat *Wasp* arrived on 3 December at Angostura (López's headquarters at that time). Masterman tells us what happened as Washburn left his Legation for the river launch which was to take him to the safety of the American ship:

'We left the house together, but Mr Washburn walked so rapidly that the consuls and ourselves could scarcely keep up with him, and he was a few yards ahead when we reached the end of the Colonnade. There the police, who had been closing in around us, simultaneously drew their swords, rushed forward, and roughly separated us from the consuls. I raised my hat, and said, loudly and cheerfully, "Good-bye, Mr Washburn; don't forget us". He half turned his face, which was deathly pale, made a deprecative gesture with his hand and hurried away. We . . . were surrounded by about thirty policemen . . . who, with shouts and yells, ordered us to march down to the Policia.'

Once safely on board the *Wasp*, Washburn sent a letter to López so angry and threatening that if the Marshal-President had received it before the American gunboat set sail Thompson believed he would have been ordered to fire on her.

Washburn's behaviour after his escape was hardly calculated to establish his innocence of complicity in the alleged conspiracy plot. The *Wasp* was no sooner under way than he was demanding to be taken to the Allied lines so that he could provide Caxias with all the information he possessed about Paraguay's military and political position in the hope that this would help him to put an end to 'the Monster López'.[10] This Commander Kirkland (who had been hospitably received by López) refused, pointing out that he was on an official mission and that an action such as Washburn proposed would be a gross violation of neutrality.

But Commander Kirkland was unable to enforce a diplomatic discretion upon his passenger when they put in at Corrientes. To quote Washburn himself in his *History of Paraguay*:

> 'I advised everyone I met that López had arrested all the foreigners in Paraguay and had killed or would kill them all unless the Allies should show more activity and destroy him before he had time to carry his plans of indiscriminate murder into execution. . . . I observed, however, that Commander Kirkland was extremely reluctant to have anything prejudicial to López, giving as a reason that neutral gunboats passing the military lines had no right to convey intelligence from one belligerent to another'.

In Buenos Aires Washburn became even more voluble. Burton, who met him there, described him as 'living in a state of nervous excitement, in an atmosphere of terror and suspicion', and thought 'many of his assertions were those of a man who was hardly responsible for his actions'.

Washburn's state of mind is partly explained by the fact that, much to his astonishment, he had found that the part he had played was by no means universally applauded. As he plaintively put it himself during the U.S. Congress investigation:

> 'When I got away from Paraguay under the circumstances that I did, when López had set his plans to kill me as he had killed everybody else, the Allies and their press set up a howl against me. It was a great satisfaction to them to abuse me, notwith-

standing I exposed the atrocities of López, whom they hated worse than they did me. Besides, this newspaper abuse was caught up by the newspapers in this country, and throughout the country from Eastport to San Diego, in every newspaper I was severely censured.'[11]

The attitude adopted towards Washburn by some of the Allied newspapers was frankly scurrilous, several of them accusing him of exploiting his diplomatic privileges in order to conduct a shady commercial deal.

There is nothing to substantiate these accusations, but one would be happier if Washburn had not played the same game, accusing practically everyone who got on well with López, including his own fellow-countrymen, of taking bribes. There was his comment, for example, on Commander Kirkland's statement (during the U.S. Congress investigation) that López had treated him with great courtesy:

'Well he was treated with courtesy. And I was told quite a number of bales of Paraguayan yerba were brought aboard and were afterwards advertised for sale in Montevideo as Paraguayan Yerba bought by the United States steamer *Wasp*.'

Writing too, in his book on Paraguay, of the various naval officers who were hospitably received by López on various missions during the war (and who almost without exception reported favourably of him and of Madame Lynch) Washburn says:

'The naval commanders thus treated by López were either English, Italians, or Americans; and from their readiness to become his trumpeters and champions, it would seem that they were of such cheap material that a good dinner, a ring, a towel of Paraguayan manufacture or a tercia of yerba was sufficient to induce them to betray their trust and leave their countrymen to be tortured and executed.'

But this was exactly the accusation urged against Washburn himself by the hostile American press. Why, the papers demanded, if Porter Bliss and Masterman really were members of the American legation, and if López was the monster Washburn claimed, did he abandon them? Surely if he was convinced that López was putting everybody to death, as he claimed, he should have refused to accept his passports unless Bliss and Masterman were allowed to accompany him?

Washburn's reply to this challenge was that he had left Paraguay
in the belief that he could do more good for Bliss and Masterman
in the United States by presenting the 'true facts' about Paraguay
than he could have done by staying on at the risk of his life

Barrett's comment on this is that Washburn 'had talked himself
into the same kind of an impasse that he had reached in his
correspondence with the Paraguayan Government: one of his
major declarations contradicted the other'. For, Barrett argues, 'if
López was a bloody monster from whom Washburn was in
danger, then Bliss and Masterman were doomed within hours of
their capture – and long before Washburn could get started on his
mission of "doing them good" in the United States. If López were
not, the Press of the United States could see no excuse for Washburn in hauling down the flag of his Legation.'

But was Washburn right in thinking that his own safety was
threatened? Commander Kirkland at any rate did not think so.
When during the U.S. House of Representatives investigation he
was asked: 'Did you regard Mr Washburn as in any danger?' his
reply was:

'No sir, I never did. Mr Washburn, I understand, used to go
out riding on horseback from Asunción every day, and it would
have been a very easy thing for López to have killed him any
time he wanted; nobody would have known anything about it.
López needed not to go into his house and take him and put him
in prison.'

None of this, of course, has any direct bearing on the question
of Washburn's complicity in the alleged conspiracy, though it
obviously suggests that he was seriously disturbed by the events
he had lived through, that he was not a very reliable or objective
witness, and that he was eminently unsuited for the post he had
occupied.

His utter lack of any kind of finesse alone disqualified him. We
have already seen instances of his clumsy indiscretions, and it is
relevant here to note some others. There is, for example, the
extraordinary letter which Washburn wrote to his successor,
General Martin T. MacMahon, which, besides listing property
belonging to foreigners left behind in the U.S. Legation and money
and property taken out of Paraguay for foreigners, speaks of a
certain Paraguayan lady, a friend of Washburn's, as 'our spunky,
witty, confidential, López-hating little friend,' refers to 'Mrs.

Lynch and her brats' and, after passing on various official responsibilities to MacMahon, states: 'I am taking it for granted that you will not have any communication with him (López) . . .'. It is not, to put it mildly, the kind of hand-over that is customary between ambassadors of a neutral country.

A comment of Masterman's is also worth quoting: 'Mr. Washburn did talk most imprudently. Amongst ourselves it was all very well to say what we thought of the war and the character of López; but he used, in his blundering Spanish, to tell things to natives.' And Masterman goes on to say that a number of visitors to the Legation, '"Your Excellency-ied" him into the most perilous of confidences, and then betrayed all to Mrs Lynch – which, perfectly right in themselves as mere personal opinions, became treason and conspiracy if the point of view were shifted a little.'

Masterman also points out that at the very moment that Washburn was assuring the Paraguayan government that '"he hoped to see the Allies defeated"' he was recording with the same pen, in his *History of Paraguay*, 'that López was a monster of iniquity, a coward, and a knave' – and saying so to inmates of the American Legation. Masterman says that Antonio de las Carreras (the former Blanco leader, now in disgrace with López and soon to be executed) commented on Washburn's behaviour with the Spanish idiom 'He was trying to eat with both sides of his cheek'.

Again, none of this amounts to proof of complicity on Washburn's part, but it does tend to make one feel that, in his blundering way, he was quite capable of it and that the Paraguayan authorities, given the heightened atmosphere of war and crisis, had ample justification for suspecting him.

It is, of course, quite possible that they knew he was guilty of no more than ineptitude and indiscretion (he had made so many anti-López remarks that if he had been a native of the country he would obviously have been arrested for treason long ago) and were deliberately entangling him in the web.

This possibility was presumably in General MacMahon's mind when, in connection with an examination of the long correspondence between Washburn and the Paraguayan Foreign Office during the United States Congress investigation, he gave it as his opinion that either López genuinely believed that Washburn was implicated, or that he wanted to obtain as many statements as possible from him – 'playing upon Mr Washburn's fears, and thus compelling him to make a most humiliating display of himself and take a course which neither his Government nor his best friends would approve . . .'.[12]

There has, however, been no convincing explanation as to what benefit the latter course of action would bring López. It could be argued that he hoped a new American Ambassador might be better disposed towards his cause, but he could have no guarantee of this, especially as the newcomer would be briefed by Washburn, and to throw discredit on a country's ambassador was hardly the best way of enlisting its sympathy.

Most commentators on the subject have come to the conclusion that Washburn, while obviously guilty of anti-López grumblings, was not an active conspirator. Harris G. Warren for example, while admitting that Washburn had been 'very free about expressing his opinions about López and Paraguay in a way that made him a model of what a diplomat should never be' (and pointing out that two of Washburn's closest Paraguayan friends were well-known to be hostile to López) declares that 'to charge him with a plot to crown his career by eliminating López was utterly absurd.'[13] And Barrett, one of the best disposed towards López of the European writers on the subject, believed that the American Minister was merely 'the cat's-paw for men more practical than he,' who 'fed his vanity and his almost incredible credulity' and 'led him to attempt things far out of his province as a minister of a neutral power', in the process causing him to indulge in 'indiscreet meddling with the affairs of Paraguay' and filling him with incredible tales about López which he accepted as true without investigation.

As for the House Committee of the U.S. Congress which investigated the matter, it is not easy to be altogether sure what was the outcome. In presenting its report it commented that much of the testimony was 'of a conflicting character', revealing 'a feeling of bitterness and animosity between different officers of the navy, and between the naval and diplomatic officers of the government, not creditable to the parties concerned, and subversive of that efficiency in the public service which the government has a right to expect from its officials'.

A majority of the committee condemned Rear Admiral S. W. Godon for not giving sufficient help to Washburn at the time of the latter's return to Paraguay from leave; resolved that the arrest and detention of Bliss and Masterman was 'a gross insult to the honour and dignity of the United States'; and delivered a lecture to naval officers on the subject of co-operating with diplomatic officers. Warren tells us that a minority report, while agreeing that the detention of Bliss and Masterman was an insult to the U.S.A., considered that Washburn's acquiescence to it compromised the American flag, 'and could not be justified upon any consideration of personal safety'; declared that Washburn should not have accepted a passport that did not cover the whole of his staff without exception, while also declaring that Washburn had acted imprudently in adopting a hostile attitude towards the Paraguayan President, and in 'associating Bliss and Masterman with his legation (one a British subject, suspected by López of a conspiracy with his enemies and the enemies of his country – both adventurers and of doubtful reputation)' – and insisted that neither Admiral Godon or Admiral Davis should be censured.

But the Committee could not agree on any actual recommendations. In effect, Barrett says, it 'begged the issue', simply coming to the obvious conclusion that nothing had happened in Paraguay which warranted new legislation

It should perhaps be mentioned here that this was one of the least savoury periods in American politics. Not long before Washburn appeared before the House Committee (on 30 March 1869) General U.S. Grant became President. One of the men most responsible for his election was Elihu Benjamin Washburn, a Congressman from Illinois – and brother of Charles Ames.

One of Grant's first appointments, on 5 March, was that of E. B. Washburn, as Secretary of State. The outcry in the press and elsewhere was such that Washburn resigned on 16 March. But during the brief period he held office he issued an order (dated 15 March) recalling from his post as Minister to Paraguay General MacMahon, 'the man', Barrett comments, 'whose conduct of that post was a rebuke to a member of the Washburn family'. According to Barrett, the thinking behind this action was that: 'the presence of a Minister in Paraguay who was dealing satisfactorily with a man whom Washburn (Charles Ames) claimed to be a "monster" was certain to influence the judgement of the House Committee'.

In considering the question of Charles Ames Washburn's possible complicity a few final points are worth making. There is, first, the fact that there were times when Masterman, himself one of López's victims, entertained doubts on the matter. For example, when the Paraguayan Foreign Secretary sent Washburn a despatch containing a 'confession' from José Berges, 'signed by him in a trembling hand' (and exacted, undoubtedly, under torture), this included a description of the circumstances in which Berges had allegedly handed over treasonable documents to Washburn 'so exact and vivid' that 'my own belief in Mr Washburn's statements was staggered for a time.'

And a little later, Masterman records, Washburn received a further despatch 'most politely worded . . . often admirably arranged and always well written; yet full of the most serious charges against him, and so well argued, so clearly supported, and with such a mass of evidence to back them, that I often pondered with aching brain for hours over these papers, and could hardly hold my own certain conviction still that they were false, base fabrications from beginning to end.'

Far more serious, however, as a possible indication of Washburn's guilt (as well as of the existence of a movement directed against López) was a slip of the tongue which Mrs Washburn is supposed to have made on board the *Wasp*. This is best explained by looking at the following passage from the transcript of the proceedings of the U.S. House of Representatives Committee of Investigation:

'*Question:* (by Mr Orth): In your letter marked 'private' to Admiral Davis, you say this: "Mr Washburn told me that he had overheard of a revolution or conspiracy against the Government (of Paraguay); but on one occasion Mrs Washburn, when her husband was not present, stated that there was a plan to turn López out of power, and to put in his place his two brothers Venancio and Benigno"? Please state the circumstances under which you received this information.

Answer (Com. Kirkland) It was on the passage down the river, two or three days after we left the batteries. Mrs Washburn said distinctly that there was no conspiracy but that there was a plan. It was at the dinner table. Mr Washburn had finished his dinner and had gone out for something, and shortly after came back. This remark struck me as rather singular, and I wrote of it to the Admiral. I know that she made a distinction between the words "conspiracy" and "plan".

Q.: Was any person present?

A.: Yes, sir; a Mr Davie was present.

Q.: Who was he?

A.: He went up with me as an interpreter and translator, and assisted me in writing.

Q.: Did Mrs Washburn, at the time and in connection with the remarks that you just stated, say that there was no conspiracy?

A.: We were speaking of López and the country and the people, and she said there was no conspiracy but there was a plan to turn López out. . . .'[14]

An affidavit by Charles J. F. Davie, 'sworn and subscribed to' in the presence of the U.S. Consul in Montevideo was then presented. After confirming that Washburn had expressed to Commander Kirkland 'his strong wish and determination to communicate to Marshal Caxias, the Brazilian Commander-in-Chief . . . all the information that he was possessed of, and which he might have obtained in his official capacity, regarding the number of Marshal López's forces, their position and strength, and plan of operations,' it went on to state: 'was also present at table, on another and subsequent occasion, when Mr Washburn having left the table, Mrs Washburn alluded to the revolutionary plan against President López which she and Mr Washburn had been cognizant of, to upset López's Government and to put one of his brothers, Benigno and Venancio López, in his place.'[15]

With these fine distinctions between 'conspiracy' and 'plan' we are obviously in the realm of semantics. It is true that when Mrs Washburn herself came to be questioned she denied, if not very convincingly, having uttered the words sworn to by Kirkland:

'I do not remember ever to have had any conversation with him about it, more than that we were all conversing about the conspiracy. I could not have said that there was a plan or conspiracy because I did not then believe it; but I may have said that at one time we may have supposed there was, because of the arrest of people etc. I did not then believe there was a conspiracy and, of course, could not have said that there was one. I do not remember definitely what occurred on the voyage, as I was very nervous and suffered a great deal.'[16]

And finally to quote a recent opinion, Kolinski, while pointing out that Washburn, 'was vehement in his denials of complicity in any such plot' goes on to say:

'It proved difficult for him, nevertheless, to offer convincing explanations for his decision to retain his legation in Asunción instead of moving to Luque where the government had been transferred, and for his action in transforming the legation into a haven for more than 40 persons, many of whom were among the conspiracy suspects' – and he too draws attention to Mrs Washburn's alleged indiscretion.

It is difficult to see how, in the face of all this, some writers have persisted in dismissing both the conspiracy plot and the possibility of Washburn having played a part in it, as pure invention on the part of the Paraguayan authorities. It is, assuredly, a case of 'not proven', one way or the other, on both counts.

Whether a conspiracy existed or not, investigations of a most thorough kind certainly took place. López dealt with what he obviously considered a serious crisis by calling a council of war, summoned by a decree of 2 August 1868. This decided to try those under suspicion by military courts under the ordinances or *Leyes de Partida* which were then in force in Paraguay. Two-man tribunals were set up to handle the investigations. A number of these tribunals were manned by priests, including Father Fidel Maiz, who was the chief investigator. Police and army units were ordered to arrest the suspects and bring them to San Fernando, which before long took on the grim appearance of a concentration camp.

As Kolinski says: 'The roll of those in custody came to read like a roster of Asunción's first families': the vendetta against the 'old Spanish' aristocracy, initiated by Dr Francia, was being continued by his successor with a vengeance. The most prominent of the Paraguayans eventually to be executed were Benigno López (Venancio was also executed in the following year); López's brothers-in-law Saturnino Bedoya and General Barrios (the latter after an attempt at suicide); the Ministers Berges and Benítez; Bishop Palacios, Dean Bogardo and General Bruguez.

Among the foreigners arrested were John Watts, the British engineer, and James Manlove, the American adventurer (both of whom were apparently executed); Leite Pereira, the former acting Portuguese consul, and Antonio de las Carreras, the former Uruguayan Blanco diplomat (both of whom died); Alonzo Taylor, López's British architect and von Treuenfeldt, the telegrapher (of whom more in a moment), the ill-fated Prussian observer von Versen – and Masterman and Bliss – who all survived.

It is difficult to arrive at the exact number of people executed in what Burton described as 'the conspiracy that has been so fiercely asserted and denied, the new Reign of Terror called by some the Reign of Rigour.' The Allies were continually publishing lists of the victims which they claimed to have found abandoned in the Paraguayan camps they had overrun. But there were too many of these to be convincing, and Barrett points out that 'several of the witnesses' before the U.S. Congress House Committee 'testified to the general inaccuracy of the lists.' One of these lists, published in the *Tribuna* of Buenos Aires, on 20 February 1869, purported to be taken from the captured diaries of General Resquín, but Burton says that 'even this paper was looked upon with suspicion. It might, after all be nothing but a *ruse de guerre*.' We would do well, he suggests 'to exercise a certain reservation of judgement' on all such accounts of killings and atrocities. He tells us that when he himself visited the Allied camp in September 1868 'all were talking of the butcheries . . . they talked so much that the less credulous portion of the public began to disbelieve the reports generally.' He found that 'the victims were killed and brought to life again half a dozen times'. Burton also tells us that just as he was embarking to return to Buenos Aires he was told of the discovery of 'six corpses laid out straight, with their feet towards the enemy, and each bearing pinned to his breast a paper inscribed "thus perish the traitors."' By the time he reached Buenos Aires, he tells us, 'the figure of six had grown to sixty-seven, and included women and children: it there advanced, temporarily halting at 64 . . . at 70, and at 400 to 800 victims'.

Cunninghame-Graham, of course, goes the whole hog, quoting an Italian source to support the ludicrous claim that by September 1869, 'eight thousand victims had been despatched by López'.

Interestingly enough Burton points out that we would be in a better position to arrive at the truth if Thompson had 'been explicit upon the subject' – but that all the same Thompson had refused to indulge in wild speculation, stating 'I know very little about the subject myself, and probably hardly anyone knows much'.

In these circumstances obviously no figure of the executions can be relied upon, though Kolinski seems inclined to accept that of 500, while acknowledging that it was derived from Masterman, who cannot be regarded as an unbiased source.

Masterman himself gives us a most vivid picture of the sufferings of the suspects, from fetters, forced marches, bad food and accommodation, and interrogations under torture. The description is so vivid, indeed, so full of the details of horror, that generally speaking it compels acceptance. But if there were so many exaggerations on the number of executions it seems reasonable to suppose that the same thing may have happened in this respect also. Burton tells us that when he was in Buenos Aires he called upon the crusty American Admiral Davis, a man not at all likely, Burton points out, 'to be imposed upon by mere "amiability and plausibility"' on López's part, who nevertheless declared that Marshal López had 'affected him favourably' and believed that the atrocities 'had been grossly exaggerated'.

Burton also scoffs at the claims made by both Masterman and Bliss that they had themselves been put to the torture. In this case we can certainly share his scepticism.

These two were released on 10 December, a week after the *Wasp* returned bearing on board the new American Minister, General MacMahon, who refused to present his credentials until Masterman and Bliss were safely on board. They were both treated by the American officers as prisoners whose cases would need to be investigated on their return home. They were also medically examined and at the Congress House Committee of Investigation Commander Kirkland testified:

> 'I ordered him (Surgeon Gale) to examine them. I think he said that Bliss had a slight diarrhoea, probably caused by long confinement or change of diet. I ordered him then to examine the persons of these men to see if they had been subjected to torture, with a view to entering it in the log book of the ship. The doctor reported that there was no sign of torture about them.'

Furthermore, as Warren points out, 'before throwing all caution aside in shedding tears for these interesting characters,' we should also note the 'sworn testimony of Thomas Q. Leckron, who talked with Bliss when he came aboard the *Wasp*.'

Leckron, the Captain's clerk, testified as follows:

> 'I remarked . . . that after three months of torture and confinement which he had undergone it must indeed be a relief to find himself once more with those who had the power and the will to protect him. He then said that as far as torture was concerned he had never been subjected to it, or even threatened with anything of the kind; that he had not been in irons; that he and

Mr Masterman had a hut as comfortable as any of those occupied by the Paraguayans; that they were given every day a sufficient allowance of beef and mandioca, as well as yerba; and that the only thing he complained of was that he could not go any distance from his quarters without being accompanied by a Paraguayan soldier.'

It is true that Porter Bliss himself was in a somewhat special position, because López had commissioned him to write a highly uncomplimentary book about Washburn and his alleged share in the conspiracy called *História Secreta*, though Porter Bliss asserted later that it was written under duress. Nevertheless both he and Masterman persisted in claiming that they had been tortured, and Dr William Stewart (who, however, had by then deserted to the Allies) confirmed everything that Bliss and Masterman had said. On the other hand, in addition to the sworn testimonies of Kirkland and Leckron, we have Captain Ramsay's report that Dr Frederick Skinner had told him that neither Masterman nor Bliss had been tortured, and a statement by Dr Marius Duval that they showed no signs of it. As Warren so rightly says 'someone certainly was lying,' and with the evidence at our disposal we can really do no more in this instance than agree with Warren's own conclusion: 'Perhaps we had better let this matter of veracity rest there'.

A similiar uncertainty surrounds the question of López's own part in the conspiracy trials and executions. There seems little doubt that there was a marked hardening of his nature at this time. As Burton puts it, 'the suspicion of treason, and the firm resolve to fight his last man, seem to have acted unfavourably upon the Marshal President', though he insists that before this López 'had preserved a certain character for moderation', and that 'despite the reports which are always set on foot concerning an enemy, he could not be accused of cruelty'. He admits, too, that the executions, 'if they really took place,' must be explained either as 'the most fatal of necessities' or as 'the dementia preceding destruction'.

Burton also draws attention to the fact that about this time López 'had become addicted to port wine and piety; to mass-going and hard drinking', which both Thompson and Masterman confirm. It should also be noted, though, that Burton also points to reports 'which show heart of a softer stuff' citing, for example, López's affection for his children by Elisa Lynch; and Thompson tells us how at San Fernando López 'used to go out with his children to fish in a lagoon near the headquarters'.

López himself does not figure in any of the accounts as having been directly involved in the workings of the tribunals, although he acted as a final judge in the case of the chief suspects. These, of course, would include members of his own family. As might be expected Washburn put matters in their blackest colours, declaring in a statement in Buenos Aires on 20 September 1868, quoted by Burton, that López had imprisoned, flogged and tortured his mother and his sisters. As also might be expected both Masterman and Cunninghame-Graham follow Washburn's lead.

But again, the situation is not as clear-cut as this would suggest. When, for example, General MacMahon was asked, during the U.S. Congress House Committee investigation, to comment on the report that López had maltreated his sisters he replied, 'I never heard of it until I left Paraguay and I do not believe it'.

He was even more emphatic in his reply to a similar question about López's mother:

'I never heard of it in Paraguay or until I came into the camp of his enemies; on the contrary, I know that while I was in Paraguay, his mother and sisters were treated as the first ladies of the land by himself and by everybody. Their residence was at the time a few miles from Piribebuy and when I left, my house, being one of the best in Piribebuy, was given over to the mother of the President where she lived with her daughters, and on many occasions it occurred to me that his devotion to her was exceedingly filial. He always treated her with the utmost respect, frequently communicating with her by telegraph, and was constantly sending messages to her. On the anniversary of her birthday I was invited to dine at her house with a number of people. I could not go that day but I remember his sending all of his children and Mrs Lynch there to dine with her; he also sent presents to her.'

Other witnesses gave similar evidence, and Burton quotes a letter which López sent to his mother on 10 September, couched in terms which fully bear out MacMahon's testimony.

If López was the unmitigated monster his enemies gave him out to be, this attitude towards his mother at this particular juncture is all the more surprising in view of the fact that he was almost certainly aware of her feelings about the war. We know from Thompson, for example, that Doña Juana had visited López at his headquarters at Paso Pucu after the first battle of Tuyutí, when 'it was whispered' she had begged her son 'to give up the war against such overwhelming Powers, and to retire to Europe'. She visited him again in July 1868, Thompson tells us, to plead for her sons and daughters who were under arrest.

According to Father Maiz, drawing on reports from several people, including Father José I. Acosta, chaplain to the López family, López probably knew that both his mother and his sisters had, at the least, been aware of a plot being hatched against him.

Kolinski agrees that López was 'lenient with his mother, for whom he continued to hold sincere affection'; but his claim that Venancio López 'was kept in custody like a common prisoner' does not square with this comment by Masterman (who certainly had no desire to whitewash López):

'I had often watched with hungry envy the many "encomiendas" (gifts of eatables, etc.) the two brothers of the President received, and longed to share them, especially the bread, which arrived new nearly every morning from their mother's house. . . .'

Kolinski thinks that 'there is reason to believe that López may not have been fully aware of the extent to which his tribunals went in their hunt for suspects'. He refers to an episode from the narrative of Alonzo Taylor,[17] López's former architect, which took place on 25 December:

'. . . López and Mrs Lynch rode through the Guardia, with several officers, and I think she drew his attention to us. We were ordered to stand in a row, and he came up to us, and asked, "are you all prisoners?" We replied, "Yes", and then Mr von Treuenfeld appealed to his Excellency, who asked him why he was there. Mr Treuenfeld said he did not know, and the President told him he was at liberty, and might retire. I then approached, and said I should be grateful for the same mercy. López asked me who I was, and affected great surprise when he heard my name, and said, "What do you do here? You are at liberty." Then the other prisoners, ten in number, came up and received the same answer.'

The rest of Alonzo Taylor's narrative, which is very similar in tone to Masterman's and full of much the same descriptions of tortures and executions, was used frequently in anti-López propaganda publications, but, as Barrett points out, with the above passage about his release omitted.

In commenting on the passage at the U.S. Congress Investigation, however, General MacMahon said:

'This statement was entirely voluntary on his part, no reference having been made to the treatment he received while in prison. He premised the remark by some such expression as this: "I do not care what others say; President López never treated me otherwise than as a gentleman." He was not then under the surveillance of López; he was within the jurisdiction of the Allies.'

Elisa Lynch also claimed, in her *Exposición y Protesta*, that López was unaware of the atrocities, and that they were deliberately committed, largely at the instigation of Bishop Palacios, as part of the conspiracy, so that details could be given to the Allies for their anti-López propaganda campaign. In doing so, of course, she tacitly admitted that there *were* atrocities, and in any case she could hardly be called a disinterested party. Barrett, however, suggests that: 'the evidence from the many souces quoted in these notes would indicate that Palacios was responsible for most of the cruelties and that López held him responsible . . .'.

According to Washburn, it was Elisa Lynch herself who was mainly to blame. He writes, 'to this bad, selfish, pitiless woman may be ascribed many of the numberless acts of cruelty of her paramour'.

MacMahon disagreed completely, informing the U.S. Congress that in his opinion Elisa Lynch was 'a woman who has been grossly maligned . . . by the press of Buenos Aires, which charged her with all sorts of immoralities, such as being cruel, instigating the President to unheard-of deeds of atrocity and with everything that could be written about a woman.'

In an additional statement MacMahon came back to the subject, in order to read to the committee an extract from a Buenos Aires paper which had just reached him:

'"We publish today an interesting narrative of one of the English Paraguayan sufferers just come down. He speaks in the highest terms of the kindness shown to himself and his wife and also to all the other English in López's employment by Madame Lynch, and he, in common with all the sufferers, denounced in indignant terms the calumnies and slanders that have from time to time appeared in some of the organs of the Press against this heroic woman who has ever exerted herself to mitigate the suffering which the war entailed upon the Paraguayan people.'''

Burton, too, states that:

'All are agreed that during the war Madame Lynch has done her utmost to mitigate the miseries of the captives and to make the so-called "détenus" comfortable.'

Burton, incidentally, is also one of the few writers on the subject to spare a thought for what, in human terms, the war meant for Elisa, as a woman and a mother. No wonder, he says in effect, that by now she was showing signs of ageing, her blonde hair 'sprinkled with grey', and her figure tending to bulkiness (though she was still a handsome woman): for 'her nerve must have been terribly tried since the campaign began, by telegrams which were delivered even at dinner time, while every gun, fired in a new direction, caused a disturbance. She and her children have been hurried from place to place, and at times she must have been prey to the most wearying and wearing anxiety.'

In spite of all this, Burton says: 'Her manners are quiet and she shows a perfect self-possession'. While both she and López were still secretly hoping against hope for some sort of foreign inter-vention, 'only on one occasion', Burton's informant told him, 'did she betray . . . some anxiety – as to whether the British Minister would visit Paraguay'.

But to complete these examples of opinions contrary to Wash-burn's wholesale condemnation – even Masterman provides evidence that Elisa was not callously indifferent:

'One evening an officer came round with a number of little boxes containing gifts from Mrs Lynch . . . I received some cigars, sugar, yerba, and a bottle of rum.'

Where, then, does the truth lie? Somewhere between the two extremes, no doubt – or, rather, one must, as with most human beings, take a handful from first one, then the other, side of the scale.

The same justice, of course must be afforded to Francisco Solano López himself.

*   *   *   *   *

But to return to the war. Reference has already been made to the Allied passage of the batteries on the River Tebicuary after the fall of Humaitá. López now decided to withdraw his forces – supplemented by the garrisons from Mato Grosso, which had all been evacuated with the exception of a squadron of cavalry left near the disputed border-line of the river Apa – to new positions higher up the river, near the small river-port of Villeta. Thompson was placed in charge of the evacuation of Fortín (the enemy again being deceived by the use of 'quaker' guns) and of the preparation of new batteries at Angostura, where a small river called the Pikysyry runs into the Paraguay. It was now that Thompson was promoted from Major to Lieutenant-Colonel (López was very sparing of promotions to higher ranks, especially where foreigners were concerned) and presented with a sword of honour.

The withdrawal was accomplished with few losses and the guns at Angostura were all in position, including the *Criollo* which was brought down from Asunción by steamer, together with all the other guns in the capital and its garrison, by the time the Allies moved in any strength. They crossed the Tebicuary on 1 September 1868 after a sharp skirmish with the Paraguayan rear guard, in which the most famous of the Paraguayan patrol leaders, Captain José Matiás Bado was wounded and captured: unable to endure the thought of being removed from the conflict he tore off his bandages in order to ensure a speedy death. Seven days later the ironclads began to bombard Angostura and to be bombarded in their turn: the *Criollo*, for example, striking one of them at the water-line. Meanwhile the Paraguayan army waited behind their new lines for the renewal of the Allied onslaught. Ammunition was short; none of the guns had more than 100 rounds (and many far less) and none of the infantry more than 60 to 100 rounds.

The onslaught, however, was delayed for some time. Caxias had decided that the Pikysyry lines were too strong for a frontal assault, despite his overwhelming superiority in men and munitions. Taking a leaf out of López's book he, too, started work on a road through the Chaco, parallel to the river Paraguay, to a point opposite San Antonio, four miles to the north of Villeta, with the idea of then re-crossing the Paraguay to take López in the rear.

While these plans were in preparation the ironclads continued to bombard Angostura, and from 8 October to pass and repass the batteries. 'It was capital sport,' Thompson tells us, in true British style, 'looking out for these steamers at night. They used to extinguish every light on board, and when going down the stream would go with the current, only putting on full speed when they found they were detected.' Although the Paraguayan shells could not sink them, the ironclads, besides losing a number of men, suffered considerable damage. Thompson describes how, when they had to retire in order to repair the damage, he and his men would watch the splinters that had been removed from them and thrown into the river 'drifting down for four or five hours, and among other small splinters came pieces of doors and other inside work, which showed they had been perforated'.

This was the period of intense activity by neutral shipping – a portent of the serious crisis that was gathering for the Paraguayan forces. Besides the *Wasp*, which took Washburn away in mid-September and returned on 3 December to land General Mac-Mahon (and take Masterman and Bliss on board) several British ships arrived. One of these, the *Linnet*, brought Gould on another unsuccessful attempt to take away the British subjects. Captain Parsons of the *Beacon* (who was treated to English plum pudding made by Elisa Lynch) fared better, embarking Dr Fox and twelve Englishwomen with their children. During October and November, French and Italian ships, arriving 'almost daily', Thompson says, evacuated a number of their nationals, though Thompson states that 'the Brazilian ironclads several times came up and insulted them, going even to the length of firing at the battery over the bows of the Italian steamer'.

Caxias and his Chaco army crossed the river Paraguay to San Antonio on 6 December and began to move inland along the road to Villeta. The last set campaign of the war (though not the end of the fighting) was under way – the Lomas Valentinas campaign as it is known, after the name of the low-lying hills (or *lomas*) in the area.

When the Allied army reached the narrow bridge crossing a swift-flowing stream named Ytororó, they found their passage blocked by 5,000 men and 12 guns, under the command of General Caballero. The bridge was the only way in which the stream could be crossed, which meant a direct assault by the Brazilians, who were led by General Alexandre Gómez de Argolo. The action which followed was regarded by several allied witnesses,[18] as one of the most hard-fought battles of the whole war. Caballero's outnumbered Paraguayans stubbornly defended their positions and in ferocious hand-to-hand fighting the bridge changed hands no less than three times, at the end of which the Paraguayans were in possession. Caxias himself, however, now arrived with reinforcements and the sixty-five year old commander himself led the final charge: Brazilian legend has it that he was wearing an old curved sword which had remained unused in its scabbard for so long that when he drew it, a cloud of rust, spiders and crickets flew out of it.

The Paraguayans were now dislodged from the bridge and forced to retreat, leaving six of their twelve guns behind. They had lost 1,200 men out of their small force; one of the battalions which went into action with 300 effectives, had only nine men unwounded by the end of the battle. But Allied losses were far higher – well over 3,000 casualties – while among the wounded were General Argolo and a number of other senior officers.

The Allies were badly shaken by the closeness of the decision at the battle of Ytororó, and it was not until 11 December that they resumed their advance southward towards Villeta – López's Dunsinane, one is almost tempted to call the advance, for it was an exceptionally hot day and the Allied soldiers used the branches to shield their heads from the sun, so that they looked like a forest on the march.

Caballero again engaged the enemy with about 4,000 men and twelve guns, at a place called Avay. Another ferocious battle took place. The Paraguayans – who 'all fought like lions', Thompson tells us – held their ground in pouring rain for four hours against overwhelming odds and wave after wave of frontal assaults, until they were completely surrounded by the enemy cavalry. They were now practically cut to pieces. There were few prisoners, for the simple reason that Caballero's men would not lay down their arms until they were literally hacked out of their hands. Most of those who were taken (nearly all of them badly wounded) managed to escape a few days later. General Caballero himself was pulled off his horse and his poncho and silver spurs were taken, but he was not recognized, and miraculously made his way back through the surrounding enemy unscratched. Thompson says that 300 women 'belonging to the Paraguayan army' were also captured – and that the Allies 'did not treat them well'.

The Allies had once again suffered far heavier losses than the Paraguayans. They had at least 4,000 casualties, among them General Osório, who was badly wounded in the jaw by a bullet, though he insisted on being carried round the field of battle in a cart so that he could still be seen by his soldiers – and when he eventually returned to the army he had to wear a black silk cloth tied under his chin in order to support his lower jaw and to cover the still unhealed wound. At one stage in the battle, Lima Figueiredo relates, it was only a series of charges by fresh cavalry under General José Antônio Corrêa de Câmara that saved three of the Brazilian infantry battalions from almost certain annihilation.[19]

As at Ytororó, the Battle of Avay was an action decided only by superior Brazilian manpower. Indeed Brazilian losses had been so heavy that Caxias had to disband six of his battalions and incorporate the survivors into other units, and once again to delay the final assault, on the rear of López's positions.

Frantic attempts were now made by the Paraguayans, at Thompson's suggestion, to construct new trenches from Angostura to López's headquarters at Itá-Ibaty in order to protect the rear, but there were not enough women left to dig them in time or soldiers to man them. A plan to construct a string of 'star' forts had to be abandoned for the same reason, and eventually López concentrated his forces (consisting now of only 3,000 men according to Thompson) together with the remaining guns, among them the Whitworth 32-pounder, at Itá-Ibaty itself. Even so there was not time to dig a trench all the way round, though Thompson caustically comments, 'this . . . did not signify with a general like Caxias, who was certain to find out which was the strong side, and attack it'.

Nevertheless, in Thompson's view it was a good position, and he believed that if López had saved all his men to defend it instead of sending them to fight in the open field, 'he might have destroyed the Brazilian army this month'.

The battle of Lomas Valentinas, often described as 'the Waterloo' of the war, began at 2 a.m. on 21 December, as 25,000 Brazilians set out from Villeta, leaving their packs behind them and in their best uniforms and with their rifles freshly cleaned.

According to Thompson, Caxias had received 'positive orders from the Emperor to risk his last man in bringing the war at once to a conclusion', and perhaps the parade-ground appearance of the troops was an earnest of his determination to try and comply.

Marching in two dense columns the Brazilians reached the perimeter of the semi-circular line of the Paraguayan positions by noon, and as Thompson had predicted, 'sat down before the strongest portion of it, to have their dinner'. In the meantime one of the columns, commanded by General J. L. Mena Barreto, was detached to deal with the Pikysyry trenches from the rear. These were defended by only 1,500 troops, nearly all of them boys or invalids. They put up a fierce resistance but were soon overpowered by sheer weight of numbers, losing 700 killed and 200 taken prisoner, the remainder either fighting their way through to join López at Itá-Ibaty or seeking refuge with Thompson in the fortress of Angostura, which was now completely cut off.

At three o'clock Caxias, although there were no defences to the rear of the Paraguayan lines, ordered a direct frontal assault on Itá-Ibaty. For three hours, almost without pause, Brazilian infantry and cavalry charged at the defenders. General MacMahon, who was present at the battle – at his own request and not, as an Allied propaganda story had it, because he was being held prisoner by López – declared that the fighting was as desperate as anything he himself had witnessed or participated in during the American Civil War.[20] MacMahon had by now, despite his briefing by Washburn, become a staunch supporter of López and Elisa Lynch (who was also present throughout the battle), and afterwards he declared that at Lomas Valentinas the Paraguayans

'fought as no other people ever fought to preserve their country from invasion and conquest. Many, too, had crawled away from the prison pens of the invaders, into whose hands they had fallen. And in the face of these things, there are men here even in the United States who gravely tell us that all of this is done because their ruler is a barbarian and a monster from whose clutches they are ever trying to escape and whose rule is a blight upon the age which these gentle civilians of the Allied nations, with unprecedented philanthropy, are spending countless millions to remove. Thinking of these things, we are sometimes tempted to lose our patience at this insult to the common sense of the world.'[20]

The boys and old men of López's army certainly gave a good account of themselves, fully justifying Thompson's claim that 'a very few Paraguayans were able to defeat a great many of the Brazilians.' They beat back attack after attack, and fought on even when they had been several times wounded. They placed their guns, dismounted by continuous enemy bombardment, on mounds of earth so that they could continue firing them, although fourteen of them had to be surrendered, including the precious Whitworth. At one stage the Brazilians broke through the line and reached López's own headquarters, but were thrown out by a charge of his personal escort. At the end of the three hours fighting all the attacks had been repulsed, and the Allies broke off the action. They had lost at least 4,000 men, among them many senior officers. Young sub-lieutenant Diouísio Cerqueira, who was himself wounded, later wrote that his battalion lost 78 per cent of its officers and 58 per cent of its men – a ratio comparable, Kolinski points out, 'to losses suffered by Union and Confederate units at such desperate battles as Antietam and Shiloh'.

But by now López had lost most of his own army – which, according to some estimates was reduced to a mere 2,000 – though during the next few days he brought from his main army base at Cerro León the few troops that still remained there, numbering about 500, and collected a few other reinforcements, including the sailors from his remaining steamers. He also succeeded, after several attempts, in getting a message through to Thompson at Angostura, ordering him to cut his way through the Allied army and join him at Itá-Ibaty, but cancelled the order just as Thompson was getting ready to lead his garrison out. Thompson quotes from this counter-order to explain what had caused López to change his mind: 'The chief drawback of the enemy is the immense number of wounded he has, which he cannot attend to, as the road he has opened through our trench barely permits him to convey his most distinguished wounded'. 'The situation has changed', he told Thompson.

'I sustain myself well and the enemy can only attack me very weakly, being completely demoralised. You must therefore sustain yourselves at all hazards . . .'.

The Marshal-President's renewed confidence received a more dramatic expression in a reply which he sent to a summons to surrender, which he received on 24 December from Caxias, who believed that the Paraguayan army had to all intents and purposes been destroyed. In his reply, which was apparently written in consultation with his senior officers, and was delivered to the Brazilian lines under a flag of truce by Colonel Silvestre Aveiro, López's staff aide, and by the Marshal-President's eldest son, the fourteen year old Major Juan Francisco López, he referred to the abortive conference at Yataíty-Corá in 1866 in which he sought 'the reconciliation of four sovereign nations of South America which had already begun to destroy each other in a remarkable manner' – and went on to state:

'My initiative met with no answer but the contempt and silence of the Allied governments, and new and bloody battles on the part of their armed representatives, as your Excellencies call yourselves. I then more clearly saw that the tendency of the war of the Allies was against the existence of the Republic of Paraguay and, though deploring the blood spilled in so many years of war, I could say nothing; and placing the fate of my country and its generous sons in the hands of the God of Nations, I fought its enemies with loyalty and conscience, and I am disposed to continue fighting until that God and our arms decide the definite fate of the cause.'

The reply at least provided the Allies with further proof, if they needed it, of the temper of the man they had to deal with. But in fact the Marshal-President's new access of confidence was hardly justified. His forces had kept the enemy out but, even during the comparative lull of 22 and 23 December, they had been further depleted by an almost continuous artillery and rifle fire from the Brazilians. 'The rifle-bullets, by thousands,' Thompson relates, 'did not cease from 21 to 27 December, both by day and night, and all the wounded were exposed to this fire, as well as the combatants.' It was the height of the Paraguayan summer and the temperature registered 101 degrees. By now, too, the infantry and cavalry charges had been renewed.

General MacMahon noted in his journal:

'The headquarters began to swarm with wounded, yet none withdrew from the lines except those whose wounds were such as to positively and immediately incapacitate them from further fighting. There were children of tender years who crawled back, dragging shattered limbs or with ghastly bullet wounds in their half naked bodies. They neither wept nor groaned nor asked for surgical attention. When they felt the merciful hand of death heavy upon them, they would lie down and die as silently as they had suffered.'

On 23 December, as his position became more desperate, López sent MacMahon, together with his children – though not Elisa who insisted on staying with their father – to Piribebuy, a village to the east of Cerro León, which was soon to become the new 'Capital'. Before MacMahon left, López entrusted him with a will bequeathing all his possessions and property to Elisa, asking him to be his executor and begging him to look after his children in the event of his death.

On 25 December, the Brazilians opened what was probably the heaviest cannonade of the whole war. It was followed by a further frontal assault, which was again repulsed, though by now López only had six guns which were not dismounted and his ammunition was nearly exhausted. In the evening, when the Brazilian cavalry appeared at the rear of his headquarters, López sent his dragoons into action, but they were surrounded and cut up before his eyes, as he had no reinforcements to send them: only 50 managed to return to his side. His force had now dwindled to 1,000 men, and the fact that the Brazilians by now, according to Thompson, had 'only 20,000 sound men left, out of the 32,000 they had at the beginning of December', could not affect the issue.

On the morning of 27 December, after another furious bombardment, the Allied army, headed by the Argentine contingents, committed to the battle for the first time, advanced for the final assault. The few remaining Paraguayans, now under the personal command of their Marshal-President – who, according to Thomson, was under direct fire for the first time at Lomas Valentinas – put up a desperate resistance, 'and fought individually,' Thompson says, 'against whole battalions, till they were cut down.'

When he saw that the situation was hopeless, López set off for Cerro León accompanied by a few of his aides, in such haste that for a time he was separated from Elisa, who according to Thompson, 'went about among the bullets looking for him'. Eventually she too managed to get away, as did Generals Resquín and Caballero, with the few dozen cavalry-men who were still mounted. Caxias claimed later that only some 90 men managed to follow the fleeing Marshal-President, and that of these, only twenty-five reached Cerro León, and though he thinks this is an exaggeration Thompson agrees that it cannot be far from the truth.

This leads Thompson to ask a very pertinent question, and one that has frequently been asked since:

'Why did not Caxias, the Commander-in-Chief of the Allied army, being at war *not with the Paraguayan nation but with its Government*, and having 8,000 magnificently-mounted cavalry, with nothing to do, pursue López, whom he might have taken without the loss of another man?'

The possible answers which Thompson, with soldierly bluntness, offers to these questions more or less correspond to the speculations that have vexed historians ever since:

'Was it from imbecility, or from a wish to make more money out of the army contracts? Was it to have an excuse for still maintaining a Brazilian army in Paraguay, or was there an understanding between Caxias and López? Or was it done with the view of allowing López to re-assemble the remainder of the Paraguayans, in order to exterminate them in "civilized warfare"?'

These are all terrible possibilities, and the last and most terrible may well be the most likely. As early as 1867, Masterman tells us that he and his friends wondered whether 'the wretched mismanagement of Caxias . . . which prolonged the war' was 'done intentionally, in order to make it one of utter extermination.'

Thompson, too, asserts that the Allies were 'determined that the war should not yet be brought to an end,' and that they were resoved 'not to leave a Paraguayan of any age or sex alive . . .'.

In Burton's view, 'any service in the world would have called upon Marshal Caxias to justify himself before a court-martial, and a strict service like the French or the Austrian would probably have condemned him to be shot. In Brazil, he was created a Duke . . .'. And he draws attention to the very odd fact that when eventually Caxias did agree to a pursuit of López, he sent after him not cavalry but infantry.

As for Thompson, he roundly declares that whatever the explanation for this curious behaviour, 'the Marquês de Caxias is responsible for every life lost in Paraguay since December 1868, and for all the sufferings of the poor men, women and children in the power of López'.

Some of the conspiracy suspects in fact were liberated by the Brazilians at Lomas Valentinas, among them the Prussian observer Max von Versen and the Brazilian major Ernesto Augusto Cunha Mattos, who was later to repay Elisa Lynch for the kindness she had shown him while he was a prisoner. López's sisters, Inocencia and Rafaela, had already been sent to Cerra León, and it was on 25 December, when the disastrous outcome of the battle as far as the Paraguayans were concerned was becoming increasingly clear, that Benigno López, Bishop Palacios, José Berges, Colonel Alén and the wife of Colonel Martínez, had been shot.

That López had not expected so disastrous an outcome to the battle is evident from the remark addressed to Cuverville, the French Consul, by Elisa Lynch, when he met her and López not long after the flight from Lomas Valentinas. 'We have had a terrible disaster,' she is reported by Burton to have exclaimed; in great agitation, adding, 'we owe it to M. Caminos'.

Luis Caminos, the War Minister, is described by Burton as the 'Grouchy of the Paraguayan Waterloo'. He had been left in Asunción, with a flying column of 2,000 men and eighteen guns, with instructions to fall upon any Brazilian force that might land from the Chaco. According to Burton, López had deliberately left San Antonio undefended in order to lure the Brazilians into a trap, and Burton believed that there was little doubt 'that so strong a force attacking in the bush would have thrown the Brazilians into complete confusion'. As it was Caminos had decided to retreat to Cerro León.

How complete was the final collapse of the Paraguayan lines is proved by the fact that López was forced to leave behind him, Thompson tells us, 'his carriages, clothes, papers, hat, gold-embroidered "poncho" etc., and even some of his female slaves with the baggage'. Burton was later shown one of the carriages in the allied camp – 'a carriage-bed, a kind of *fourgon*, somewhat like the old wagon of the Suez road', and he confirms that it was filled with 'a wealth of damaging documents'.

In the meantime, Angostura was the only point still held by the Paraguayans in the whole of their defensive system. The survivors from the Pikysyry trenches – 'most of them having lost their arms', Thompson tells us (in previous battles) and 'the greater part being small boys' – as well as over 400 badly wounded men from other parts of the battle area, and about 500 women – crowded into the fortress, so that Thompson suddenly found that he had 2,400 to feed instead of the 700 who had formed the original garrison. He managed to do so for a time by careful rationing, and by sending out skirmishing parties to raid the enemy's provision dumps and cattle pens. He was subjected all this time to an almost continuous bombardment by the Brazilian ironclads.

Thompson claims that as late as the night of 26 December (the eve of the final Allied assault), he received a message from López saying:

'Here we are getting on very well, and there is no fear. The enemy is in his last agony and desperate, and nothing troubles him so much as the impossibility of moving with the great number of wounded he has.'

This helps to explain why on 28 December, when Allied forces began to invest Angostura, while the bombardment from the river was redoubled, Thompson and his men at first refused to believe messages sent to them under a flag of truce, informing them that López had been utterly routed and calling upon them to surrender.

The Allied commander, however, then sent Thompson 'a private letter from an Englishman who had been a witness of everything . . . and who was taken prisoner on the 27th, in which he told the true state of the case'.

Presumably this Englishman was Dr Stewart, who had apparently surrendered to the Brazilians in the course of the battle. Presumably, too, the letter was the one General MacMahon had in mind when, in his statement to the U.S. Congress Committee of Investigations, he stated that Thompson had been tricked into surrendering Angostura by a false message from Dr Stewart.

Thompson, however, tells us he also sent a group of his officers, at the Allies' suggestion, to inspect López's headquarters and interview the wounded Paraguayans left there. With the defeat thus confirmed, Thompson called a conference of his officers. He pointed out to them that although they could undoubtedly inflict heavy casualties on the enemy, ammunition and provisions would only last a few days longer and the position was ultimately untenable.

Only one officer, according to Thompson, voted against the decision to surrender, though young Lieutenant José María Fariña, who had achieved fame as a commander of *chatas* along the upper Paraná in 1866, refused to allow the surrender of the Paraguayan flag, handing it down from its staff, wrapping it around a cannon ball and throwing it in the river.[21]

The formal capitulation, on honourable terms, took place on 30 December. Caxias offered to send Thompson either to Buenos Aires or to England at the Allies' expense, but he proudly insisted upon paying his own way. Before leaving he went to Itá-Ibaty, where he found '700 of our wounded in López's house alone, their wounds not having been even dressed,' and the battleground 'still covered with dead in different stages of decomposition'. He successfully demanded medical attention for the Paraguayan wounded, and then boarded a British ship at Villeta which was to take him to his brother's house at Buenos Aires, to recuperate from his experiences – and so out of this story.

But before he sailed from Paraguay for ever he left the ship for a brief visit to Asunción; he found it practically deserted of its inhabitants – and being systematically sacked by Brazilian troops.

The first of them had landed on 1 January 1869, and the bulk of the army, which had marched northwards from Villeta and Lomas Valentinas, entered the city four days later, dressed once more in their best uniforms, their bands playing. Caxias celebrated his victory with a *Te Deum* in the Cathedral, during which he fainted in the intense heat. On 12 January he asked to be relieved of his command – and issued an order proclaiming that the war was over.

The proclamation was premature indeed, for while Francisco Solano López was alive, Paraguay was still undefeated. Incredible though it may seem (the repetition of the adjective becomes monotonous but it is fully justified), another Paraguayan army came into being.

López arrived at Cerro León, his training-camp in the Cordillera, the low range of hills some 40 miles from Asunción, in late December 1868, with no baggage, no artillery, and only a handful of survivors from Lomas Valentinas. He found there Luis Caminos and the 2,000 men from Asunción, (only 1,500 according to Kolinski). There were also a few garrison troops and, Thompson says, several thousand wounded in the military hospitals.

This nucleus of an army gradually grew. In ones and twos or in small groups, soldiers who had escaped from Itá-Ibaty or Angostura, sick or wounded men who had escaped or been released, managed to make their way through the enemy lines, now spread out far beyond Asunción, stealing guns, food and equipment wherever they had the chance, to join their Marshal-President. Among them, Barrett says, were soldiers who had been harboured by the wild Indians of the Chaco after they had been cut off by the enemy, and who in several cases brought Indian recruits with them.

By the end of January López had an army again, though estimates vary widely as to its size, ranging from Burton's 6,000 to Kolinski's 13,000. In addition López had managed to install some of the equipment saved from the arsenal at Asunción at Caacupé, where under the direction of General Resquín thirteen light field-guns were cast. As many as possible of the reformed infantry units were armed with weapons collected from old battlefields or Allied prisoners, by raids on enemy outposts, and by sporting guns or antique firearms taken from civilians; but as both weapons and ammunition were so scarce, the long Paraguayan lance became increasingly important.

With such resources miraculously at his disposal, López was able to prepare a new defence line along the escarpment of the Cordillera – the western edge of the Paraná plateau which falls slightly to the east of lake Ypacarai and the railroad. This position on the Azcurra heights was a strong one in itself – except for the fact that the flanks were in danger from a numerically superior enemy.

A number of factors lie behind this astonishing revival. First and foremost, of course, was the continuing devotion of the majority of the ordinary people of Paraguay to their Marshal-President, and Barrett is perfectly justified in pointing out that López, the defeated Dictator, 'could exist now only by the will of those whom he had ruled.'

But the Allies contributed substantially to the revival, if not by deliberate policy, then by a complete failure to offer any attractive alternative. The sacking of houses in Asunción continued, and Cerqueira reports that immense quantities of booty, including silver and furniture were being loaded on to outgoing ships. Marshal Guilherme Xavier de Souza, successor to the Marquês de Caxias – who had to face a Senate inquiry when he arrived home on his failure to capture López and his premature declaration of the end of the war, though his explanations were accepted – was a weak man who exercised little control over his men, and the looting was accompanied by a great deal of violence and drunkenness. Citizens of Asunción who had managed to stay behind or who succeeded in returning to the city soon regretted it. They received no help from the Allies – and General MacMahon's statement on the subject to the U.S. House of Representatives Committee of Enquiry, though strongly anti-Brazilian and pro-López in tone, sums up the situation fairly accurately:

'I was told by a foreign resident of Asunción that they (the Paraguayan refugees) were brought in laden with packs and various things, paraded around the streets, sometimes two or three days, to be exhibited, almost entirely naked, no provision being made for clothing them or providing for their comfort or necessity; that they were treated with insult and abuse and turned loose upon the streets, subjected to the caprices of the brutalized soldiery of Brazil. And the Gentleman who told me this was in the interest of the Allies. He said that formerly he thought it a piece of great barbarity on the part of López to drive the population back within his own lines, but that now, since his residence in Asunción, he was satisfied that López acted wisely and humanely in so doing as it preserved them from the brutal indifference of the Allied authorities and the more brutal lusts of their soldiery.'

The Paraguayan people, therefore, could hardly be blamed for concluding that what the Allies had to offer in the way of government was a good deal worse than the dictatorship to which they had, over the generations, become accustomed, or for regarding the provisional administration which the Allies eventually set up in June, 1869, manned by Paraguayans who had left the country some years before or who had deserted from López, as a puppet government of traitors.

The deterioration in Asunción affected the Allies themselves. Many officers applied for permission to be relieved of their commands and sent home, urging sickness, family crises and other causes, and in most cases, Barroso says, Xavier de Souza, who was himself in poor health, agreed,[22] while Taunay tells us in his *Memoirs* that a number of other officers, convinced that it would only be by killing practically every Paraguayan that López himself could be got at, urged the opening of peace negotiations. When, for example, the able and subtle Counsellor José Maria da Silva Paranhos (later Visconde de Rio Branco) arrived in Asunción to investigate the state of affairs, Major Anfrísio Fialho, former commander of the Rio Grande do Sul German artillery, argued at a formal banquet given to welcome Paranhos that an early peace would check the demoralization that now affected the whole of the Brazilian army, besides reducing the heavy financial burden that war was placing on Brazil.

At the same time Asunción had become a hot bed of pro-López spying and intrigue. According to Burton, the Hungarian Colonel Wisner von Morgenstern, who after his capture had been allowed to reside in Asunción, 'kept a small *pulperia* at the street corner, where officers came for their periodical dram, and visited a pretty "daughter", who was reported to reward important intelligence'. Burton also says that Colonels Iturburú and Baez, officers in a new special force of anti-López Paraguayans formed by the Allies, were in fact spies for López, gathering much valuable information for him.

However, the presence of Paranhos in Asunción soon checked the demoralization. He reported the state of affairs to Rio de Janeiro, and it was decided to renew the war effort without delay, though it was rumoured that there was, in some quarters, a marked reluctance to do so, and that Dom Pedro had to hint that he would abdicate if his determination to continue the fighting until López was dead was not implemented.

As a first step towards the renewal of the war, the ailing Xavier de Souza was replaced as commander-in-chief by the Emperor's son-in-law (and grandson of Louis Philippe of France), Luíz Felipe Maria Fernando Gastão d'Orléans, the Conde d'Eu. Although the blonde, blue-eyed Frenchman was only 26 years old, spoke indifferent Portuguese and was somewhat deaf into the bargain, he had long been begging his father-in-law to send him to the war, and in fact proved himself a firm and reasonably vigorous commander.

He set himself to reorganize his army of 26,000 battle-hardened and well equipped veterans, dividing it into two corps, commanded by the two most famous and experienced of Brazil's Generals – Osório (his chin still bound up in a black silk scarf) and Polidoro, the former Commandant of the Escola Militar. The war effort by now was almost entirely Brazilian, though a token force of Argentinians under Mitre remained at Luque; the Uruguayans had disappeared from the scene, apart from a few individuals incorporated into Brazilian or Argentine units.

It was, nevertheless, López who reopened hostilities, by sending what Burton calls 'a railway battery' – two light guns mounted on a railway car (in effect the first armoured train in South American history) – down the line to Aregua. 'The Paraguayans' Burton tells us 'after doing damage, leisurely retired, and stopped the train to pick up two of their wounded who had fallen out of it.'

Although the 'railway-battery' did not produce major results, it caused a good deal of confusion and reinforced López's legendary reputation for ingenious innovations. At the same time he sent out raiding parties to capture horses and weapons, and, Kolinski says, to destroy railway bridges and cross-ties on the track behind the Brazilian advanced positions. Morale in his makeshift army was high and he began to talk of shortly recapturing Asunción. Meanwhile life behind the Paraguayan lines had assumed a settled, at times almost peaceful, aspect, as the men built houses and the women cultivated the hastily improvised fields.

The small town of Piribebuy (with about 3,000 inhabitants) had taken on something of the air of a real capital, with the acquisition of the treasury and the remaining state archives, and the presence of state officials and foreign representatives.

Among these was General MacMahon, who provides us with a vivid picture of the house which had been prepared for him and of Piribebuy itself; he begins with a description of the house:

'It consisted of two principal rooms, one floored with brick, the other with a hard earthen floor. The windows were without glass and opened, as did the doors on both sides on wide corridors, as the open space sheltered by the over-hanging eaves is generally called in these countries. The furniture consisted of a circular centre-table, quaintly carved of native wood, a large writing desk with drawers, and a side-table with a decanter, several glasses, and a bundle of cigars. The tables, like all the others in the country, were uncomfortably high. The decanter was comfortably full of *caña* (Paraguayan rum).

'The village of Piribebuy consists of four streets intersecting each other at right angles, and enclosing an open space or grass-covered plaza, about a quarter of a mile across. It is situated on a gentle slope or knoll, with higher ground or crests on all sides at a distance of about a mile and a half. The houses are of one storey, and generally roofed with thatch. On the crown of the knoll was the cemetery, enclosing about an acre of ground, and marked by a single large wooden cross in the centre. The market-place was under a dense orange grove at one extremity of the village, and always presented during the day a spectacle full of life. Scores of women, old and young, assembled there to sell their wares, and kept up an incessant chatter all day long. The Piribebuy – a clear and rapid stream, very sudden in its rises and falls – passed at the foot of the slope on which the town was built. The whole population bathed there every day, the women generally after nightfall.'

MacMahon was recalled before he could witness the savage disruption of this peaceful scene.

During April and May 1869, López actually began to advance from the Cordillera in the direction of Asunción. When word reached him that the Conde d'Eu was moving against him with practically the whole of the Brazilian forces (together with the remaining Argentine contingents) he divided his army into three wings, each resting on a fortified position. If Caxias had been in command of the enemy, the Paraguayan leader could have counted with reasonable certainty on a direct attack against his strong, central positions on the Azcurra heights. This time he was outwitted, for the Conde d'Eu, after a council of war at his field headquarters at Pirayú, a small station on the railroad in front of the Azcurra escarpment, decided on a flanking movement against López's left, while keeping a force at Pirayú in order to convince López that the attack would come in the direction he had anticipated.

The Brazilian flanking operation began on 1 August. A small Paraguayan force was routed at Sapucay, and the Conde d'Eu and Osório led their forces through the village of Valenzuela by a route which led to Piribebuy to the south, and well behind the flank of the Paraguayan position on the Azcurra heights.

The Brazilians reached the neighbourhood of Piribebuy on 11 August. On the following morning they began a heavy bombardment with forty-seven guns, which lasted for four hours. When the little town had been practically blasted to pieces, the cavalry charged into the Paraguayan trenches. The defenders put up a fierce resistance, reduced at the end to using stones, dirt, bottles and broken glass as weapons. It was now that the Allied troops first began to comprehend the tragedy which had befallen Paraguay, for many of the dead were women and very young boys.

When resistance in the trenches had been overcome, the Brazilians swept into the town itself. Brazilian sources, and the Conde d'Eu himself, later denied the allegations, but Paraguayan historians complain with great bitterness that the Brazilians now perpetrated the worst massacre of the whole war, against a town whose garrison consisted of only 2,000 men, half of them convalescents from the hospital, and crowded with women and children, most of them families of officers and men in López's army. Most of these Paraguayan historians accept the account of Father Fidel Maiz, who declared that the Brazilians at Piribebuy 'committed the most execrable cruelties; savagely splitting the throat of the brave and stoic garrison commander, Lieutenant-

Colonel Pedro Caballero and other prisoners, including the children in their mothers' arms; the burning of the hospital with all the sick and wounded, over six hundred being horribly burned to death; and to this must be added the complete loss of our national archives and library and a large amount of gold and silver which was divided among the Allies with satanic greed.'

Other sources, cited by Kolinski, say that it was the sight of their General, Meno Barreto, mortally wounded in the stomach by practically the last Paraguayan shot fired, that made the Brazilian infantry go 'berserk'.

According to Barrett, when the news reached López he reversed his plan of campaign for the first time in his career, ordering an immediate march on Piribebuy, until realizing that this would invite almost certain disaster, he cancelled the order, and decided instead upon an attack on the flank of the Brazilian army at Yagarí.

His plan in itself was strategically sound; between him and the enemy was a small river and much broken ground, so that the overwhelming superiority of the Brazilian cavalry was to some extent nullified. But the Brazilians had apparently massed their artillery at exactly the points López had chosen to attack. His men made a desperate attempt to get beyond the Brazilian guns but after losing 2,000 men, were forced to withdraw. Barrett, taking his cue from Paraguayan historians, believes it was now that López became convinced that his battle plans were somehow being leaked to the enemy.

Meanwhile, the allied commanders had gradually restored order in Piribebuy. Not long after the firing had stopped young Taunay searched out the house in which Elisa Lynch and her children had been living. Her piano was still there, and in spite of the presence of a shell-shattered and decapitated Paraguayan soldier, Taunay sat down to play. The sound of the piano created a bizarre effect in the silence that had fallen over the battlefield.

A brother-officer called Taunay to the *quinta* at the back of the house where a wine-cellar had been discovered. When he had toasted the Allied victory in champagne, Taunay searched among the abandoned belongings of Elisa Lynch and Francisco Solano López, which were scattered in all directions. He came across the beautifully bound second volume of *Don Quijote*. He searched, but to his regret he could not find the first volume. The soldiers who were now ransacking the house were better pleased: they had discovered a store of silver coins bearing the arms of Castile and Aragon.

The Conde d'Eu now moved north from Piribebuy, but López, appreciating the new threat, evacuated his Azcurra positions and retired northwards towards Campo Grande. The Brazilians reached Caacupé (where López had set up his small arsenal) on 13 August. They found there 1,200 wounded in the charge of the Italian doctor Diego Domingo Parodi – to whom, General Resquín claims, López had given most of his remaining money for the care of the wounded – and some 70 Europeans. They also found a portable printing press still containing the half finished 12 August edition of the Paraguayan army's last newspaper, *La Estrella*.

It was at Caacupé that General Osório, still not completely recovered from his wound, came near to physical collapse and asked to be relieved of his command. General Polidoro also fell ill. Osório was replaced by General J. L. Mena Barreto, and Polidoro by Genral Victoriano Carneiro Monteiro.

But the Conde d'Eu would not allow his army to linger at Caacupé and quickly set off in pursuit of López. His cavalry (numbering 30,000 according to Barrett) found the Paraguayan rearguard under General Caballero entrenched at Campo Grande. The battle that followed (known as the battle of Acosta Nú in Paraguay) was the last major action of the war. It was fiercely contested but the outcome was, in the end a Brazilian victory with terrible losses for the Paraguayans. It was found that many of Caballero's soldiers were boys as young as ten years old, wearing false beards. Young Lieutenant Dionísio Cerqueira (who was promoted after the battle) reports that the battlefield was literally covered with dead boys, most of whom had not reached the age of adolescence. Many of them were armed with weapons of such antiquity that, Taunay comments, they could normally only be seen in museums.

Caballero's stubborn holding-action had given López time to withdraw his remaining forces, but the army which had so proudly and devotedly rallied to his cause, was now reduced to 2,000. At Campo Grande López had, moreover, lost the whole of his baggage train, and practically all his remaining guns. The possibility of American intervention had disappeared with the recall of General MacMahon in late May, and the only hope now remaining to López was either that some other foreign power might intervene to stimulate peace negotiations, or that the Brazilians themselves would grow tired of the prolonged struggle. The terrain to which he had withdrawn, however, was not really suited to guerilla tactics of the kind, for example, that Juárez had been able to employ in Mexico against Maximilian, and the inhabitants, in any case few in number, were not of the semi-nomadic, gaucho type such as those of the Argentine pampas.

The war, therefore, was now a matter of straightforward pursuit on the part of the Brazilians, and a more or less continuous retreat by the half-clothed and half-starved remnants of López's army.

Nevertheless, when he reached the village of San Estanislao, López was able to stay long enough to hold a formal review, at which he conferred decorations upon many of the survivors of the battle of Campo Grande, promoted a number of officers, and made one of his highly popular speeches. The ceremony helped to raise morale, besides serving as a gesture of defiance against the provisional puppet government in Asunción, which had recently proclaimed him an outlaw.

From San Estanislao López withdrew first to Caraguatay and then to Itanará, deeper and deeper into the wilderness that forms the extreme north-east corner of Paraguay.

His army was now less than 1,000 strong, but it was accompanied by hundreds of civilians, most of them women and children, so that the retreat had something of the appearance of an Exodus, recalling in some respects those earlier migrations of the Guaraníes under their Jesuit leaders, described earlier in this book: it is as if the first exodus had thrown a long delayed echo, to enclose the two extremities of Paraguayan history.

These civilians were divided into two groups, families of proven loyalty to López, who had obeyed his orders to evacuate their homes and accompany the army, and members of families whose loyalty was suspect, and whose lot was little better than that of the wretched prisoners themselves. But before long all distinctions were swallowed up in a universal suffering, as they staggered on through an almost unknown wilderness, plagued by insects, with no food supplies and entirely dependent on the few edible roots and dried fruits that could be found. During the early summer months of November and December, pursuing Brazilian troops found hundreds of these civilians, lying along the trail, either dead or in the last stages of exhaustion and starvation.

The soldiers were in not much better plight, and many of them, too, collapsed from hunger or exhaustion, or, unable to face the privations of the retreat any longer, left the column at night and gave themselves up to the allied patrols.

Worse horrors were to follow, as the word 'conspiracy' began to be heard once more. In those nightmare conditions, with nerves stretched to breaking point, an objective assessment could not perhaps be expected, and Kolinski is probably right when he says that 'evidence of suspect activities was not always convincing'. Barrett, on the other hand, accepts the version derived from General Resquín and other Paraguayan sources.

According to this, López had been convinced that there were traitors in his small army ever since, at the battle of Yagarí, he had found that the Brazilians apparently knew his plan of attack. These suspicions became centred on a Lieutenant Aquino, a member of López's own bodyguard. He had been among those scattered in the last hopeless charge at Yagarí, and when three days later he rejoined the army with several of the stragglers, he had been personally welcomed by López. He was also among the several hundreds missing after the battle of Campo Grande, most of whom found their way back to the Paraguayan lines. The fact that he had twice had the opportunity of deserting but had not taken it, was obviously a circumstance in his favour, and he was in fact among those whom López decorated at San Estanislao. At Caraguatay, however, Resquín arrested Lieutenant Aquino. He had (this version of the story goes) found on him a sheet of paper containing eighty-six names of other Paraguayan officers and soldiers in the army and a pouch of Brazilian gold pieces: when questioned, he is said to have proudly declared himself a true patriot – and a 'Captain of Guides', a group which believed that the only chance of ending the foreign occupation was to eliminate López and which had, it was alleged, joined him at Azcurra.

Aquino and the eighty-six whose names appeared on his list were handed over to Resquín for execution. What followed was, as Barrett says, 'the grimmest scene of the Paraguayan war'. Ammunition was so low, that a hundred lancers were detailed to carry out the sentence. The boys and old men who formed the detail were so emaciated they could hardly raise their lances, let alone thrust cleanly with them. 'Hardly a man died as the result of a single wound,' Barrett recounts, 'the strength of the executioners was not equal to the task, and some of them fell across their victims from exhaustion before the task was done.'

The same sources declare that about this time a wagon containing López's family arrived at his camp under an escort. This escort claimed that the prisoners had been arrested in Piribebuy after an attempt to desert to the enemy before the shelling of the town began, and that Venancio López had, on the way back, again tried to desert, wounding the boy-sergeant of the escort in the process.

Barrett quotes a paper which, it is alleged, the Brazilians had managed to convey to Venancio, and which he still had with him. Referring to a law under consideration by the provisional government in Asunción to confiscate all the property and possessions of the López family (which was in fact later enacted), it included the words: '. . . you must declare your loyalty before it is too late if you wish to save your property. The men who bring you this can be trusted.' Whether there is substance in these allegations or not, the outcome was that Venancio too was executed by the lancers.

Both Barrett and Cunninghame-Graham claim that López had his mother and sisters flogged for their share in the attempted escape, and, according to Resquín, for having plotted to poison López, though it appears that López could not bring himself to sign their death warrants.

It was at some stage during this *Via Dolorosa* (as the last retreat of López is often called by Paraguayan historians) that what remained of Paraguay's treasury was secretly buried, or so it was rumoured, for the frequent treasure-hunts in later years failed to discover anything.

Caraguatay meanwhile had been turned into a temporary base for the Allied armies. While there the Conde d'Eu learned that, astonishingly enough, there was still a Paraguayan navy of sorts. It consisted of six small vessels which had been withdrawn along the river Manduvira (another tributary of the Paraguay) in order to escape the Brazilian squadron. General Câmara was sent to capture the ships. He arrived too late. The Paraguayans set fire to the ships (they included the *Yporá*, the *Añambay*, and the *Pirabebé*, which had played such a heroic part in the earlier actions along the rivers Paraná and Paraguay) and according to Taunay a number of Brazilians were killed when one of the magazines exploded. The rusted remains of the hulks can still be seen, and their end is still commemorated in a Paraguayan folk song.

But the Conde d'Eu was also having his difficulties. As the result of a dispute with the main Brazilian contractors the flow of supplies was suddenly halted, and there was a severe food shortage.

This in turn led to quarrels between the Allies, because the Argentinians took to stealing the horses of the Rio Grandense cavalry for food.

Eventually the problems were overcome, and the Conde d'Eu despatched a force to occupy the port of Concepción, about 200 miles to the north of Asunción along the river Paraguay, and established another temporary base at Rosario, which lies roughly midway between the two. The last scene of the last act in Paraguay's tragedy was soon to take place.

In Argentina, meanwhile, the new President, Domingo F. Sarmiento (Mitre's successor) was deploring in a letter of 30 December 1869, to his American friend – Mary Mann – General MacMahon's statements in favour of López. 'Such representatives of the United States,' he declared 'produce a deplorable effect upon public opinion.' He also wrote 'La Guerra está concluido aunque López queda como Blackeagle en los bosques' – 'the war is ended even though López persists like Blackeagle in the forests.'[23]

López had in fact emerged from the forests. On 14 February 1870, he entered Cerro Corá, or 'Corral of Hills', a natural amphitheatre among the wooded foothills of the Amambay mountain-range, in the extreme north-eastern region of Paraguay, not far from the Brazilian border, about thirty miles along the Concepción road west of the border towns of Pedro Juan Caballero and Ponta-Porá. Within the amphitheatre is a stream called the Aquidaban-Niqui, a tributary of the larger River Aquidaban.

There are no towns and villages nearby and the landscape has a wild, dramatic beauty of a kind one only seems to find in South America. Great hardwood trees surround the amphitheatre, wreathed and crowned with flowering lianas. The dense tangle of branches and creepers are alive with monkeys. The *ais*, or three-toed sloths, lie flattened against the highest branches like so many great slugs, at night time uttering their weird, sighing calls. The air vibrates with the whine and hum of insects and wild bees, and the whirring of the wings of humming birds, poised like tiny filagree helicopters over the flowers of the *Ceibas*. Jaguars and tapirs can still be found in the recesses of the forests.

Some historians have suggested that López may have come to Cerro Corá en route for a march across the Chaco to Bolivia, or even northward into the Brazilian province of Mato Grosso, but there is no firm evidence to this effect. It seems more likely that he hoped that the isolation and natural defensive nature of the area might allow time for his tiny army, now little more than 500 (considerably less according to some sources) to recuperate, so that he might reorganize it for yet further resistance. But there was in fact little chance of the walking skeletons in their rags of uniforms regaining their strength. There were no farms in the area, and daily rations consisted of one cow or ox among the 500 men. Even the hides, Resquín reports, were devoured by the hungry men.

Still López tried to keep up a show of military purpose and cohesion. On 24 February 1870, he authorized the last of his medals, for 'the campaign of Amambay', to commemorate the six-month march from Piribebuy and Campo Grande, and bearing the legend: 'Vencio Penurias y Fatigas', to signify that the bearer had overcome the most arduous of trials and tribulations.[24]

'Plans were drawn out, a ribbon chosen, and officers appointed,' Cunninghame-Graham comments, 'exactly as if he had been in his own palace in Asunción. In all the history of the world, no military order was instituted in stranger circumstances.'

It was one of his last official acts. The very last appears to have been the signing, on the last day of February, of the death-warrants of his mother and sisters. The executions were never carried out: it was the eve of his own death.

As with so many of the events in his life, his end has been the subject of the most varied and contradictory statements. In some accounts he was said to have committed suicide; in others, he was reported to have been killed in the Chaco while attempting to flee to Bolivia; in yet others he was reported to have been executed after being taken prisoner. The version given here, however, seems to be the one that best accords with what firm evidence is available.

Brazilian patrols – and possibly Paraguayan prisoners and deserters – had reported the whereabouts of López to General Corrêa da Câmara, and by the end of February, 1870, the strong force of Riograndense cavalry, together with several infantry units, had gradually converged in a half-circle on Cerro Corá.

There were two 'gateways' or forest-paths leading into the amphitheatre. At dawn on 1 March, part of the Brazilian forces, in a sudden, surprise thrust, descended on the small Paraguayan outpost guarding one of these entrances, overwhelmed it, and pressed on to the main camp. Behind them other troops were pouring into the neighbourhood, to the number probably of 8,000.

A survivor from the Paraguayan outpost managed to reach the camp ahead of them. López had with him about 400 soldiers, Elisa Lynch and their children, the Paraguayan Vice-President, Francisco Sánchez, the Secretary of State, Luis Caminos, Father Fidel Maiz, the ever-faithful General Resquín, and his aides-de-camp. The attack had been a surprise and there was a good deal of confusion. In the midst of it López managed to persuade Elisa and her children to enter the coach which had been carried in sections down the long trail and recently been reassembled, and, harnessed to two of the remaining half dozen horses, it set off on the road south.

It had barely departed before the first Brazilian cavalrymen appeared and bugles sounded a charge. For about fifteen minutes the tiny half-famished remnants of the Paraguayan army fought with their old fury, until they were scattered. It was long enough for their Marshal-President to mount his white horse and, accompanied by some of his staff, to make his escape. A group of Brazilian cavalrymen on their strong well-fed horses set off in pursuit and soon began to overhaul the fugitives. The bullets began to fly. Caminos was hit and fell from his saddle. Vice-President Sánchez, it appears, was also killed. General Resquín's horse stumbled, and momentarily fell behind.

Most eye-witness reports agree that the lance that pierced López's stomach was wielded by a Corporal Lacerda, known to his comrades as 'Chico Diabo', though there seems to be some doubt as to whether it was thrust or hurled. López at any rate was badly wounded, but he managed to break away from his assailants, and bleeding profusely (some accounts say he had pulled the lance out with his own hands) reached the banks of the Aquidaban-Niqui. Some of his staff were still with him, and they helped him across the shallow muddy stream. He was too badly wounded to climb the steep bank on the other side. While his aides ran in search of an easier slope, he lay, half in half out of the water, hanging on to a small palm tree that grew at the edge of the stream.

It was thus that his pursuers found him. At this point, according to some accounts, a lieutenant called upon him to surrender, and López drew his revolver and shot him; according to others, it was General Câmara himself, who had been called to the spot, who issued the summons, and López threw his sword at his enemies. All accounts are agreed that he refused to surrender, and that he uttered the words for which he will always be remembered by his countrymen and which even his worst enemies have not sought to belittle or deny: 'Muero con mi Pátria' – 'I die with my native land'.

Either before or immediately after these words (there is no absolute certainty on the point) a cavalryman, who is generally supposed to have been João Soares, a Riograndense, waded across the stream, turned López round, and with his Spencer carbine shot him in the back at close range.

The body of Marshal-President Francisco Solano López, blood-spattered and mud-stained, was flung over two poles and carried back across the stream. After a brief autopsy, probably performed by Surgeon Manoel Cardosa da Costa Lôbo (even this is not known for certain), which established that the lance-wound had been mortal in itself, though it was the Spencer carbine which had administered the coup-de-grâce, the corpse was apparently thrown on the ground for exhibition to the troops. Among the souvenirs removed from the body, were a watch bearing the official Paraguayan motto, 'Paz y Justicia,' (Peace and Justice), a ring (a present from Elisa according to some accounts) engraved with the words 'Vencer o Morir' (Conquer or Die), the battle-cry with which the Marshal-President had led his troops into action at the very beginning of the war; several tufts of hair pulled out of his scalp; and (it is said) an ear cut off by an officer in order to win a wager. As for 'Chico Diabo', he received a reward of one hundred pounds sterling.

When news of her son's death was brought to her, Doña Juana Carillo de López is said to have wept, to the astonishment and indignation of her daughters, and in spite of the fact that she was apparently aware that López had signed her death-warrant the day before.

The horses drawing the carriage with Elisa Lynch and her children were too feeble to travel at high speed, and they were soon overtaken by Brazilian cavalrymen. Riding alongside the carriage they called upon the occupants to surrender. Juan Francisco López, now at 15 a full Colonel, refused, and drawing his revolver, fired through the open window. The thrust of a Brazilian lance laid him on the floor of the carriage; but in his case the wound was almost immediately mortal.

With her three other children – and the dead body of 'Panchito' – Elisa Lynch was escorted back to the camp. There she was shown the body of her lover. She asked and obtained permission to bury it. Using bits of sticks and their bare hands, Elisa and her sons, aided (some reports say) by her companion, Isidora Díaz, sister of General Díaz, the hero of Curupaíti (and once López's boon companion) scooped out a shallow grave, for Francisco Solano López and his eldest son. According to Father Fidel Maiz the Paraguayan prisoners of war were then forced to dishonour the memory of their dead leader by marching over his grave.

NOTES

1 Quoted by Masterman. Kolinski puts the total of the Allied army at this date at 45,000.
2 Quoted by Masterman. Kolinski agrees to the total of 20,000 for the Paraguayan forces at this stage.
3 *Vultos de Pátria*, Antônio da Rocha Almeida. Rio de Janeiro 1961.
4 Quoted by Masterman.
5 See for example letters to the Condessa de Barral quoted by Alcindo Sodre.
6 See for example *Eliza Lynch: Regent of Paraguay*, Henry Lyon-Young. London 1966.
7 *Datos históricos de la guerra del Paraguay con la Triple Alianza*, Francisco Isidoro Resquín. Buenos Aires 1896. Quotations from Resquín are taken from this book.
8 Actually Cuverville, not Cuberville.
9 U.S. House of Representatives Report No. 65, 41st Congress, 2nd Session.
10 Testimony of Commander W. A. Kirkland. U.S. House of Representatives Report No. 65, 41st Congress, 2nd Session; and affidavit of Charles J. F. Davie, Note 115.
11 Testimony of Charles Ames Washburn, 30 March 1869, Washington D.C. House Report No. 65.
12 Testimony of General M. T. MacMahon, U.S. House of Representatives Report No. 65, 41st Congress, 2nd Session.
13 *Paraguay: an informal history*, Harris G. Warren. Norman 1949. Quotations from Warren are taken from this book.
14 U.S. House of Representatives Report No. 65, 41st Congress, 2nd Session, 28 October 1869.
15 Affidavit of 9 July 1869.
16 Testimony of Mrs Washburn, 29 October 1869, at New York City. U.S. House of Representatives Report No. 65, 41st Congress, 2nd Session.
17 Included in Masterman's *Seven Eventful Years in Paraguay*.
18 See *Reminiscências da campanha do Paraguaí*, Cerqueira, *op. cit*, and *A guerra de López*, Barroso, *op. cit*.
19 *Grandes soldados do Brasil*, José de Lima Figueiredo, *op. cit*.
20 'The War in Paraguay,' Martin T. MacMahon. *Harper's New Monthly Magazine*, XL, April 1870.
21 *El libro de los héroes*, Juan E. O'Leary. Asunción 1922.
22 *A guerra de López*.
23 Letters of Sarmiento to Mary Mann, *Hispanic American Historical Review*, XXXII, 3 August 1952.
24 *Jornadas de agonía*, Manuel Gálvez. Buenos Aires n.d.

Epilogue

The death of Francisco Solano López and the end of the war were celebrated in the Brazilian camp at Cerro Corá with the noise, abandon, and stamina of carnival in Rio de Janeiro. In the wild release following the years of tension, bloodshed and suffering, strange friendships and liaisons flourished. General Corrêa de Câmara, the Brazilian commander entered, almost immediately it seems, into a union with Inocencia, the sister of López and widow of the executed General Barrios, from which a daughter resulted. Similar relationships are said to have developed between López's other sister Rafaela, the widow of the former treasurer Saturnino Bedoya, and Commander Pedra; and between one of Venancio López's daughters and Captain Teodoro Wanderley. Perhaps these liaisons played their part in establishing the pro-allied bonafides of the dead Marshal-President's family, for although their property had been confiscated by a decree of the provisional Paraguayan Government, it was before long restored to them and they lived, as they had always wished to do, in aristocratic comfort in Asunción.

The prolonged celebrations at Cerro Corá were a prelude to many more of a similar nature as the news gradually spread. When it reached the Conde d'Eu on 4 March 1870, he was on board a steamer en route for Concepción, but as soon as he arrived at his destination the victory was celebrated amid scenes of wild rejoicing by a dance, though by all accounts it belonged to the category which was popularly known among the troops as 'bailes sifilíticos'. The Conde d'Eu returned to his temporary headquarters at Rosario on 6 March, where the news, Captain Taunay tells us, caused 'delirium to reign among the troops'. Many of the Paraguayan inhabitants of the river ports appear to have shared in the enthusiasm, but Lieutenant Dionísio Cerqueira noted tears on the faces of the gaunt and ragged Paraguayan soldiers, who had returned to their homes after their release at Cerro Corá.

There was great excitement in Rio de Janeiro, too, when the

news arrived, though the Emperor was not altogether happy at the manner of Marshal-President López's death, feeling that he should have been taken prisoner, and suggesting that money was the most fitting reward for 'Chico Diabo', and that he should receive no further mark of recognition. The first of the troops to be repatriated, landed at Rio de Janeiro on 2 May, to a popular demonstration which the newspapers described as 'unique',[1] and to a reception by Dom Pedro and the royal family.

In a letter of 15 February, to his friend Mrs Mann, President Sarmiento of Argentina had reported that he had ordered the repatriation of part of the Argentine forces (before the final episode) 'with astonishment and public satisfaction', and that he had arranged for the returning soldiers to receive their back pay. In Buenos Aires, too, there was rejoicing when the death of López was announced, tempered by some regret that the end of the war might be bad for business: in the provinces the rejoicings were noticeably more muted.

As for the survivors of the Marshal-President's little band at Cerro Corá, the officers were taken to Concepción, where they were 'encouraged' to sign statements condemning the policies of their former leader. Most of those who did so were released – and most of them then repudiated the declaration they had signed.

Of López's immediate entourage Vice-President Sánchez and Secretary Caminos had been killed during the final skirmishes. Father Fidel Maiz, who, as López's Grand Inquisitor during the conspiracy trials, was high on the Brazilian list of 'war criminals', was subjected to a horrifying mock-execution ceremony, reminiscent of that undergone by Dostoyevsky and the members of the Petrashevsky plot at the hands of the Russian Tsar Nicholas I. In his book Maiz claimed that the execution was halted by the intervention of Colonel Floriano Peixoto, the future 'Iron Marshal' of Brazil after she had become a republic.

General Caballero had been absent on a foraging expedition when the Brazilians broke into the camp at Cerro Corá, and completely surrounded by Brazilians had been forced to surrender. Together with Father Fidel Maiz, General Resquín, Colonel Aveiro and a few other senior Paraguayan officers, he was kept aboard a Brazilian ship, in order to thwart the vengeance of the provisional government in Asunción. General Resquín was taken to Humaitá where he, too, was encouraged to sign a statement deploring his part in the war – which he, too, later repudiated. Father Fidel

Maiz was taken to Brazil for a time, but was eventually allowed to return to Paraguay.

Elisa Lynch's situation at Cerro Corá had been a particularly daunting one. Reviled by López's family and threatened by the starving survivors of the Paraguayan civilian prisoners, she was more than once in danger of her life. But she found a thoroughly gentlemanly protector in Cunha Mattos, the Brazilian major to whom she had shown kindness while he was a prisoner at Lomas Valentinas and who was now commander of Brazil's 12th Battalion. The other senior officers also behaved with some courtesy. Elisa and her children were placed aboard the Brazilian steamer *Princesa*. Apart from the fact that a sentry was stationed at the door of their stateroom they were treated as ordinary passengers. It is reported by Barrett that Elisa's youngest child cried for hours on end while she comforted him, and that once during the night the sentry heard her cry out 'Dear God, let me forget!' The story must be regarded as at least emotionally true.

At Asunción, Paranhos, the Emperor's special envoy in Paraguay, boarded the *Princesa*. He had a long conference with Elisa, who, with her usual courage, wished to land in order to vindicate herself before the provisional government and to fight for the property of herself and her children. Paranhos informed her that a decree had been passed condemning her for having commanded troops, conferred decorations and held reviews.[2] He also showed her a petition he had received through the provisional government, from the ladies of Asunción requesting him not to allow 'Madame Lynch, against whom is raised the voice of a justly indignant people, to leave the field of her crimes with the spoils stripped from so many victims; leaving those victims without just reparation . . .'.

Paranhos then presented her with his reply:

'*To His Excellency Señor Laizago, etc.*

Your government presumed in the petition signed by the ladies and submitted to this Legation that Madame Lynch carried great wealth with her. That is not true, as an inventory of what she had in her carriage at the time of her capture proves. The natural generosity of the conqueror has left that intact.

'The inventory was made by a responsible group of Brazilian officials on board the vessel to which the prisoner was taken and was ordered by his Excellency, Conde d'Eu, with the approval of the undersigned, having in mind the best interests of all concerned at the moment of victory over the ex-Dictator.

'The personal effects in this inventory are not of great value and certainly represent much less than what Madame Lynch must legitimately have acquired in Paraguay.

José. M. da Silva Paranhos'.[3]

When Elisa still persisted in her intention to land and face her accusers, Paranhos was obliged to place her under arrest as a prisoner of war.

When the *Princesa* reached Buenos Aires, however, she was allowed to land, in order to engage a French solicitor named Edmond Berchon des Essart to handle her claims and her affairs in Paraguay, and to take charge of the various documents she had brought with her.

Many of the newspapers in Buenos Aires, and in particular *La Tribuna*, were hostile to Elisa, reviving the most scurrilous gossip of the past. But in other quarters she met with kindness, especially from those she had helped in Paraguay during the war, or who had been entertained by her in Asunción before it started.

From Buenos Aires she went to England. The greater part of the money which Francisco Solano López had set aside for her and her children had been entrusted to Dr William Stewart, who was now living in Edinburgh. Stewart had been a medical technician in the British Army who had arrived in Asunción penniless after the failure of one of the Paraguayan colonization projects. He and his Paraguayan wife had been befriended by both Elisa Lynch and López, and Stewart had risen to become chief surgeon in the Paraguayan army. After his surrender to the Brazilians at Lomas Valentinas, however, he had become a propagandist for the anti-López cause. Charles Ames Washburn himself came to London to consult him before he faced the Congressional Inquiry, and Stewart made a sworn deposition on his behalf.

Elisa applied to Stewart for the money which had been entrusted to him. When she did not receive a satisfactory answer she put the matter in the hands of her London solicitors.

Before the case came to court she received the news that des Essart, her solicitor in Buenos Aires, had been murdered – possibly in an attempt to seize Elisa's papers which, it was rumoured, might contain material of a politically dangerous nature, or perhaps in the hope of obtaining maps showing the whereabouts of the treasure reputedly buried during López's last retreat – and that these papers had been impounded by the French Consul and sent to France. Elisa could, of course, obtain their release by filing a claim with the French Government, but it might take some considerable time.

Perhaps Stewart had heard of this and had assumed that none of Elisa's papers was now available. At any rate when he was called to the stand in Edinburgh he swore on oath that he had not received any money from Francisco Solano López for the purposes Elisa alleged, and that he had not signed an acknowledgement of its receipt, as she had claimed. As this was the point on which the whole case hinged, the judge asked Stewart to repeat his denial, which he did with the utmost confidence.

Elisa Lynch herself has described what happened then:

'As I presented the receipts and acknowledgements which testified to the contrary, the judge, most surprised at their existence in the hand and letter of Dr Stewart, asked him if he recognized them. To which he replied, "Yes, But I had forgotten them".'

No wonder Kolinski speaks of Stewart's reputation as having in consequence acquired 'some tarnish', and of course he lost the case. But he had already made his dispositions in the eventuality of such an outcome – and promptly went bankrupt, so that Elisa and her children never received their money.

It appears that Elisa now visited Ireland, her homeland, but then divided her time between France and England, where her sons were at school.

'I saw her several times in London in 1873 or 1874,' Cunning-hame-Graham informs us, 'getting into her carriage at a house she had, I think, in Thurloe Square or Hyde Park Gate. She was then apparently about forty years of age. Of middle height, well made, beginning to put on a little flesh with her abundant fair hair just flicked with grey. In her well-made Parisian clothes, she looked more French than English, and had no touch of that untidiness that so often marks the Irish woman. She was still handsome and distinguished-looking. Her face was oval and her lips a little full: her eyes were large and grey, if I remember rightly, and her appearance certainly did not seem that of one who had looked death so often in the face, lived for so long in circumstances so strange and terrifying, buried her lover with her own hands, and lived to tell the tale.'

Eventually she received her papers from the French authorities, and in 1875 she returned to South America. In Buenos Aires she met and talked with Enrique Wisner von Morgenstern, the Hungarian soldier who had been perhaps the most loyal friend she and Francisco Solano López had possessed. Short of money now, she sued the Argentine Government for the value of the furnishings looted from her home in Asunción, which had found their way to Buenos Aires. She won her case, but the lawyer's fees swallowed up most of the money she was awarded. Most of the remainder went on a series of suits for slander and defamation of character against a number of Argentine newspapers.

When she announced her intention of revisiting Asunción an anonymous letter in *La Tribuna* on 26 September 1875, asserted that she would not dare to do so, because she knew she would be kidnapped and tortured to make her tell where Paraguay's treasure was buried. Regarding this as a challenge she sent a demand to the Paraguayan Government to be tried on any charges which could be brought against her, and went to Asunción.

The Paraguayan government was acutely embarrassed. The President was now Juan B. Gill, (a close friend of Washburn during the period of his embassy) and for various political reasons (quite apart from the fact of Elisa's confiscated property) he did not want the publicity of a public trial. Acting apparently without constitutional authority, he ordered Elisa to re-embark under a military guard, three hours after she had landed in Asunción. It appears that during that brief period she was warmly welcomed by a number of old friends and adherents.

Back in Buenos Aires the lawsuits continued to eat up her resources. She returned to Europe, where her youngest son died. When her two surviving sons Carlos and Enrique had completed their education she returned once more to Buenos Aires, taking them with her. There she assigned to them all her claims to the lands and property which their father had bequeathed to her in Paraguay. Later Carlos and Enrique sold their rights to an Argentinian named Francisco Cordero, who tried to make an international grievance out of it when the Paraguayan Government contemptuously dismissed his application.

In 1885 Elisa returned to Europe, alone. She visited Ireland for a time, then travelled to Constantinople, where she remained for about a year. From Constantinople she went to the Holy Land. For the next three years she was a familiar figure at the various shrines. Always alone, speaking to no one, it appears that she had severed all her old contacts, except for her sons with whom she still corresponded.

Then, her funds nearly exhausted, she returned to Paris, where she took a room in a cheap lodging house. The landlord found her dead in her bed one morning, and the woman who had once dreamed of becoming an Empress was buried in a pauper's grave.

What, though, of the countries which had participated in the longest and most bitter war in the history of South America? The aftermath was not without its ironies. Uruguay, whose civil war between Blancos and Colorados had sparked off the conflict, was least affected. There had never been any strong popular enthusiasm for the war. When the small Uruguayan force practically disappeared in the early stages, there were no serious attempts to send replacements. The return of Venancio Flores, his assasination, and the revival of international dissensions seemed of much greater moment than the far-away war in Paraguay.

Neverthless there were indirect consequences. For one thing the Allied support of Flores had finally established the predominance of the Colorado party in the nation's slowly developing political democracy – and the independent status of Uruguay as a buffer-state between Argentina and Brazil was permanently established.

The two major Allies came to regard Paraguay in something of the same light. They kept their forces of occupation in the defeated country for six years, but the reawakening of traditional rivalries and suspicions ensured their eventual withdrawal and Paraguay's independence. They also served to keep territorial ambitions within limits. At the peace settlement Argentina's old claims to the former Jesuit mission area east of the river Paraná were recognized, but her territorial aspirations in the Chaco, which if satisfied would have given her a common frontier with Mato Grosso, were contested by Brazil and the matter had to be put to arbitration. The Rutherford B. Hayes decision of November 1878, fixed the Argentine border in this area at the river Pilcomayo, across the Paraguay from Asunción.

Argentina's disappointment, however, was offset by the fact that freedom of the river Paraná to international commerce was now guaranteed, and the no doubt sorrowing ghost of Dr Francia finally exorcised. In any case Argentina had not done badly out of the war: the economic losses of its earlier years had been largely cancelled out by the fact that after the Paraguayan threat to the Paraná had been removed, Buenos Aires became the main *entrepôt* for traffic along the river and the chief centre of all the commercial activity connected with the waging of the war.

One of the major results of the war as far as Argentina was concerned, indeed, was the consolidation of Buenos Aires as the undisputed capital of a united Argentine republic. Provincial hostility towards Buenos Aires had by no means disappeared – and has not done so even today. But the presence (however, reluctant in many cases) of provincial troops in a national Argentine army had undoubtedly helped to minimize it. As Kolinski says 'the last great chance' for the victory of the provinces over Buenos Aires had in effect disappeared 'with the death of Francisco Solano López and the subsequent assassination in Entre Ríos of Justo José de Urquiza' – and in retrospect the natural community of interests between these two representatives of an older, more feudal system and way of life emerges with increasing clarity.

As far as Brazil was concerned, it might be said that, in the long run, Francisco Solano López had his revenge. The Empire had, it is true, achieved her maximum territorial aims (short of the complete annexation of Paraguay, that is), acquiring the whole of the disputed frontier zone between the rivers Apa and Blanco, while astute diplomacy in connection with Argentina's claims in the Chaco had prevented Argentina from acquiring a common frontier with the Empire in Mato Grosso, and thus ensured that Paraguay would remain a genuine buffer state, and one, moreover, which would have some cause for gratitude to Brazil and would, therefore, be more likely to be amenable to Brazilian influence.

In some respects, too, the war had provided a stimulus to economic activity in various parts of the huge Brazilian Empire. Military necessities had speeded up the construction of roads, railways and telegraphic communications, and the improvement of navigational facilities on the waterways. The naval arsenal at Rio de Janeiro had developed to the point at which it could build its own ironclads, while munition works had been established in various parts of the country, and textile factories had been opened at São Paulo. In many respects, in fact, the war marked the beginning of Brazil's industrialization, supported by the more up-to-date methods of banking and finance introduced by the Baron of

Maua, and of a partial shift away from the excessive dependence on a few primary products such as sugar and coffee.

Of equal importance for the future was the fact that the presence of troops (and to some extent the visit of the Emperor to Rio Grande do Sul) had stimulated interest in the extreme western provinces while, at the other end of the vast country, the opening of the Amazon to international navigation towards the end of 1866 was to have profound economic importance.

On the other hand, Brazil as the major – and most persistent – partner in the Triple Alliance, had been subjected to the greatest strains, both political and economic. Of the estimated 190,000 allied deaths from battle or disease,[4] Brazil's amounted to at least 100,000.[5] Brazilian expenditure on the war has been estimated at $300 million. It was met partly by loans and partly by highly unpopular taxes, but even so it placed an enormous strain on the country's banking and financial systems, and was largely responsible for a series of severe economic crises, amounting at times to near collapse.

The war, moreover, provoked far-reaching social changes. The most important of these concerned the institution of slavery. This was already being strongly challenged in some quarters before hostilities started, and inevitably the war increased the pressure for abolition. Slaves who were recruited into the armed forces were offered their liberty as an inducement to service. They found themselves fighting side by side with allies who had already abolished slavery – and against a country which had done likewise. In a statement to the Brazilian Senate after the war, the Visconde de Rio Branco (as Paranhos had become) pointed out that these circumstances had made a profound impression not only upon him but upon the whole of the Brazilian army.[6] And it was largely as a result of his testimony that on 28 September 1871, the first instalment of emancipation was enacted, the 'Rio Branco' law, as it is usually called, which provided that children of slaves should henceforth be free. This still left nearly two million enslaved, but the strength of the abolitionist movement was tremendously strengthened.

The social upheaval caused by the war, however, spread wider than this. The *caboclos* or poor whites, who next to the negro slaves had formed the largest group in the army, taken from their native provinces probably for the first time in their lives and coming into contact with people of different nationalities and outlooks, also demanded an improvement in their social and economic status. Many veterans in fact received small plots of land, in reward for their war service, and these further consolidated their sense of social and economic identity.

All these changes inevitably led to the release of new political forces, and these increasingly tended to find their focus in the army, which had itself undergone radical changes. Before the war the army had as often as not been the tool of whichever political party or grouping controlled the budget; its officers had been allowed little say in its management, and were often promoted for their political allegiances rather than for their soldierly attainments. Sheer military necessity had altered much of this: the high casualties among the officers, for example, had meant that men of humble origin, who had previously had little expectation of social advancement, entered the officer class, and in many cases made the army their career. In addition, the shared experiences of war had forged a bond of unity between men of all ranks, every section of the Brazilian class-structure, and every part of the empire, of a kind that had never previously existed. When the war was over, of course, the size of the army was gradually reduced to peace-time proportions, but the new sense of cohesion and purpose survived the demobilization period – and extended to the large numbers of discharged veterans. At the same time, a group of new commanders had come to the fore who owed their positions entirely to military factors; who, as war heroes, could not be ignored by the politicians; who, whatever their private political sympathies, tended to think first and foremost as army men – and who could count on the backing of soldiers, reserves and veterans alike.

In other words the army had emerged, as it has on several occasions since in Brazil's history up to the present day, as an independent political force. It was not, moreover, one that looked with particular sympathy upon the imperial form of government. As so often happens when an army has served abroad, it had imbibed new ideas from the foreigners with whom it had come into contact, and in particular the republicanism and liberal democracy exemplified by Bartolomé Mitre and Buenos Aires.

This was especially true of the younger officers and those who had emerged from anonymity as a result of their war service, while many of the older ones, though still personally loyal to Dom Pedro, had no wish to see the army revert to a minor role in the nation's affairs – and both sections began to doubt whether the retention of the imperial form of government best served their interests.

Kolinski is undoubtedly right, in fact, when he suggests that the Paraguayan war 'may have represented the empire's high water mark,' and when he argues later that 'its several effects upon Brazil's peoples and institutions – changes in class structure and social organization, impact upon land settlement, effect upon slavery, rise of the army as a new force – all combined to operate against the continued retention of a monarchical system of government and its dependence upon the rural latifundia class'.

The Empire was to survive for nearly twenty years more, but it can be said with some justice that the process of erosion began with the death of Francisco Solano López. The circumstances of its passing abound in ironies. It was in large part due to the efforts of the Emperor that the act of May 1888, finally abolishing slavery was passed – but as a result of it he lost his most considerable support, that of the wealthy conservative slave-owning *fazendeiros*. It was as the result of his liberal policies, too, that he also offended the church. It was at this juncture that the army decided that Brazil must become a republic. And when in November 1889 Dom Pedro abdicated and quietly sailed away in a British warship, the *caudillo* President of Venezuela declared when he heard the news: 'The only republic in South America is ended, the Empire of Brazil'.

These are ironies of a kind which Francisco Solano López, the man who was reputed to have aspired to the hand of one of Dom Pedro's daughters, who had perhaps hoped to become an Emperor, and who had been thwarted in his aims by the Emperor of Brazil, might well have appreciated.

But what of Francisco Solano López's Paraguay? If at the end he himself had achieved something of the heroic stature of Macbeth, tied 'bear-like' to a stake, it was to Paraguay herself that the real tragedy belonged. The appalling figures of the country's losses must be repeated – at least 220,000 people killed in battle or dead of disease, hunger or exhaustion, leaving a population which von Versen estimates at only 221,000 (not much more, that is, than those who had died). Of these only 28,000 were men, so that women over 15 outnumbered men by more than four to one,[7] and it was many years before a normal ratio between the sexes was re-established.

The economic collapse of the country was almost complete. In the earlier stages of the war the women had continued to cultivate the land, but the policy of calling them up for auxiliary services, combined with the evacuation of civilian populations in the face of the enemy's advance, had resulted in the abandonment of most of the farms, while the large herds of cattle and horses that had once existed had virtually disappeared. The country's treasury had disappeared too – in the costs of the war, and, López's enemies said, into his own pockets or into secret hiding places. Although too, the Allies eventually cancelled the enormous indemnities which they had demanded (there was not the wherewithal, in any case, to pay them) they did nothing to help in the country's economic recovery, and during the six years of the occupation Paraguay was exploited in ways which, Kolinski suggests, 'Could be likened in several aspects to the "carpetbag' period of the vanquished Confederacy after the American Civil War.'

Politically the nation experienced a sense of collapse almost as complete. It was not only that few people with education or administrative experience had survived, or that the aftermath of so devastating a way inevitably gave rise to bitter animosities and recriminations, but that the only system of government the county had ever known had been destroyed, and there were no alternative political traditions to fill the vacuum. Although the new constitution of November, 1870 was more 'democratic' than anything Paraguay had known before, the concept of democracy itself was well-nigh meaningless, and in consequence it produced instability and lack of confidence for a long time to come: between 1870 and 1932 Paraguay, in addition to the triumvirate set up as a more or less puppet-government by the Allies, had no less than 32 presidents, most of whom acquired power or lost it in circumstances of violence and anarchy.

Paraguay, it is true, was not unique in this respect among Latin American countries – but in some respects the anarchy that followed the death of López was of that special kind that belongs to any people which have been forcibly detached from their immemorial habits and traditions. Those who have regarded the War of the Triple Alliance as fundamentally a racial one, indeed, can point not only to the near-extermination of the Guaraníes, but also to the virtual extinction of a form of cultural and social organization which reached back to the Jesuit missions, and beyond them to the ancient tribal communities.

It was these factors which the *Manchester Guardian*, in an article on 14 April 1870, had in mind when it came to assess a war which, it declared, had 'made a profounder impression on the minds of competent observers' than almost any other conflict:

'It has destroyed a remarkable system of government. It has overturned the only South American state wherein the native Indian race showed any present likelihood of attaining or recovering such strength and organization as to fit it for the task of government. No other state in South America has been able to boast of so much internal peace.'

And later the article suggests that if the Paraguayans had 'been somewhat more numerous, though even by only a few thousands', it is likely that López would have won the war and Paraguay might in consequence 'have become to modern South America what the Incan dominion made of Peru in times anterior to the Spanish Conquest – an all-extending because an all-embracing nation'.

The article does not ask whether such a state was worth having, though it acknowledges the obvious threat that the existence of López's Paraguay posed to her more Europeanized neighbours. It is here, perhaps, that the ambivalence so often experienced in connection with Latin America, and above all in the case of Paraguay, inevitably comes into play. On the one hand, one regrets the passing of what may have been a first chance for a predominantly Indian race to reassert itself against the descendants of the European conquerors; and on the other, one heartily deplores the absolutist and backward form of government in which the challenge manifested itself. The answer, of course, *should* be that there are other and better ways for the Indian populations of South America to rehabilitate themselves, socially, politically and economically. In practice, though, they have not so far been able to do so; they are still predominantly a submerged people – even in Mexico, in spite of the Revolution with its stress on the ancient Indian cultures and the disappearance from public places of the statues of Hernán Cortés, the Conqueror.

As far as Paraguay itself is concerned, the ambivalence of feeling persists as one contemplates the aftermath of the War of the Triple Alliance. For out of the chaos and anarchy produced by the attempt to conform to alien forms of political and social organization, the single stabilizing factor that eventually emerged was the very one which the allies had been at most pains to eliminate – the spirit of Francisco Solano López.

It was not only the kind of rehabilitation mentioned in the Introduction to this book – the statues and busts of the Marshal-President at Cerro Corá, Piribebuy, Ytororó, and elsewhere, the transfer of his remains to the Pantheon of Heroes in Asunción, the memorial to his soldiers in the form of the shell-blasted towers of Humaitá church on the outskirts of the capital, the naming of streets and squares after his generals and so on – but a positive reassertion of the kind of national solidarity he had evoked. It was a reassertion, moreover, which demanded vindication by the same terrible means Francisco Solano López himself had employed – that of a bitter and bloody war.

To complete the picture of history repeating itself, the Chaco War of 1932 also arose as the result of Paraguay's unusual geographical position and of border disputes.

From 1879 to 1883, while Paraguay was still gradually recovering from her defeat, the War of the Pacific was being fought, on the far western side of the sub-continent, between Chile and the combined forces of Peru and Bolivia. The victory of Chile deprived Bolivia of her vital Pacific coastline, so that, like Paraguay, she became a landlocked country with no direct access to the sea.

Unable, therefore, to look to the Pacific for an outlet for her trade, she began to revive her old claims, dating back to colonial times, to possession of a part of the Chaco, which would give her access to the River Paraná, and thence to the Atlantic.

Both countries, then, were recuperating after a disastrous defeat; both were smarting under a sense of national frustration and humiliation. Skirmishes between the *fortines* or outposts, which both sides had established in the Chaco began in 1928. The traditional patriotism of the Paraguayans soon reasserted itself, and indignation against the Bolivians mounted. In 1931 there was a popular uprising against the government of the day in protest against what was considered a lack of firmness in its policy towards Bolivia. When it was learned that not only was national honour at stake, but that oil deposits existed in the Chaco, the determination to throw out the intruders was redoubled.

In the middle of 1932 a Paraguayan garrison in the Chaco was seized by Bolivian troops and in spite of the efforts of other South American countries and of the League of Nations to prevent it, full-scale war broke out.

It was assumed by the Bolivians (and by most other observers) that they would have an easy victory. They greatly outnumbered the Paraguayans; they had employed a German General, Hans Kundt, to train their army; and they had acquired large quantities of surplus military equipment from the First World War, including a number of aeroplanes. It had, apparently, been forgotten that Paraguayan soldiers could thrive against worse odds than these.

There were a number of natural advantages in their favour. As in Francisco Solano López's time, they had the interior lines and were closer to their bases. They were much more familiar with the Chaco than their enemies, and they made the best military use of the difficult, inhospitable terrain. It was not the sort of country in which large bodies of men could operate effectively, and under their able commander, José Félix Estigarribia (himself to become a Marshal-President), the Paraguayans resorted to the kind of tactics which had so frequently been successful when the Allies had been invading their country, splitting into small groups and conducting raids behind the Bolivian lines, cutting their communications – and seizing their supplies.

But it was, once again, in sheer fighting spirit that the main natural advantage lay. Whereas the bulk of the Bolivian army consisted of Indians, brought from the Altiplano to fight in an utterly unfamiliar territory, for a cause they did not understand, and for a country which had never absorbed them into its social, political and economic structure, the Paraguayans, whether of Guaraní or Spanish descent, were united in a common national purpose.

In what nevertheless proved a long and bitterly contested war, the Paraguayans steadily advanced, making up their own deficiencies by capturing vast supplies of the enemy's munitions and armaments (including a British tank which now stands in one of Asunción's squares) in the time-honoured manner of López's soldiers. Strategically Estigarribia had decidedly the better of it over his German opponent, and gradually the Paraguayans cleared the whole of the disputed Chaco. In the process they killed or captured large numbers of Bolivians; many others deserted, and of the 77,000 troops Bolivia had sent into the Chaco, by the end of 1933 only some 7,000 remained. But the Paraguayans did not themselves have the numbers or the strength to invade the highlands of Bolivia itself. Eventually, on 12 June 1935, a truce was arranged, and four neighbouring republics, together with the

U.S.A., began mediation efforts. They lasted a long time, and at one stage it looked as if the Paraguayan army officers might force a resumption of hostilities. At last, however, in July 1938, a settlement was arrived at, whereby Paraguay acquired the lion's share of the disputed area in the Chaco – about three-quarters of it – and Bolivia, instead of the passage to the sea she had gone to war for, received only the cold comfort of land transit through a few carefully selected and limited zones.

It is the Chaco War that forms the natural conclusion to the story of Francisco Solano López and his Paraguay. As Justo Pastor Benítez, one of Paraguay's leading twentieth century writers, has said:

> 'The country needed a landmark to indicate the termination of decadence and to conclude the process of territorial demarcation; a victory which would revive the faith that had been slumbering and which would waken the moral forces that lie in the depths of history.'[8]

The revival of this faith did not, it is true, lead to political peace. The victory which had largely exorcised the bitterness of defeat in 1870 had also raised the prestige of the army, and for the next twenty years power passed, usually by violent means, from the hands of one soldier to another. Nevertheless, the tradition of Francisco Solano López had been firmly re-established, transcending the most violent of political rivalries. Most Paraguayans would have echoed the sentiments of Colonel Rafael Franco, one of the heroes of the Chaco War, founder of the *Febrerista* party, and later leader of a revolt against the government of the day, when in 1936 he declared:

> 'The people of Paraguay can be assured that the immortal spirit and genius of our race has returned to the palace of Solano López, and that in future Paraguay will follow the path which carried it in the past to prosperity, greatness, and to its greatest destinies.'[9]

When, moreover, political stability was at last re-established, by another hero of the Chaco War, President Alfredo Stroessner, it was by means of a type of authoritarianism which was fundamentally much the same as that of the Marshal-President and his predecessors.

It was perhaps a reversal to traditional preferences, to the sort of government Paraguayans at present best understand. It is certainly not for the insufficiently informed outsider to pass judgement. But in contemplating the story of this strange and fascinating country, in which one is torn so often between admiration for the courage and devotion of its people, and revulsion against the circumstances in which they have been forced to display these qualities, the last word must go to the further 36,000 men of the Chaco War – who joined their comrades of the War of the Triple Alliance in the vast army of Paraguay's dead.

NOTES

[1] For example *Jornal do Comércio*, 3 May 1870.
[2] Decree of the Provisional Government of Asunción, 1870, quoted by Barrett.
[3] See *La regeneración*, No. 75, *Exposición y protesta*, Elisa Lynch, quoted by Barrett.
[4] História da Guerra do Paraguai, von Versen, *op. cit.*
[5] Kolinski, *Independence or Death*.
[6] *A History of Brazil*, João Pandía Calogeras, trans. Percy Alvin Martin.
[7] Chapel Hill 1939.
See for example, *Empire in Brazil: a new world experiment with monarchy*, C. H. Haring. Cambridge, Mass. 1958.
[8] *Estigarribia, el soldado del Chaco*, Justo Pastor Benítez. Buenos Aires 1943.
[9] *Um voluntário da pátria*, Francisco Pinheiro Guimaraes. 2nd ed., Rio de Janeiro 1958.

Select Bibliography

Alberdi, Juan B., *Grandes y pequeños hombres del Plata*, Paris n.d.
— *Los intereses argentinos en la Guerra del Paraguay con el Brasil*, Paris 1865.
— *Las disensiones de las repúblicas de la Plata y las maquinaciones del Brasil*, Paris 1865.
— *El imperio del Brasil ante la democracia de América*, (Colección de artículos escritos durante la Guerra del Paraguay contre la Triple Alianza), Asunción 1919.
Amerlan, Alberto, *Nights on the Río Paraguay. Scenes of war and character sketches*, Trans. from the German by Henry S. Suksdorf, Buenos Aires 1902.
Azvedo, M. de, *Rio da Prata é Paraguaï: quadros guerreiros*, Rio de Janeiro 1871.
Baez, Cecilio, *El Mariscal Francisco Solano López*, Asunción 1926.
Barrett, William E, *Woman on Horseback: the biography of Francisco López and Eliza Lynch*, London 1938.
Barroso, Gustavo, *A guerra do López*, 3rd. ed., São Paulo 1929.
— *História militar do Brasil*, São Paulo 1938.
Benites, Gregorio, *Anales diplomático y militar de la guerra del Paraguay*, 2 vols, Asunción 1906.
Benítez, Justo Pastor, *Estigarribia, el soldado del Chaco*, Buenos Aires 1943.
Bolton, H. E., 'The Mission as a frontier institution in the Spanish American Colonies', in *American Historical Review*, XXIII, 1917, and in *Wider Horizons of American History*, New York and London 1939.
Box, Pelham Horton, *The Origins of the Paraguayan War*, 2 vols, University of Illinois, Urbana, 1927.
Boxer, C. R., *Salvador de Sá and the Struggle for Brazil and Angola: 1602–1683*, London 1952.
Bray, Arturo, *Solano López*, Buenos Aires 1945.

Burton, Richard F., *Explorations of the Highlands of Brazil*, 2 vols, London 1869.
— *Letters from the Battlefields of Paraguay*, London 1870.
Calogeras, João Pandía, *A History of Brazil*, trans. Percy Alvin Martin, Chapel Hill 1939.
Carlyle, Thomas, 'Dr. Francia', in *Foreign Quarterly Review*, No. 52, July 1843.
Centurión, Juan C., *Memorias de Juan C. Centurión ó sea reminiscencias históricas sobre la guerra del Paraguay*, 3 vols, Buenos Aires 1894–7.
Cerqueira, Dionísio, *Reminiscências da campanha do Paraguaï*, Rio de Janeiro n.d.
Chaves, Julio César, *La revolución paraguaya de la independencia*, Asunción 1961.
Chaves, María Concepción de L., *Madame Lynch*, Buenos Aires 1957.
Codman, John, *Ten Months in Brazil with notes on the Paraguayan War*, New York 1872.
Cunninghame-Grahame, R. B., *Portrait of a Dictator*, London 1933.
— *A Vanished Arcadia: being Some Account of the Jesuits in Paraguay, 1607–1765*, London 1901.
Díaz, Antonio, *Historia política y militar de las repúblicas del Plata, desde el año de 1828 hasta el de 1866*, 12 vols, Montevideo 1877–8.
Díaz, César, *Memorias inéditas del General oriental Don César Díaz*, publicadas por Adriano Díaz, Buenos Aires 1878.
Domínguez, Manuel, *Causas del Heroísme Paraguayo*, Asunción 1903.
Funes, Gregorio, *Ensayo de la Historia civil del Paraguay, Buenos Aires y Tucumán*, Buenos Aires 1816.
Gálvez, Manuel, *Los caminos de la muerte*, 2nd, ed., Buenos Aires 1928.
— *Humaitá*, Buenos Aires n.d.
— *Jornadas de agonía*, Buenos Aires n.d.
González, J. Natalicio, *Solano López, diplomático*, Asunción n.d.
— *Cuentos y parábolas*, Buenos Aires 1922.
— *Proceso y formación de la cultura Paraguaya*, Asunción and Buenos Aires 1938.
Haring, C. H., *Empire in Brazil: a new world experiment with monarchy*, Cambridge, Mass., 1958.
Haydon, F. Stansbury, 'Documents relating to the first Military

Balloon Corps organized in South America', in *Hispanic American Historical Review*, XIX, 4th November, 1939.

Hernández, Pablo, *Organización social de las doctrinas Guaraníticas de la Compañía de Jesus*, 2 vols, Barcelona 1913.

Hutchinson, Thomas J., *The Paraná, with incidents of the Paraguayan War, and South American recollections from 1861–1868*, London 1868.

James, Preston E., *Latin America*, 3rd. ed., New York 1939.

Jones, T. B., *South America Rediscovered*, University of Minnesota 1949.

Jourdan, Emílio, *História das campanhas do Uruguaï, Mato Grosso, e Paraguaï*, 3 vols, Rio de Janeiro 1893–4.

Kennedy, A. J., *La Plata, Brazil, and Paraguay during the present war*, London 1869.

Koebel, W. H., *Paraguay*, London 1917.

Kolinski, Charles J., *Independence or Death: the story of the Paraguayan War*, Gainesville 1965.

Lima Figueiredo, José de, *Grandes soldados do Brasil*, Rio de Janeiro 1944.

— *Brasil militar*, Rio de Janeiro 1944.

Lima, Oliveira, *O Império Brasileiro, 1822–1889*, São Paulo 1927.

López, Francisco Solano, *Proclamas y cartas del Mariscal López*, Buenos Aires 1957.

Lynch, Alicia, *Exposición y protesta*, Buenos Aires 1877.

Lyon-Young, Henry, *Eliza Lynch, Regent of Paraguay*, London 1966.

MacMahon, Martin T., 'Paraguay and her enemies' in *Harper's New Monthly Magazine*, XL, 239, April 1870.

— 'The War in Paraguay', in *Harper's New Monthly Magazine*, XL. 239, April 1870.

Maiz, Fidel, *Etapas de mi vida, contestación de las imposturas de Juan Godoy*, Asunción 1919.

Mansfield, C. B., *Paraguay, Brazil and the Plate. Letters written in 1852–53*, Cambridge 1856.

Masterman, George F., *Seven Eventful Years in Paraguay*, London 1869.

Meyer, Gordon, *The River and the People*, London 1965.

Mörner, Magnus, *The Political and Economic Activities of the Jesuits in the La Plata Region*, Stockholm, 1953.

— *The Expulsion of the Jesuits from Latin America*, ed., with introduction, New York 1965.

O'Leary, Juan E., *El libro de los Héroes*, Asunción 1922.
— *El Mariscal López*, Asunción 1905; 2nd ed., Madrid 1925.
Olleros, Mariano L., *Alberdi, á la luz de sus escritos en cuanto se refieren al Paraguay*, Asunción 1905.
Orléans, Gaston de, Conde d'Eu., *Viagem militar a Rio Grande do Sul*, São Paulo, 1936.
Paz, José Maria *Memorias póstumas*, 2 vols, Buenos Aires 1917.
Pendle, George, *Paraguay: a riverside nation*, 3rd. ed., London 1967.
Pereira da Silva, J. M., *Memórias de meu tempo*, Rio de Janeiro 1895.
Pereyra, Carlos, *Francisco Solano López y la guerra del Paraguay*, Buenos Aires 1945.
Peterson, Harold, F., Efforts of the United States to mediate in the Paraguayan War, in *Hispanic American Historical Studies*, XII, 1 February, 1932.
Pinheiro Guimaraes, Francisco, *Um voluntário da pátria*, 2nd ed., Rio de Janeiro 1958.
Pitaud, Henri, *Madame Lynch*, Asunción 1958.
Raine, Philip, *Paraguay*, New Brunswick, 1956.
Rebaudi, Arturo, *Guerra del Paraguay: la conspiración contra el Mariscal López*, Buenos Aires, 1917.
— *Guerra del Paraguay, vencir o morir*, Buenos Aires 1920.
— *La declaración de guerra de la República del Paraguay a la República Argentina. Misión Luis Caminos, misión Cipriano. Ayala, declaración de Isidoro Ayala*, Buenos Aires 1924.
Rengger, Johann Rudolph and Marcelin Longchamps, *Essai historique sur la révolution du Paraguay et le gouvernement dictatorial du docteur Francia*, Paris 1827 (English trans., London 1827).
Resquín, Francisco Isidoro, *Datos históricos de la guerra del Paraguay con la Triple Alianza*, Buenos Aires 1895.
Rocha Almeida, Antônio da, *Vultos de Pátria*, Rio de Janeiro 1961.
Robertson, J. P. and W. P., *Letters on Paraguay: comprising an account of a four years' residence in that republic under the government of the Dictator Francia*, 3 vols, 2nd ed., London 1839.
Sarmiento, D. F., Letters of Sarmiento to Mary Mann, in *Hispanic American Historical Review*, XXXII, 3 August, 1952.
Schmitt, Peter, 'Las relaciones diplomáticas entre el Paraguay y

las potencias europeas, 1840–1870,' in *Historia Paraguaya*, 111, Asunción 1958.

Service, Elman R. and Helen S., *Tobatí: a Paraguayan town*, Chicago 1954.

Snow, William P., Paraguay in 1852 and 1968, in *American Geographical Society, Occasional Publications*, No. 2, 1968.

Sodre, Alcindo, *Abrindo um cofre*, Rio de Janeiro 1956.

Southey, Robert, *History of Brazil*, London 1810–19.

Spalding, Walter, *A Invasão paraguaia no Brasil*, São Paulo 1940.

Taunay, Alfredo d'Escragnolle, *Memórias do Visconde de Taunay*, São Paulo, 1948.

—   *A retirada da Laguna*, 24th ed., São Paulo 1957.

Thompson, George, *The War in Paraguay: a historical sketch of the country and its people, and notes upon the military engineering of the war*, London 1869.

Urquijo, José M. Mariluz, 'Los Guaraníes después de la expulsión de los Jesuítas,' in *Estudios Americanas*, VI, 1953.

Varela, Hector F. (pseud. Orion), *Elisa Lynch*, Buenos Aries 1934.

Versen, Max von, História da Guerra do Paraguaï, in *Revista do Instituto Histórico e Geográfico Brasileiro*, LXXVI, Part 11, Rio de Janeiro 1913.

Victorica, Julio, *Urquiza y Mitre, Contribución al estudio histórico de la organización nacional*, Buenos Aires 1906.

Warren, Harris G., *Paraguay: an informal history*, Norman 1949.

Washburn, Charles A., *The History of Paraguay*, 2 vols, New York and Boston 1871.

Wey, Walter, *La poesía paraguaya: historia de una incógnita*, Montevideo 1951.

White, Edward L., *El Supremo, a Romance of the Great Dictator of Paraguay*, New York 1916.

Wisner, Francisco, *El Dictador del Paraguay, José Gaspar de Francia*, notes by Julio. C. Chaves, Buenos Aires 1957.

(Paraguayan Investigation. H. R., 41st Congress 2nd Session. Report No. 65, Vol. II, Washington 1870).

Index

absolutism, 16, 25, 28, 35–7, 58–9
Acosta Nú, battle of, 252
Aguirre, Anastasio C., 81, 83
Alberdi, Juan B., 31
Alén, *Col.* Paulino, 125, 127, 206–7, 208, 209, 210, 243
Alfaro, *Father* Diego, 4
Allen brothers, 181
Angostura, 235, 237–8, 243–4
Antequera, José de, 11, 17
Apa, River, 45, 189
Aquino, *Lt.*, 254
Aquino, *Col.*, 159–60
Argentina
  armed forces, 105, 191
  claim to Paraguay, 17–18, 20, 40, 44, 267–8
  feeling against War, 163, 170
  rebellions, 173, 187
  relations with Brazil, 29–30, 78–9, 81–2, 93, 96, 101
  relations with Paraguay, 29–30, 40–4, 46, 63, 82–3, 96–8
  relations with Uruguay, 76, 82–3
Argolo, *General* Alexandre, 192, 235–7
armaments
  Brazilian, 109
  Paraguayan, 102, 106–8, 110, 112
Artigas, *General*, 26
Asboth, *General*, 184
Asunción, 199–202, 245, 246–7
atrocities, 79–80, 92, 210–11, 219
Avay, battle of, 236–7
Azcurra heights, 246, 250, 252

Baez, *Dr* Cecilio, x
Baiende, battle of, 189
balloons, 181
Barrett, William E., 48, 51, 56, 72, 74, 94, 126–7, 144, 182, 184, 200, 201, 210, 211, 215, 217, 220, 222, 223, 227, 232, 245, 246, 251, 252, 254, 255, 263

Barrios, *General* Vicente, 55, 89, 125, 128, 150, 151, 164, 194, 212, 215, 226, 245
Barroso, Gustavo, 106, 131, 160, 247
Barroso da Silva, *Admiral* Francisco, 115, 116, 117–18, 120, 123
Bedoya, Saturnino, 174, 205, 213, 226
Belgrano, *General*, 18
Benítez, Gumesindo, 215, 226
Benítez, Justo P., 276
Berges, José, 83, 87, 97–8, 103, 116, 205, 211, 213, 215, 216–17, 224, 226, 243
Blanco, River, 45
Blancos, 77, 79, 80, 81–2, 83–6, 92–5, 198, 267
Bliss, Porter, 200, 210, 211, 215, 217, 219–20, 222–3, 226, 228–9, 235
bogovantes, 141, 203, 208
Bolivia, 43, 93, 102, 134, 163, 274
Box, Pelham Horton, xiv, 16, 27, 28, 59, 63, 75–6, 82, 84, 91, 94, 97
Boxer, C. R., 9
Bray, Arturo, 103
Brazil
  armed forces, 104–5, 191, 247–8, 270
  effects of War, 268–71
  feeling against War, 170
  navy, 110–12, 115–17, 138
  relations with Argentina, 29–30, 78–9, 81–2, 93, 96, 101
  relations with Paraguay, 29–30, 42–3, 44–6, 64–5, 79, 83, 85–6
  relations with United States, 85–6
  relations with Uruguay, 76, 78–81, 83–6, 92–4
Britain
  intervention, 94–5, 100–1, 233
  relations with Paraguay, 39–40, 43, 46, 62

Britons in Paraguay, 185–7, 200–1, 235
Brizuela, Juan J., 49–50
Bruguez, José M. 116, 119, 123, 133, 159, 176, 178, 197, 211, 212, 215, 226
Bucareli y Ursúa, Francisco, 13–14, 15
Buenos Aires, 17, 19, 28–9, 40, 41–2, 46, 59, 60, 62, 93, 262, 268
Burton, Richard F., x, xii–xiii, 16, 20, 25–6, 28, 34, 35–7, 48, 52, 53, 72, 73, 74, 85, 103, 107, 109, 112, 130, 134, 136, 142–3, 145, 146, 152, 163, 172, 177, 181, 185, 186–7, 193, 211, 218, 226, 227–8, 229, 230, 233, 242, 243, 245, 247, 248

Caacupé, 252
Caballero, General Bernardino, 194, 195, 208, 209, 235–6, 241, 252, 262
Câmara, General José Corrêa de, 237, 255, 257–8, 261
Caminos, Luis, 185–7, 215–17, 243, 245, 258, 262
Camisão, Col. Carlos, 188–9
Campo Grande, 252, 253
Canavarro, General David, 128, 129
Canstatt, Santiago, 37, 39–40
Caraguatay, 255
Cárdenas, Bernardino de, 10–11
Carlyle, Thomas, 25
Carpentería, battle of, 76
Caxias, Marquês de, 176–81, 184, 186, 192, 198, 199, 200, 212, 215, 218, 225, 234, 235–6, 237–8, 239, 241–2, 244–5, 246
Centurión, Juan C., 213
Cepeda, battle of, 60
Cerquerira, Lt. Dionísio, 239, 246, 252, 261
Cerro Corá, 256, 261–2
Cerro León, 241, 245
Chaco see Gran Chaco
Charles III of Spain, 12–13
chatas, 118, 139–40
'Chico Diabo', 258–9, 262
Chile, 92, 102, 163, 274
Chodasiewicz, R. A., 180–1, 184
Cochelet, Mme, 55–6
Coimbra, battle of, 89
Colorados, 77, 78, 80, 267
commercial classes, 19, 28, 59

Concepción, 256
conspiracy of 1862, 69–70
conspiracy of 1868, 205–6, 210–18, 224–7, 229–30
conspiracy of 1869, 254
Corrientes, 29, 42–3, 96–9 115–16, 124–5, 132–4, 136
Cunha Mattos, Maj. Ernesto, 242, 263
Cunninghame-Graham, R. B., 3, 6–7, 14, 33, 38, 39, 90, 125, 163, 166, 227, 230, 255, 257, 265
Curupaíty, 156, 160–3, 167–71, 178, 192–3, 197, 199, 204
Curuzú, 160–2
Cuverville, M., 213, 243

Davie, Charles J. F., 224–5
Davis, Admiral, 223, 224, 228
Decoud brothers, 37–8, 47
Derqui, Santiago, 62
Des Essart, Edmond B., 264
Díaz, César, 46
Díaz, General José, 116, 137, 141, 144, 146, 149, 150, 151, 168, 170, 178, 180
Drago, Col., 188
Duarte, Maj., 128–30
Duval, Dr Marius, 229

Elizalde, Rufino de, 81, 83, 101, 184
Entre Ríos, 43, 63, 93
Estero Bellaco, battle of, 145–6, 148–9
Estigarribia, Col. Antonio de la Cruz, 116, 124–5, 128–9, 130–1
Estigarribia, José F., 275
Eu, Conde d', 74, 107, 248, 250, 252, 255–6, 261, 264

Federales, 49, 77
Flores, Venancio, 77–9, 80–2, 83, 86, 92, 93–5, 98, 106, 129–30, 135–6, 146–7, 149, 151, 159, 162, 165, 173, 198, 267
Francia, Dr José G. R., 19–22, 24–32, 35, 36
Franco, Col. Rafael, 276
Funes, Dr Gregorio, 15

Gálvez, Manuel, 178
Genés, Capt. Ignacio, 203
Gill, Juan B., 266
Godon, Rear-Admiral S. W., 183–4, 222–3

Gómez, *Col.* Leandro, 92
Gould, G. Z., 154, 185–7, 191, 235
Gran Chaco, 1, 41, 63, 204–6
 War of, 1932, 274–7
Guaraníes, 1, 3–12, 15–16, 20, 24,
 27–8, 148, 272, 275
 language, 1–2, 98
Guaycurú Indians, 155

Hayes decision, 1878, 267
Henderson, C. A., 39
Hopkins, Edward R., 39
Humaitá, 38, 103, 106, 108–9, 142,
 153, 156, 172, 192–3, 198–9,
 203, 204, 206–10
Hutchinson, Thomas J., xiii, 105,
 106, 110, 112, 118, 121, 135–6,
 144, 152, 163, 166, 186–7, 191,
 204

Ignacio, José J., 176, 178
Ildefonso, Treaty of, 45
Indians, 1–2, 27, 155, 188, 245, 273,
 275
Itá-Ibaty, 237–8, 244
Itapirú, 141–2, 146
Itapuá, 30
Ituzaingó, battle of, 30, 76

Jesuit state, 2–16, 28–9, 32, 272
'Jesuit War', 12
Juana, *Doña*, 34, 126–7, 157, 230–1,
 255, 257, 259

Kennedy, *Cmr.* A. J., xiv, 110, 111,
 121, 153–4, 197–8
Kirkland, *Cmr.* 218–20, 224–5, 228
Koebel, W. H., xiii, 40, 102
Kolinski, Charles J., 92, 103, 104,
 106, 137, 167, 181, 210, 211–12,
 213, 214, 225, 226, 227, 231,
 239, 245, 248, 251, 254, 265,
 268, 271, 272
Krüger, 106, 116, 155
Kundt, Hans, 275

La Barra, Federico de, 49
Lamas, Andrés, 84
Leckron, Thomas Q., 228
Lescano, Pedro, 69
Lettson, H. G., 100
Liberals, x, 59–60, 62, 64, 77, 85
Lima Figueiredo, José de, 237
Lomas Valentinas, battle of, 237–43
López, Benigno, 47, 48, 53, 69, 117,
 127, 128, 164, 200, 205,
 212–13, 215, 224, 226, 243

López, Carlos Antonio, 28, 33–5,
 37–40, 42–5, 46, 48, 60, 63–5,
 66–7
López, Francisco Solano
 after Curupaíty, 170
 alleged paranoia, 125–6, 128
 ambition to become emperor, xi,
  48, 73–5, 83
 atrocities, 210–11, 219
 and battle of Piribebuy, 250–1
 becomes President, 69–70
 before battle of First Tuyutí, 150
 before battle of Riachuelo, 119
 and Britons in Paraguay, 185–6
 canvasses marriage to Pedro II's
  daughter, 74
 care for ceremony, 173–4
 at Cerro Corá, 256–7
 at Cerro León, 245
 character and actions, ix–xi, 47–9,
  73, 84, 162, 229
 as commander, 107, 116–17
 and commercial classes, 58–9
 council of war, August, 1868, 226
 death, 257–60
 declares war on Argentina, 97, 99
 diplomatic acts on eve of War,
  82, 84–6
 discusses peace with Mitre, 163–7
 economic policy, 70–1
 education, 47–8
 educational measures, 71–2
 escape from Lomas Valentinas,
  241–3
 evacuates Asunción, 199–200
 fails to intervene in Brazilian-
  Uruguayan war, 86, 93–5
 fear of assassination, 136
 fear of being under fire, 143, 145
 final retreat ('*Via dolorosa*'),
  252–9
 and Humaitá, 142, 199, 206
 in campaign against Argentina,
  1845–6, 43–4
 loots Tuyutí, 194–7, 199
 and Manlove, 182
 and Mato Grosso campaign, 91
 meets Elisa, 49–52
 morale-building, 137, 140
 mother *see* Juana, *Doña*
 as negotiator, 60–2, 65, 83
 popular support, 27–8, 72–3, 102,
  246
 possible alliance with Urquiza,
  133–4, 173

Lôpez Francisco – *cont.*
  principles, 35
  and prisoners forced to enter Allied armies, 134–5
  punishes deserters' relatives, 132
  reaction to battle of Uruguiana, 131–2
  refuses to surrender, 1868, 239–40,
  rehabilitation, x, 274
  religious fervour, 176
  requests transit for troops through Corrientes, 96–7
  responsibility for War, 47, 58, 60, 65–6, 73, 75–6, 84, 87–8
  retreats from Paso de la Patria, 143
  retreats into the Chaco, 204–6
  suspects cholera, 1867, 176
  treatment of arrested foreigners, 231–3
  and hopes of United States intervention, 184
  and Uruguayan Blancos, 80
  visit to Europe, 48, 49, 52–3, 58, 73
  and Washburn, 217–22
López, Venancio, 128, 164, 213, 215, 224, 226, 231, 255
Luque, 200, 248
Lynch, Elisa Alicia, 49–58, 74, 90, 117, 126–7, 137, 143–4, 174, 182, 199–200, 204, 217, 220–1, 231, 232–3, 240–1, 243, 258, 259–60, 263–7

MacMahon, *General* Martin T., 52, 220–1, 223, 228, 230, 232, 235, 238, 240–1, 244, 246, 249, 252, 256
Maiz, *Father* Fidel, 47, 48, 54, 69–70, 176, 180, 203, 213, 226, 231, 250–1, 258, 260, 262–3
Mallet, Emilio, 149, 151
Mamelucos, 2–5
Manlove, James, 182, 202, 226
manpower, 191–2, 241
  Argentinian, 105
  Brazilian, 104–5, 177
  Paraguayan, 82, 102–4, 132, 136, 142
  Uruaguyan, 105–6
Mansfield, C. B., 34
Marquez de Olinda, seizure, 87–8
Martínez, *Col.* Francisco, 206, 207, 209–10

execution of wife, 210, 243
Masterman, George F., xiii, 33, 34, 47, 48, 52, 71, 73, 84–5, 89, 91, 103, 106, 117, 119, 120, 124, 126, 132, 136, 140, 143, 153, 170, 182, 200–1, 202, 204, 207, 210, 211, 213, 215, 216, 217, 219–20, 221, 222–3, 224, 226, 227–9, 230, 231, 233, 235, 242
Mathew, G. Buckley, 185–6
Mato Grosso, 45, 64, 86, 190
  Paraguayan invasion, 88–92
Mena Barreto, *General* J. L., 238, 251, 252
Mesa, *Capt.* Pedro I., 112, 117, 119, 122
Mischkovsky, 155–6
Misiones, 41, 93, 96, 267
Mitre, Bartolomé, 18–19, 28, 60, 62–4, 77, 78, 81–2, 93, 94–7, 99–100, 101, 105, 129, 131, 134–6, 146–7, 148, 150, 152, 157, 162, 163–6, 168–9, 173, 176, 183, 187, 192, 198, 248, 270
Molina, Juan E., 213
Monte Caseros, battle of, 45
Monteiro, *General* Victoriano C., 252
Montevideo, siege of, 45, 77
Montoya, Ruiz de, 3–4
morale
  Brazilian, 91
  Paraguayan, 91, 97–8, 112–13, 121, 249
Morgenstern, Enrique Wisner von, 217, 247, 266
Mörner, Magnus, 9–10, 11, 13, 15

Napoleon III, xii, 53, 58, 73–4, 75
Netto, *General* Felipe, 80–1
Nueva Burdeos, French colony, 55, 63

Olabarrieta, *Maj.*, 199, 203
'old Spaniards', 1, 26–7, 70, 153, 226
O'Leary, Juan, x
Oliveira, Pedro Ferreira de, 65
Oribe, Manuel, 45, 76–7
Osório, *General* Manoel L., 129, 142, 146, 149, 153, 192, 207, 236–7, 248, 250, 252

Pakenham, J. J., 196

Palacios, *Bishop* Manuel Antonio, 54, 132, 140–1, 181, 212, 226, 232, 243
Pallejas, *Col.*, 135
Paraguay
 armed forces, 102–3, 106–10, 148, 154–5, 191–2, 245
 Congresses, 20, 24–5, 35–7, 69, 97
 constitution of, 1844, 33
 constitution of, 1870, 272
 economic policy, 28, 30–1, 38, 59, 70
 educational policy, 71–2
 effects of War, 271–3
 foreign trade, 28–30
 frontier disputes, 41, 45, 60, 64, 76, 82, 85, 267–8
 geography, 1
 independence, 16–18, 20, 24–5, 27, 31–2, 42, 44, 46–7, 101
 isolationism, 16, 29–31, 33, 39–40, 42
 navy, 86, 112, 255
 occupation, 267
 outlet to sea, 1, 17
 political system, 28, 35–8, 59
 puppet anti-López government, 247–8, 253, 255
 relations with Argentina, 29–30, 40–4, 46, 63, 82–3, 96–8
 relations with Brazil, 29–30, 42–3, 44–6, 64–5, 79, 83, 85–6
 relations with Britain, 39–40, 43, 46, 62
 relations with United States, xii, 39–40, 43, 46
 technical superiority discussed, 106–7
Paraguay, River, 1, 40–1, 64–5
Paraguayan National Theatre, 55, 57–8
Paraguayan people, 1
Paraguayan prisoners pressed into Allied armies, 130, 134–6, 149
Paraná, River, 40–1, 115, 133, 136, 137–8, 141–2, 267–8
Paranhos, José M. da Silva, 94, 247–8, 263, 269
Paso de la Patria, 136, 146, 177
Patiño, Policarpo, 33
Paunero, *General* Wenceslao, 115, 173
Payaguá Indians, 155
Paysandú, siege of, 92

Pedro II of Brazil, 74, 80–1, 83, 131, 166, 185, 188, 209, 248, 262, 271
Peixoto, Floriano, 129, 262
Pendle, George, 14, 17
Pereyra, Carlos, 97, 105
Peru, 93, 101, 163, 274
Peterkin, Edouard, 177
Pikysyry, 234
Piribebuy, 249–51
Plate, River, 29–30
Polidoro, *General*, 167, 248, 252
Pôrto Algre, *Barão* de, 157, 160, 161–2, 170, 192, 195
Portocarrero, *Col.* Hermenegildo, 89
profiteers, 70, 100
Puntas del Rosario, Conference of, 81, 83

quadrilátero, 172–3, 191–4, 198
Quatrefages, Jean, 50–1, 54

railways, use of, 106, 248
Ramírez, Francisco, 26
Resquín, *General* Francisco, I., 89, 90, 91, 125, 127, 128–9, 132–3, 150, 151, 176, 210, 212, 213, 215, 227, 241, 245, 252, 254, 255, 257, 258, 262
Riachuelo, battle of, 117–24, 132
Río de la Plata *see* Plate, River
Rio Grande do Sul, 80, 125, 128
Rivas, *General* Antonio, 157, 207, 208, 209
Rivera, Fructuosa, 76–7
Robertson, John P., 15, 19, 20–4, 25, 26, 29, 35, 36
Robertson, William P., 19, 25, 26, 29, 35
Robles, *General* Wenceslao, 98, 115–16, 125–8, 129
Rosas, Juan Manuel de, 42–4, 45–6, 76–7

Saguier brothers, 70
Sampaio, *General* Antônio, 151
San José de Flores, Pact of, 60
Sánchez, Francisco, 258, 262
Saraiva, Antônio, 81, 83
Sarmiento, Domingo de, 256, 262
Sauce, battle of, 158–60
Skinner, *Dr* Frederick, 229
slaves, 2–3, 38, 85–6, 104–5, 271
Southey, Robert, 6, 8, 9

Spanish descent *see*, 'old Spaniards'
Stewart, *Dr* William, 201, 229, 244, 264–5
Stroessner, Alfredo, 276
supplies, Paraguayan, 66, 91, 99, 107–8, 175

Tamandaré, *Admiral*, 83, 92, 138–9, 153, 156, 160, 176, 178
Taño, *Father* Diaz, 4–5
Taunay, Alfredo, 188, 189, 247, 251, 252, 255, 261
Taylor, Alonzo, 57, 226, 231
telegraph, 106, 193
10th Battalion (Paraguayan), flight and punishment, 161–2
terror of 1821, 26–7
Thompson, George, xiii, 16, 107, 136, 140, 142, 156, 158, 162–3, 167–8, 194–5, 199, 204–5, 210–11, 214, 234–5, 237–8, 239, 243–5
quoted, 48, 66–7, 82–3, 85, 86, 87, 89, 90, 91, 92, 98, 99–100, 102, 103–4, 106, 108, 109–10, 115, 116, 119, 120–1, 122–3, 125, 128, 130, 131, 133, 134, 137, 138, 139, 141, 143, 144, 145, 149–51, 152, 153, 154, 155, 157, 159, 160, 162, 164, 165, 167–8, 169–70, 174, 175, 176, 177, 178, 179, 181, 184, 186–7, 188, 189, 193, 196, 197, 198, 199, 203, 206–7, 209, 213, 217, 218, 227, 229, 231, 240, 241–2, 245
Thorton, Edward, 39, 62, 81, 83, 101
tobacco, 8, 18–19, 30, 38
Torres, Domingo de, 5
trench warfare, 109, 142
Treuenfeldt, Fischer von, 106, 175, 226, 231
Triple Alliance, Treaty of, 100–2, 163, 165–7
Tuyutí, battle of First, 150–4
battle of Second, 192, 194–7

Unitarios, 42, 77
United States
Congress investigation, 218–25, 227, 244, 246
intervention, 94, 184–5, 252
relations with Brazil, 85–6

relations with Paraguay, 39–40, 43, 46
Urquiza, *General* Justo José de, 43–4, 45–6, 59, 60–4, 77, 78, 79, 81, 93–4, 95–7, 99–100, 125, 133–4, 173
Uruguay, 76–8, 82–6, 92–4, 105–6, 191, 198, 267
Uruguiana, 129–32

Varela, Hector, 51–2, 54, 58–60
Velasco, Bernardo de, 17, 23–4, 41, 58
Vences, battle of, 43
Versen, Max von, 108, 182, 226, 242, 271
Victorica, *Dr* Julio, 96–7
Victorino, *General*, 160
Villeta, 235–6

Wagner, Wilhelm, 106
War of the Chaco, 274–7
War of the Triple Alliance
casualties, xi–xii
causes, ix, 16, 18, 28, 76
declaration by Paraguay on Argentina, 97–9
effects, xi–xii, 267–73
first action, 87
foreshadows future, xiii
unnoticed abroad, xii–xiii
Warren, Harris g., 222–3, 228, 229
Washburn, Charles Ames, 54, 65–6, 70, 72–4, 84, 88, 91, 118, 143, 144, 182–5, 200–2, 210, 211, 212, 215–26, 229, 230, 232, 233, 264
Washburn, Elihu Benjamin, 223
Washburn, *Mrs*, 224–6
Watts, John, 118, 226
Webb, *General*, 184–5
Whytehead, William, 38, 106
women combatants, 143–4

Xavier de Souza, *Marshal* Guilherme, 246, 247–8
Ximénes, *Lt.-Col.*, 160

Yataí, battle of, 129–30
Yataíty, Corá, battle of, 157
conference of, 163–7
Yegros, Fulgencio, 24–5, 26, 36
yerba mate, 8, 14, 28, 30, 38, 59
Ynsfran, Juliana, 210, 243
Ysquibel, Juana, 20–4
Ytororo, battle of, 235–6